Story & Art by
Julietta Suzuki

CHARACTERS

Mamoru

Nanami's shikigami.

Nanami Momozono

A high school student who was turned into a kamisama by the tochigami Mikage.

Tomoe

The shinshi who serves Nanami now that she's the new tochigami. Originally a wild fox ayakashi.

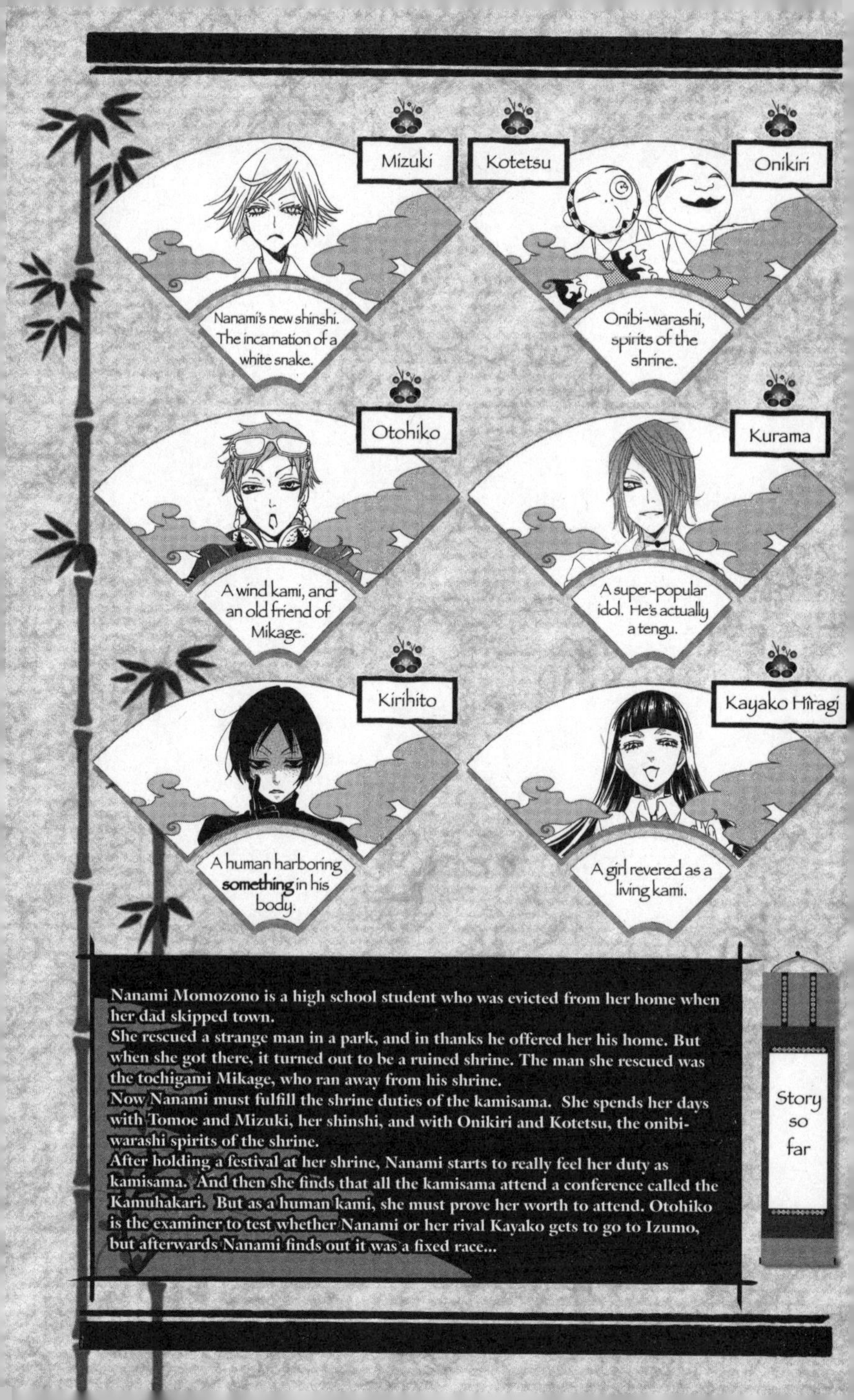

Mizuki
Nanami's new shinshi. The incarnation of a white snake.
Kotetsu
Onikiri
Onibi-warashi, spirits of the shrine.
Otohiko
A wind kami, and an old friend of Mikage.
Kurama
A super-popular idol. He's actually a tengu.
Kirihito
A human harboring **something** in his body.
Kayako Hîragi
A girl revered as a living kami.

Story so far

Nanami Momozono is a high school student who was evicted from her home when her dad skipped town.
She rescued a strange man in a park, and in thanks he offered her his home. But when she got there, it turned out to be a ruined shrine. The man she rescued was the tochigami Mikage, who ran away from his shrine.
Now Nanami must fulfill the shrine duties of the kamisama. She spends her days with Tomoe and Mizuki, her shinshi, and with Onikiri and Kotetsu, the onibi-warashi spirits of the shrine.
After holding a festival at her shrine, Nanami starts to really feel her duty as kamisama. And then she finds that all the kamisama attend a conference called the Kamuhakari. But as a human kami, she must prove her worth to attend. Otohiko is the examiner to test whether Nanami or her rival Kayako gets to go to Izumo, but afterwards Nanami finds out it was a fixed race...

Kamisama Kiss

Volume 7
CONTENTS

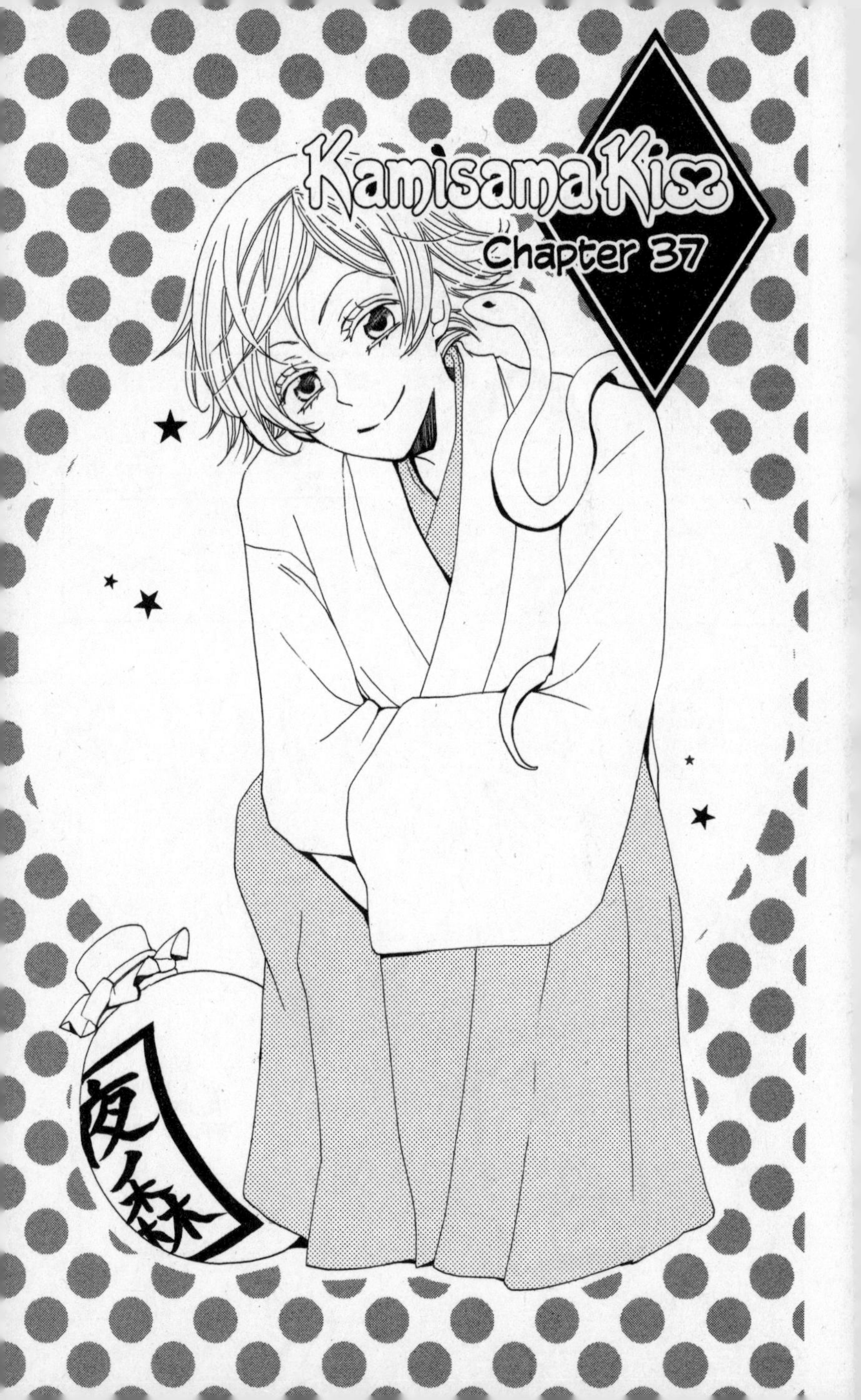
Kamisama Kiss
Chapter 37
夜鉄

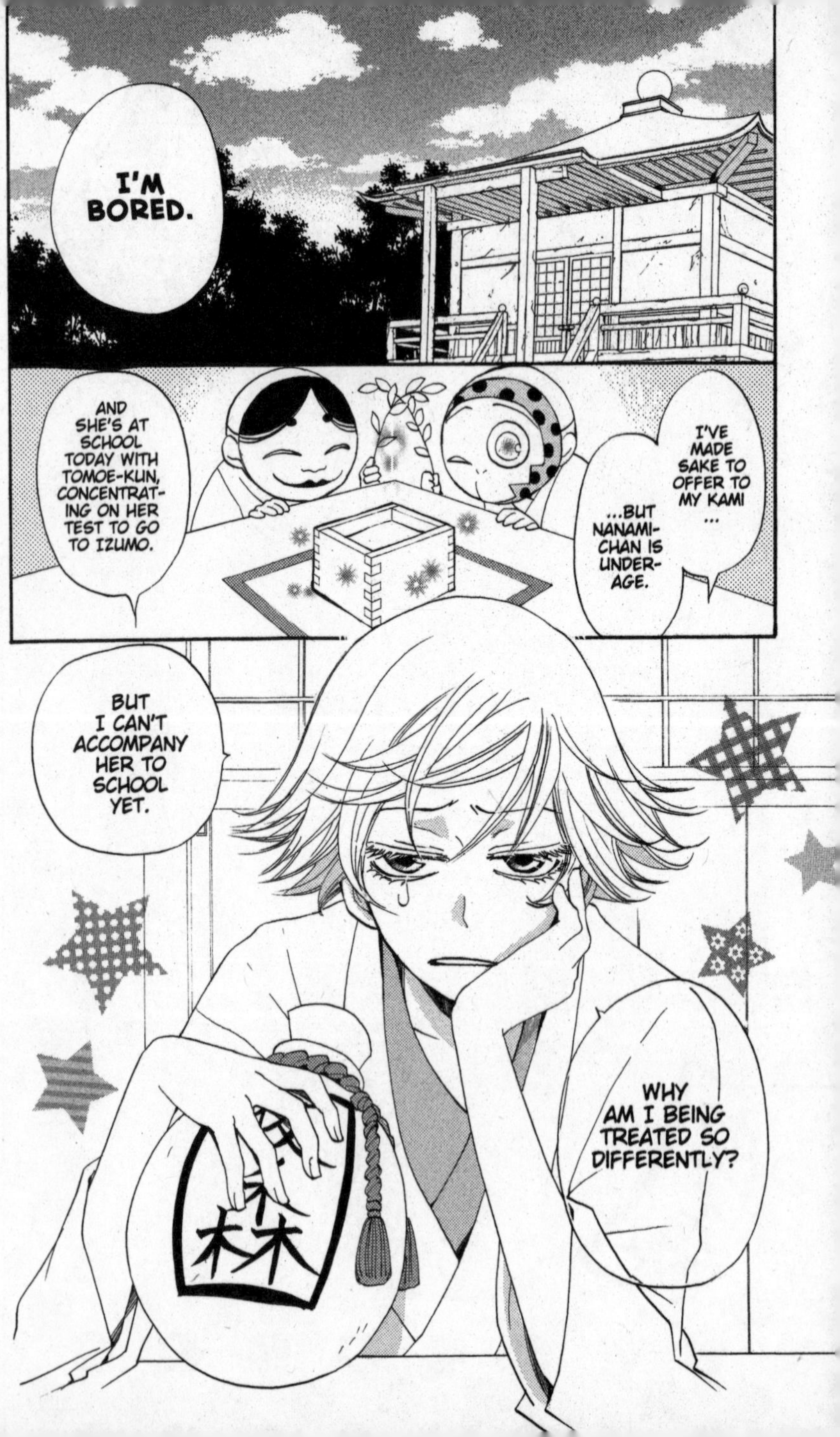
I'M BORED.
I'VE MADE SAKE TO OFFER TO MY KAMI ...
...BUT NANAMI-CHAN IS UNDERAGE.
AND SHE'S AT SCHOOL TODAY WITH TOMOE-KUN, CONCENTRATING ON HER TEST TO GO TO IZUMO.
BUT I CAN'T ACCOMPANY HER TO SCHOOL YET.
WHY AM I BEING TREATED SO DIFFERENTLY?

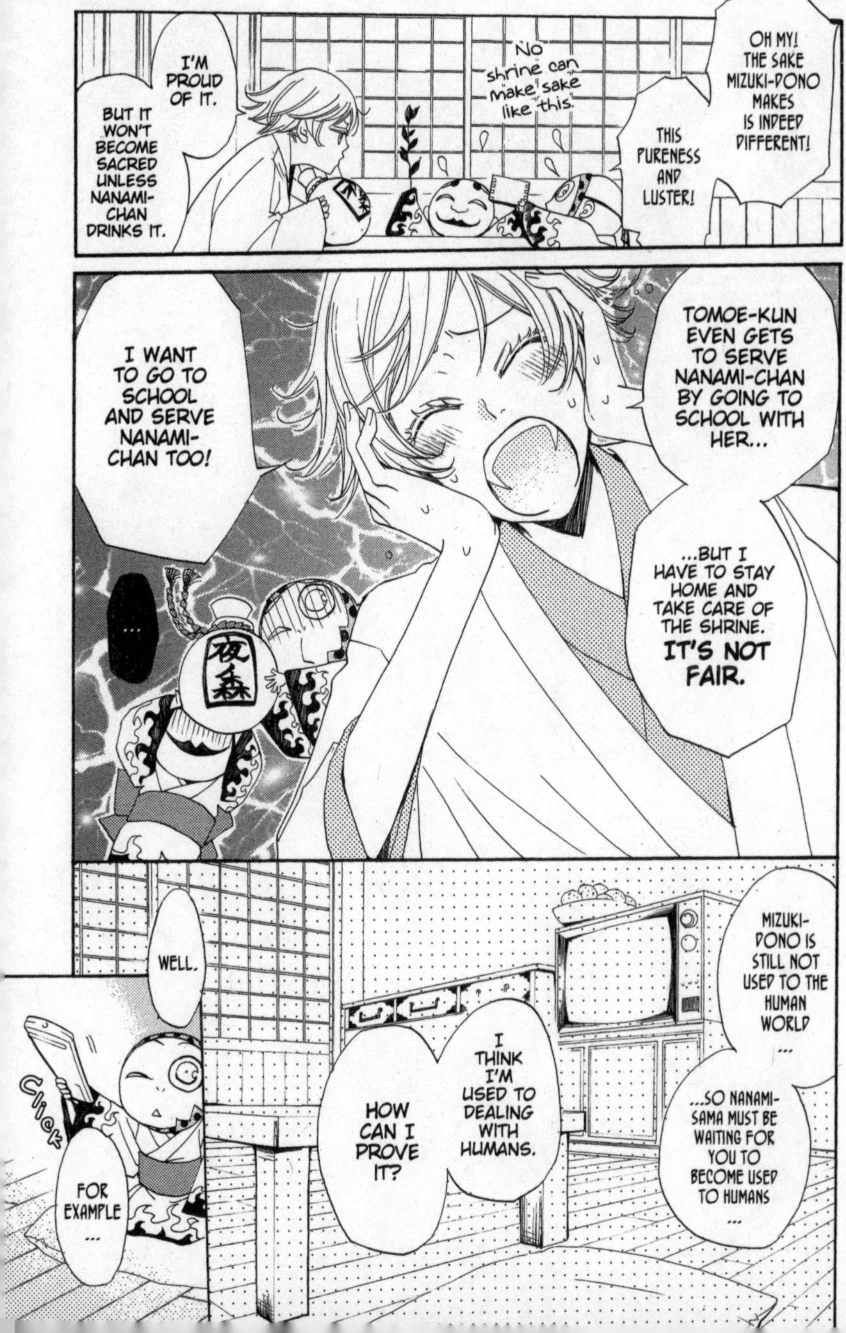
OH MY! THE SAKE MIZUKI-DONO MAKES IS INDEED DIFFERENT!
THIS PURENESS AND LUSTER!
No shrine can make sake like this.
I'M PROUD OF IT.
BUT IT WON'T BECOME SACRED UNLESS NANAMI-CHAN DRINKS IT.
TOMOE-KUN EVEN GETS TO SERVE NANAMI-CHAN BY GOING TO SCHOOL WITH HER...
...BUT I HAVE TO STAY HOME AND TAKE CARE OF THE SHRINE. **IT'S NOT FAIR.**
I WANT TO GO TO SCHOOL AND SERVE NANAMI-CHAN TOO!
...
夜森
MIZUKI-DONO IS STILL NOT USED TO THE HUMAN WORLD...
...SO NANAMI-SAMA MUST BE WAITING FOR YOU TO BECOME USED TO HUMANS...
I THINK I'M USED TO DEALING WITH HUMANS.
HOW CAN I PROVE IT?
WELL.
Click
FOR EXAMPLE...

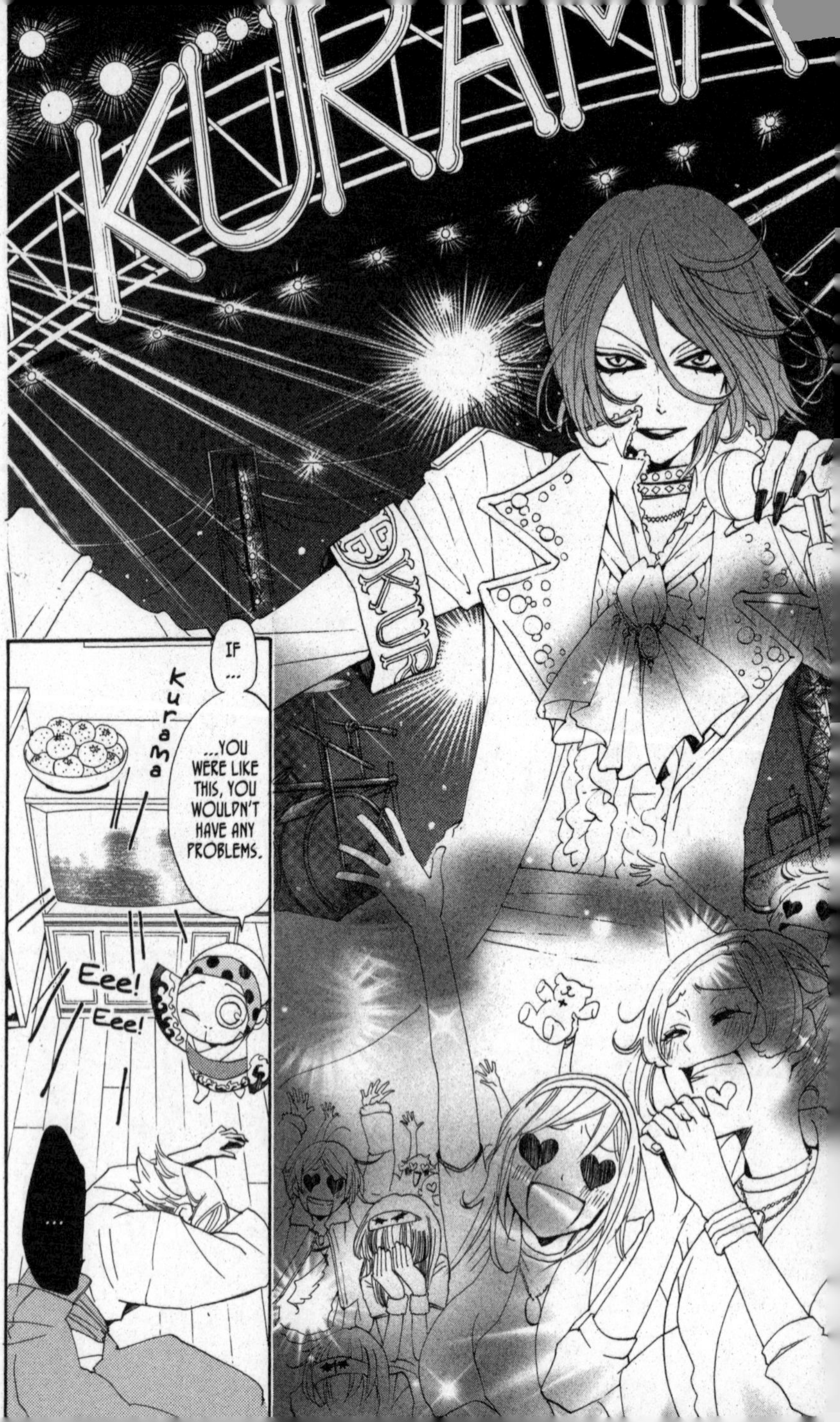
KURAMA
KUR
IF ...
Kurama
...YOU WERE LIKE THIS, YOU WOULDN'T HAVE ANY PROBLEMS.
Eee!
Eee!
...

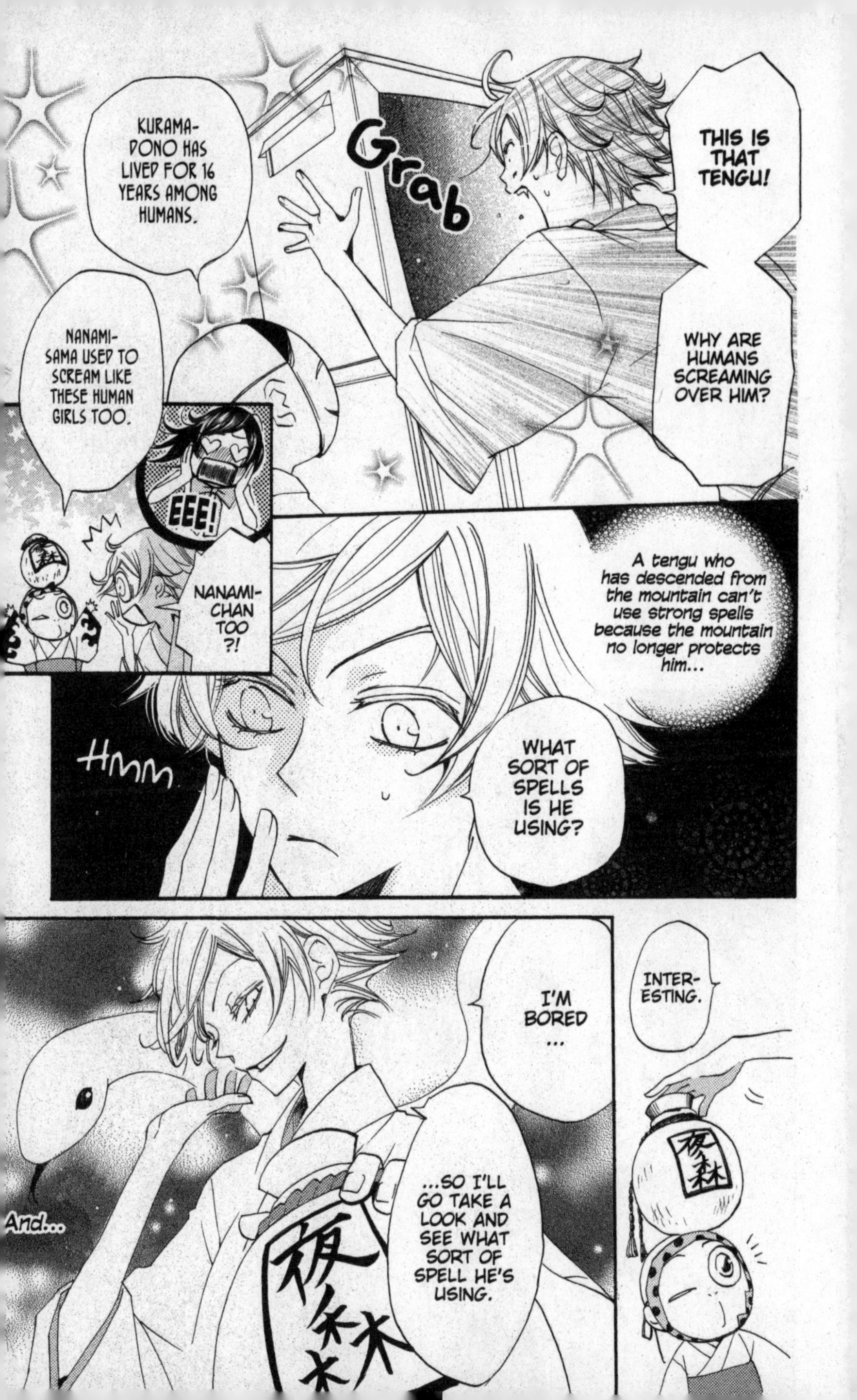
THIS IS THAT TENGU!
WHY ARE HUMANS SCREAMING OVER HIM?
Grab
KURAMA-DONO HAS LIVED FOR 16 YEARS AMONG HUMANS.
NANAMI-SAMA USED TO SCREAM LIKE THESE HUMAN GIRLS TOO.
EEE!
NANAMI-CHAN TOO?!
A tengu who has descended from the mountain can't use strong spells because the mountain no longer protects him...
WHAT SORT OF SPELLS IS HE USING?
HMM
INTER-ESTING.
I'M BORED...
...SO I'LL GO TAKE A LOOK AND SEE WHAT SORT OF SPELL HE'S USING.
And...

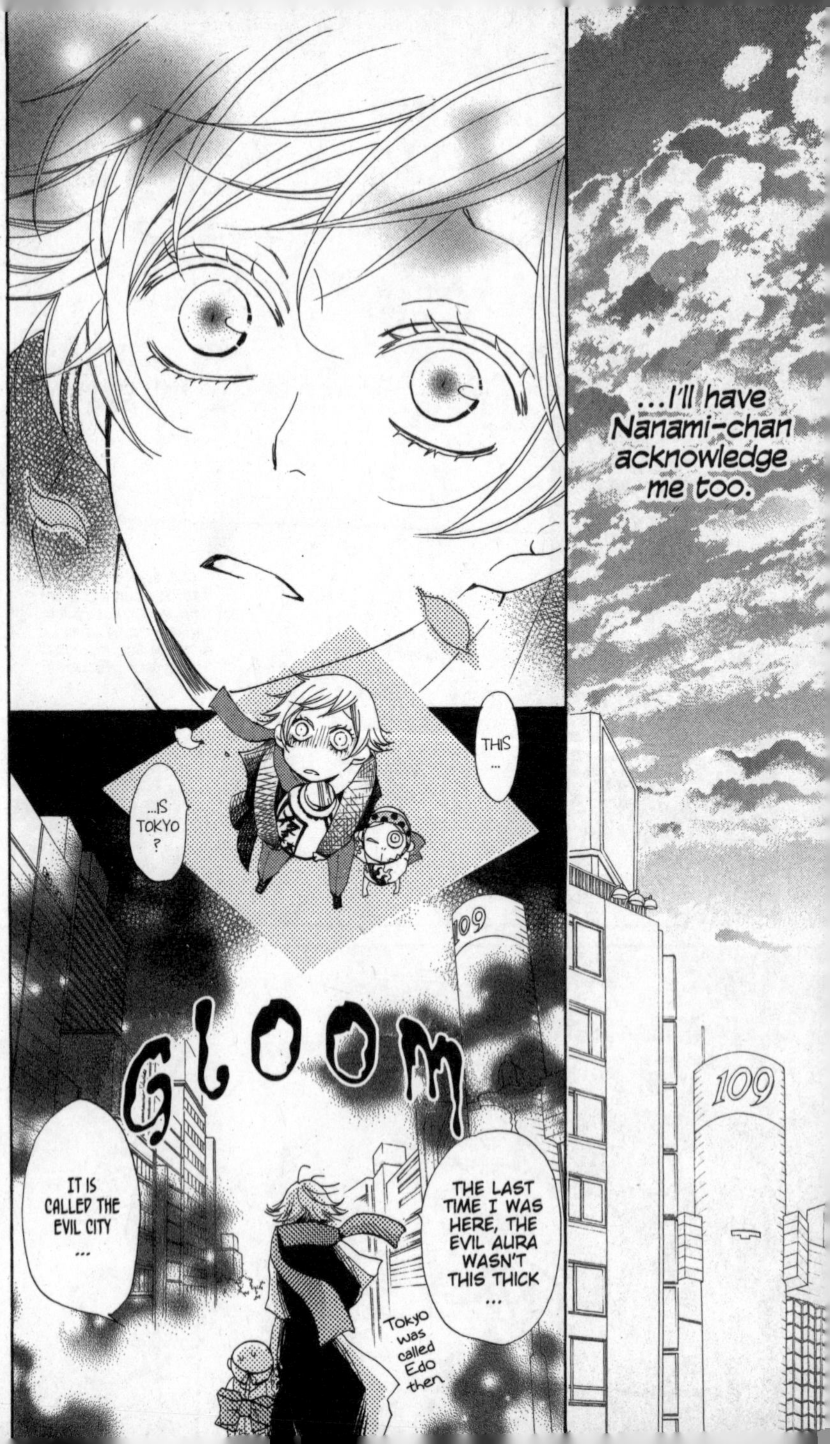
...I'll have Nanami-chan acknowledge me too.
THIS ...
...IS TOKYO ?
GLOOM
THE LAST TIME I WAS HERE, THE EVIL AURA WASN'T THIS THICK ...
Tokyo was called Edo then
IT IS CALLED THE EVIL CITY ...

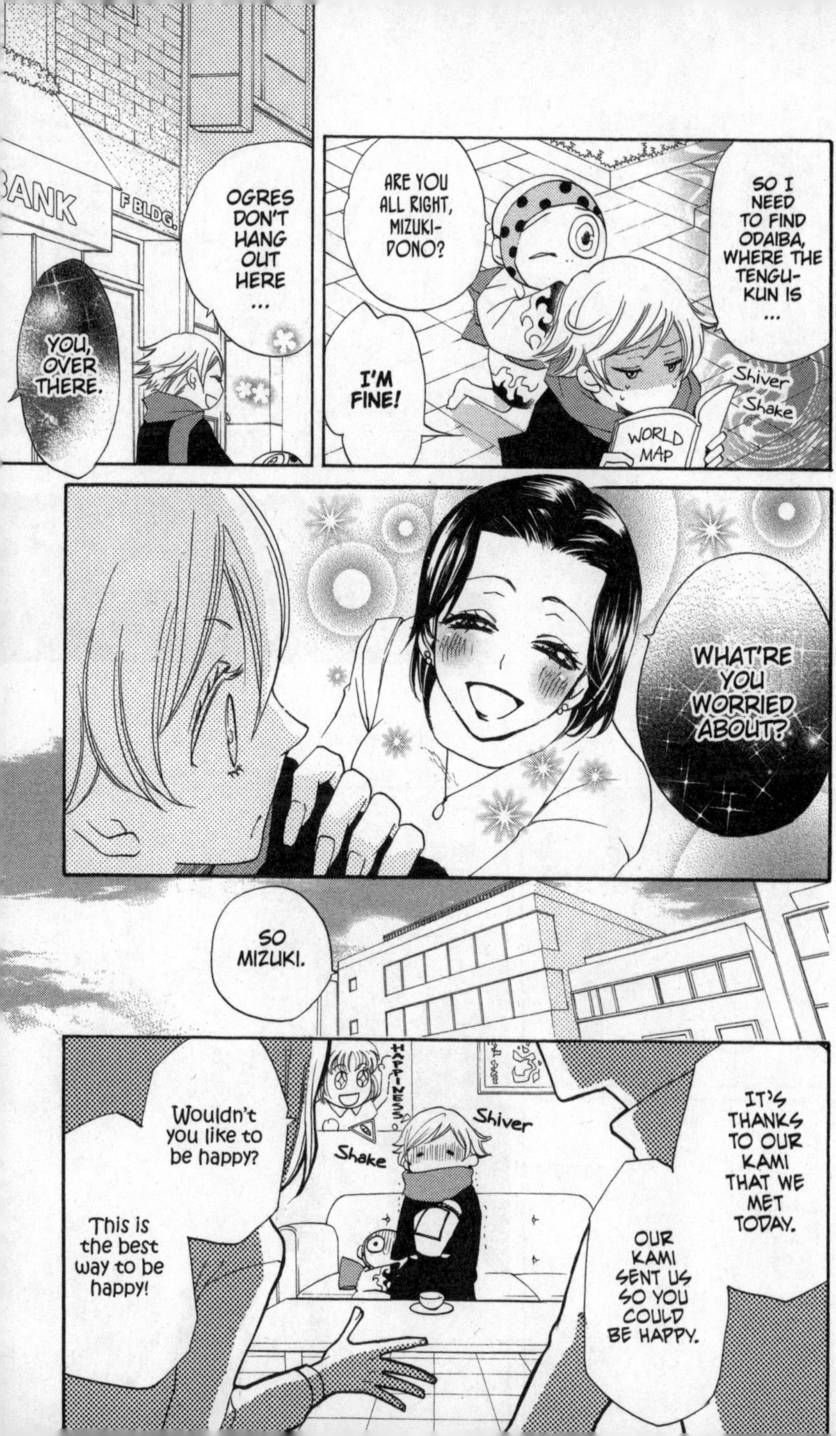
SO I NEED TO FIND ODAIBA, WHERE THE TENGU-KUN IS ...
Shiver
Shake
WORLD MAP
ARE YOU ALL RIGHT, MIZUKI-DONO?
I'M FINE!
BANK
F BLDG.
OGRES DON'T HANG OUT HERE ...
YOU, OVER THERE.
WHAT'RE YOU WORRIED ABOUT?
SO MIZUKI.
IT'S THANKS TO OUR KAMI THAT WE MET TODAY.
OUR KAMI SENT US SO YOU COULD BE HAPPY.
HAPPINESS
Shiver
Shake
Wouldn't you like to be happy?
This is the best way to be happy!

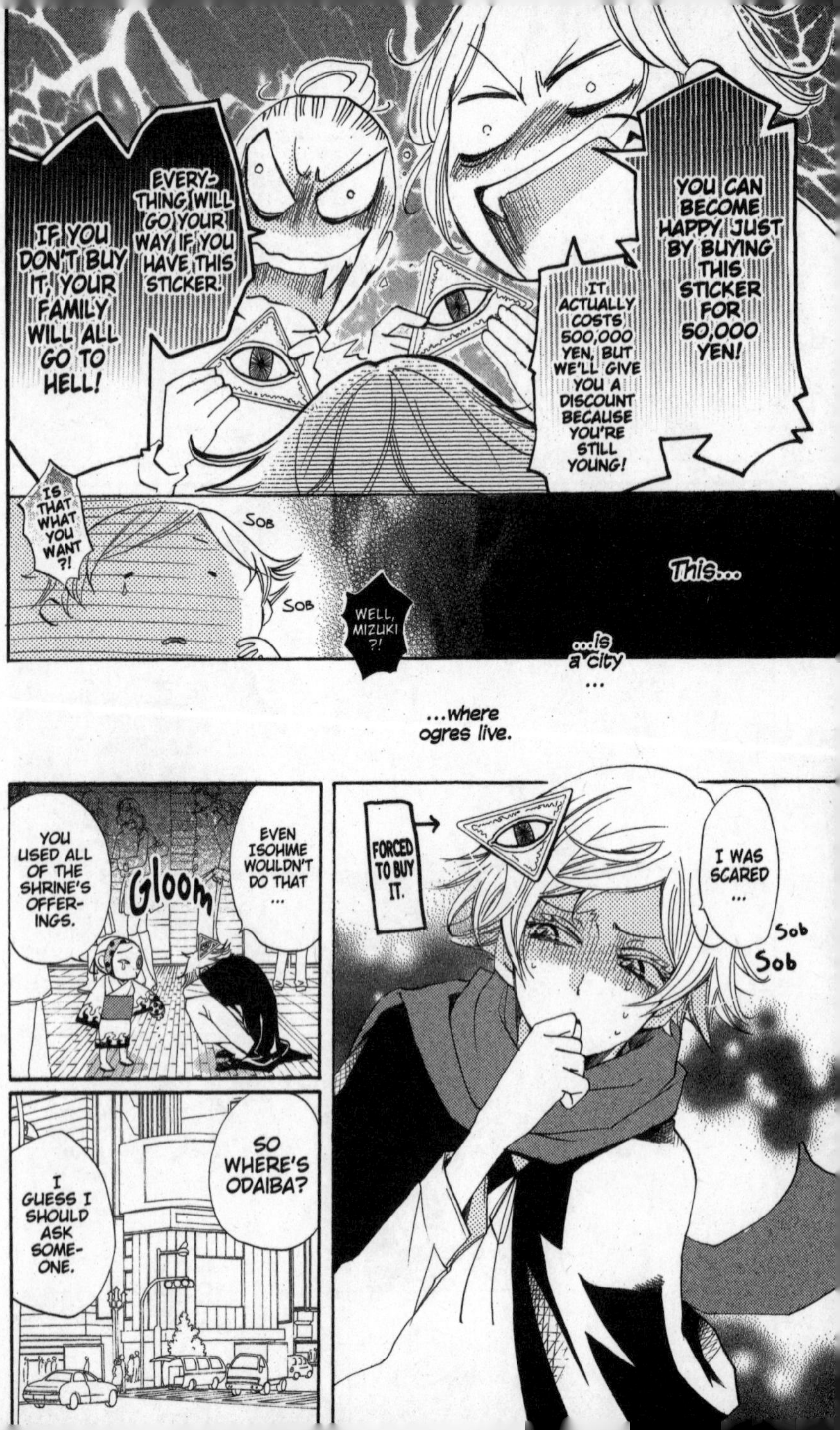
YOU CAN BECOME HAPPY JUST BY BUYING THIS STICKER FOR 50,000 YEN!
IT ACTUALLY COSTS 500,000 YEN, BUT WE'LL GIVE YOU A DISCOUNT BECAUSE YOU'RE STILL YOUNG!
EVERYTHING WILL GO YOUR WAY IF YOU HAVE THIS STICKER.
IF YOU DON'T BUY IT, YOUR FAMILY WILL ALL GO TO HELL!
This...
WELL, MIZUKI ?!
SOB
SOB
IS THAT WHAT YOU WANT ?!
...is a city ...
...where ogres live.
I WAS SCARED ...
Sob
Sob
FORCED TO BUY IT.
EVEN ISOHIME WOULDN'T DO THAT ...
Gloom
YOU USED ALL OF THE SHRINE'S OFFERINGS.
SO WHERE'S ODAIBA?
I GUESS I SHOULD ASK SOMEONE.

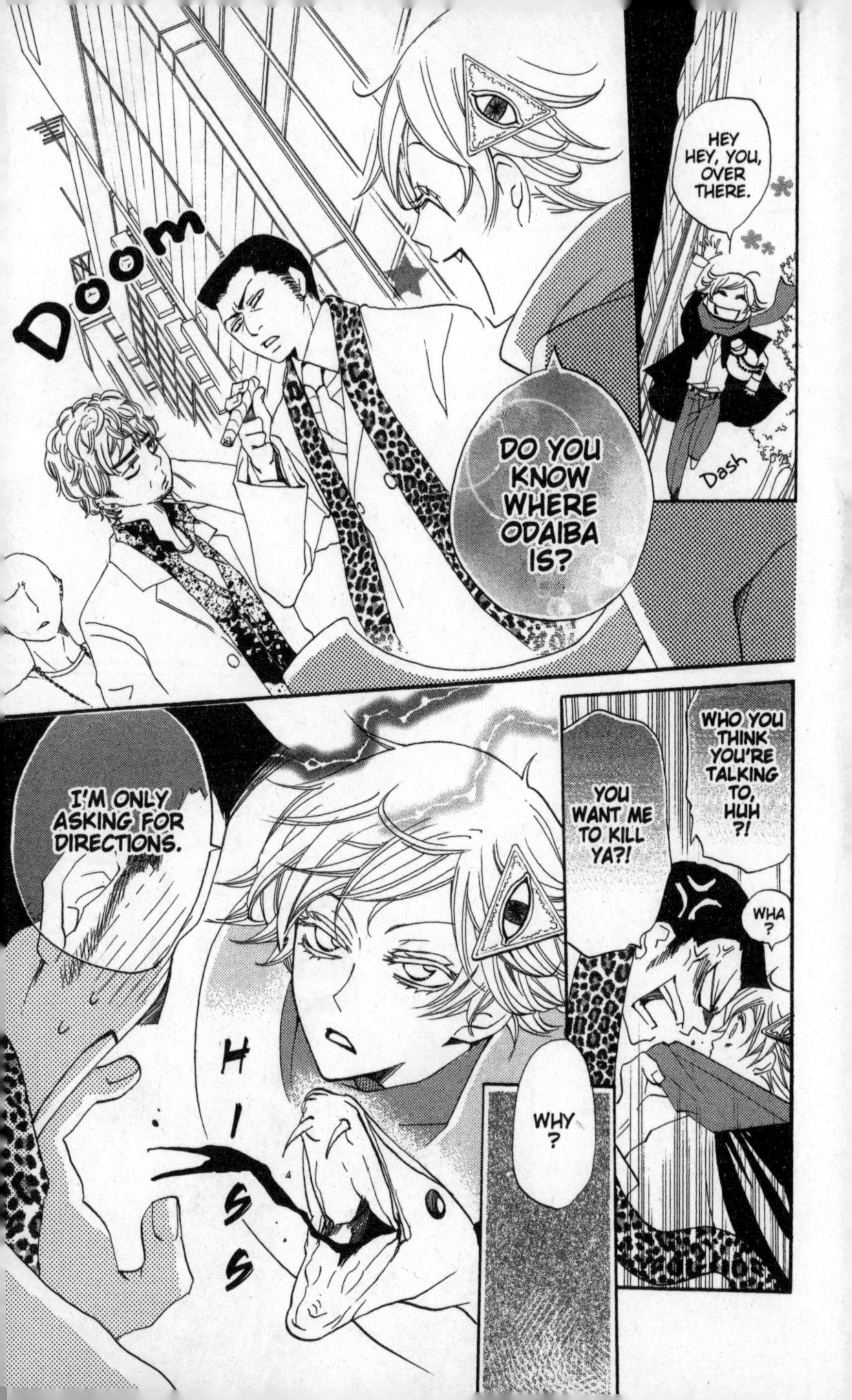
HEY HEY, YOU, OVER THERE.
Dash
Doom
DO YOU KNOW WHERE ODAIBA IS?
WHO YOU THINK YOU'RE TALKING TO, HUH?!
YOU WANT ME TO KILL YA?!
WHA?
I'M ONLY ASKING FOR DIRECTIONS.
WHY?
HISS

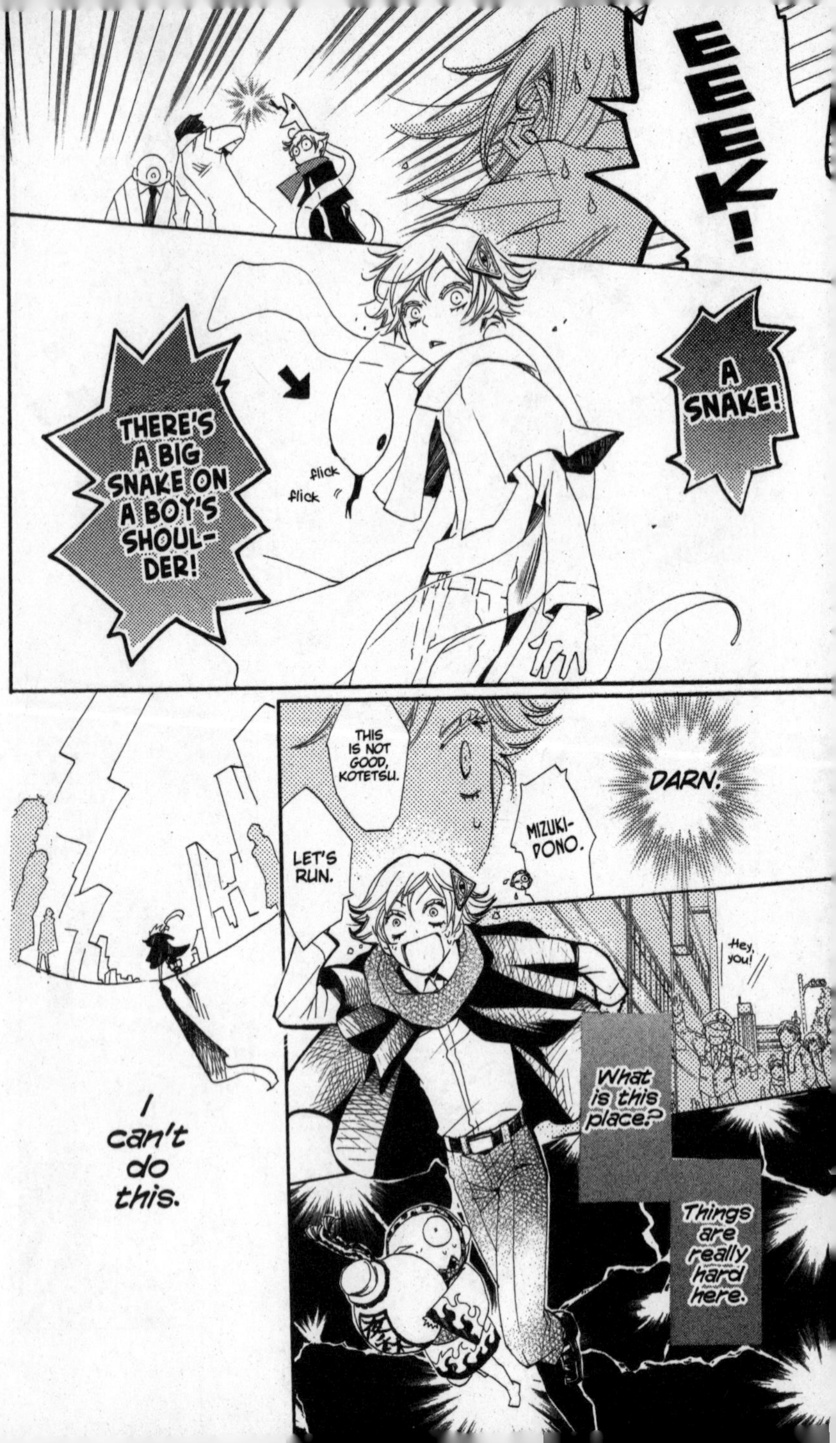
EEEK!
A SNAKE!
THERE'S A BIG SNAKE ON A BOY'S SHOULDER!
flick flick
DARN.
MIZUKI-DONO.
THIS IS NOT GOOD, KOTETSU.
LET'S RUN.
Hey, you!
What is this place?
Things are really hard here.
I can't do this.

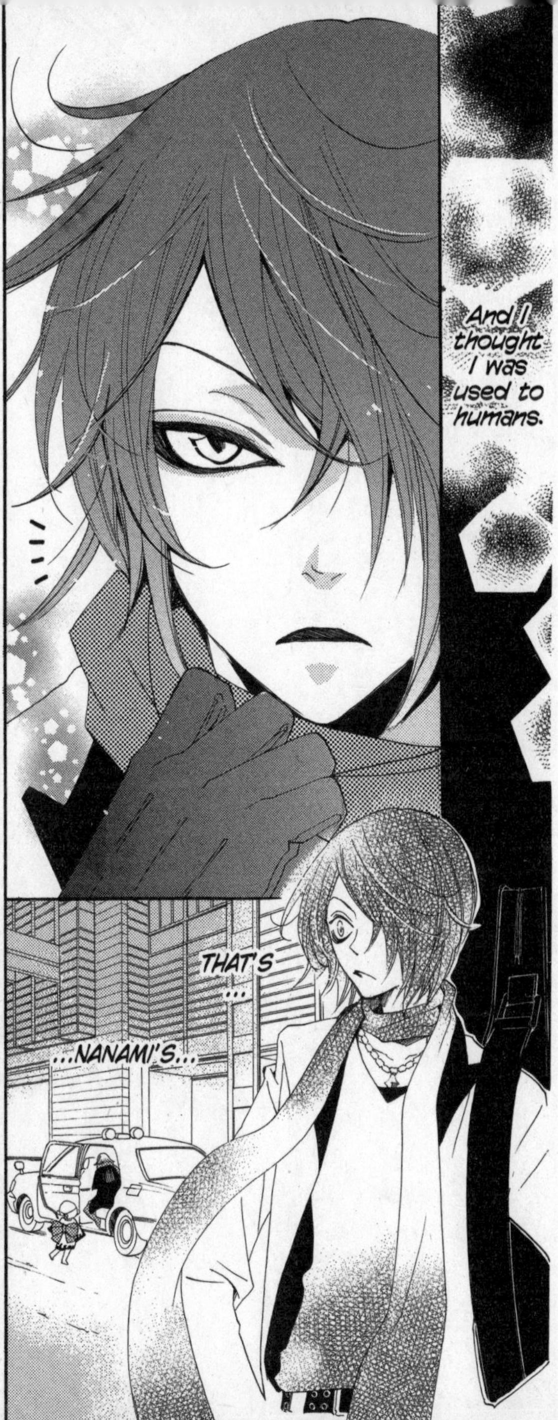
And I thought I was used to humans.
THAT'S ...
...NANAMI'S...

①

Thank you for picking up Volume 7 of Kamisama Kiss!

Volume 7 is an unknown volume number for me (because my previous series ended at volume 6), so my heart is beating fast and I'm nervous. I hope you enjoy reading it.

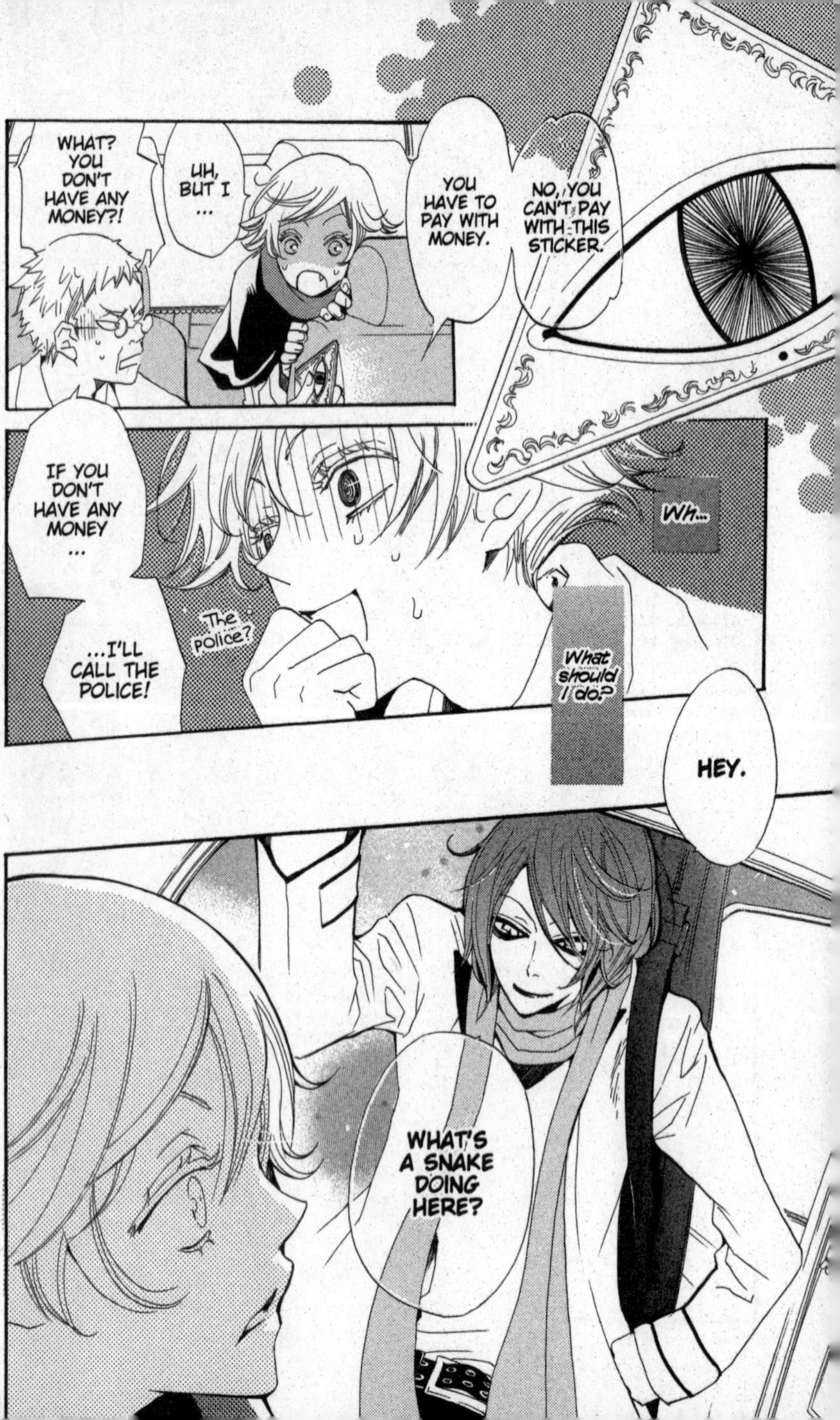
NO, YOU CAN'T PAY WITH THIS STICKER.
YOU HAVE TO PAY WITH MONEY.
UH, BUT I ...
WHAT? YOU DON'T HAVE ANY MONEY?!
IF YOU DON'T HAVE ANY MONEY ...
...I'LL CALL THE POLICE!
The police?
Wh...
What should I do?
HEY.
WHAT'S A SNAKE DOING HERE?

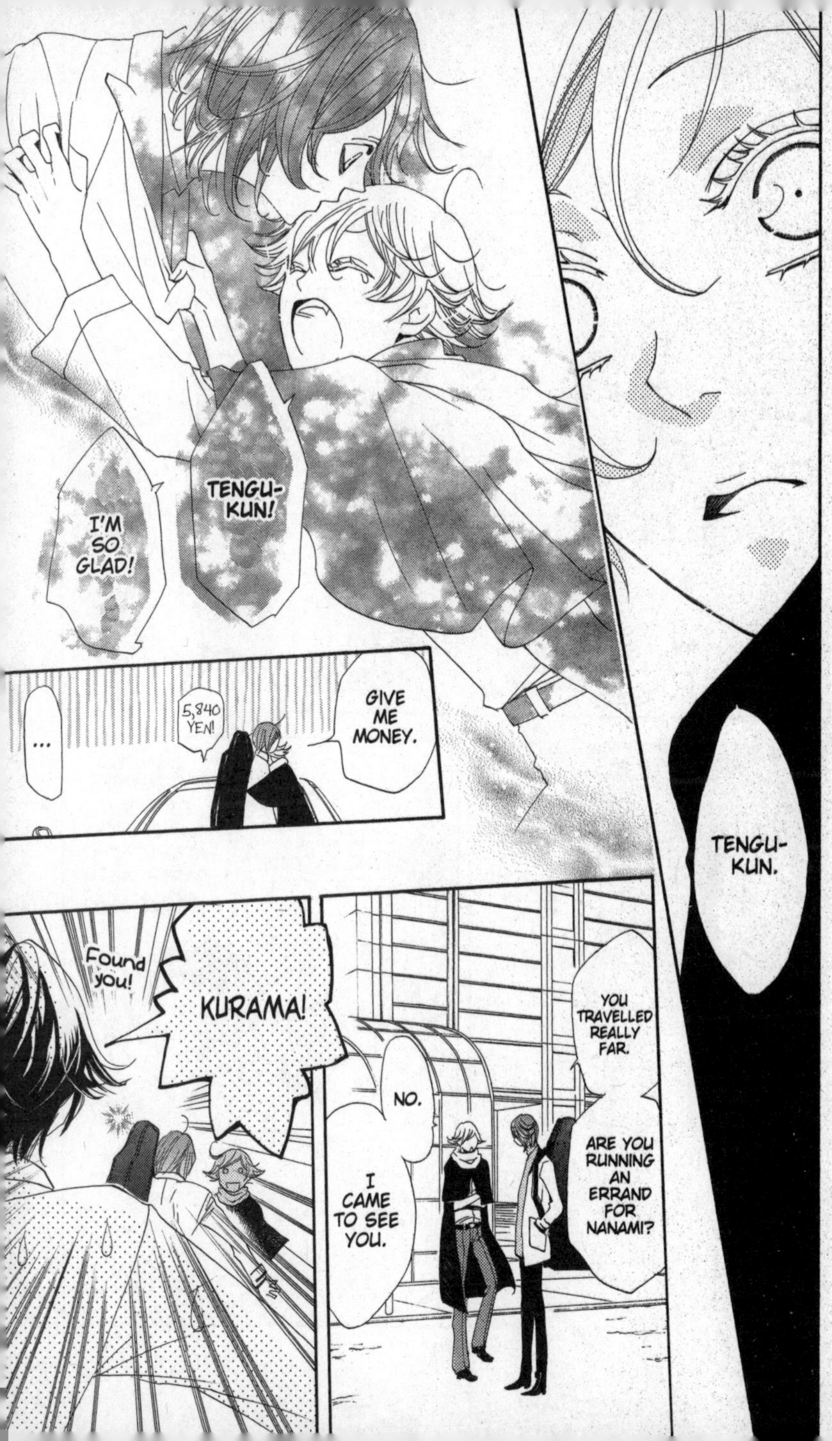
TENGU-KUN.
TENGU-KUN!
I'M SO GLAD!
GIVE ME MONEY.
5,840 YEN!
...
YOU TRAVELLED REALLY FAR.
NO.
ARE YOU RUNNING AN ERRAND FOR NANAMI?
I CAME TO SEE YOU.
KURAMA!
Found you!

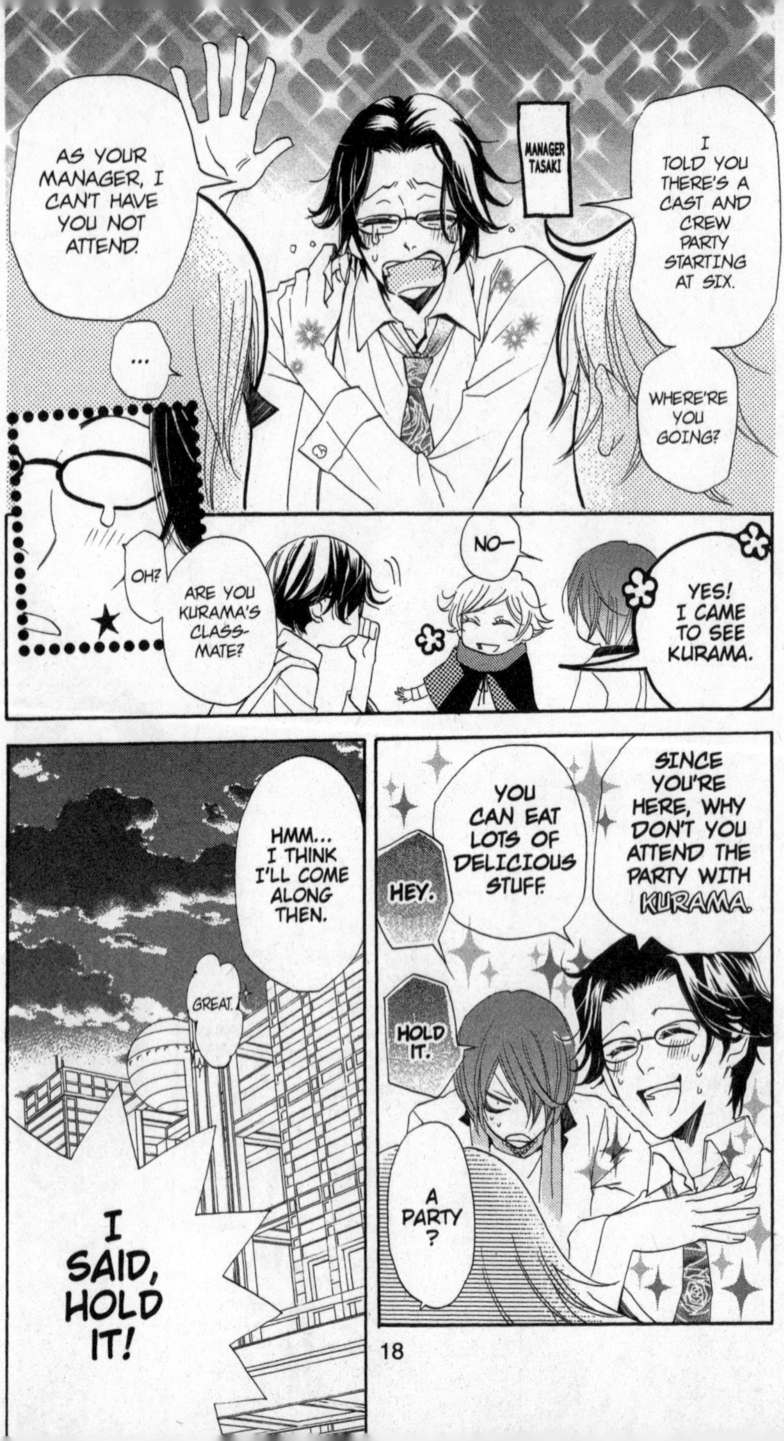
I TOLD YOU THERE'S A CAST AND CREW PARTY STARTING AT SIX.
MANAGER TASAKI
AS YOUR MANAGER, I CAN'T HAVE YOU NOT ATTEND.
WHERE'RE YOU GOING?
...
YES! I CAME TO SEE KURAMA.
NO—
ARE YOU KURAMA'S CLASSMATE?
OH?
SINCE YOU'RE HERE, WHY DON'T YOU ATTEND THE PARTY WITH KURAMA.
YOU CAN EAT LOTS OF DELICIOUS STUFF.
HEY.
HOLD IT.
A PARTY?
HMM... I THINK I'LL COME ALONG THEN.
GREAT.
I SAID, HOLD IT!

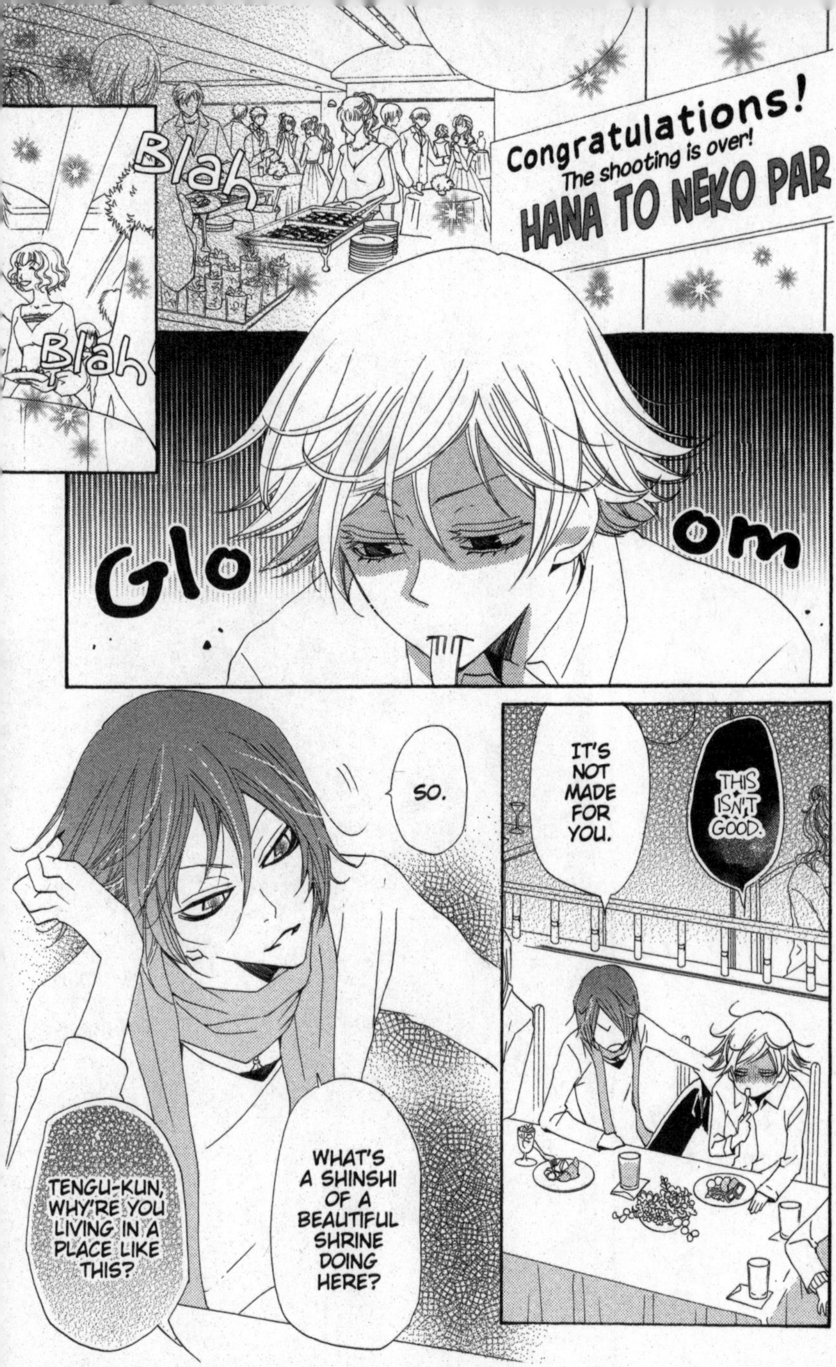
Congratulations!
The shooting is over!
HANA TO NEKO PAR
Blah
Blah
Glo om
THIS ISN'T GOOD.
IT'S NOT MADE FOR YOU.
SO.
WHAT'S A SHINSHI OF A BEAUTIFUL SHRINE DOING HERE?
TENGU-KUN, WHY'RE YOU LIVING IN A PLACE LIKE THIS?

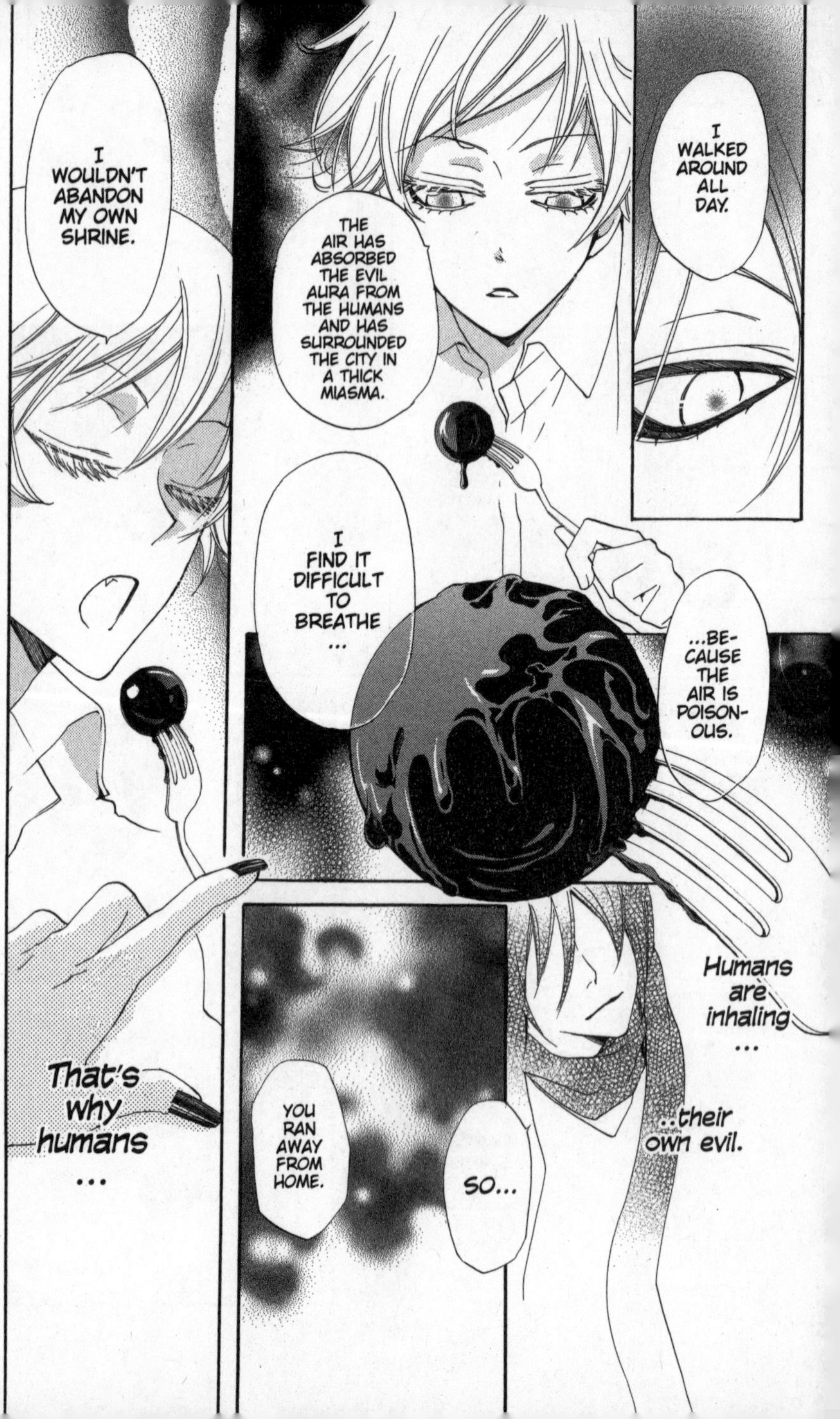
I WALKED AROUND ALL DAY.
THE AIR HAS ABSORBED THE EVIL AURA FROM THE HUMANS AND HAS SURROUNDED THE CITY IN A THICK MIASMA.
I FIND IT DIFFICULT TO BREATHE...
...BECAUSE THE AIR IS POISONOUS.
Humans are inhaling...
...their own evil.
SO...
YOU RAN AWAY FROM HOME.
I WOULDN'T ABANDON MY OWN SHRINE.
That's why humans...

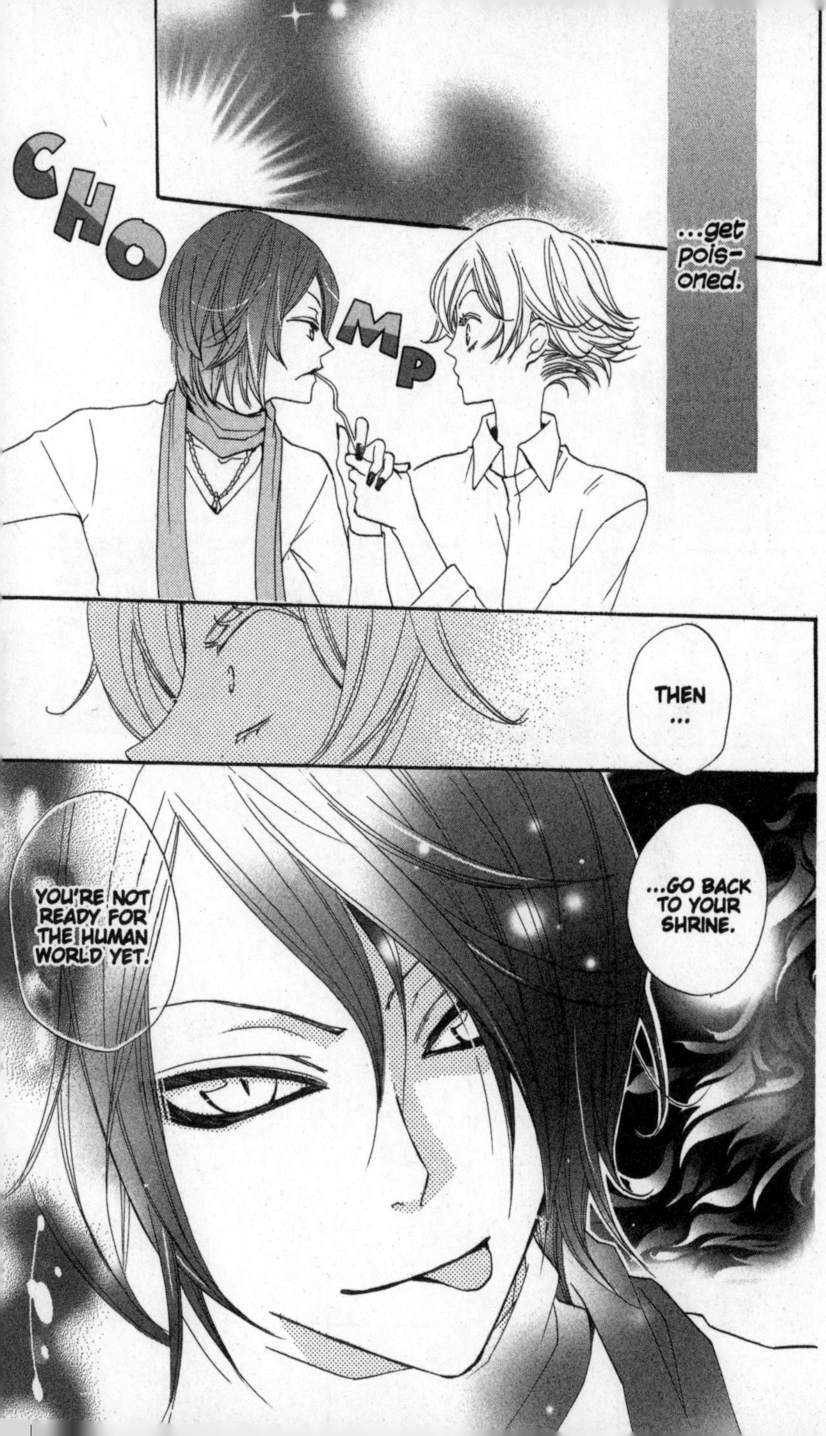
...get poisoned.
CHOMP
THEN...
...GO BACK TO YOUR SHRINE.
YOU'RE NOT READY FOR THE HUMAN WORLD YET.

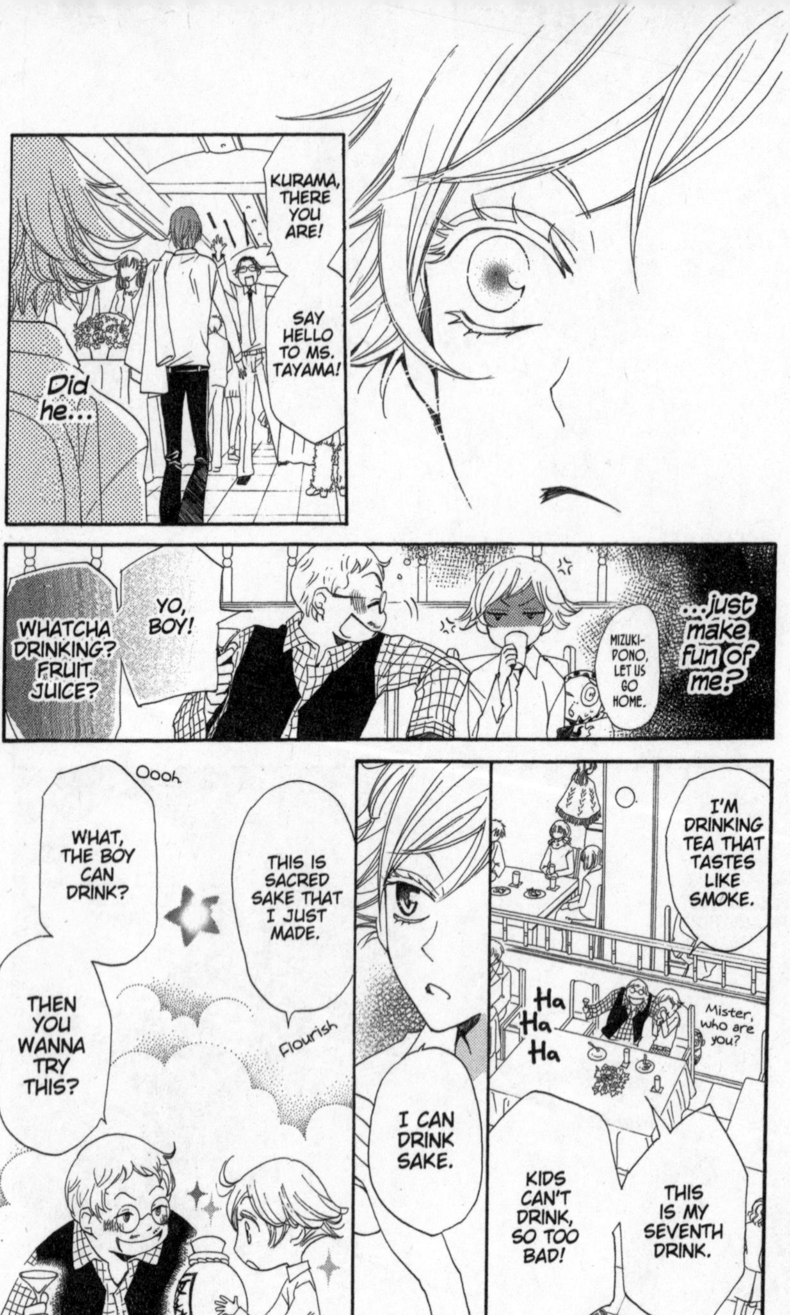
KURAMA, THERE YOU ARE!
SAY HELLO TO MS. TAYAMA!
Did he...
...just make fun of me?
MIZUKI-DONO, LET US GO HOME.
YO, BOY!
WHATCHA DRINKING? FRUIT JUICE?
I'M DRINKING TEA THAT TASTES LIKE SMOKE.
Mister, who are you?
Ha Ha Ha
THIS IS MY SEVENTH DRINK.
KIDS CAN'T DRINK, SO TOO BAD!
I CAN DRINK SAKE.
THIS IS SACRED SAKE THAT I JUST MADE.
Flourish
Oooh
WHAT, THE BOY CAN DRINK?
THEN YOU WANNA TRY THIS?

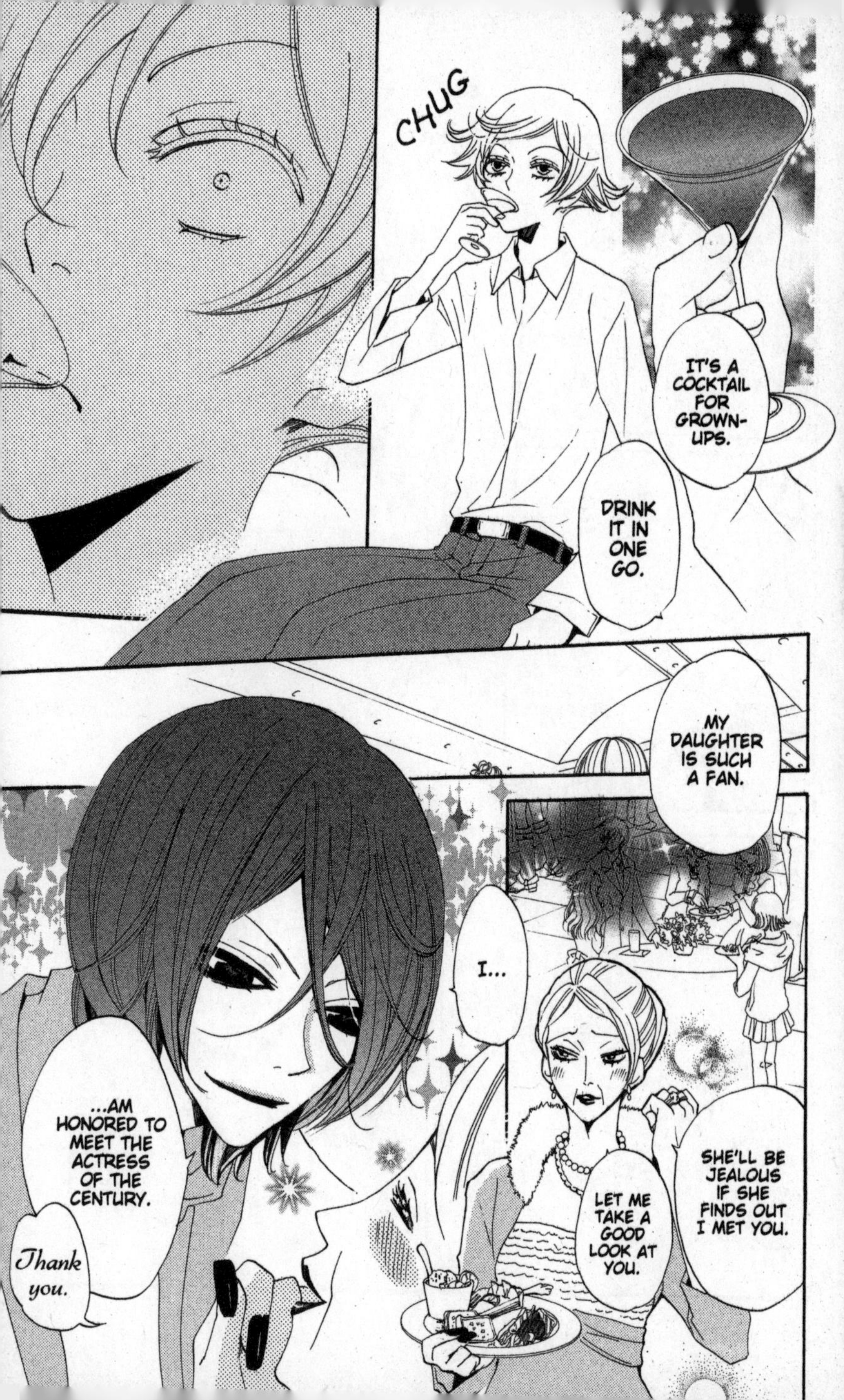
CHUG
IT'S A COCKTAIL FOR GROWN-UPS.
DRINK IT IN ONE GO.
MY DAUGHTER IS SUCH A FAN.
SHE'LL BE JEALOUS IF SHE FINDS OUT I MET YOU.
LET ME TAKE A GOOD LOOK AT YOU.
I...
...AM HONORED TO MEET THE ACTRESS OF THE CENTURY.
Thank you.

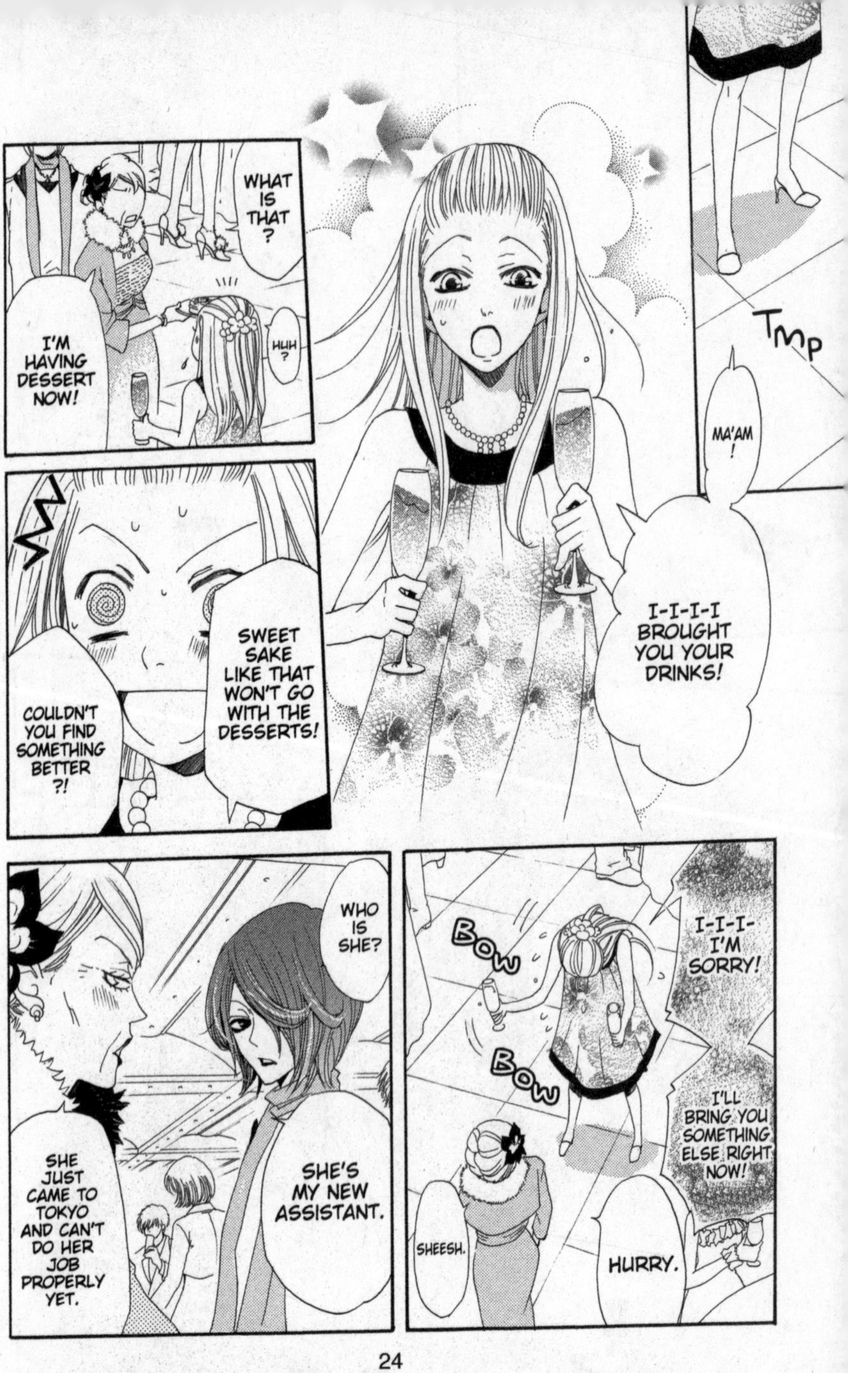
TMP
MA'AM!
I-I-I-I BROUGHT YOU YOUR DRINKS!
WHAT IS THAT?
HUH?
I'M HAVING DESSERT NOW!
SWEET SAKE LIKE THAT WON'T GO WITH THE DESSERTS!
COULDN'T YOU FIND SOMETHING BETTER ?!
I-I-I-I'M SORRY!
BOW
BOW
I'LL BRING YOU SOMETHING ELSE RIGHT NOW!
HURRY.
SHEESH.
WHO IS SHE?
SHE'S MY NEW ASSISTANT.
SHE JUST CAME TO TOKYO AND CAN'T DO HER JOB PROPERLY YET.

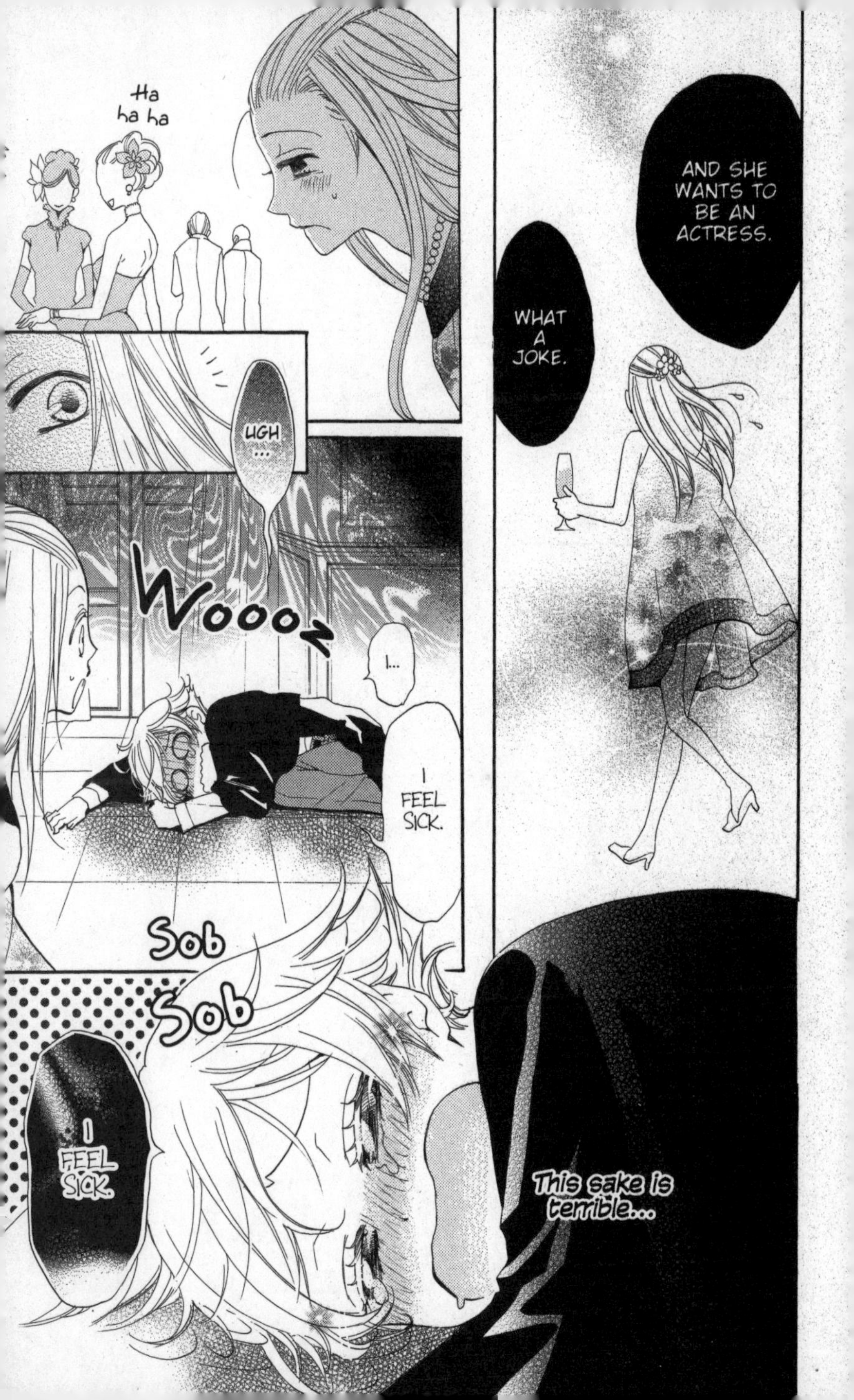

AND SHE WANTS TO BE AN ACTRESS.
WHAT A JOKE.
Ha ha ha
UGH...
Woooz
I...
I FEEL SICK.
Sob
Sob
This sake is terrible...
I FEEL SICK.

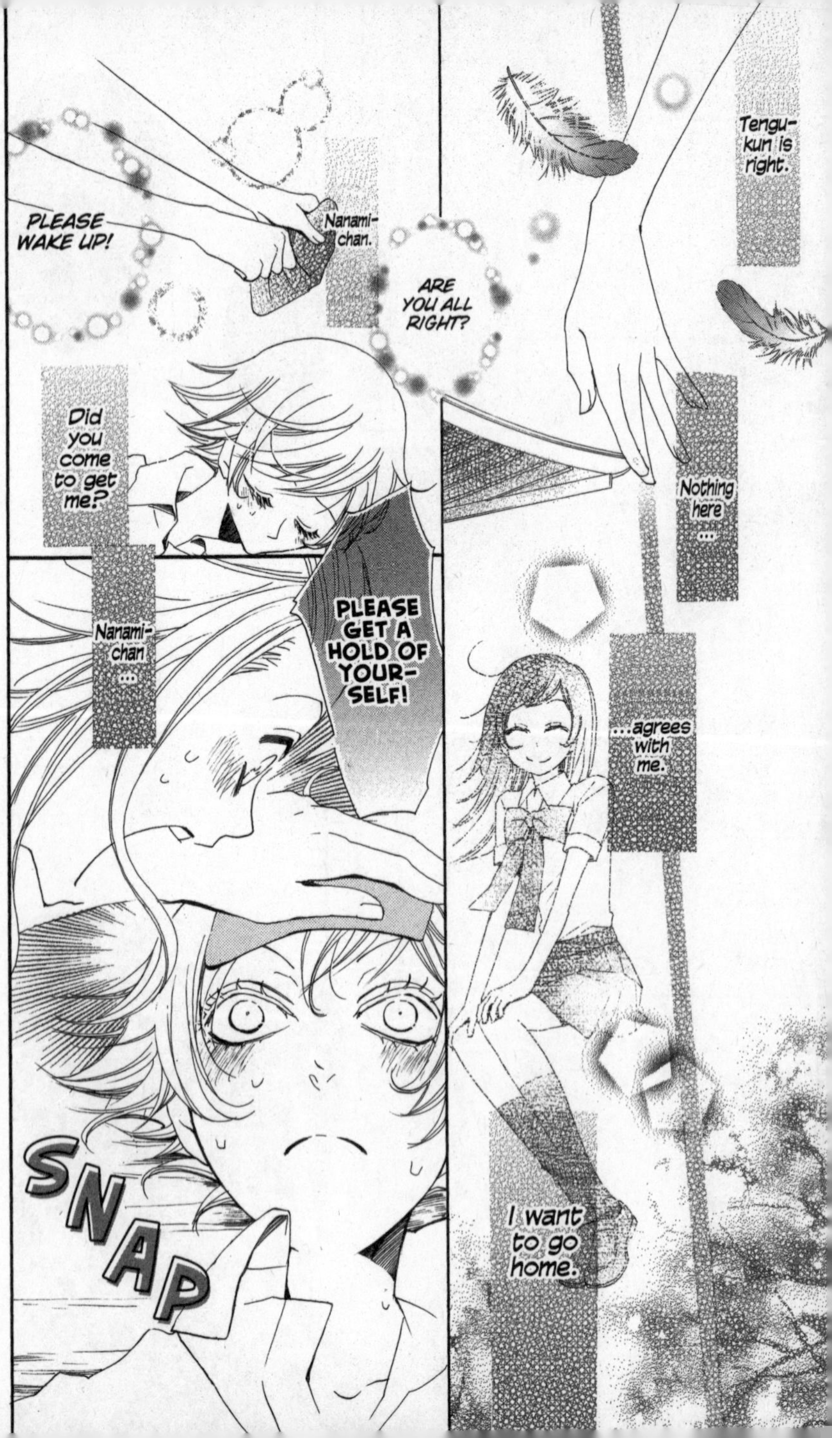
Tengu-kun is right.
Nothing here...
...agrees with me.
I want to go home.
Nanami-chan.
ARE YOU ALL RIGHT?
PLEASE WAKE UP!
Did you come to get me?
PLEASE GET A HOLD OF YOURSELF!
Nanami-chan...
SNAP

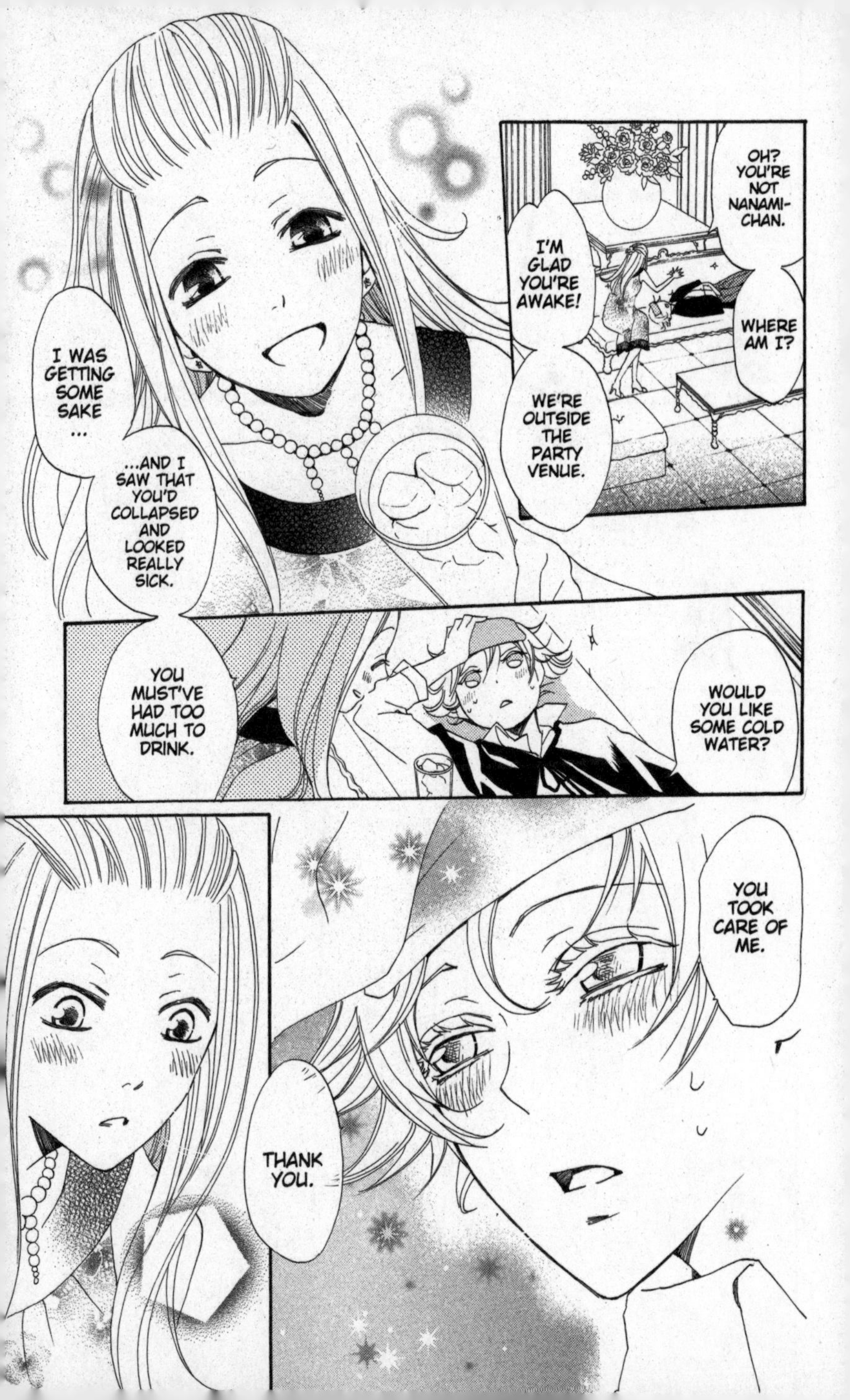
OH? YOU'RE NOT NANAMI-CHAN.
WHERE AM I?
I'M GLAD YOU'RE AWAKE!
WE'RE OUTSIDE THE PARTY VENUE.
I WAS GETTING SOME SAKE ...
...AND I SAW THAT YOU'D COLLAPSED AND LOOKED REALLY SICK.
WOULD YOU LIKE SOME COLD WATER?
YOU MUST'VE HAD TOO MUCH TO DRINK.
YOU TOOK CARE OF ME.
THANK YOU.

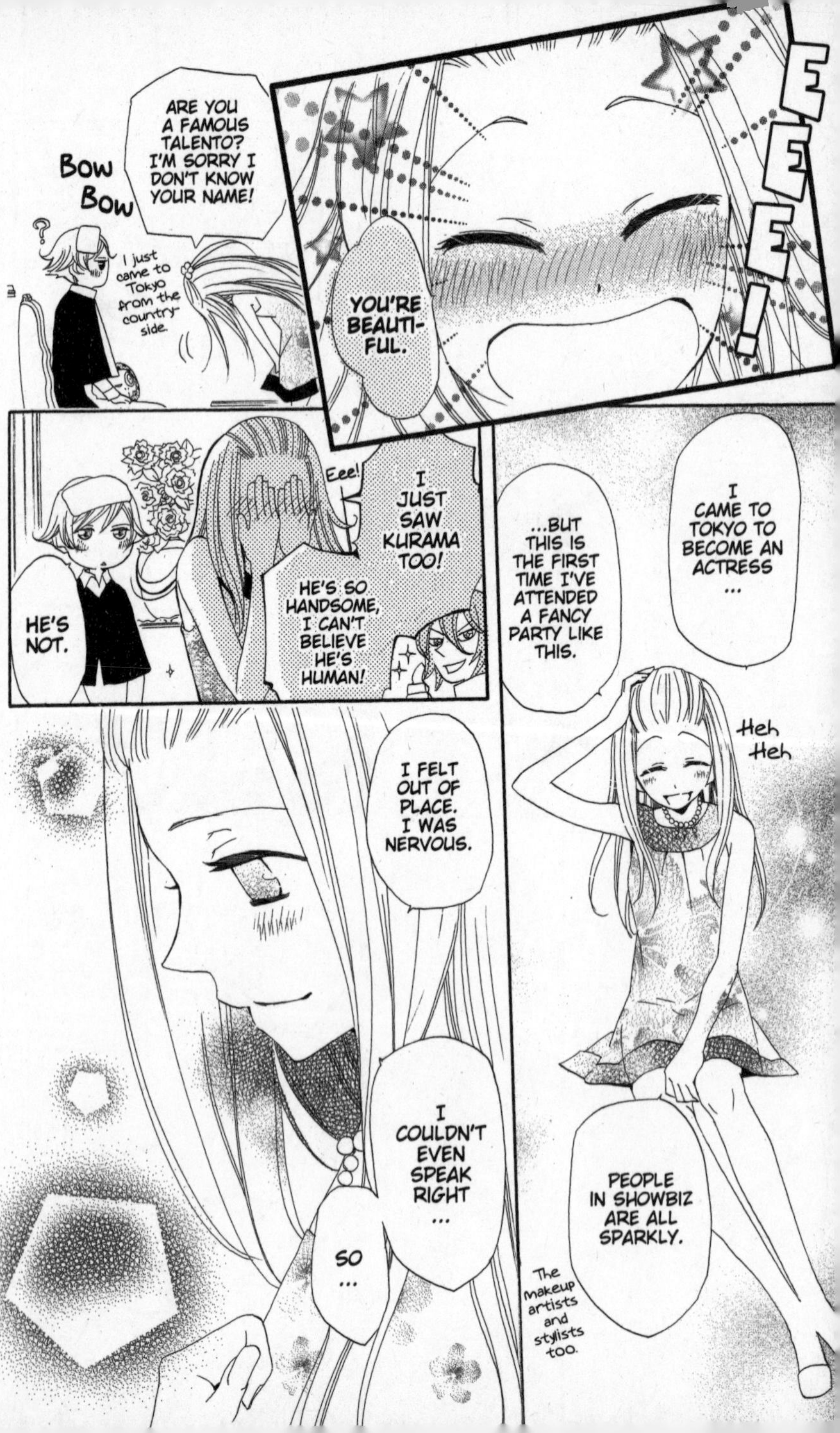
EEEE!
YOU'RE BEAUTIFUL.
ARE YOU A FAMOUS TALENTO? I'M SORRY I DON'T KNOW YOUR NAME!
BOW BOW
I just came to Tokyo from the country-side.
I CAME TO TOKYO TO BECOME AN ACTRESS...
...BUT THIS IS THE FIRST TIME I'VE ATTENDED A FANCY PARTY LIKE THIS.
Heh Heh
PEOPLE IN SHOWBIZ ARE ALL SPARKLY.
The makeup artists and stylists too.
I JUST SAW KURAMA TOO!
Eee!
HE'S SO HANDSOME, I CAN'T BELIEVE HE'S HUMAN!
HE'S NOT.
I FELT OUT OF PLACE. I WAS NERVOUS.
I COULDN'T EVEN SPEAK RIGHT...
SO...

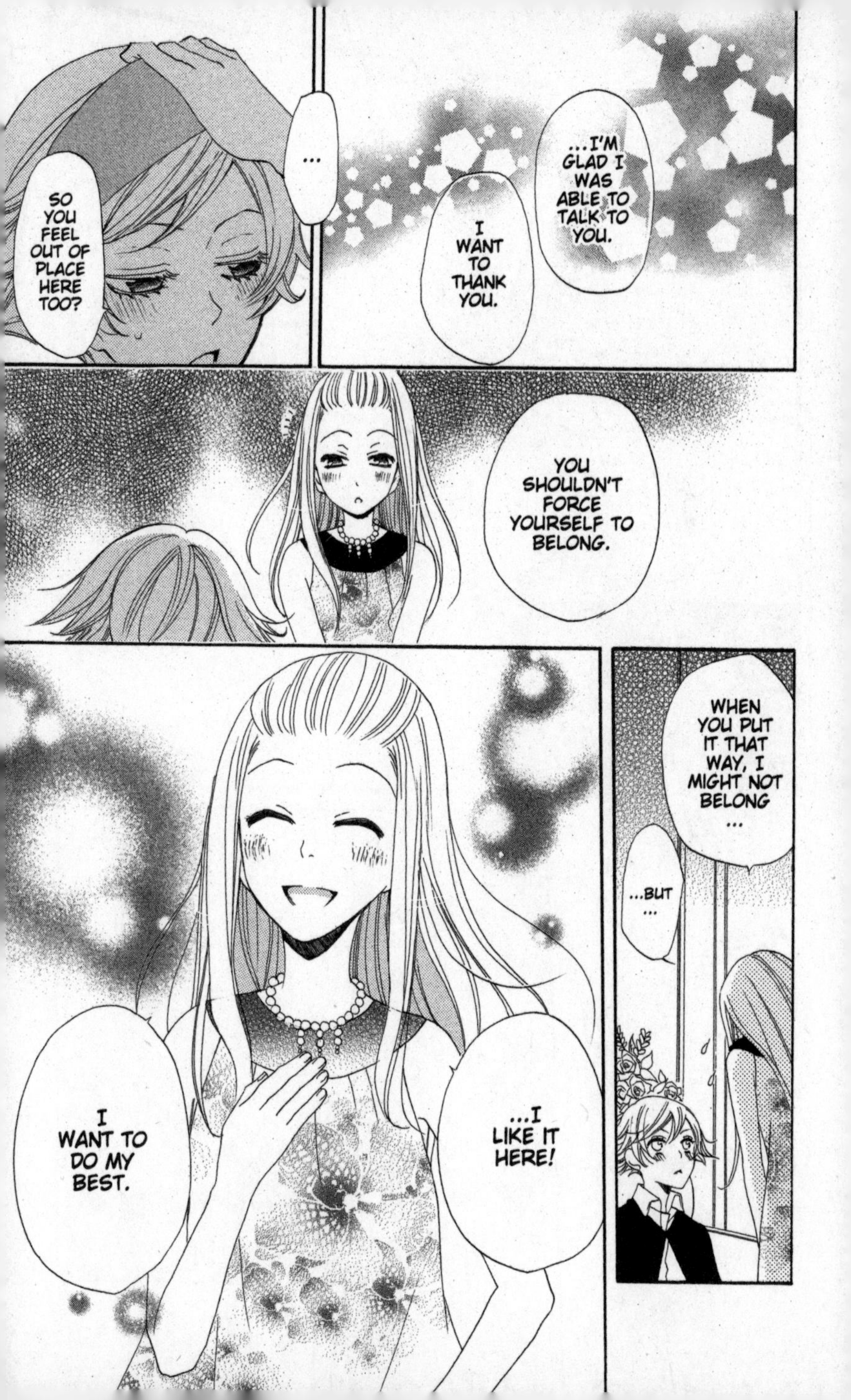
...I'M GLAD I WAS ABLE TO TALK TO YOU.
I WANT TO THANK YOU.
...
SO YOU FEEL OUT OF PLACE HERE TOO?
YOU SHOULDN'T FORCE YOURSELF TO BELONG.
WHEN YOU PUT IT THAT WAY, I MIGHT NOT BELONG ...
...BUT ...
...I LIKE IT HERE!
I WANT TO DO MY BEST.

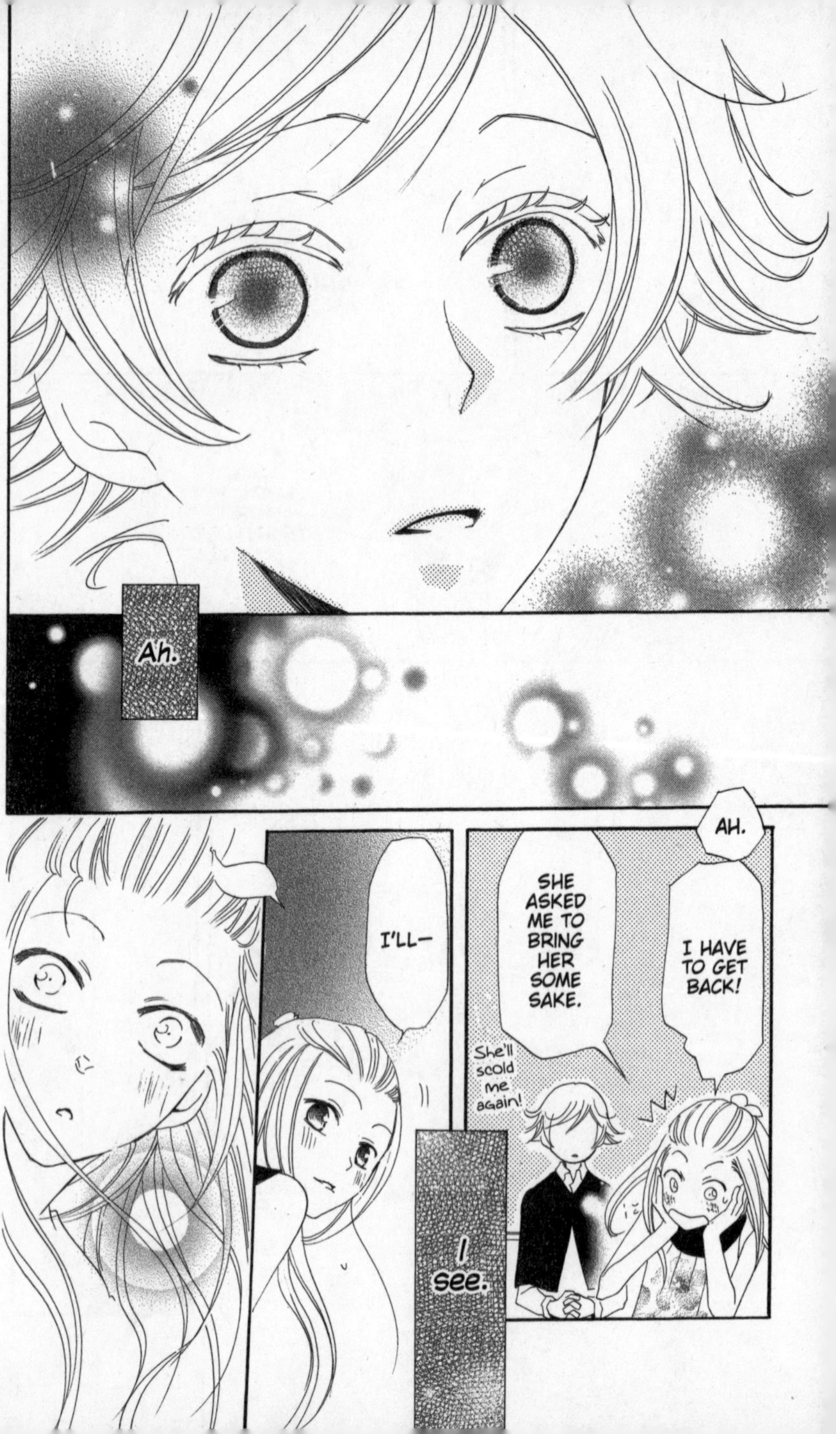
Ah.
AH.
I HAVE TO GET BACK!
SHE ASKED ME TO BRING HER SOME SAKE.
She'll scold me again!
I'LL—
I see.

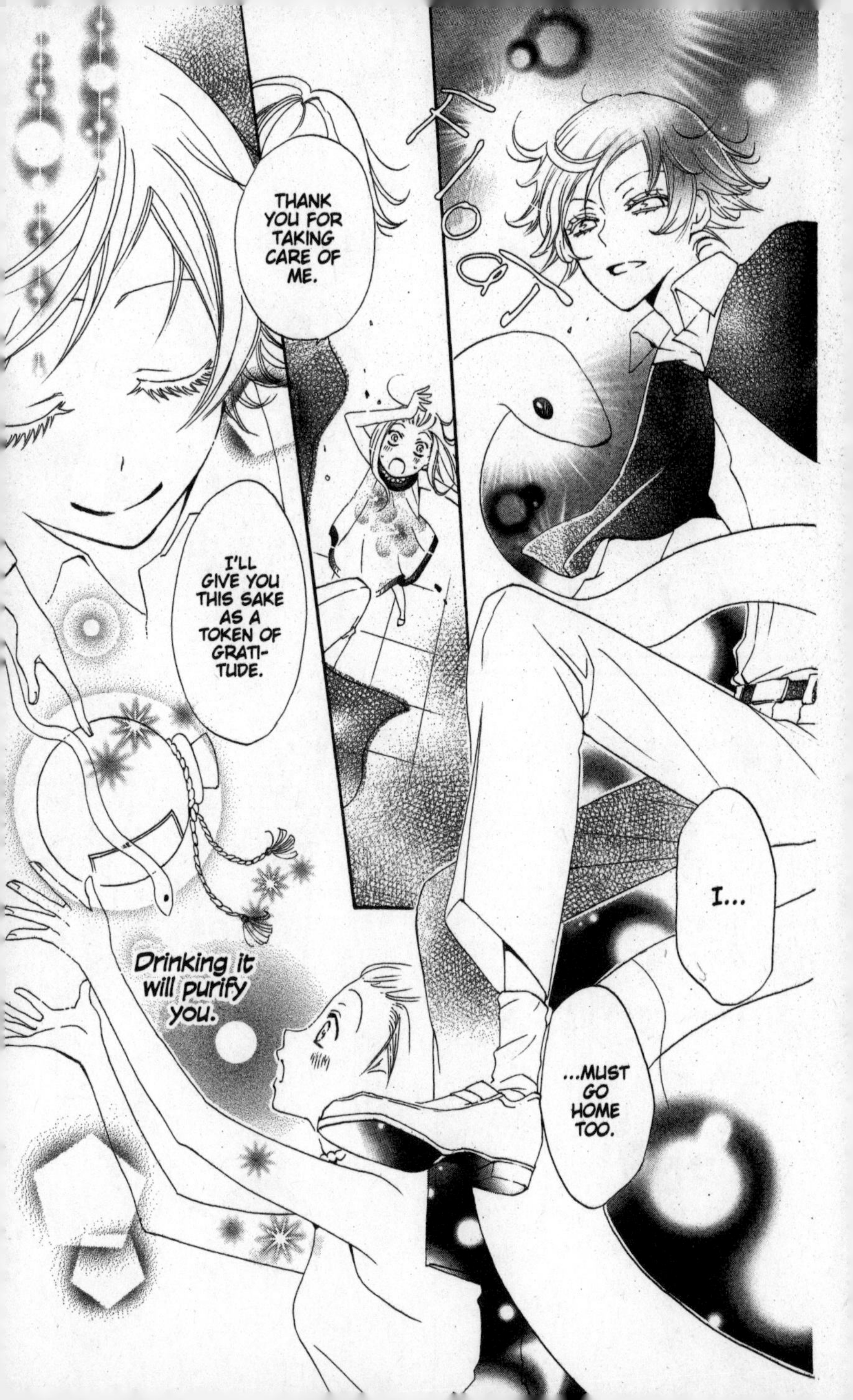
THANK YOU FOR TAKING CARE OF ME.
I'LL GIVE YOU THIS SAKE AS A TOKEN OF GRATI-TUDE.
Drinking it will purify you.
I...
...MUST GO HOME TOO.

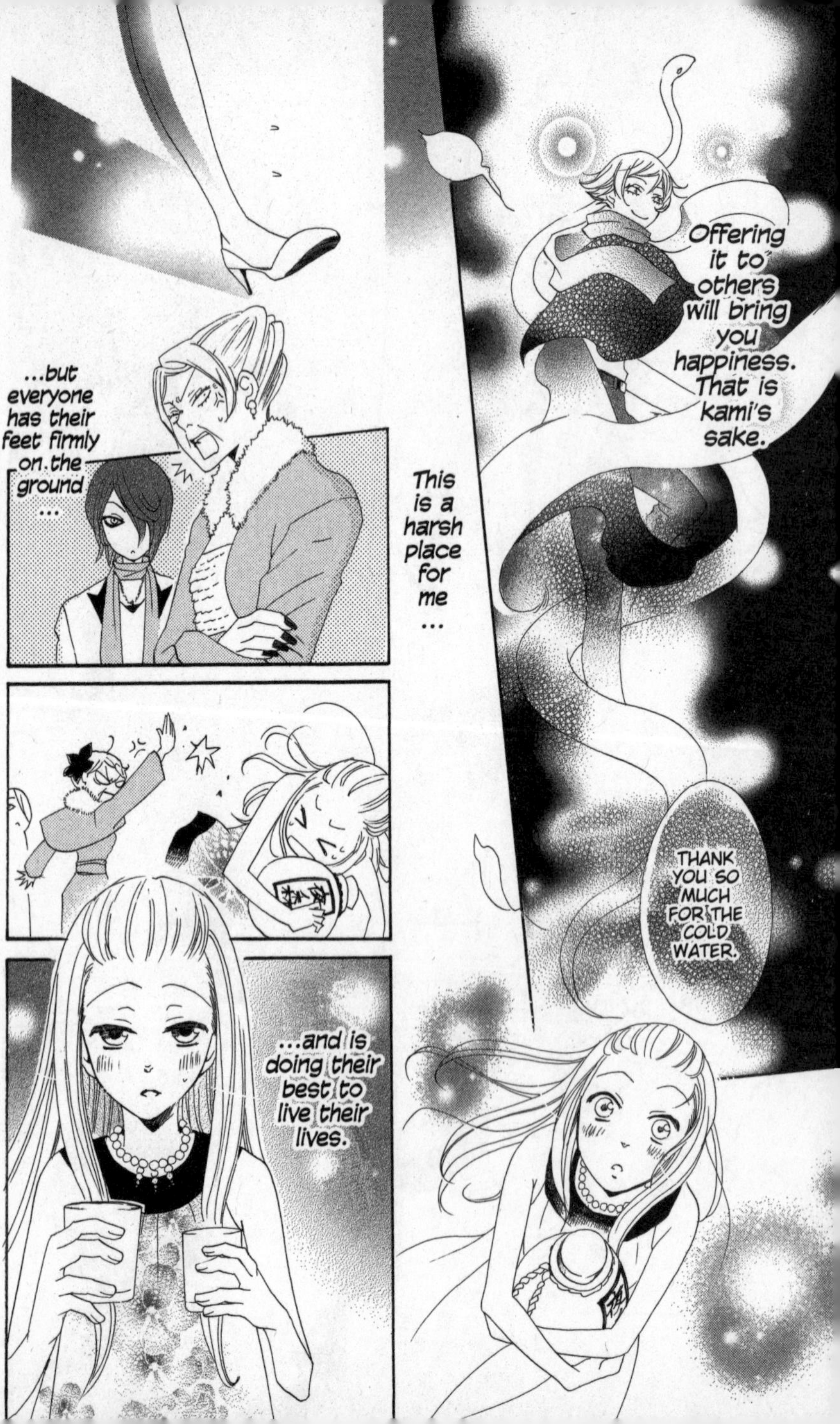
Offering it to others will bring you happiness. That is kami's sake.
THANK YOU SO MUCH FOR THE COLD WATER.
This is a harsh place for me...
...but everyone has their feet firmly on the ground...
...and is doing their best to live their lives.

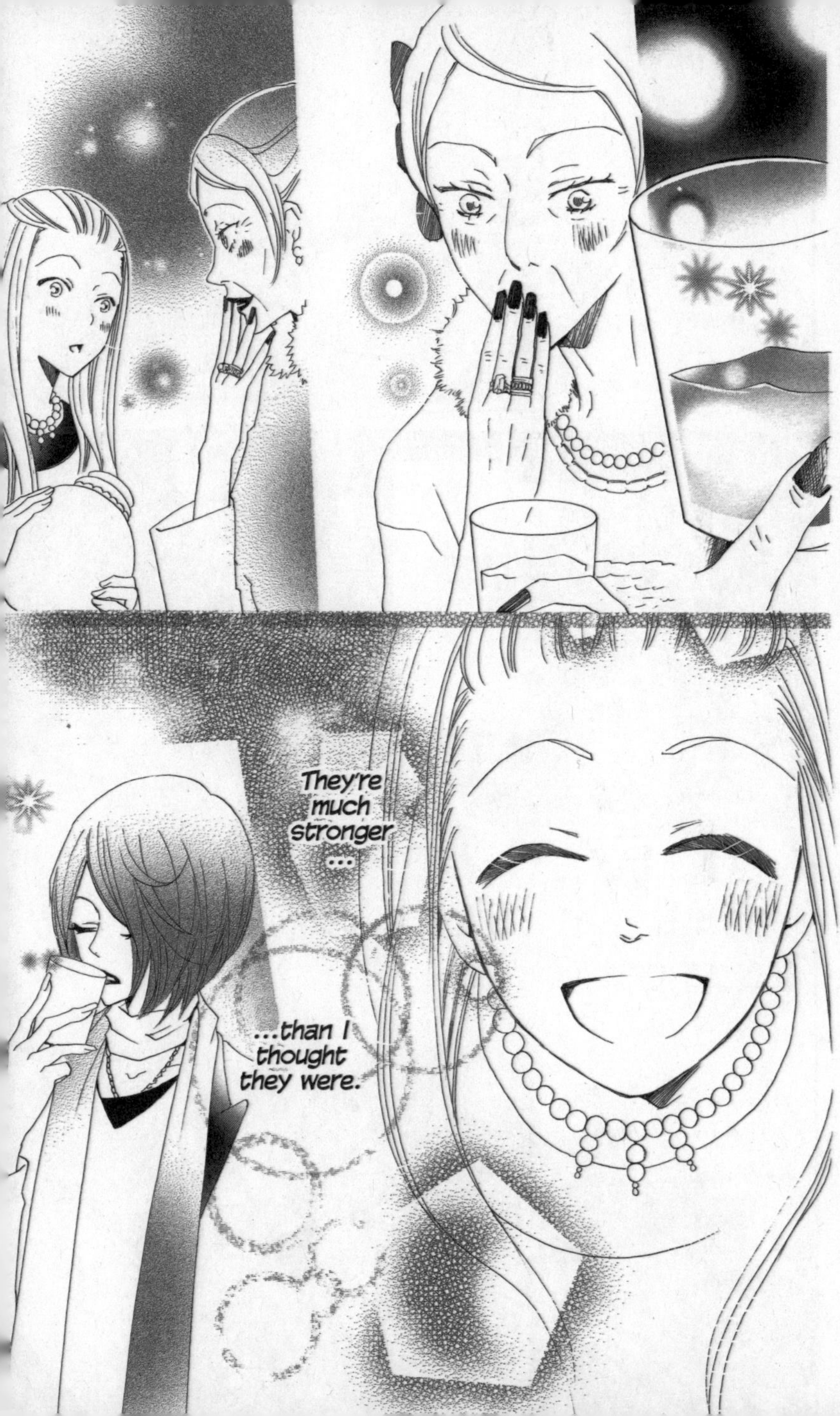
They're much stronger...
...than I thought they were.

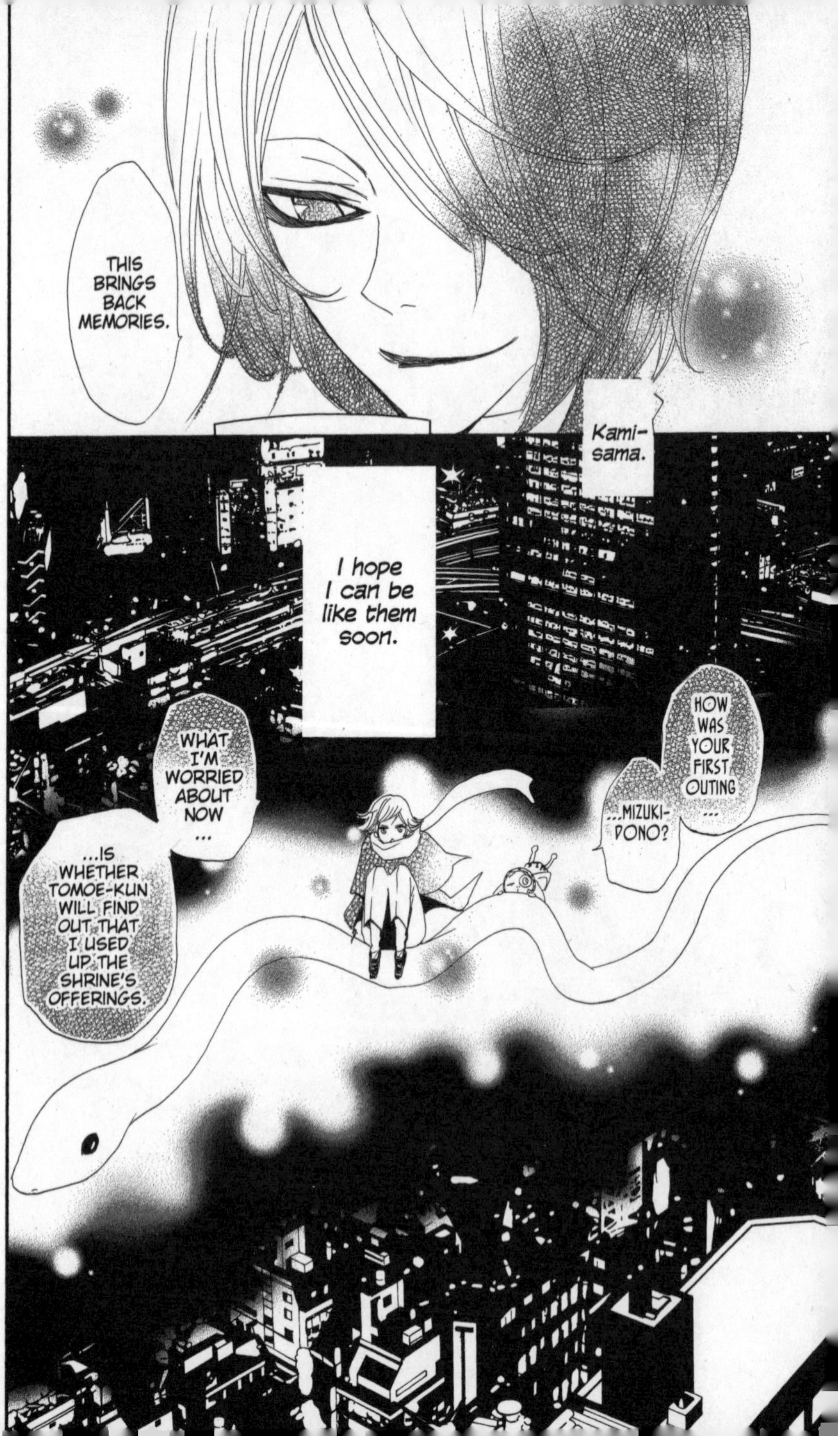
THIS BRINGS BACK MEMORIES.
Kami-sama.
I hope I can be like them soon.
HOW WAS YOUR FIRST OUTING ...
...MIZUKI-DONO?
WHAT I'M WORRIED ABOUT NOW ...
...IS WHETHER TOMOE-KUN WILL FIND OUT THAT I USED UP THE SHRINE'S OFFERINGS.

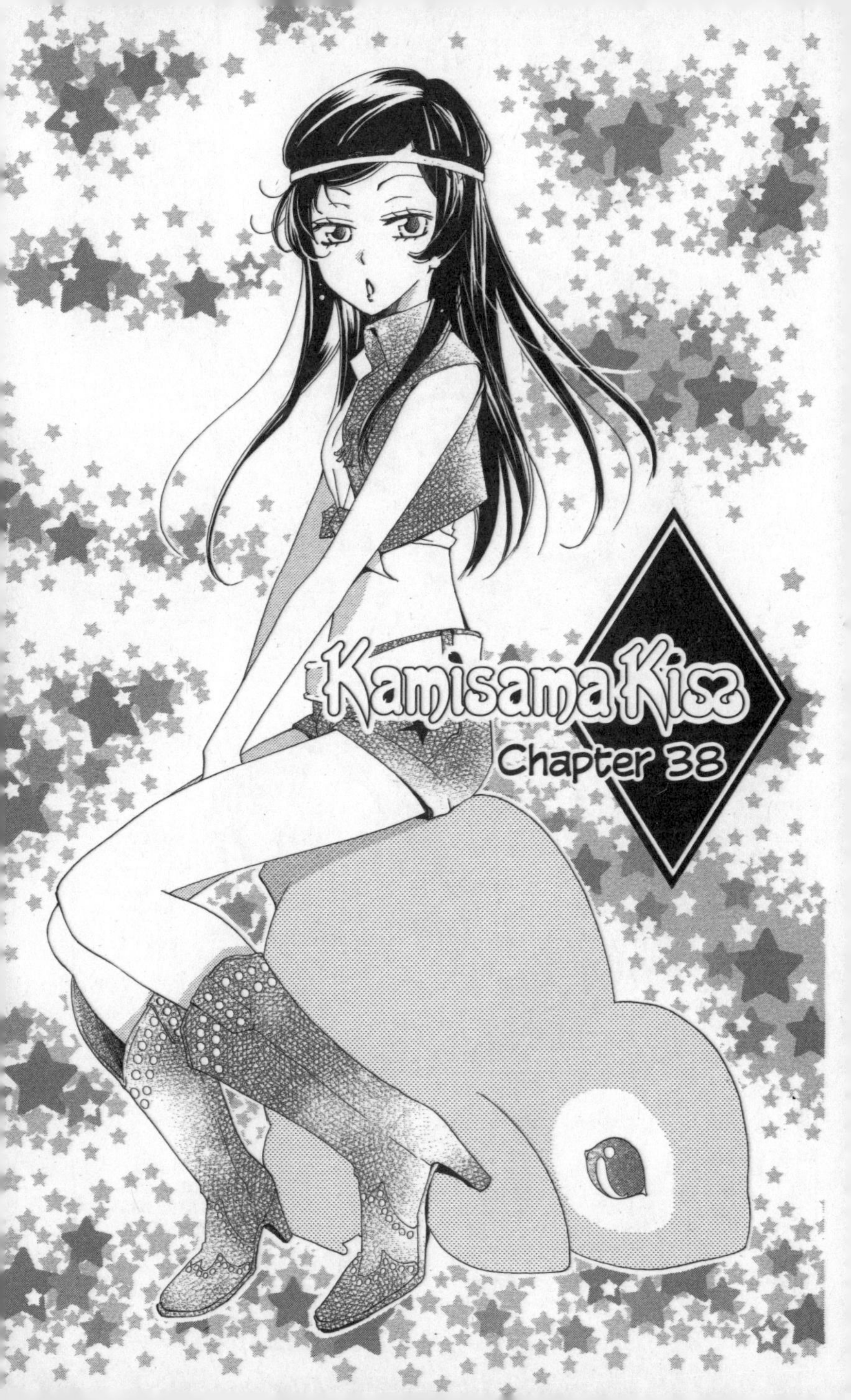
Kamisama Kiss
Chapter 38

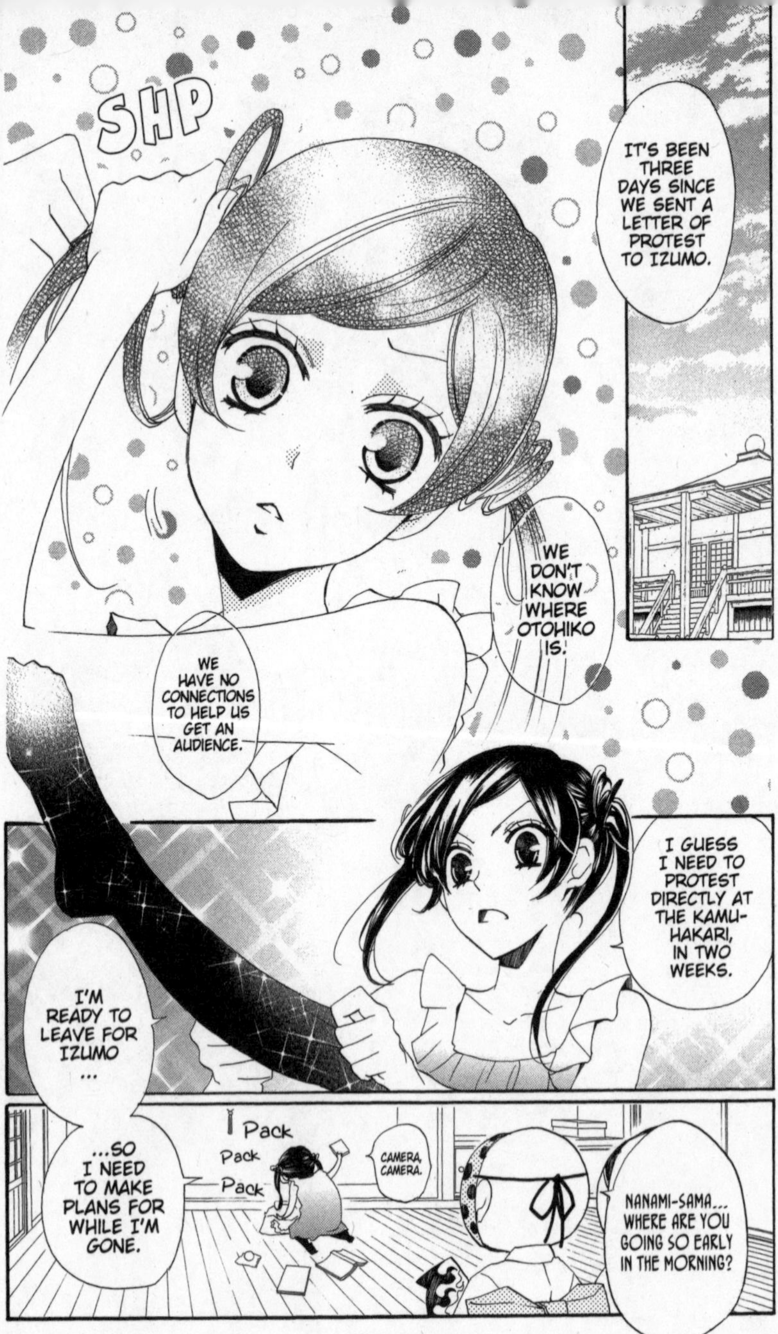
IT'S BEEN THREE DAYS SINCE WE SENT A LETTER OF PROTEST TO IZUMO.
SHP
WE DON'T KNOW WHERE OTOHIKO IS.
WE HAVE NO CONNECTIONS TO HELP US GET AN AUDIENCE.
I GUESS I NEED TO PROTEST DIRECTLY AT THE KAMU-HAKARI, IN TWO WEEKS.
I'M READY TO LEAVE FOR IZUMO ...
NANAMI-SAMA... WHERE ARE YOU GOING SO EARLY IN THE MORNING?
CAMERA, CAMERA.
Pack
Pack
Pack
...SO I NEED TO MAKE PLANS FOR WHILE I'M GONE.

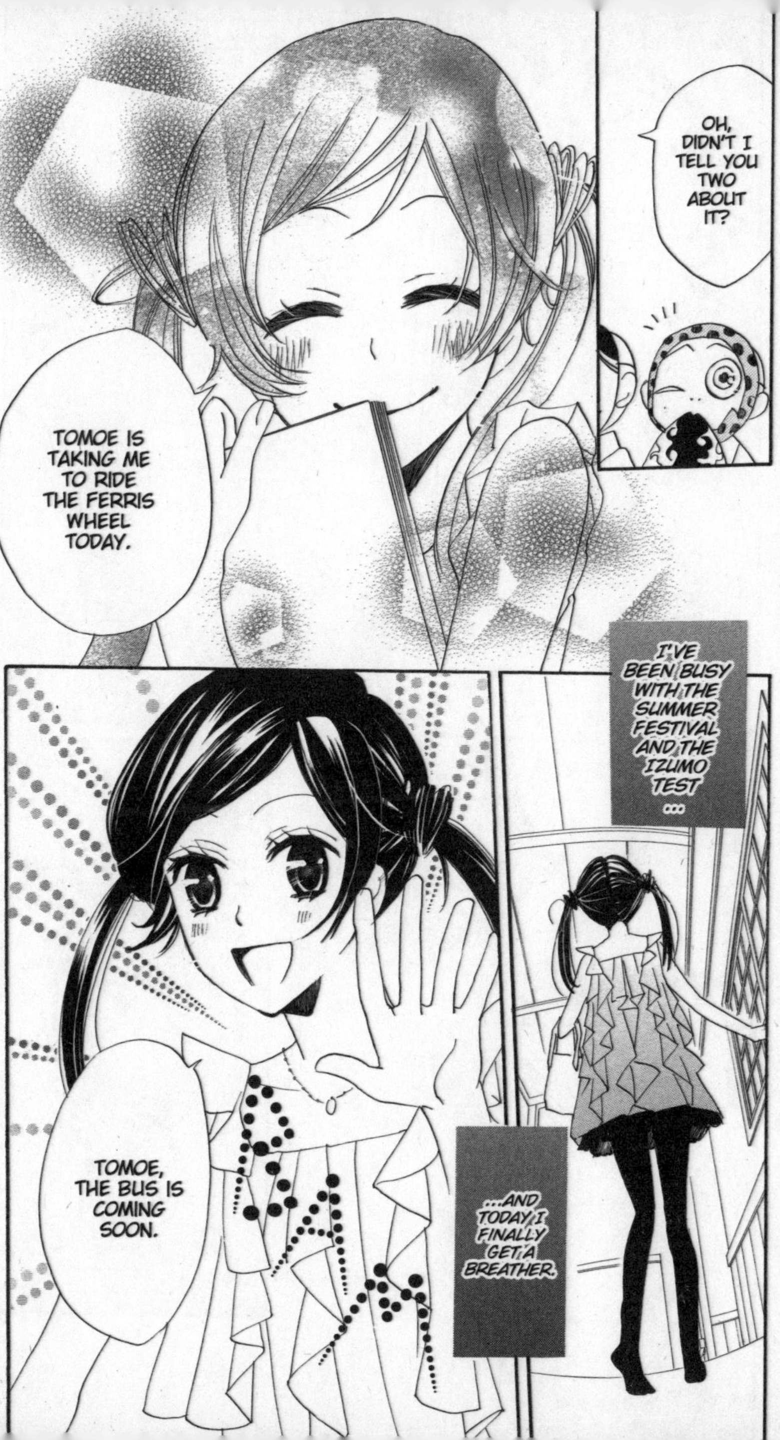
OH, DIDN'T I TELL YOU TWO ABOUT IT?
TOMOE IS TAKING ME TO RIDE THE FERRIS WHEEL TODAY.
I'VE BEEN BUSY WITH THE SUMMER FESTIVAL AND THE IZUMO TEST ...
...AND TODAY I FINALLY GET A BREATHER.
TOMOE, THE BUS IS COMING SOON.

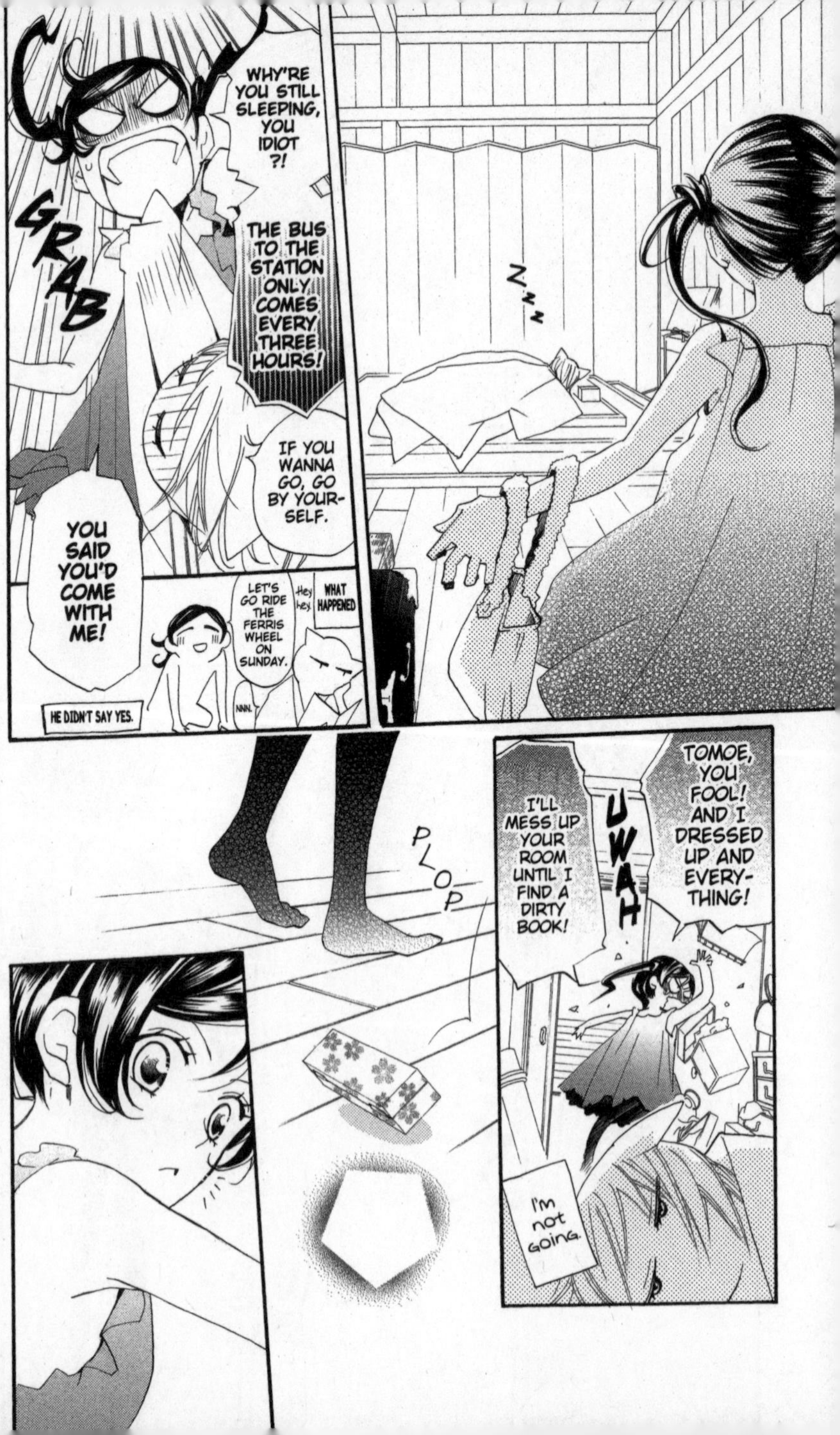

ZZZ
WHY'RE YOU STILL SLEEPING, YOU IDIOT?!
GRAB
THE BUS TO THE STATION ONLY COMES EVERY THREE HOURS!
IF YOU WANNA GO, GO BY YOURSELF.
YOU SAID YOU'D COME WITH ME!
WHAT HAPPENED
Hey hey.
LET'S GO RIDE THE FERRIS WHEEL ON SUNDAY.
NNN.
HE DIDN'T SAY YES.
TOMOE, YOU FOOL! AND I DRESSED UP AND EVERYTHING!
UWAH
I'LL MESS UP YOUR ROOM UNTIL I FIND A DIRTY BOOK!
I'm not going.
PLOP

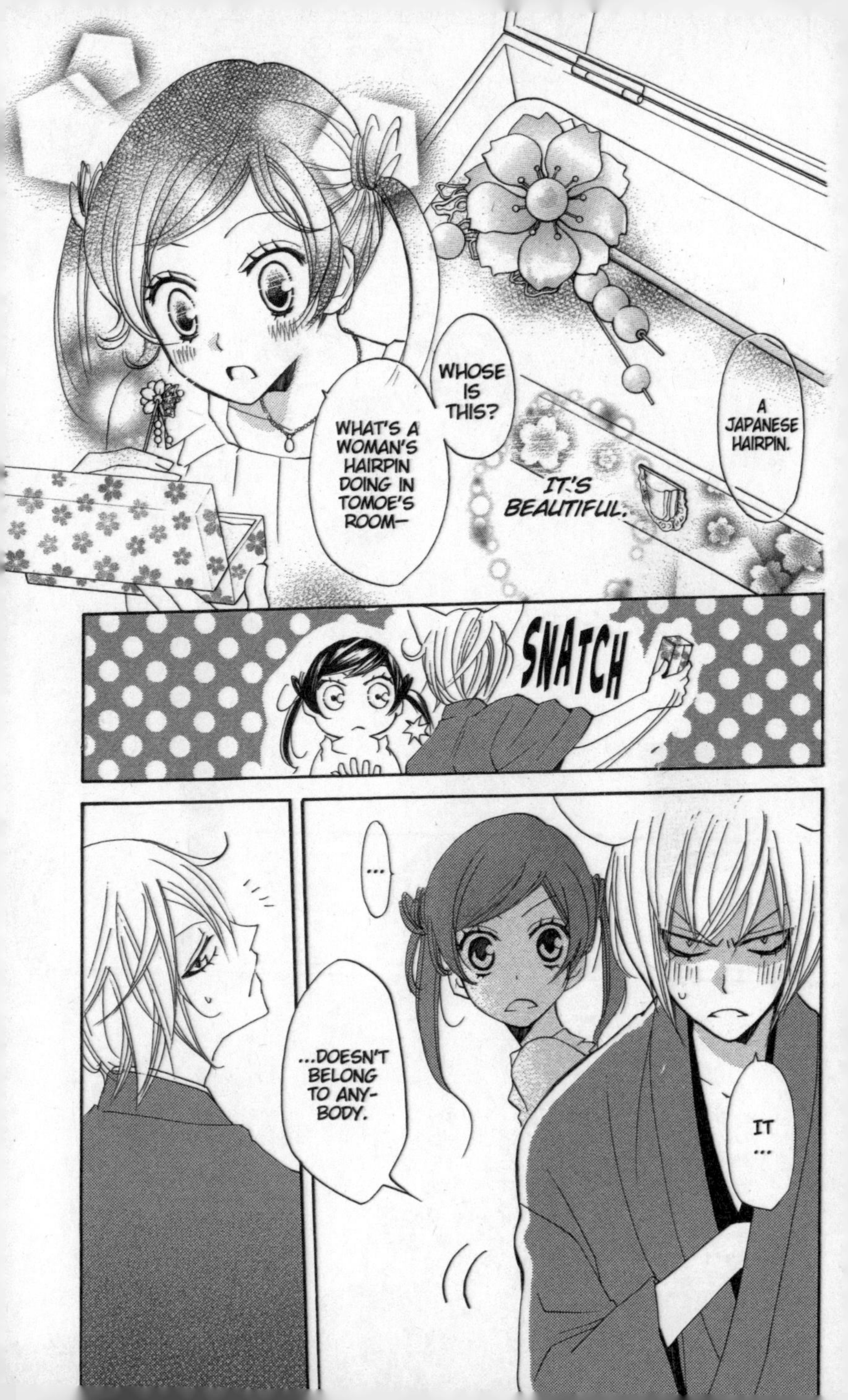
A JAPANESE HAIRPIN.
IT'S BEAUTIFUL.
WHOSE IS THIS?
WHAT'S A WOMAN'S HAIRPIN DOING IN TOMOE'S ROOM—
SNATCH
...
IT ...
...DOESN'T BELONG TO ANY-BODY.

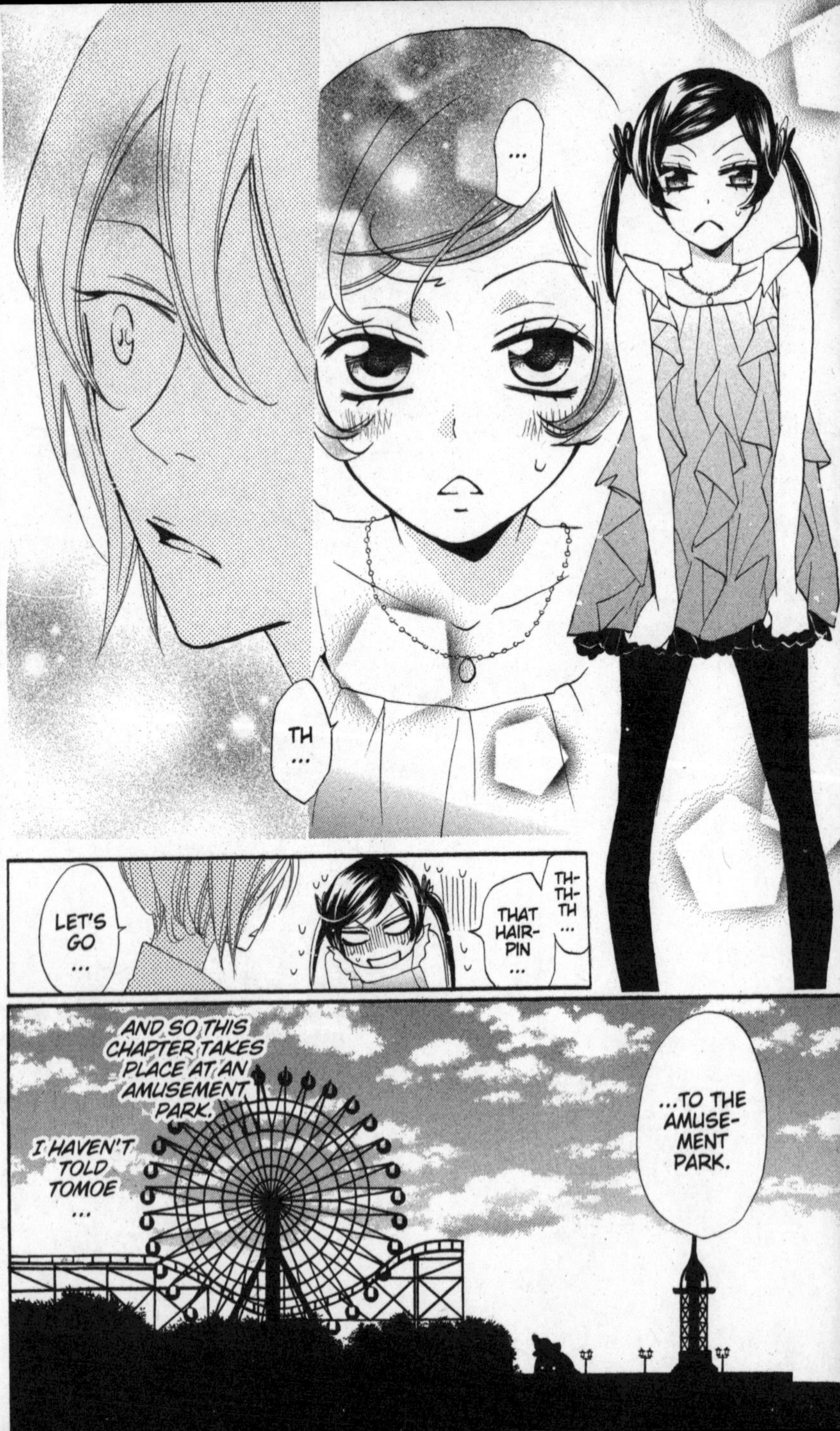
...
TH ...
TH-TH-TH ...
THAT HAIR-PIN ...
LET'S GO ...
...TO THE AMUSE-MENT PARK.
AND SO THIS CHAPTER TAKES PLACE AT AN AMUSEMENT PARK.
I HAVEN'T TOLD TOMOE ...

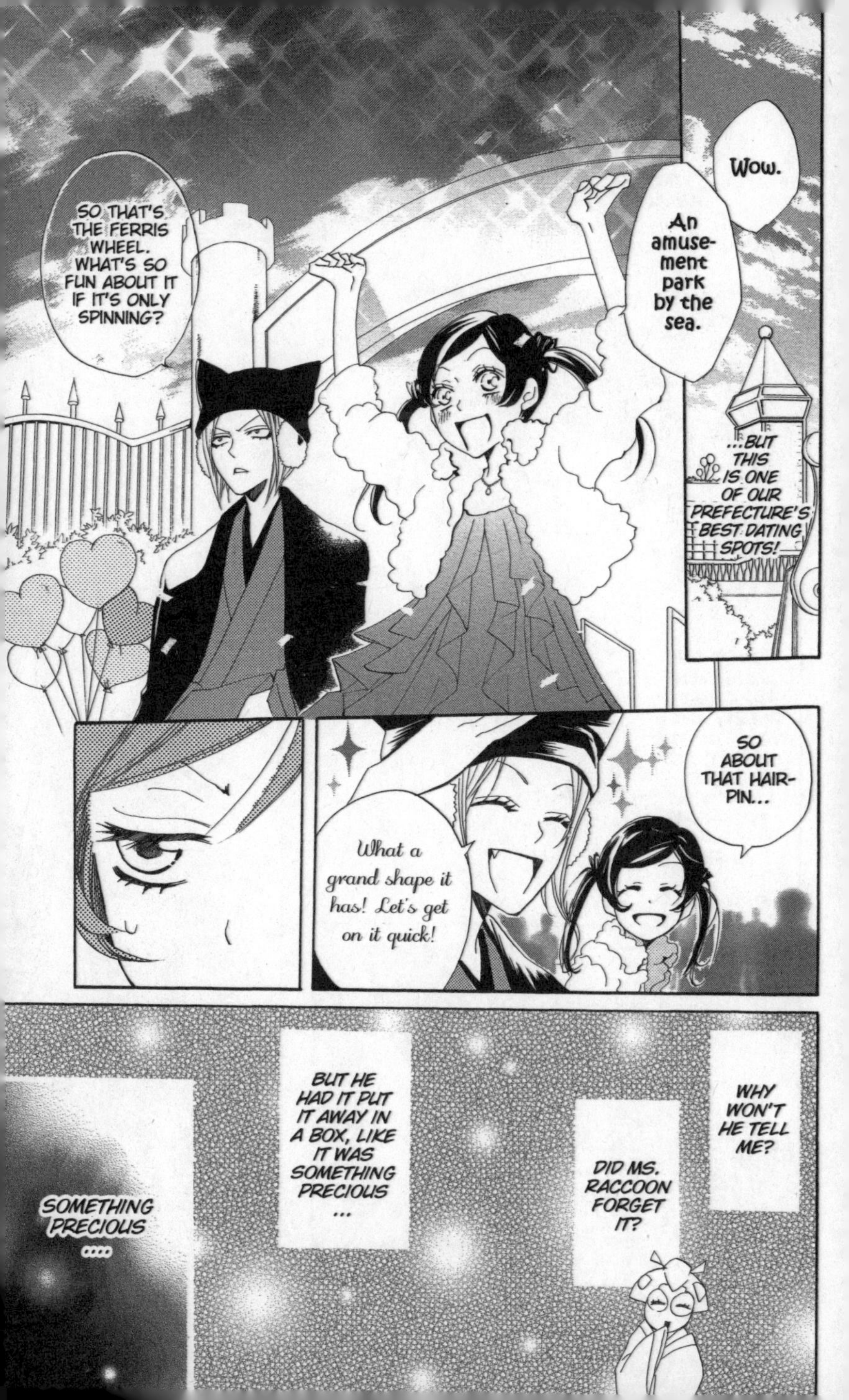
Wow.
An amusement park by the sea.
...BUT THIS IS ONE OF OUR PREFECTURE'S BEST DATING SPOTS!
SO THAT'S THE FERRIS WHEEL. WHAT'S SO FUN ABOUT IT IF IT'S ONLY SPINNING?
SO ABOUT THAT HAIRPIN...
What a grand shape it has! Let's get on it quick!
WHY WON'T HE TELL ME?
DID MS. RACCOON FORGET IT?
BUT HE HAD IT PUT IT AWAY IN A BOX, LIKE IT WAS SOMETHING PRECIOUS...
SOMETHING PRECIOUS....

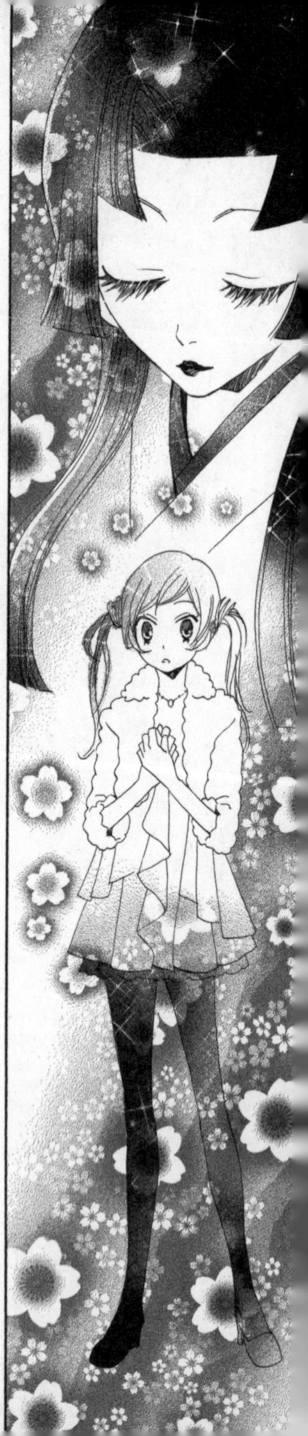

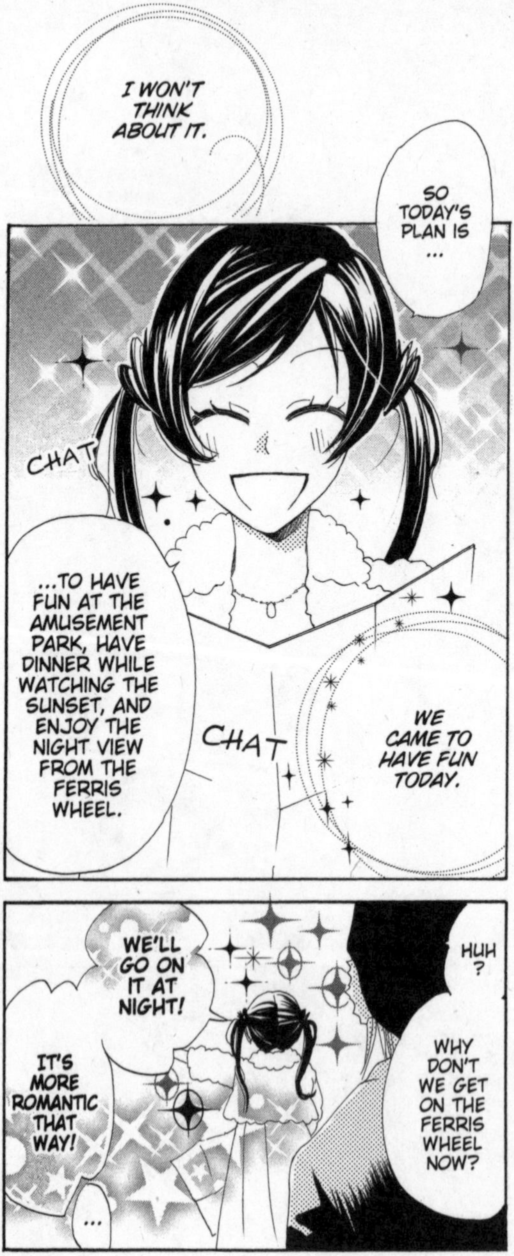
I WON'T THINK ABOUT IT.
SO TODAY'S PLAN IS ...
...TO HAVE FUN AT THE AMUSEMENT PARK, HAVE DINNER WHILE WATCHING THE SUNSET, AND ENJOY THE NIGHT VIEW FROM THE FERRIS WHEEL.
CHAT
CHAT
WE CAME TO HAVE FUN TODAY.
HUH?
WHY DON'T WE GET ON THE FERRIS WHEEL NOW?
WE'LL GO ON IT AT NIGHT!
IT'S MORE ROMANTIC THAT WAY!
...

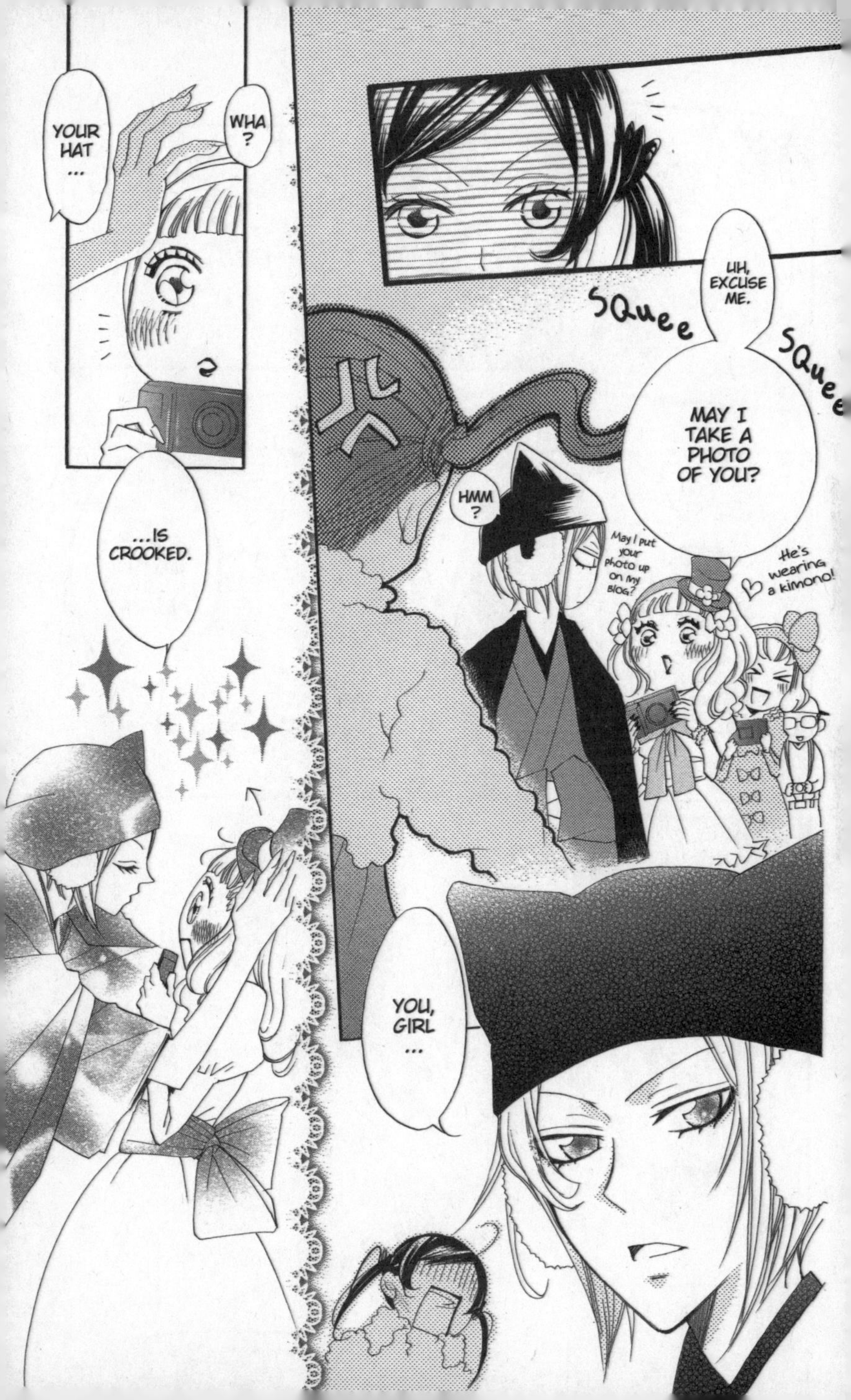
UH, EXCUSE ME.
SQuee
SQuee
MAY I TAKE A PHOTO OF YOU?
He's wearing a kimono!
May I put your photo up on my BLOG?
HMM?
YOU, GIRL ...
WHA ?
YOUR HAT ...
...IS CROOKED.

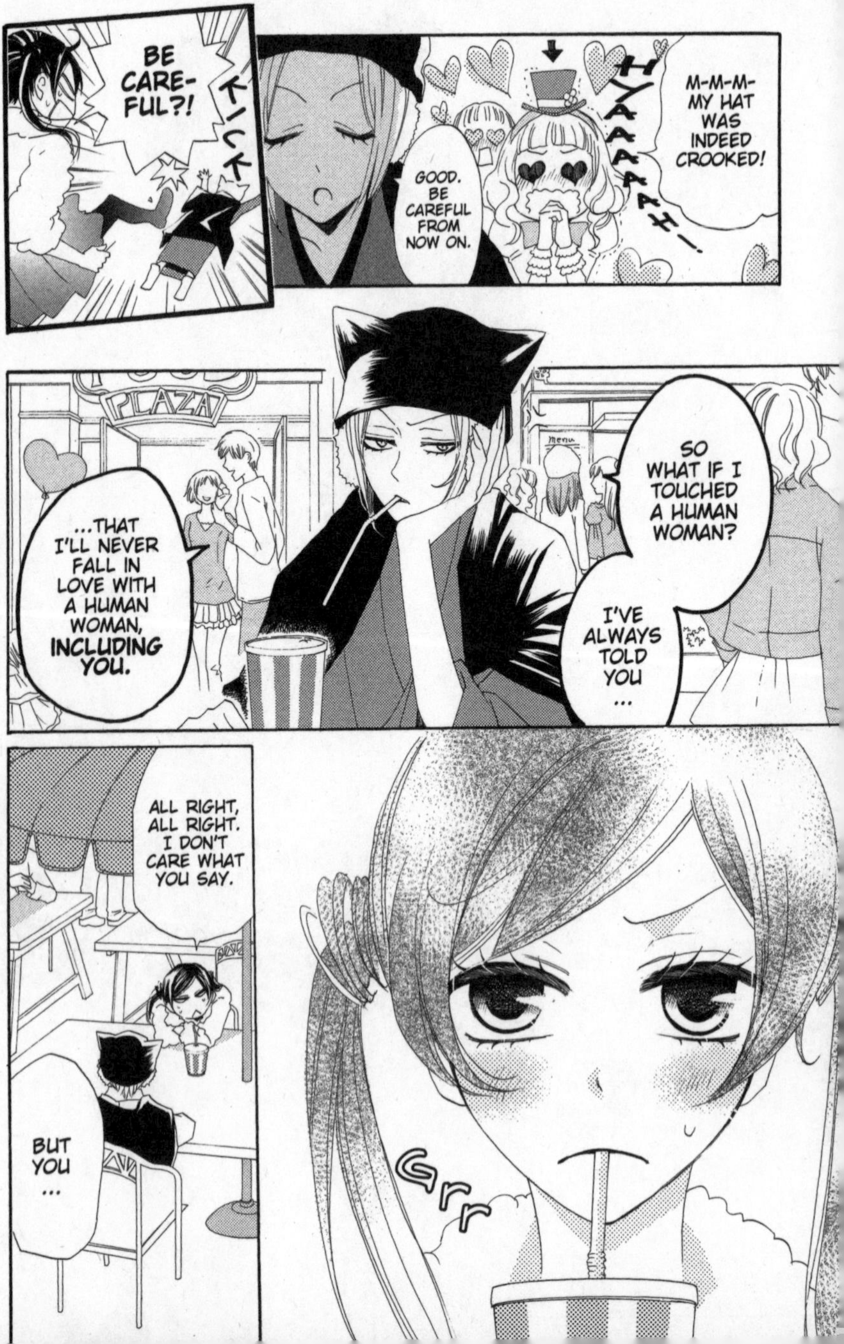
M-M-M-MY HAT WAS INDEED CROOKED!
HYAAAAAH!
GOOD. BE CAREFUL FROM NOW ON.
BE CAREFUL?!
KICK
SO WHAT IF I TOUCHED A HUMAN WOMAN?
I'VE ALWAYS TOLD YOU ...
...THAT I'LL NEVER FALL IN LOVE WITH A HUMAN WOMAN, INCLUDING YOU.
PLAZA
menu
Grr
ALL RIGHT, ALL RIGHT. I DON'T CARE WHAT YOU SAY.
BUT YOU ...

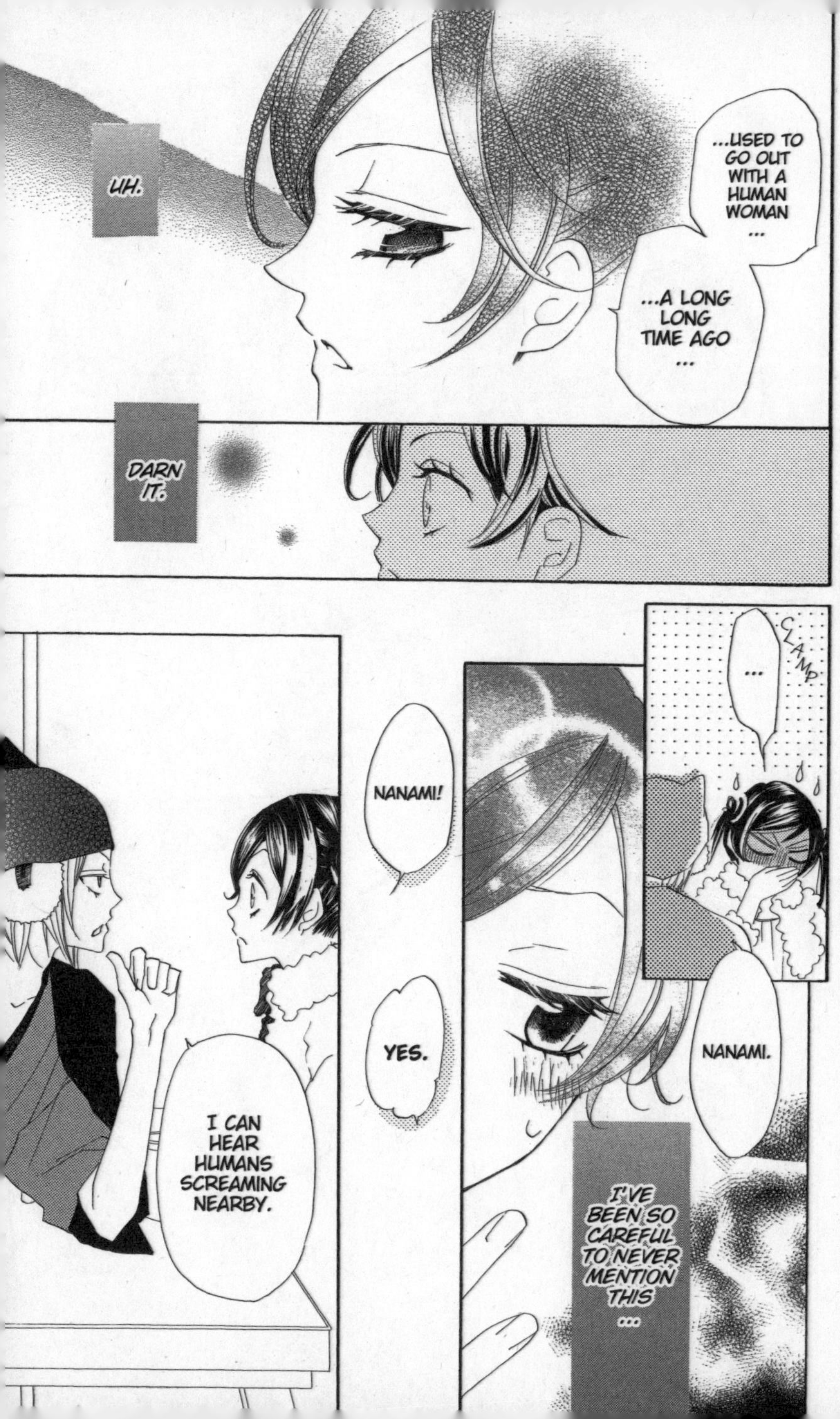

...USED TO GO OUT WITH A HUMAN WOMAN...
...A LONG LONG TIME AGO...
UH.
DARN IT.
...
CLAMP
NANAMI.
I'VE BEEN SO CAREFUL TO NEVER MENTION THIS...
NANAMI!
YES.
I CAN HEAR HUMANS SCREAMING NEARBY.

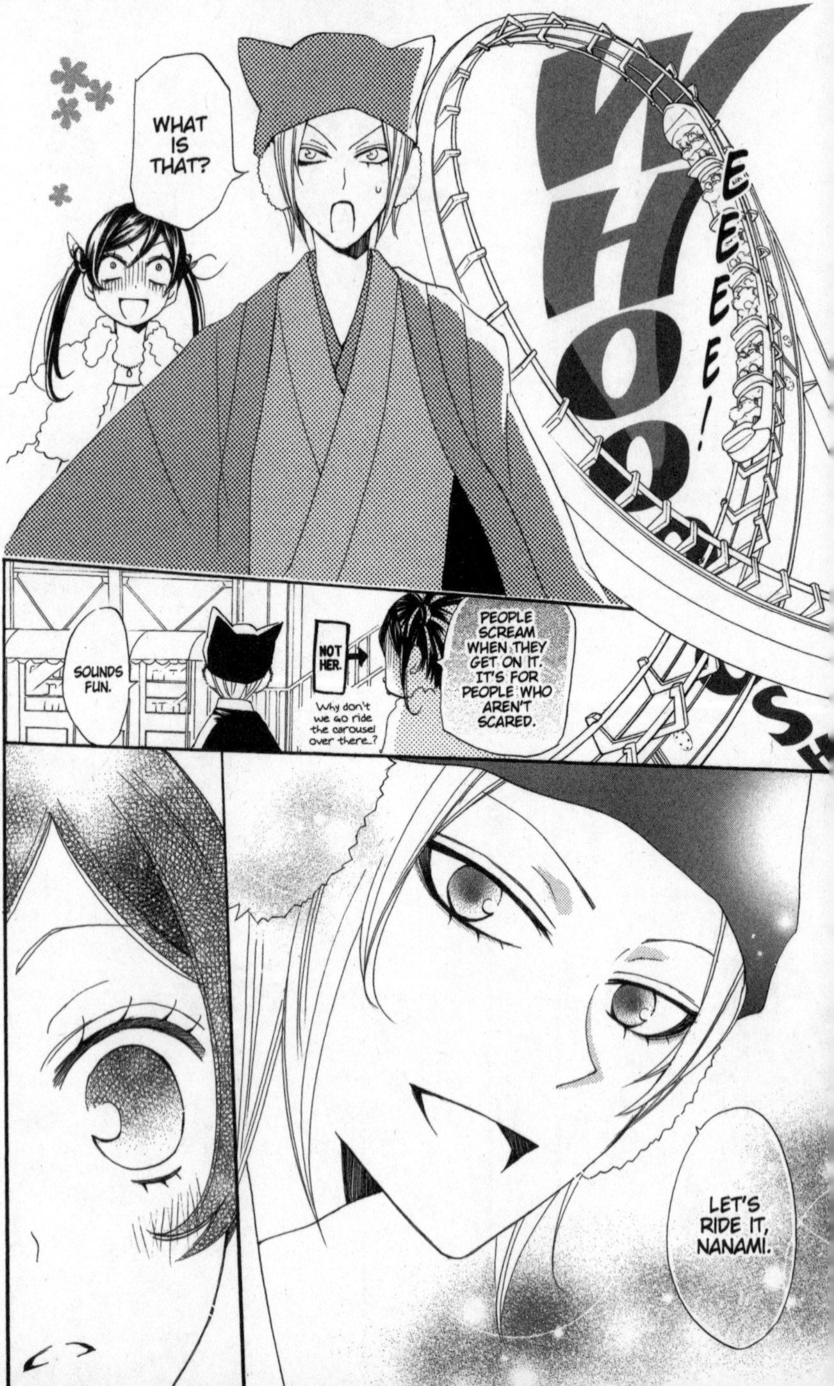
WHOOOSH
EEEEEE!
WHAT IS THAT?
PEOPLE SCREAM WHEN THEY GET ON IT. IT'S FOR PEOPLE WHO AREN'T SCARED.
Why don't we go ride the carousel over there..?
NOT HER.
SOUNDS FUN.
LET'S RIDE IT, NANAMI.

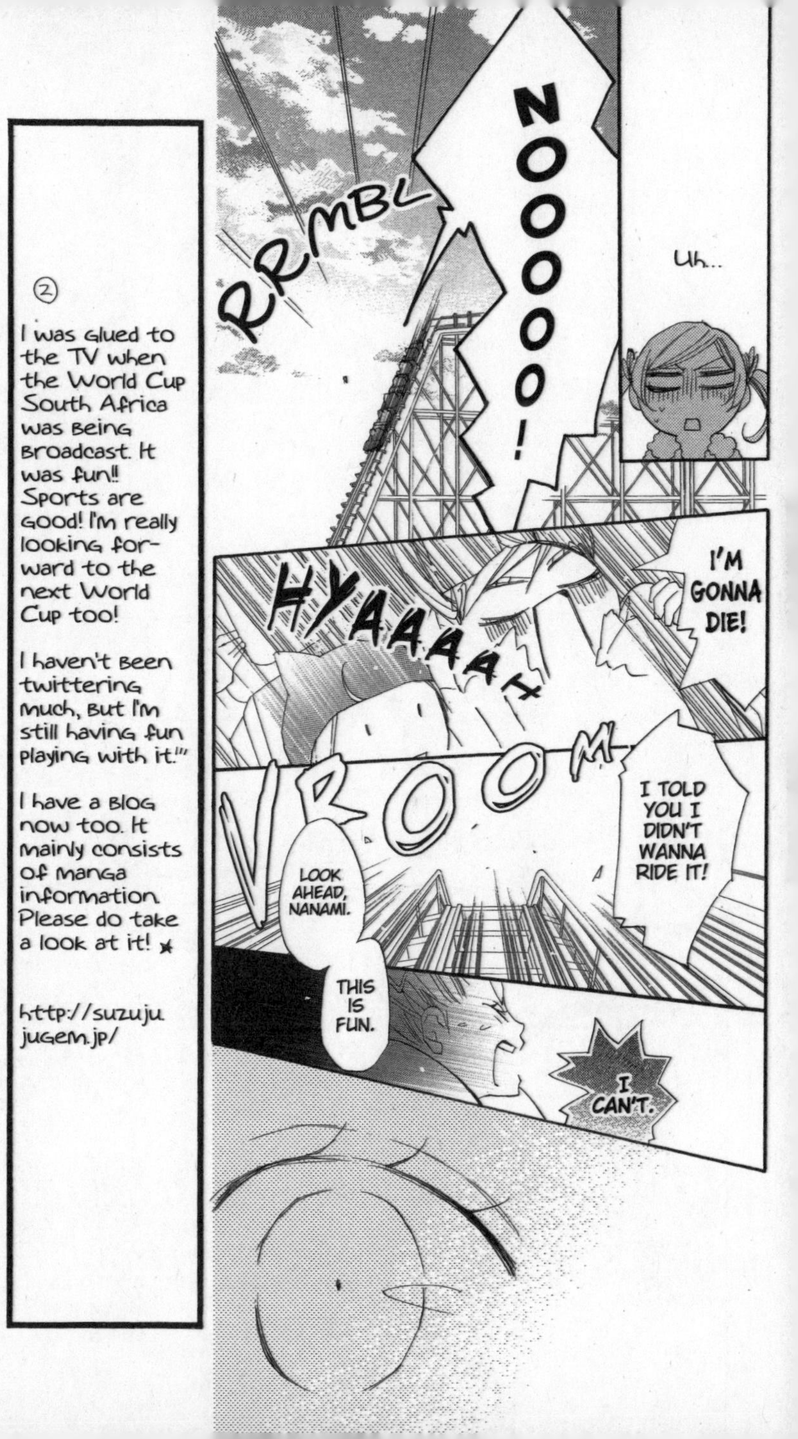
Uh...
NOOOOOO!
RRMBL
I'M GONNA DIE!
HYAAAAAH
I TOLD YOU I DIDN'T WANNA RIDE IT!
VROOOM
LOOK AHEAD, NANAMI.
THIS IS FUN.
I CAN'T.

②

I was glued to the TV when the World Cup South Africa was being broadcast. It was fun!! Sports are good! I'm really looking forward to the next World Cup too!

I haven't been twittering much, but I'm still having fun playing with it!''

I have a blog now too. It mainly consists of manga information. Please do take a look at it! ★

http://suzuju.jugem.jp/

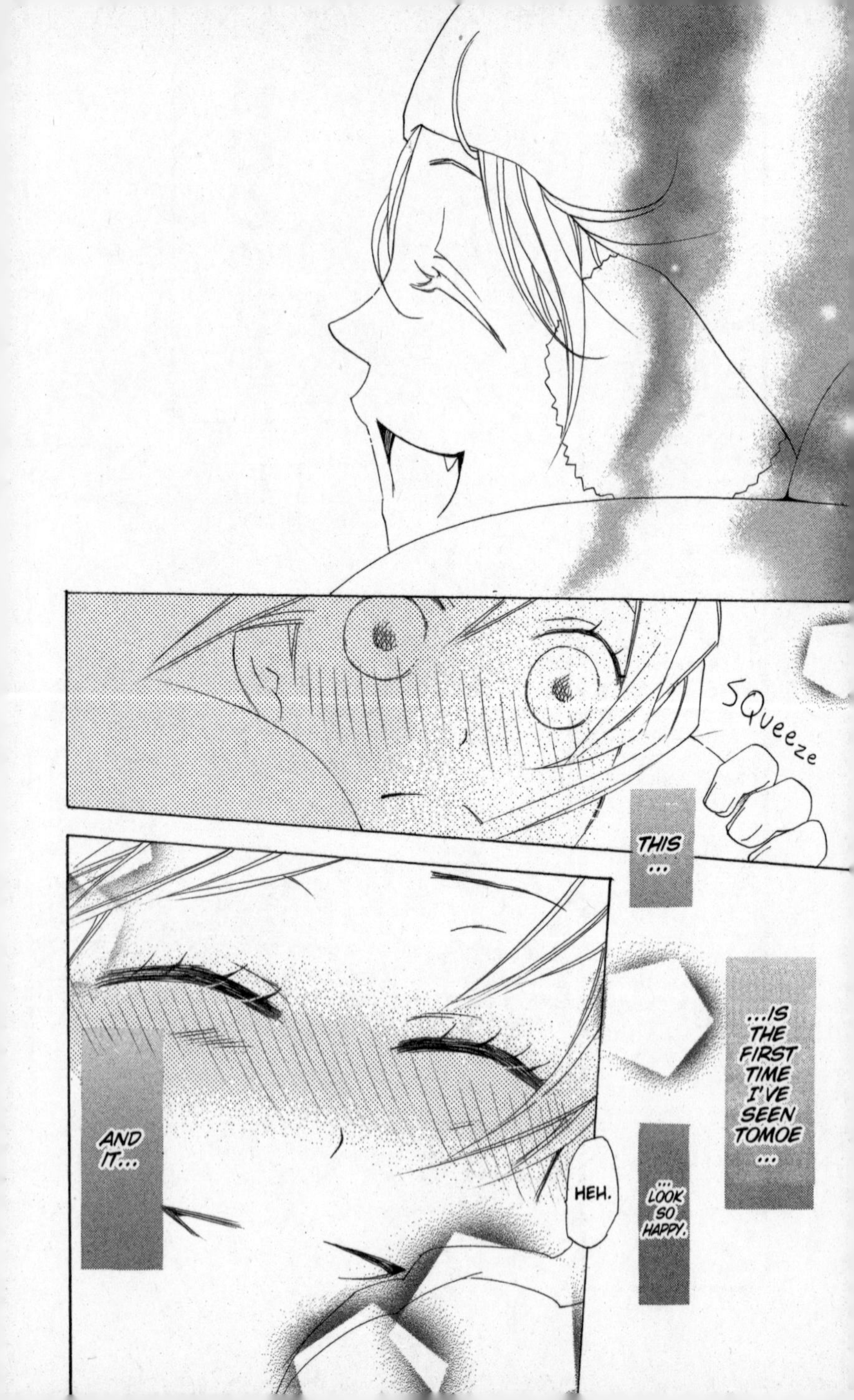
SQueeze
THIS...
...IS THE FIRST TIME I'VE SEEN TOMOE...
...LOOK SO HAPPY.
HEH.
AND IT...

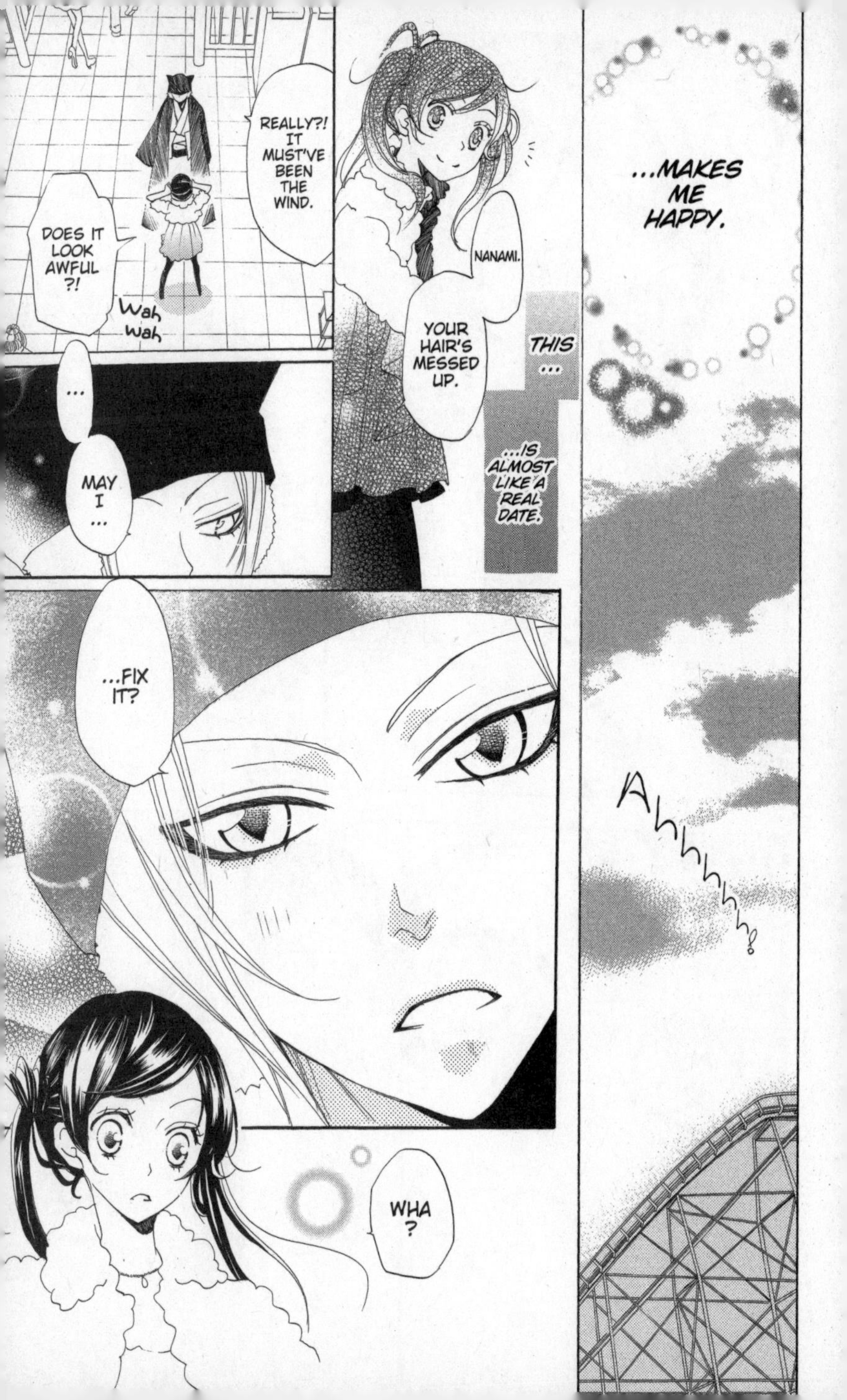
...MAKES ME HAPPY.
Ahhhhh!
NANAMI.
YOUR HAIR'S MESSED UP.
THIS ...
...IS ALMOST LIKE A REAL DATE.
REALLY?! IT MUST'VE BEEN THE WIND.
DOES IT LOOK AWFUL ?!
Wah wah
...
MAY I ...
...FIX IT?
WHA ?

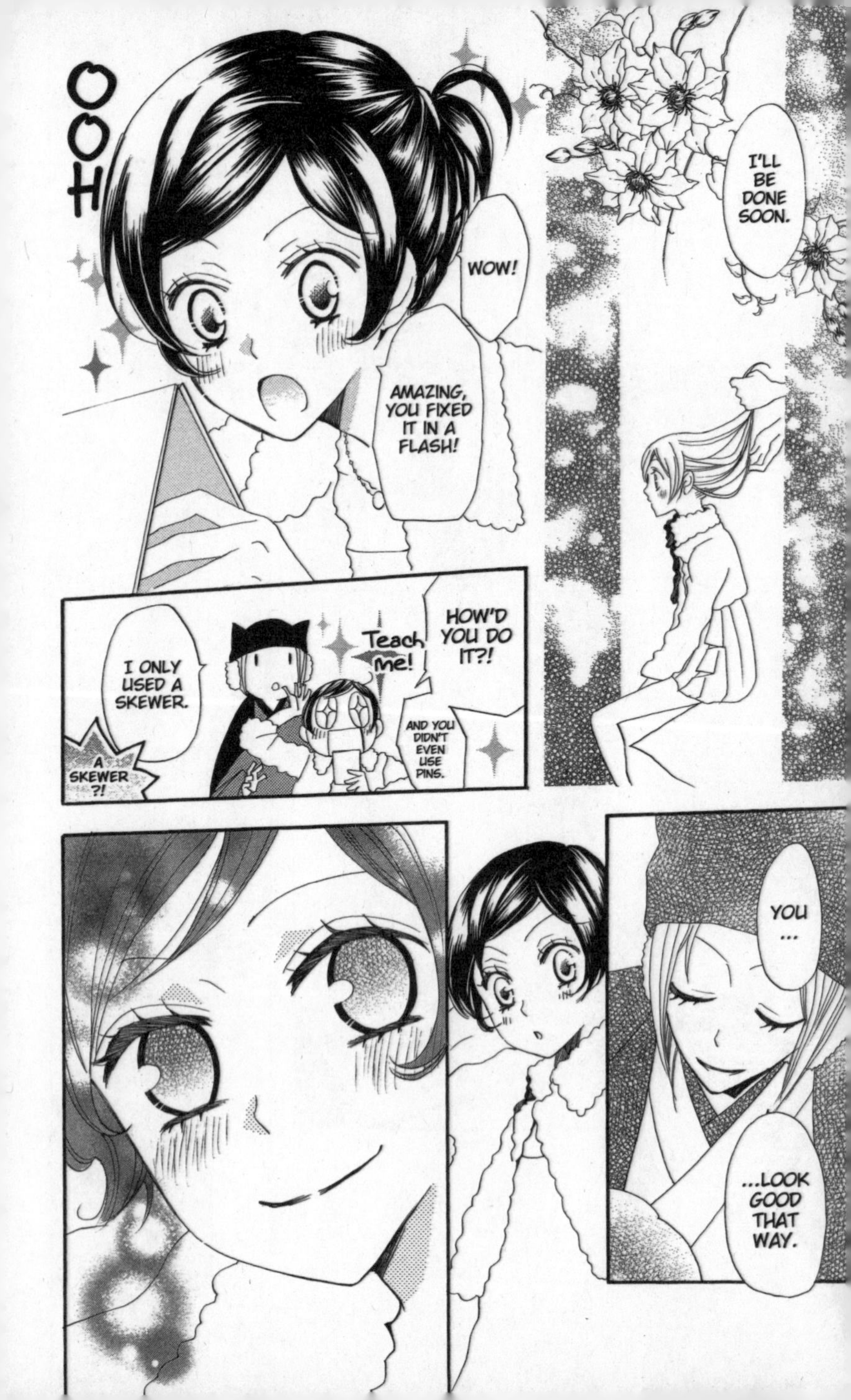
I'LL BE DONE SOON.
OOH
WOW!
AMAZING, YOU FIXED IT IN A FLASH!
HOW'D YOU DO IT?!
Teach me!
AND YOU DIDN'T EVEN USE PINS.
I ONLY USED A SKEWER.
A SKEWER?!
YOU ...
...LOOK GOOD THAT WAY.

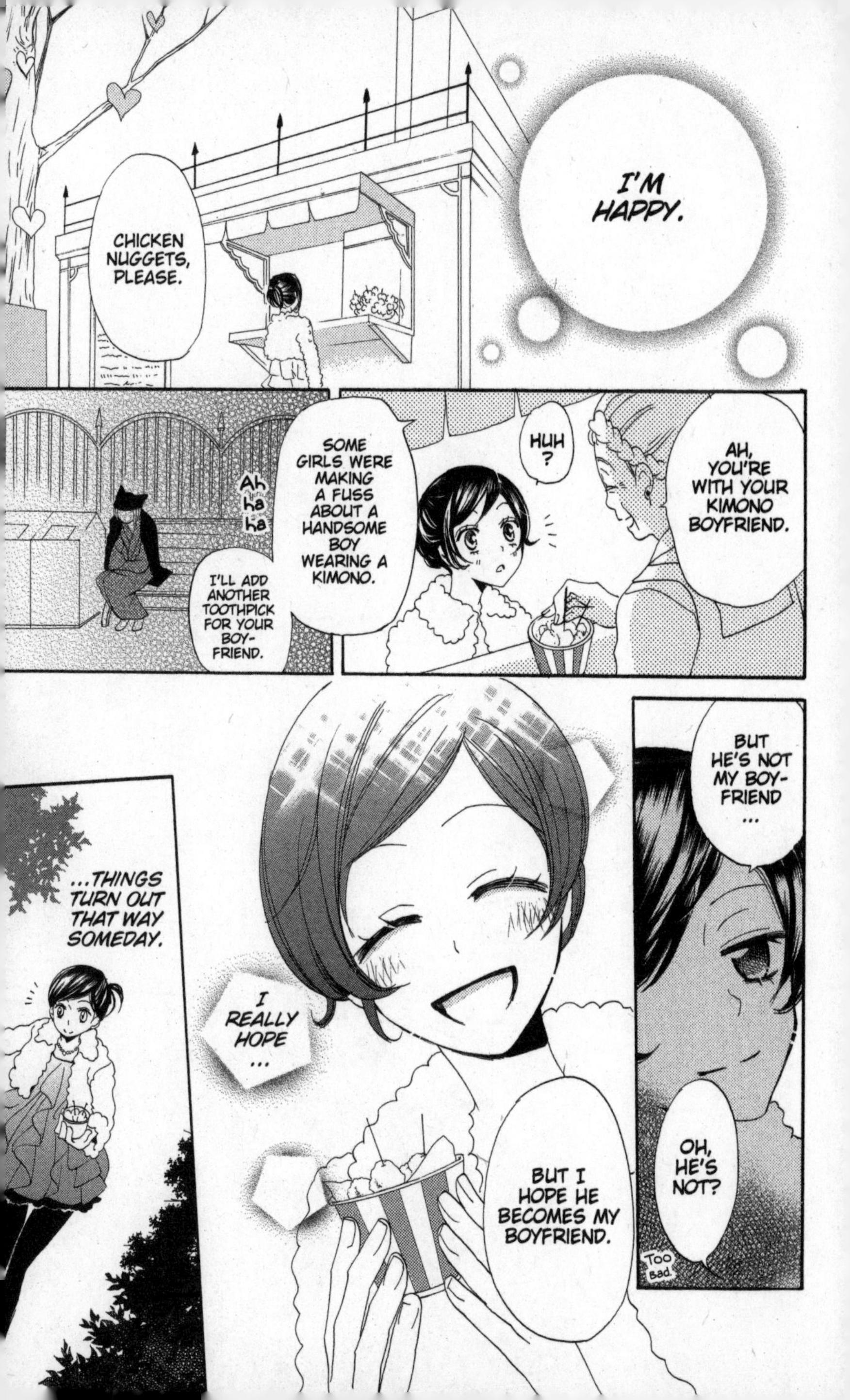
I'M HAPPY.
CHICKEN NUGGETS, PLEASE.
AH, YOU'RE WITH YOUR KIMONO BOYFRIEND.
HUH?
SOME GIRLS WERE MAKING A FUSS ABOUT A HANDSOME BOY WEARING A KIMONO.
I'LL ADD ANOTHER TOOTHPICK FOR YOUR BOY-FRIEND.
Ah ha ha
BUT HE'S NOT MY BOY-FRIEND...
OH, HE'S NOT?
Too Bad.
BUT I HOPE HE BECOMES MY BOYFRIEND.
I REALLY HOPE...
...THINGS TURN OUT THAT WAY SOMEDAY.

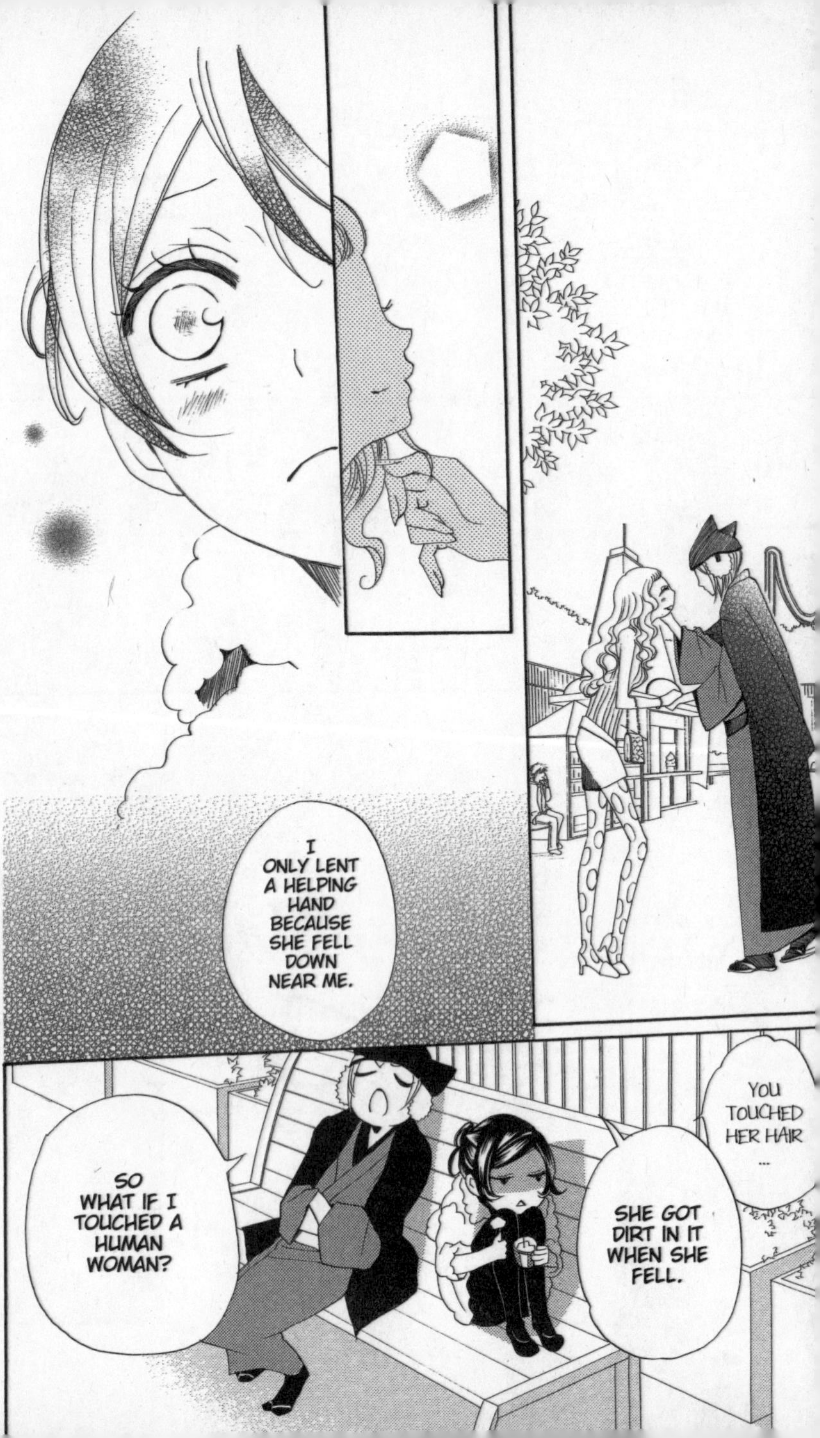
I ONLY LENT A HELPING HAND BECAUSE SHE FELL DOWN NEAR ME.
YOU TOUCHED HER HAIR ...
SHE GOT DIRT IN IT WHEN SHE FELL.
SO WHAT IF I TOUCHED A HUMAN WOMAN?

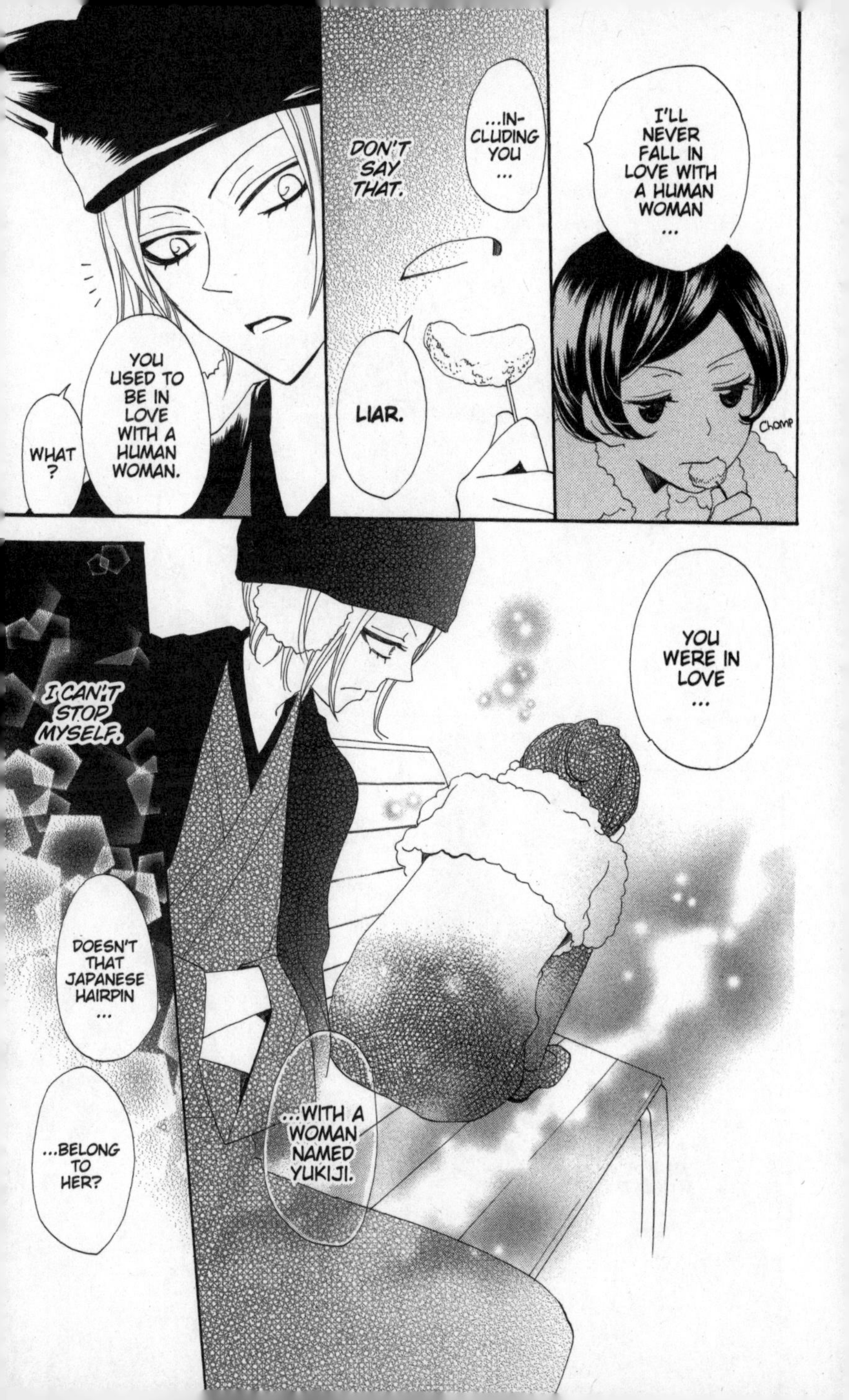
I'LL NEVER FALL IN LOVE WITH A HUMAN WOMAN ...
Chomp
...IN-CLUDING YOU ...
DON'T SAY THAT.
LIAR.
YOU USED TO BE IN LOVE WITH A HUMAN WOMAN.
WHAT ?
YOU WERE IN LOVE ...
...WITH A WOMAN NAMED YUKIJI.
I CAN'T STOP MYSELF.
DOESN'T THAT JAPANESE HAIRPIN ...
...BELONG TO HER?

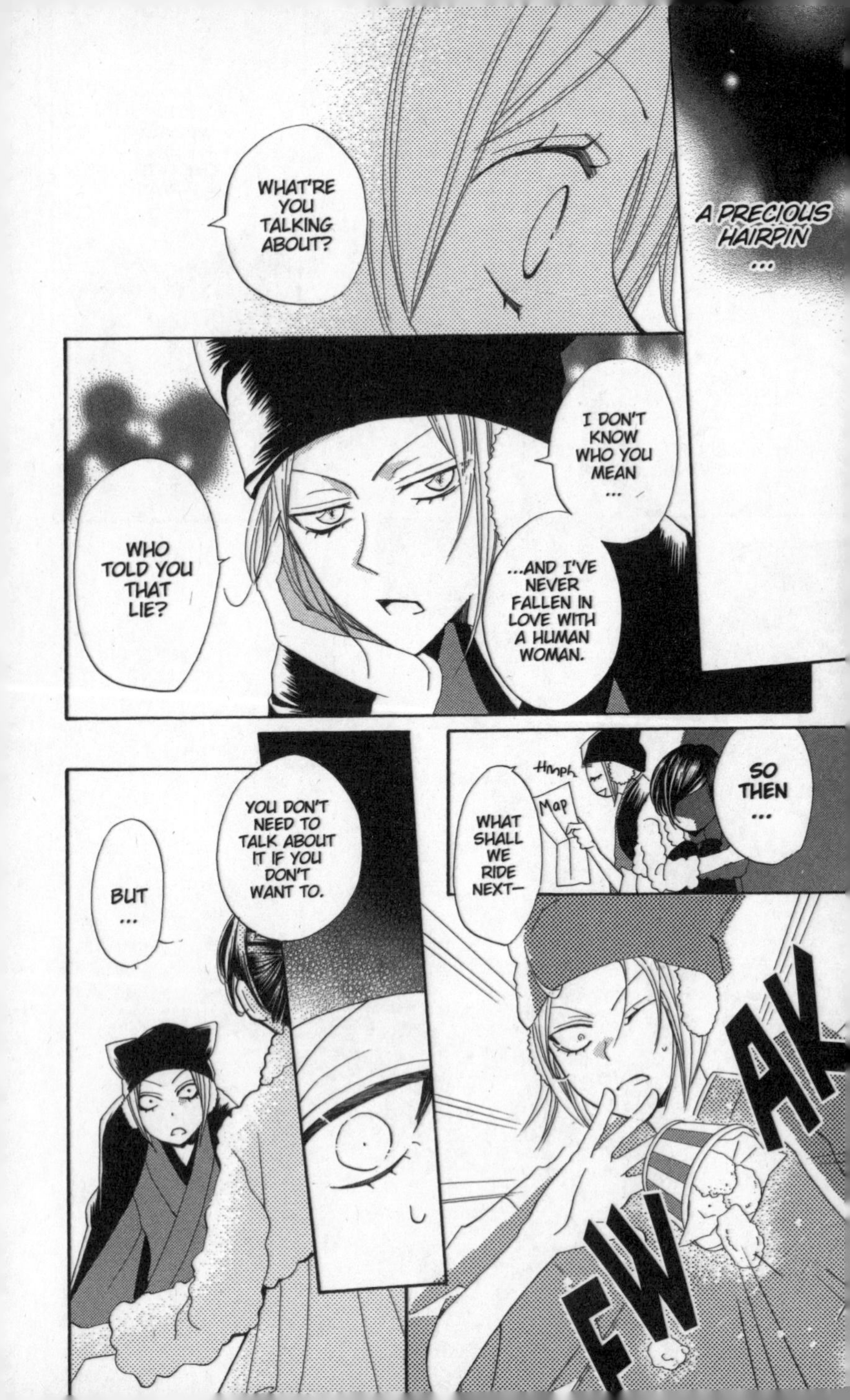
A PRECIOUS HAIRPIN ...
WHAT'RE YOU TALKING ABOUT?
I DON'T KNOW WHO YOU MEAN ...
...AND I'VE NEVER FALLEN IN LOVE WITH A HUMAN WOMAN.
WHO TOLD YOU THAT LIE?
SO THEN ...
Hmph
Map
WHAT SHALL WE RIDE NEXT—
FWAK
YOU DON'T NEED TO TALK ABOUT IT IF YOU DON'T WANT TO.
BUT ...

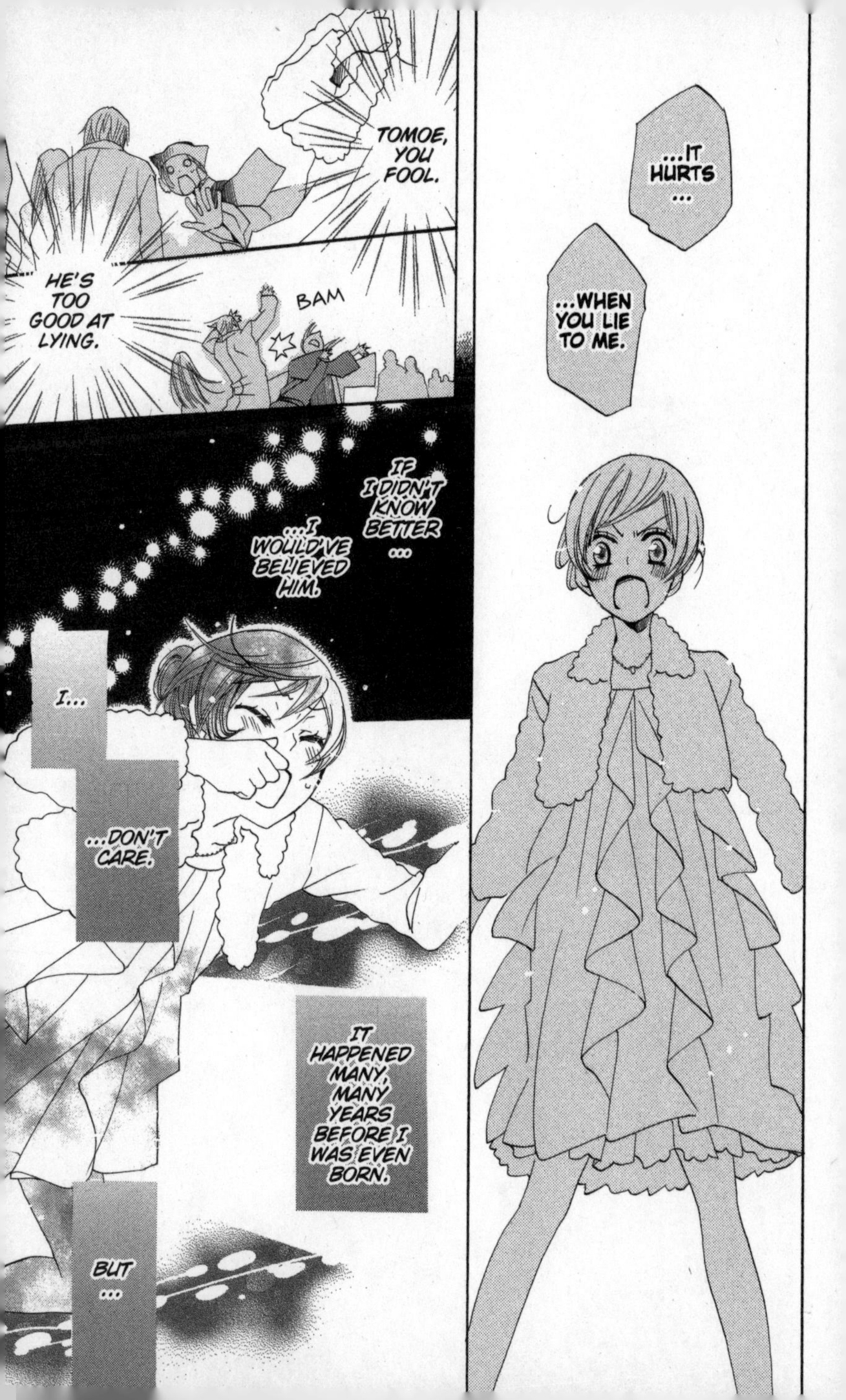
...IT HURTS ...
...WHEN YOU LIE TO ME.
TOMOE, YOU FOOL.
BAM
HE'S TOO GOOD AT LYING.
IF I DIDN'T KNOW BETTER ...
...I WOULD'VE BELIEVED HIM.
I...
...DON'T CARE.
IT HAPPENED MANY, MANY YEARS BEFORE I WAS EVEN BORN.
BUT ...

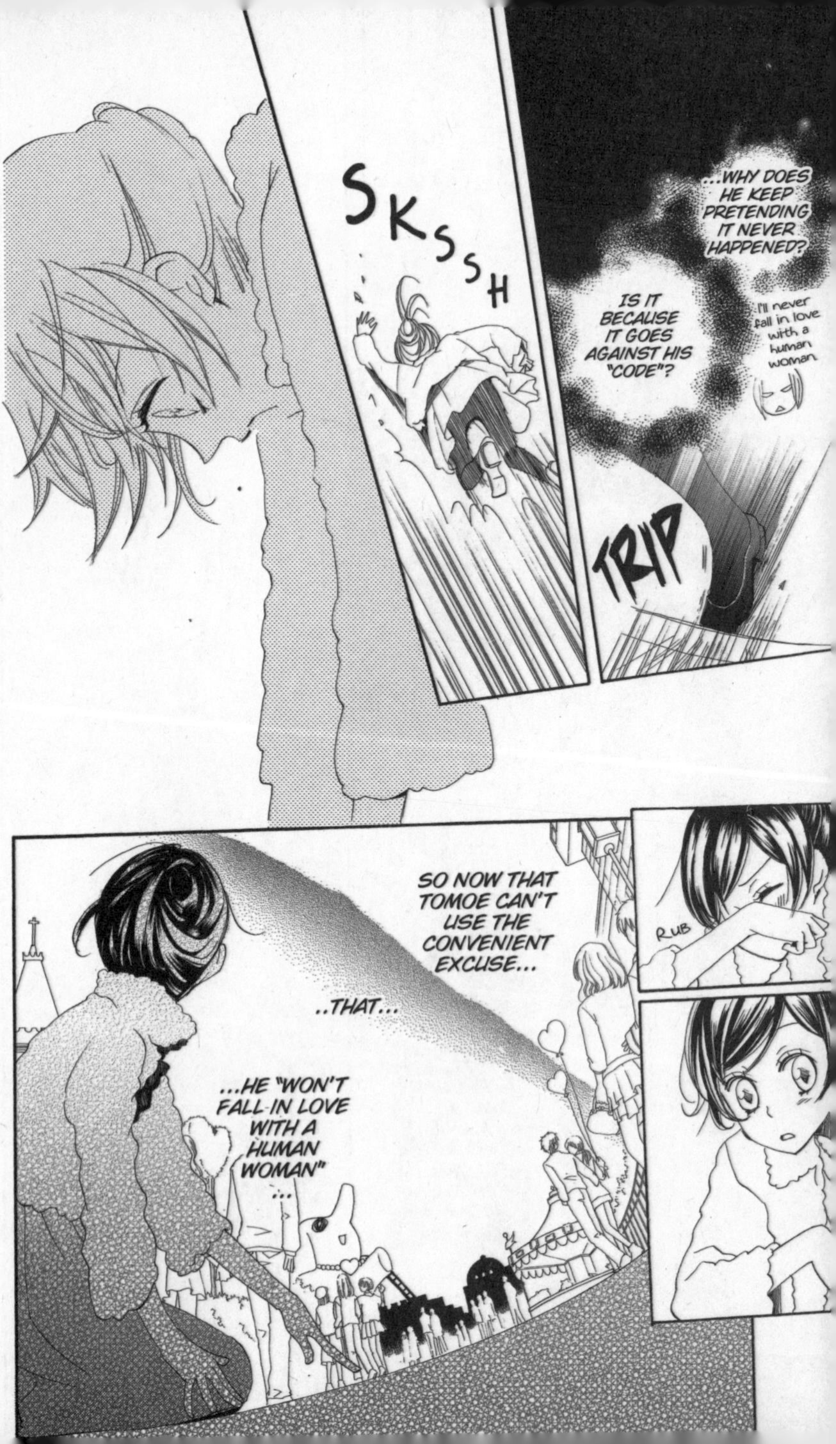
...WHY DOES HE KEEP PRETENDING IT NEVER HAPPENED?
IS IT BECAUSE IT GOES AGAINST HIS "CODE"?
I'll never fall in love with a human woman.
TRIP
SKSSH
RUB
SO NOW THAT TOMOE CAN'T USE THE CONVENIENT EXCUSE...
..THAT...
...HE "WON'T FALL-IN LOVE WITH A HUMAN WOMAN"...

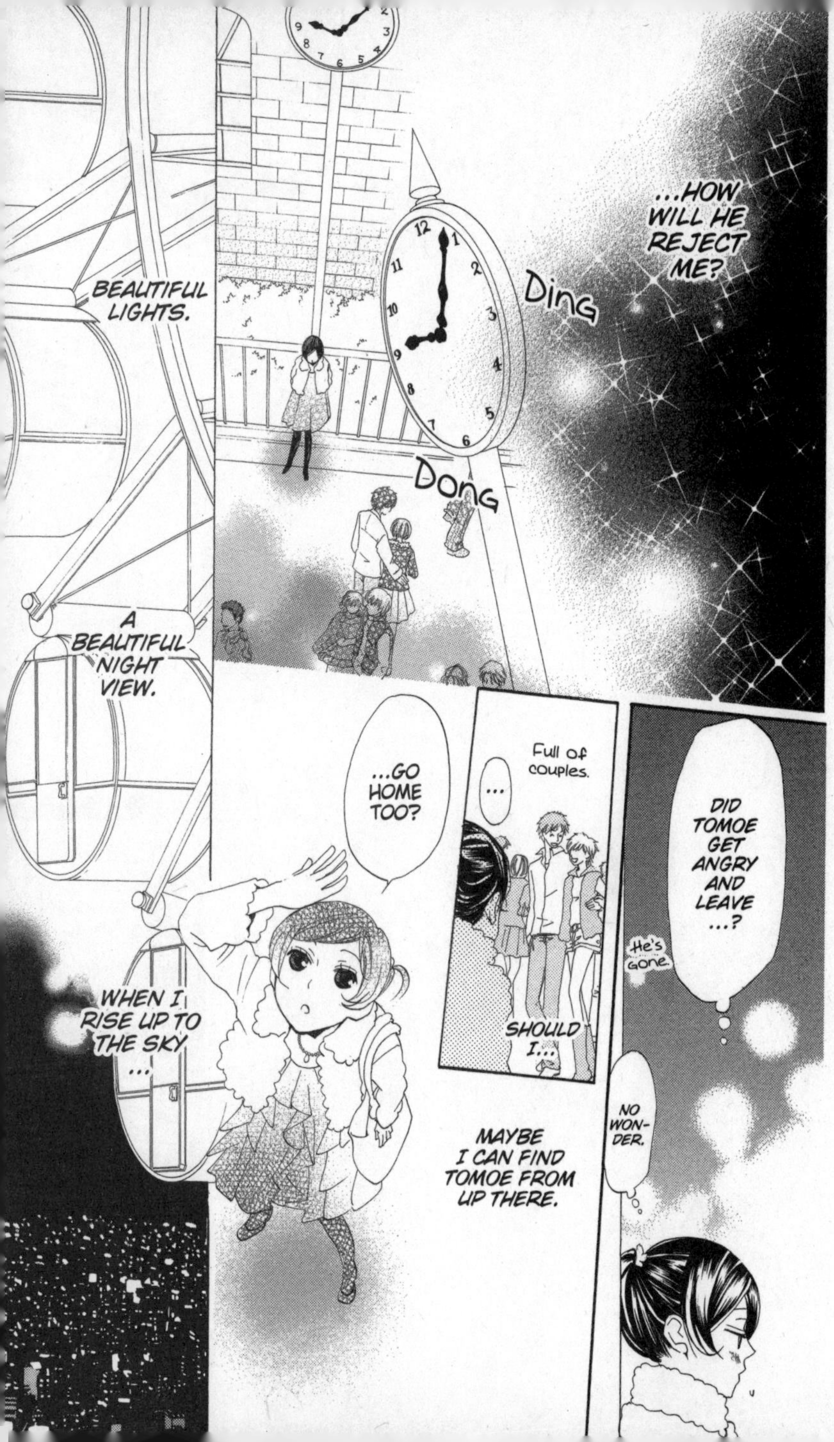
...HOW WILL HE REJECT ME?
Ding
Dong
DID TOMOE GET ANGRY AND LEAVE ...?
He's gone.
NO WON-DER.
...
Full of couples.
SHOULD I...
...GO HOME TOO?
MAYBE I CAN FIND TOMOE FROM UP THERE.
BEAUTIFUL LIGHTS.
A BEAUTIFUL NIGHT VIEW.
WHEN I RISE UP TO THE SKY ...

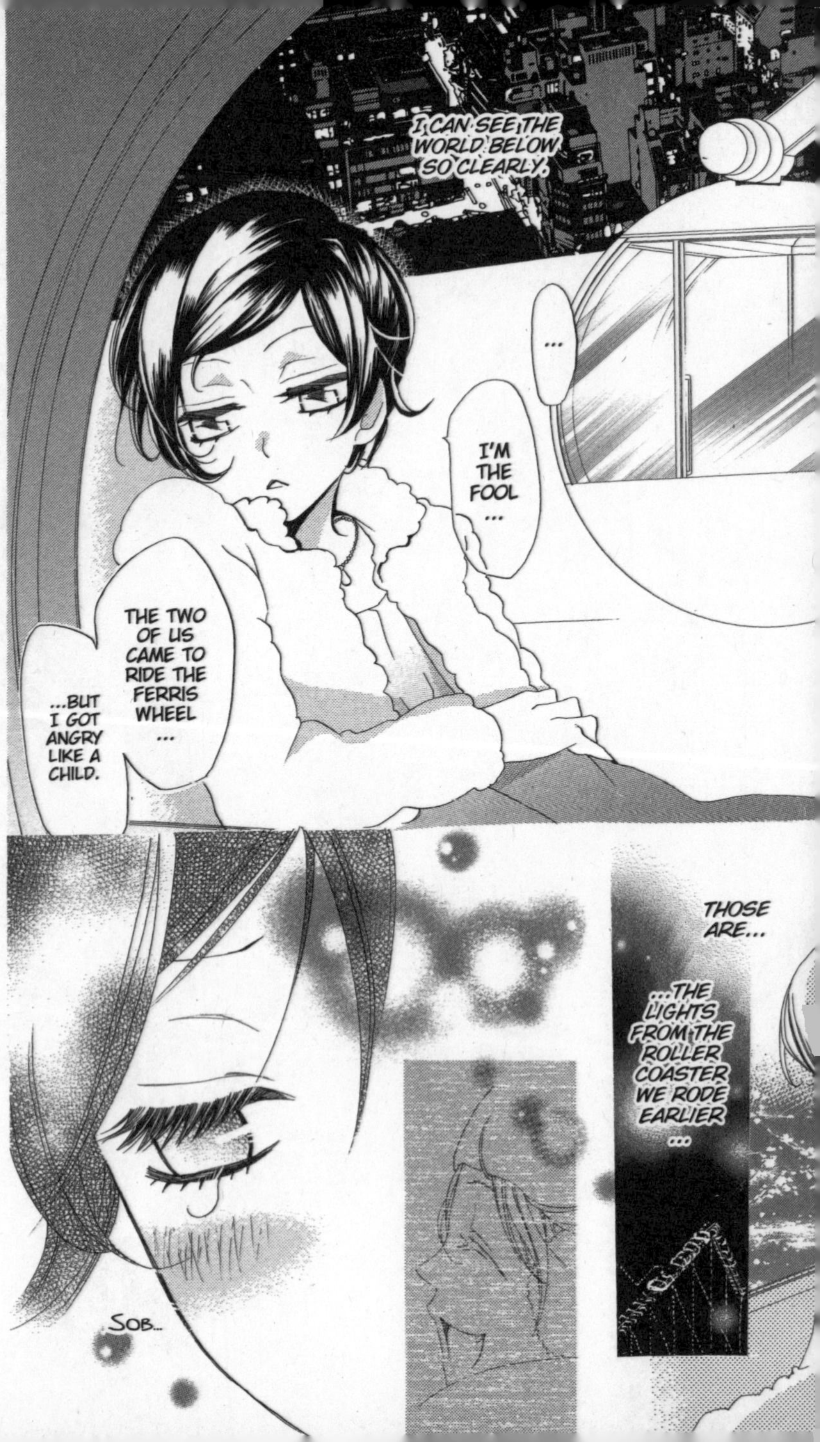
I CAN SEE THE WORLD BELOW SO CLEARLY.
...
I'M THE FOOL ...
THE TWO OF US CAME TO RIDE THE FERRIS WHEEL ...
...BUT I GOT ANGRY LIKE A CHILD.
THOSE ARE...
...THE LIGHTS FROM THE ROLLER COASTER WE RODE EARLIER ...
SOB..

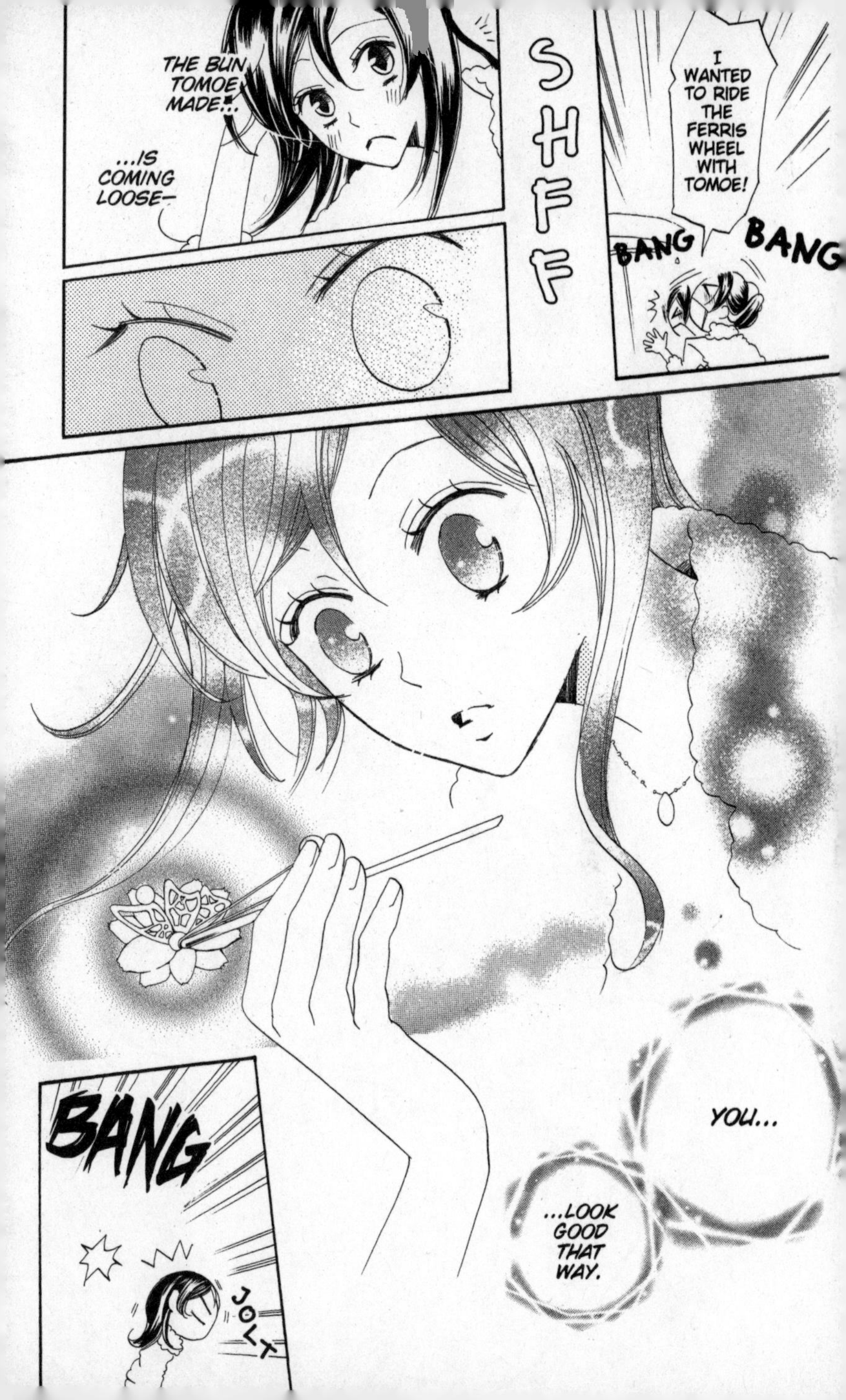
I WANTED TO RIDE THE FERRIS WHEEL WITH TOMOE!
BANG
BANG
SHFF
THE BUN TOMOE MADE...
...IS COMING LOOSE—
YOU...
...LOOK GOOD THAT WAY.
BANG
JOLT

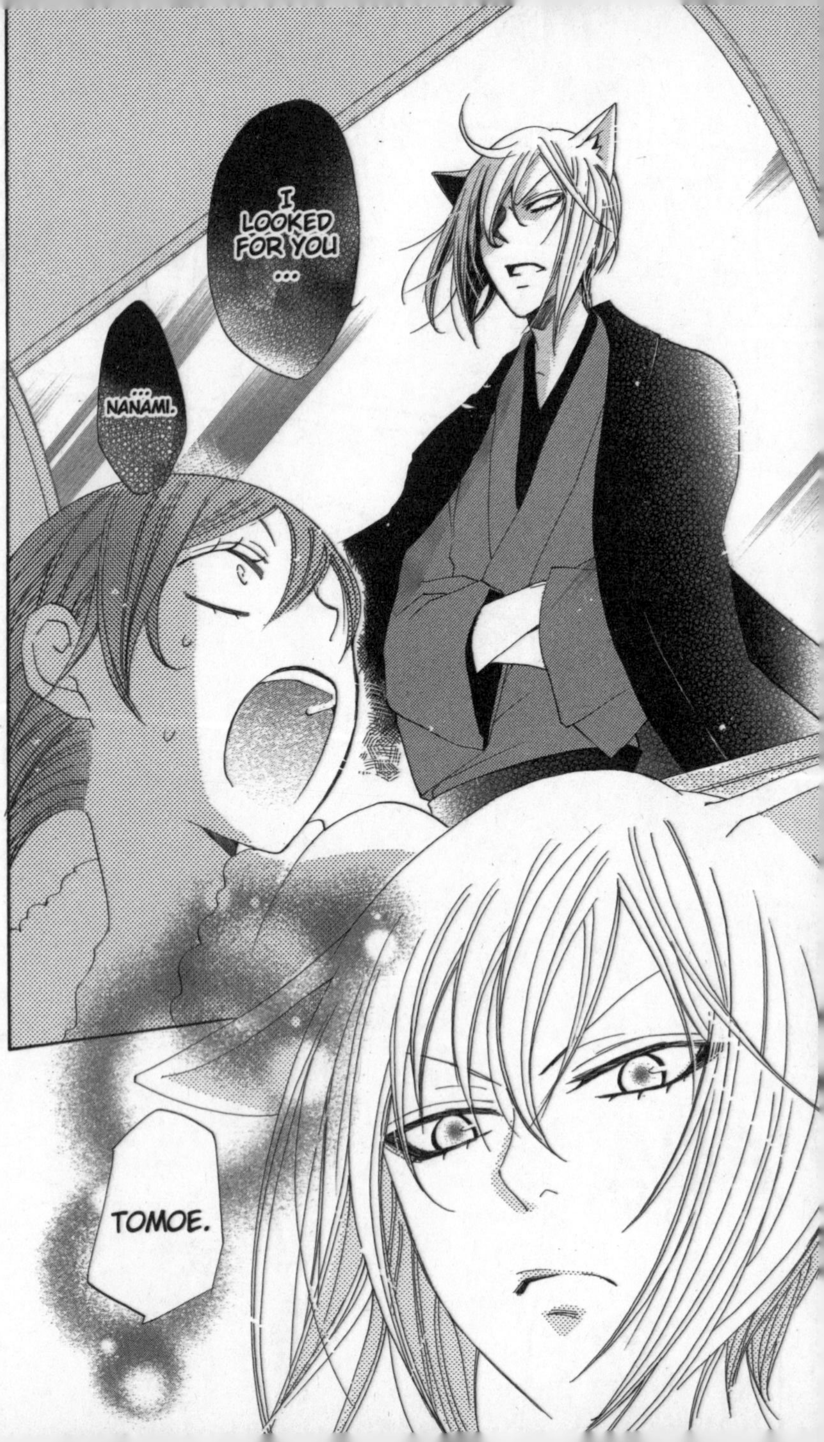
I LOOKED FOR YOU ...
... NANAMI.
TOMOE.

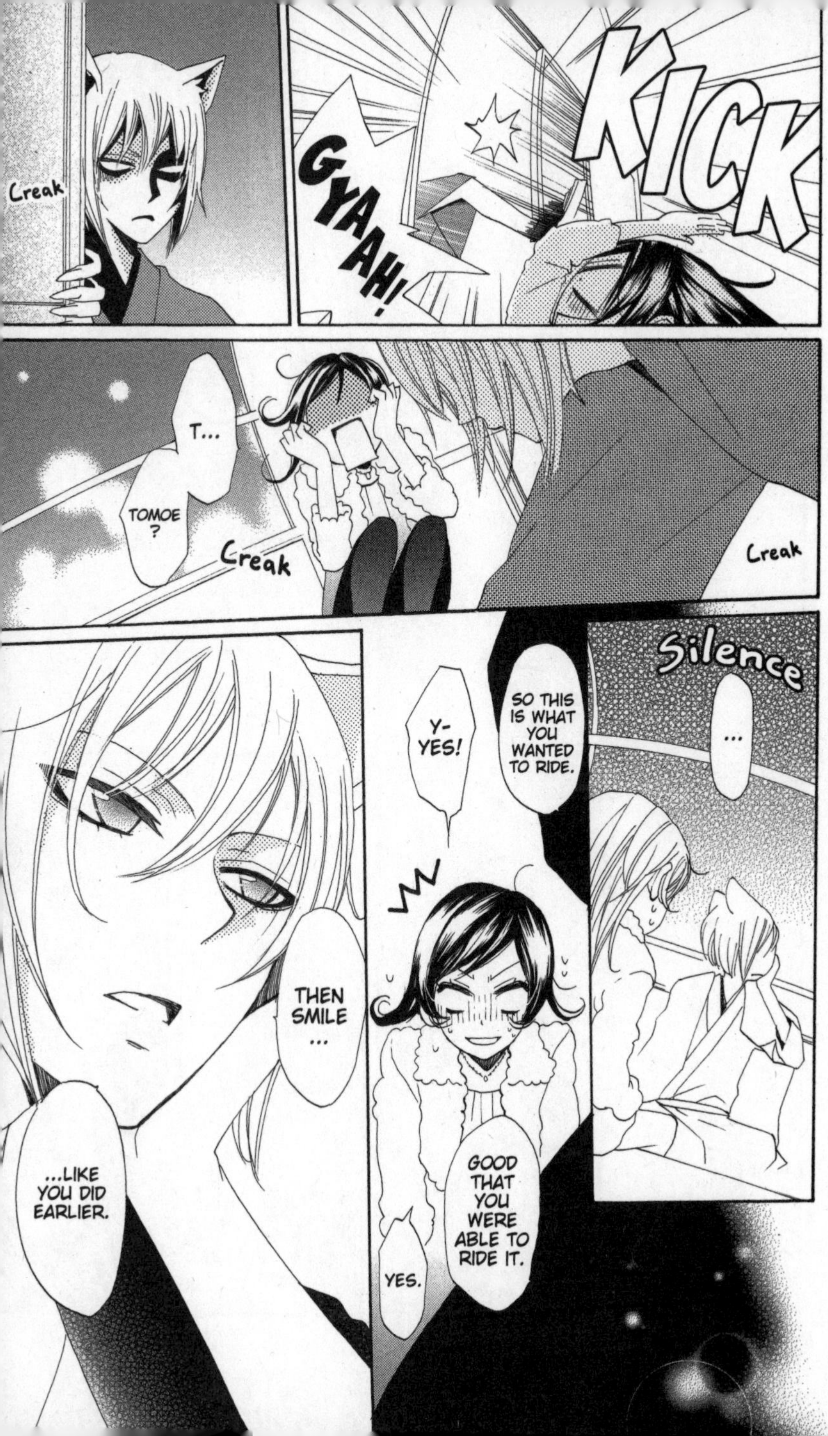
KICK
GYAAH!
Creak
Creak
T...
TOMOE?
Creak
Silence
...
SO THIS IS WHAT YOU WANTED TO RIDE.
Y-YES!
GOOD THAT YOU WERE ABLE TO RIDE IT.
YES.
THEN SMILE...
...LIKE YOU DID EARLIER.

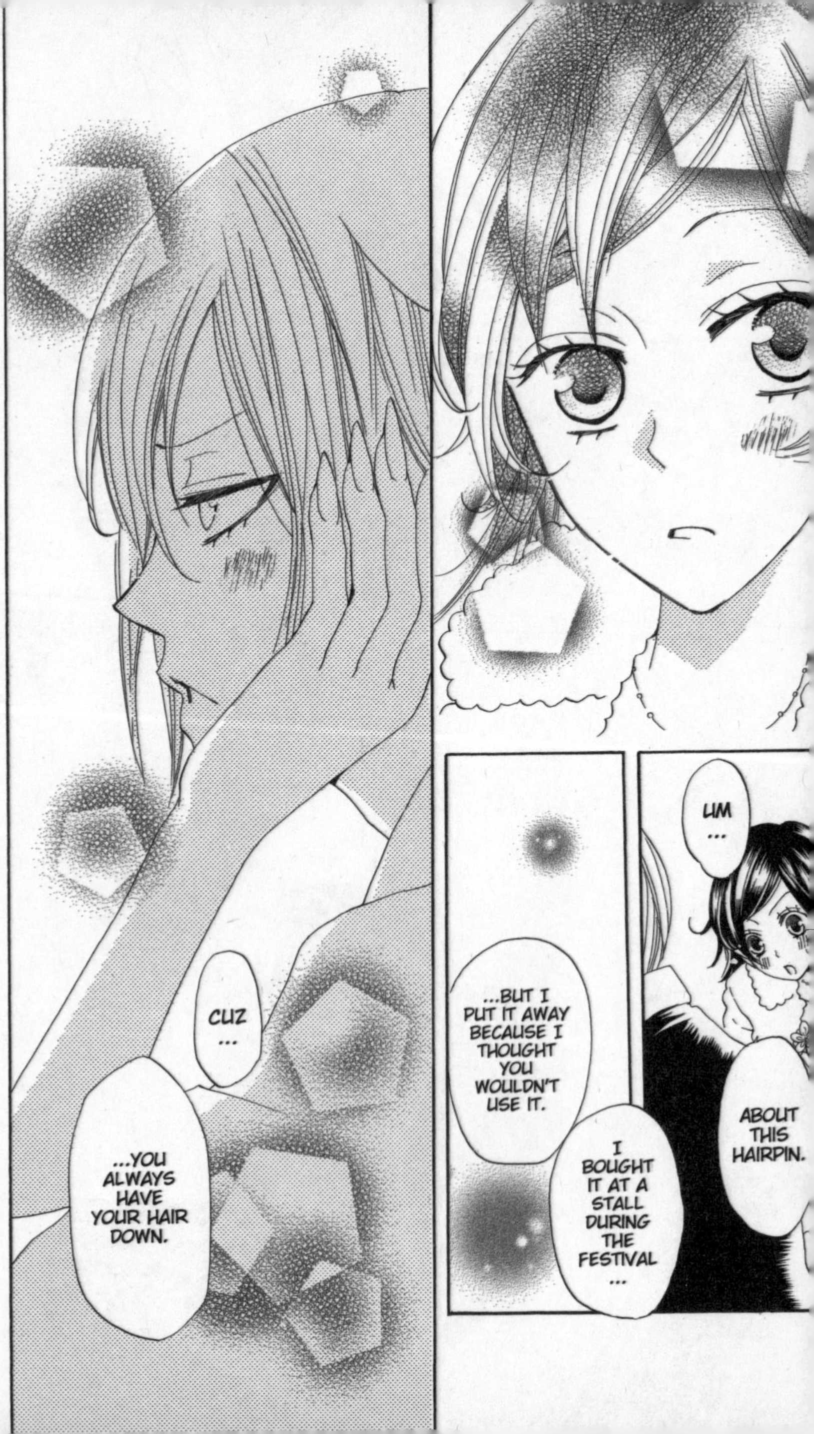
UM ...
ABOUT THIS HAIRPIN.
I BOUGHT IT AT A STALL DURING THE FESTIVAL ...
...BUT I PUT IT AWAY BECAUSE I THOUGHT YOU WOULDN'T USE IT.
CUZ ...
...YOU ALWAYS HAVE YOUR HAIR DOWN.

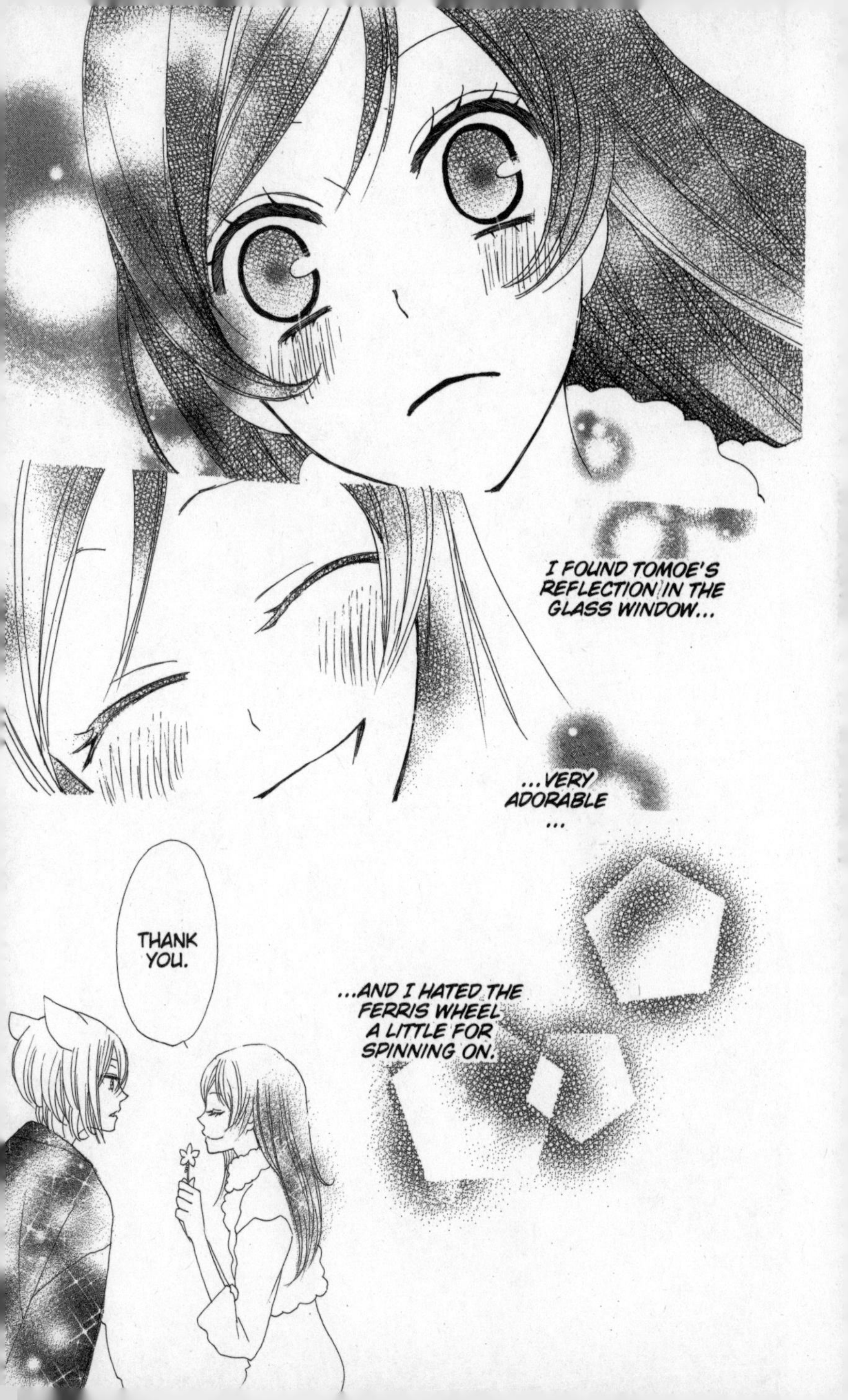
I FOUND TOMOE'S REFLECTION IN THE GLASS WINDOW...
...VERY ADORABLE ...
...AND I HATED THE FERRIS WHEEL A LITTLE FOR SPINNING ON.
THANK YOU.

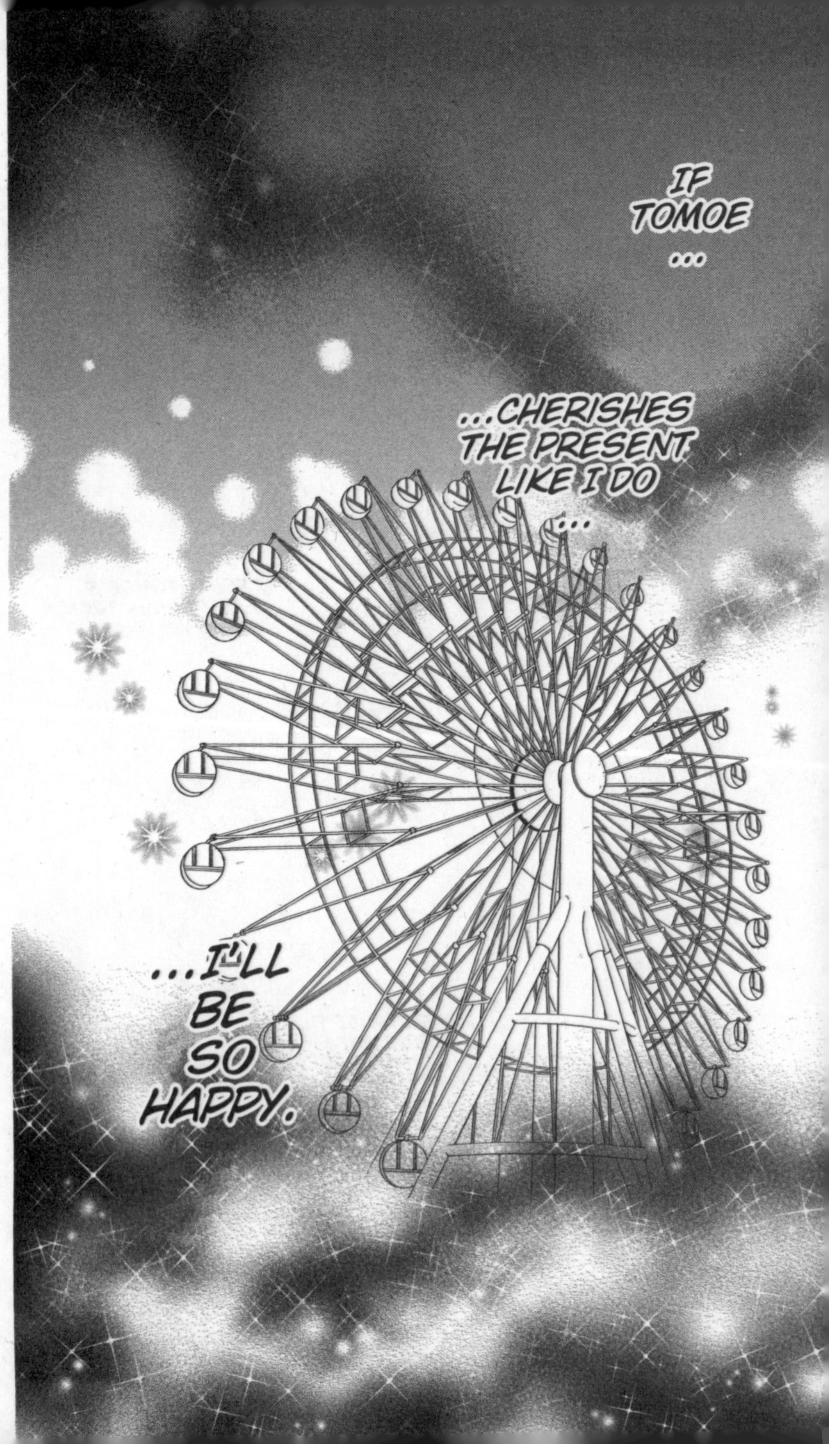
IF TOMOE ...
...CHERISHES THE PRESENT LIKE I DO ...
...I'LL BE SO HAPPY.

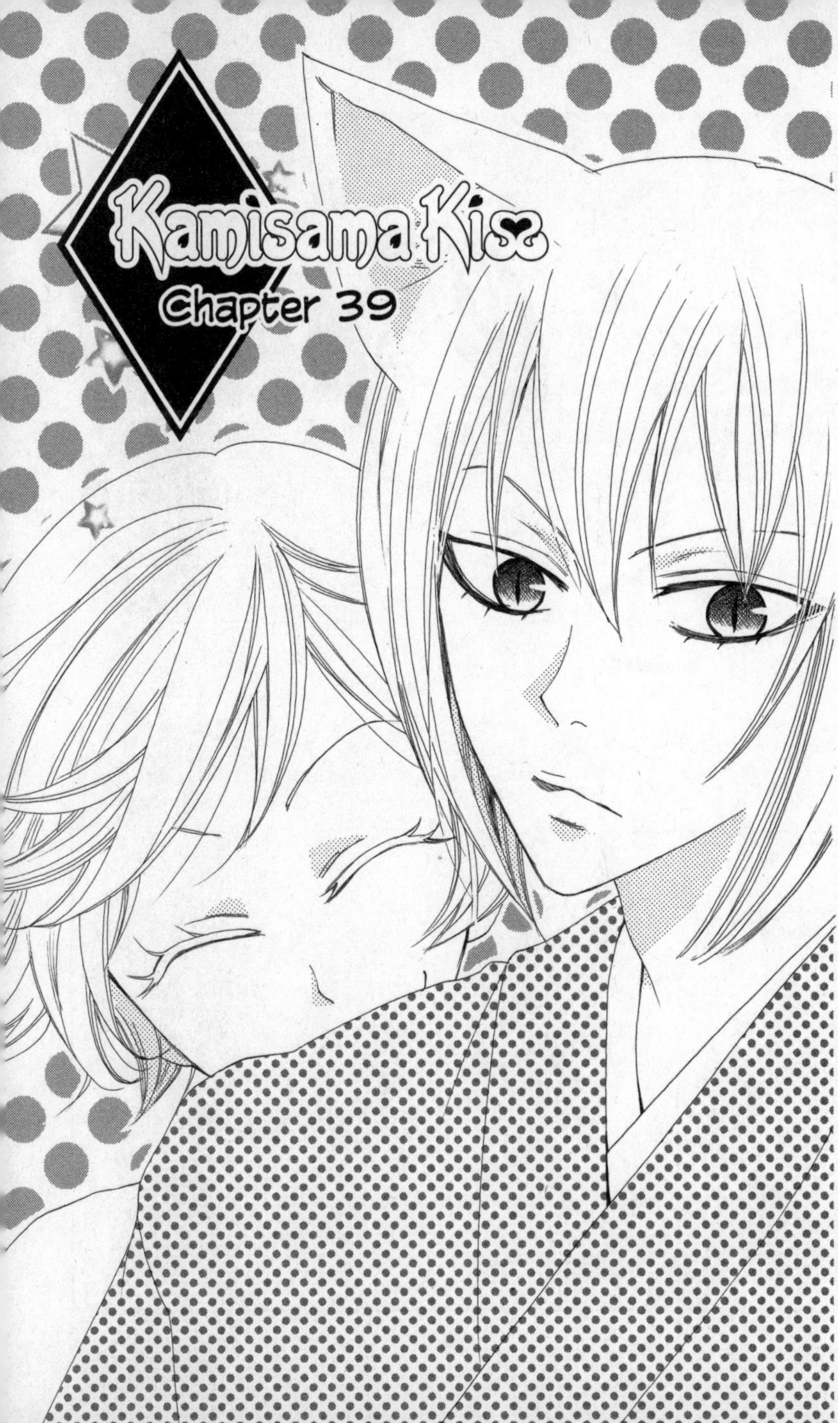
Kamisama Kiss
Chapter 39

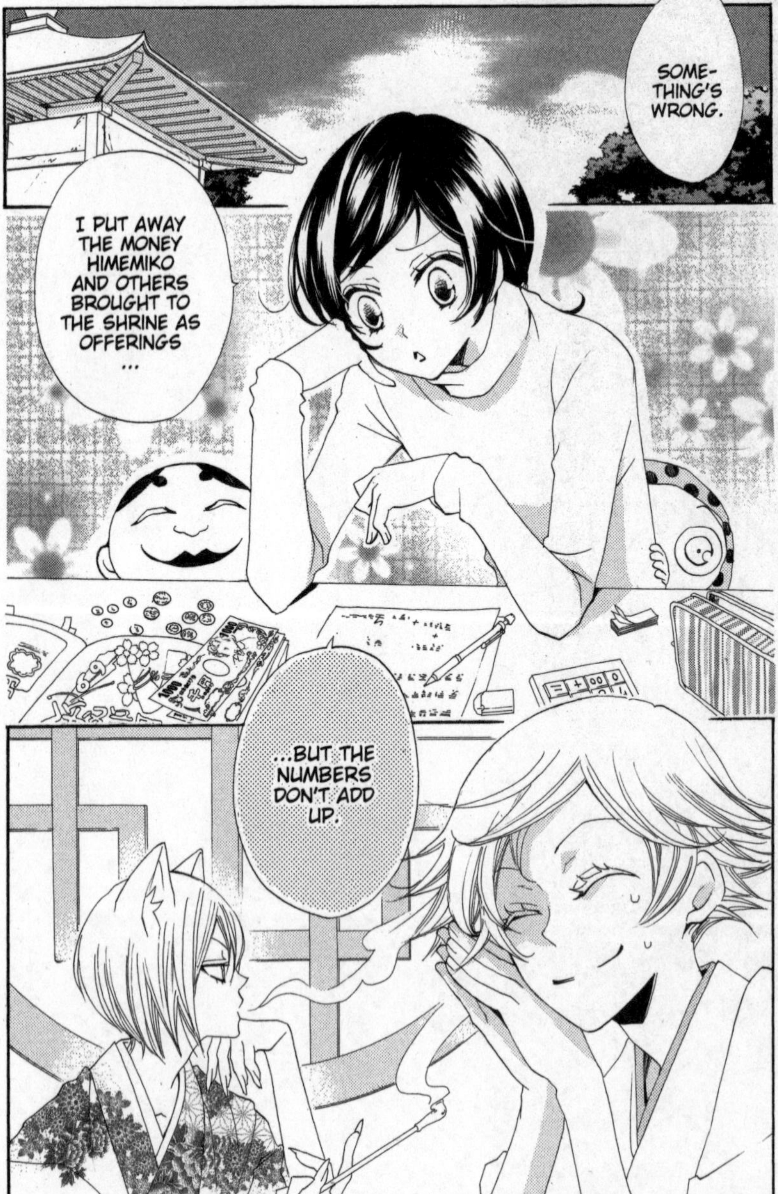
SOME-THING'S WRONG.
I PUT AWAY THE MONEY HIMEMIKO AND OTHERS BROUGHT TO THE SHRINE AS OFFERINGS ...
...BUT THE NUMBERS DON'T ADD UP.

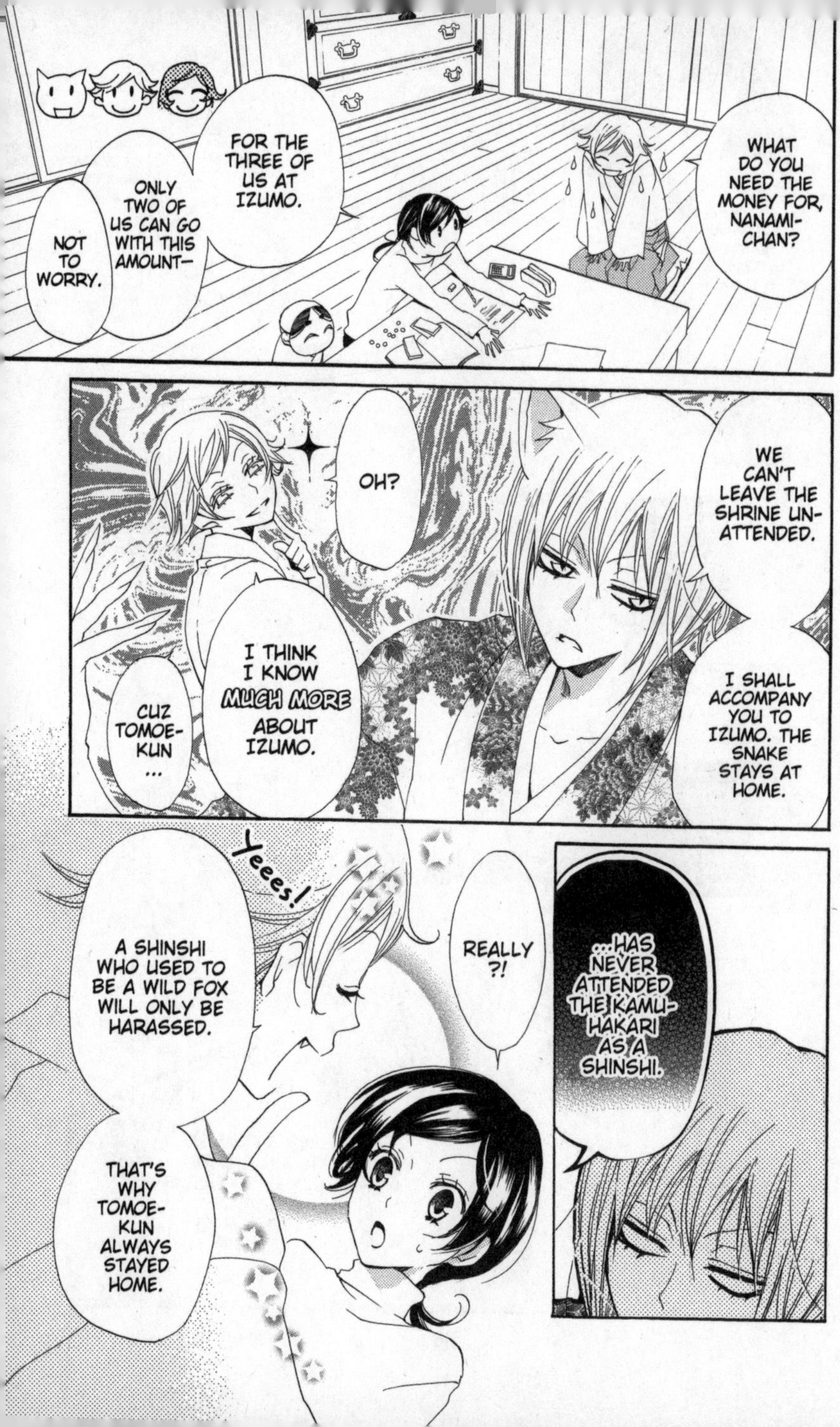
WHAT DO YOU NEED THE MONEY FOR, NANAMI-CHAN?
FOR THE THREE OF US AT IZUMO.
ONLY TWO OF US CAN GO WITH THIS AMOUNT—
NOT TO WORRY.
WE CAN'T LEAVE THE SHRINE UN-ATTENDED.
I SHALL ACCOMPANY YOU TO IZUMO. THE SNAKE STAYS AT HOME.
OH?
I THINK I KNOW MUCH MORE ABOUT IZUMO.
CUZ TOMOE-KUN ...
...HAS NEVER ATTENDED THE KAMU-HAKARI AS A SHINSHI.
REALLY?!
Yeees!
A SHINSHI WHO USED TO BE A WILD FOX WILL ONLY BE HARASSED.
THAT'S WHY TOMOE-KUN ALWAYS STAYED HOME.

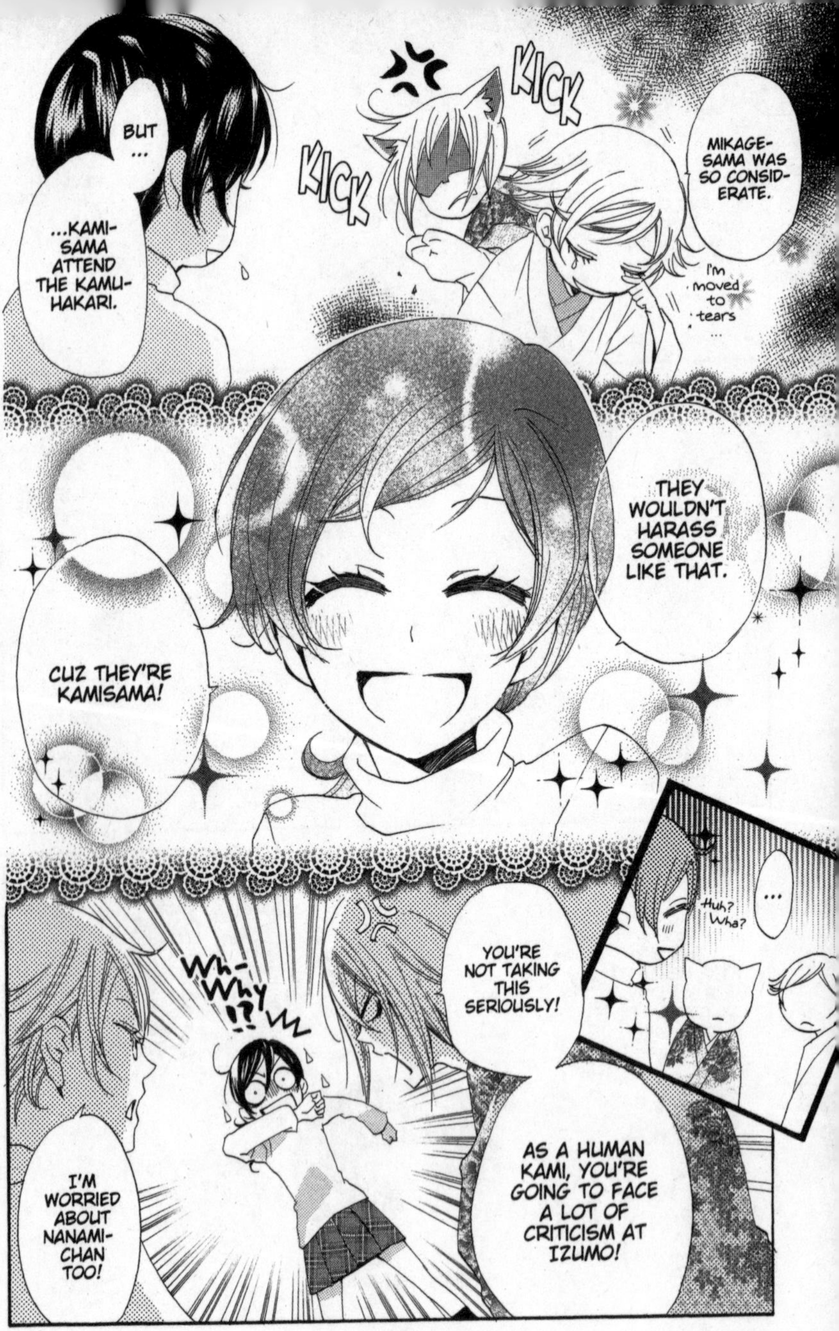
MIKAGE-SAMA WAS SO CONSIDERATE.
I'm moved to tears ...
KICK
KICK
BUT ...
...KAMI-SAMA ATTEND THE KAMU-HAKARI.
THEY WOULDN'T HARASS SOMEONE LIKE THAT.
CUZ THEY'RE KAMISAMA!
...
Huh? Wha?
YOU'RE NOT TAKING THIS SERIOUSLY!
AS A HUMAN KAMI, YOU'RE GOING TO FACE A LOT OF CRITICISM AT IZUMO!
Wh-Why!?
I'M WORRIED ABOUT NANAMI-CHAN TOO!

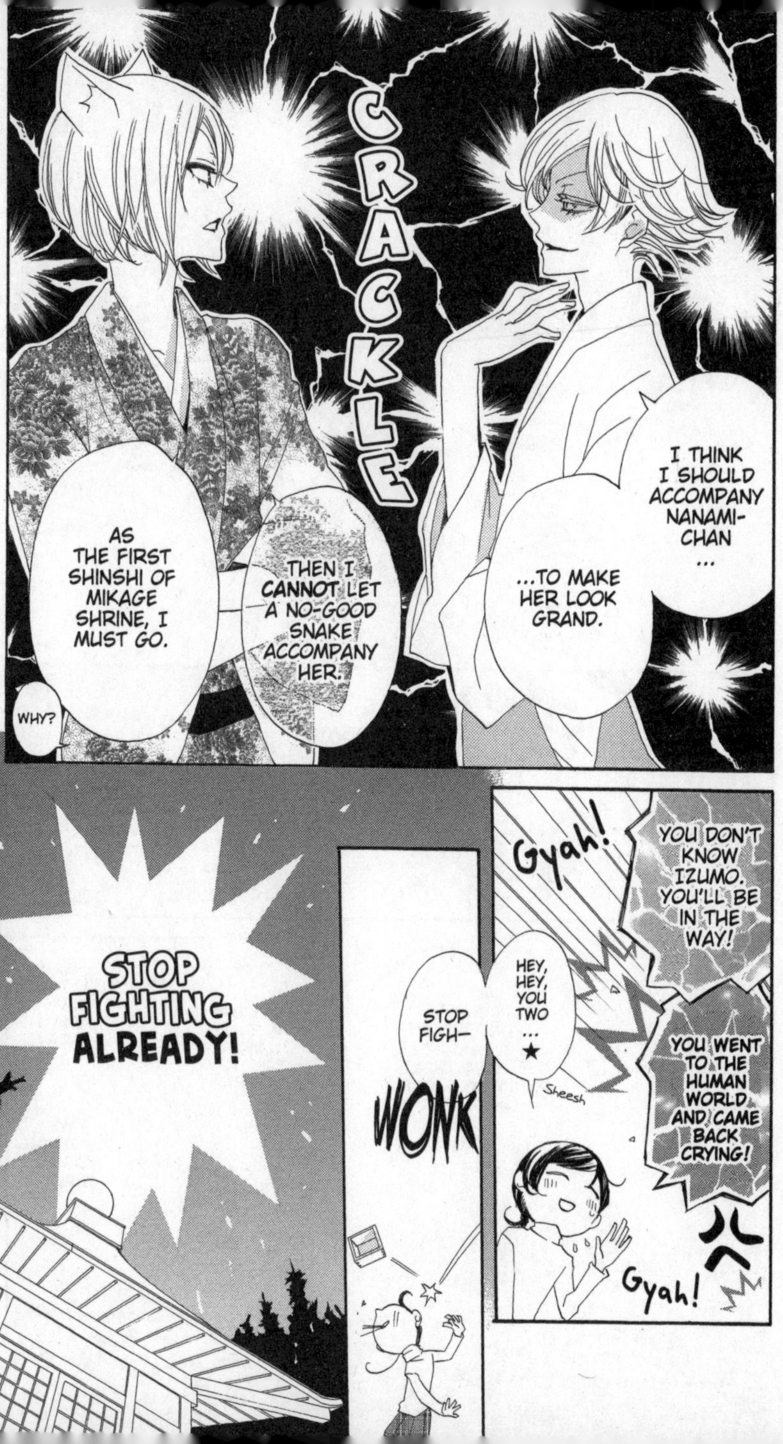
I THINK I SHOULD ACCOMPANY NANAMI-CHAN ...
...TO MAKE HER LOOK GRAND.
CRACKLE
THEN I CANNOT LET A NO-GOOD SNAKE ACCOMPANY HER.
AS THE FIRST SHINSHI OF MIKAGE SHRINE, I MUST GO.
WHY?
Gyah!
YOU DON'T KNOW IZUMO. YOU'LL BE IN THE WAY!
HEY, HEY, YOU TWO ... ★
Sheesh
YOU WENT TO THE HUMAN WORLD AND CAME BACK CRYING!
Gyah!
STOP FIGH—
WONK
STOP FIGHTING ALREADY!

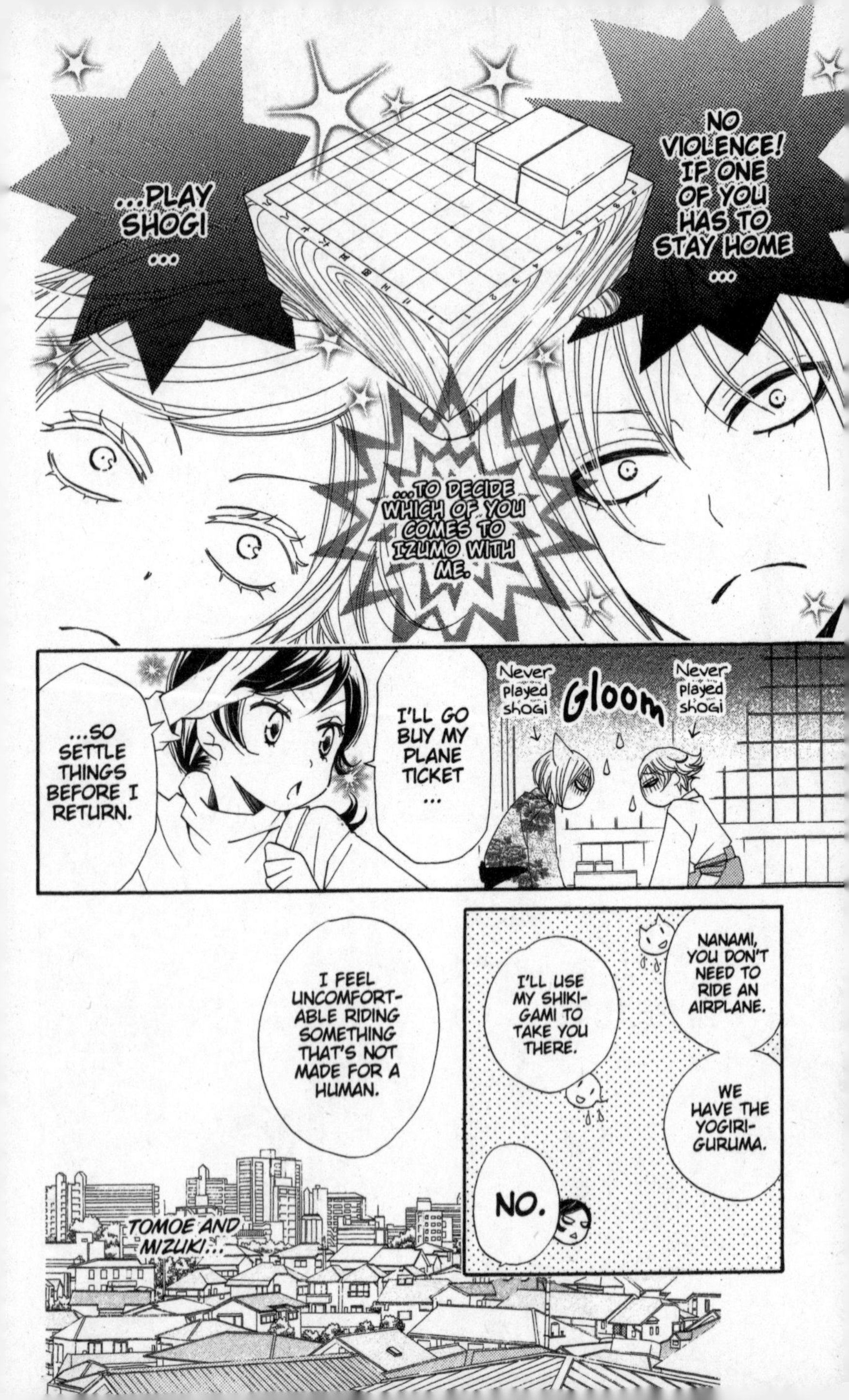
NO VIOLENCE! IF ONE OF YOU HAS TO STAY HOME...
...PLAY SHOGI...
...TO DECIDE WHICH OF YOU COMES TO IZUMO WITH ME.
Never played shogi
Gloom
Never played shogi
I'LL GO BUY MY PLANE TICKET...
...SO SETTLE THINGS BEFORE I RETURN.
NANAMI, YOU DON'T NEED TO RIDE AN AIRPLANE.
I'LL USE MY SHIKI-GAMI TO TAKE YOU THERE.
WE HAVE THE YOGIRI-GURUMA.
NO.
I FEEL UNCOMFORT-ABLE RIDING SOMETHING THAT'S NOT MADE FOR A HUMAN.
TOMOE AND MIZUKI...

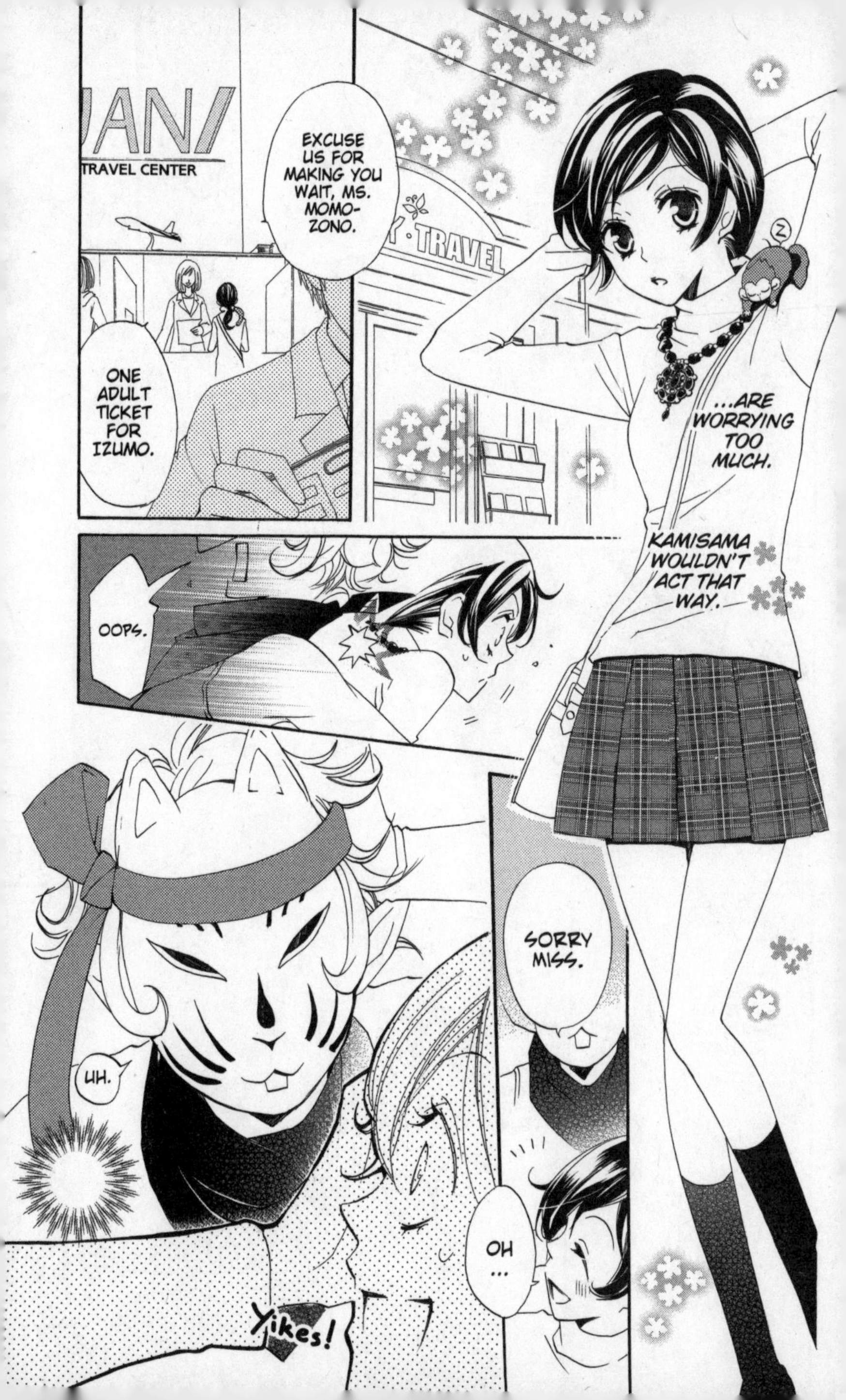
·TRAVEL
...ARE WORRYING TOO MUCH.
KAMISAMA WOULDN'T ACT THAT WAY.
JAN/
TRAVEL CENTER
EXCUSE US FOR MAKING YOU WAIT, MS. MOMO-ZONO.
ONE ADULT TICKET FOR IZUMO.
OOPS.
SORRY MISS.
UH.
OH ...
Yikes!

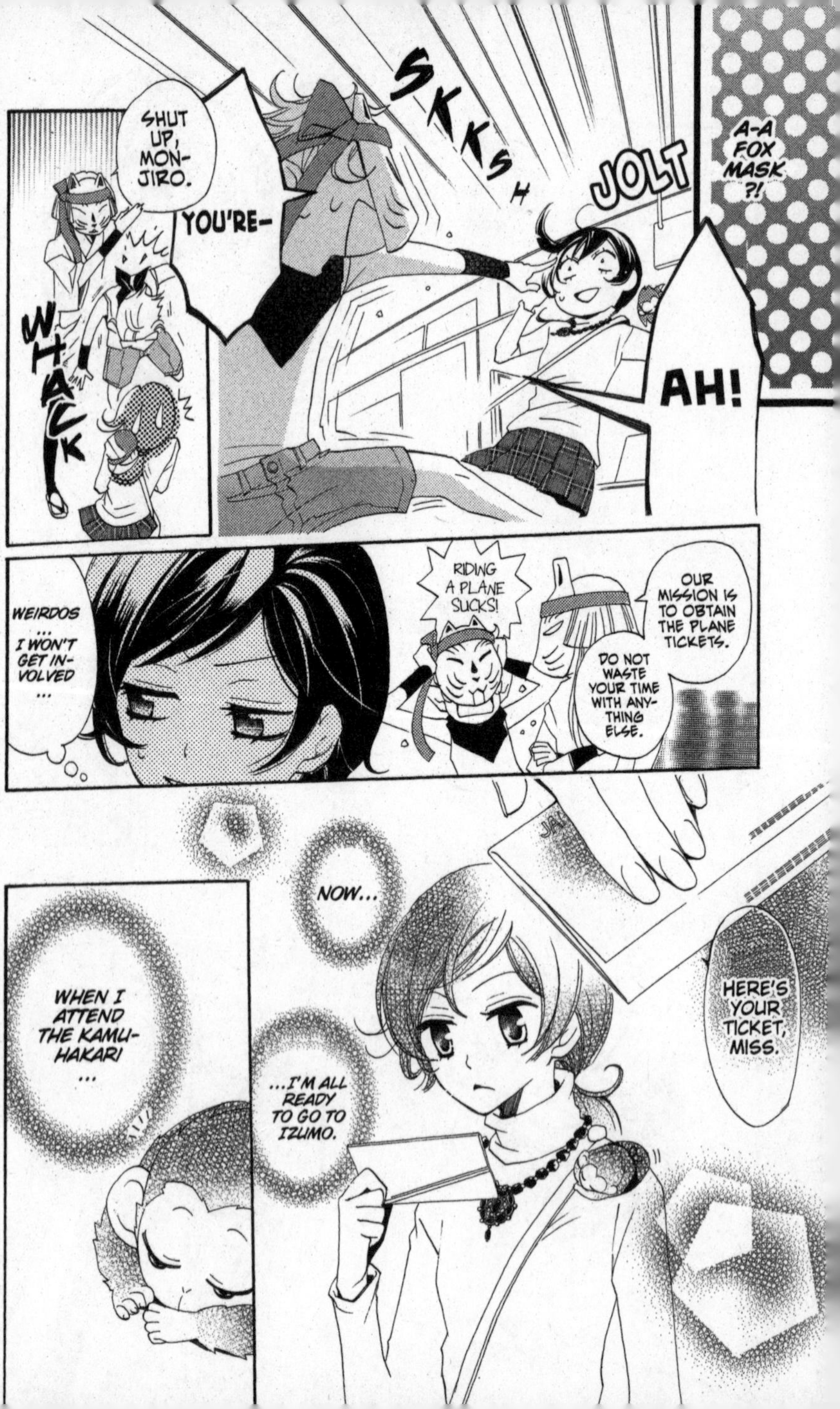
A-A FOX MASK ?!
SKKSH
JOLT
AH!
YOU'RE-
SHUT UP, MON-JIRO.
WHACK
OUR MISSION IS TO OBTAIN THE PLANE TICKETS.
DO NOT WASTE YOUR TIME WITH ANY-THING ELSE.
RIDING A PLANE SUCKS!
WEIRDOS ... I WON'T GET IN-VOLVED ...
HERE'S YOUR TICKET, MISS.
NOW...
WHEN I ATTEND THE KAMU-HAKARI ...
...I'M ALL READY TO GO TO IZUMO.

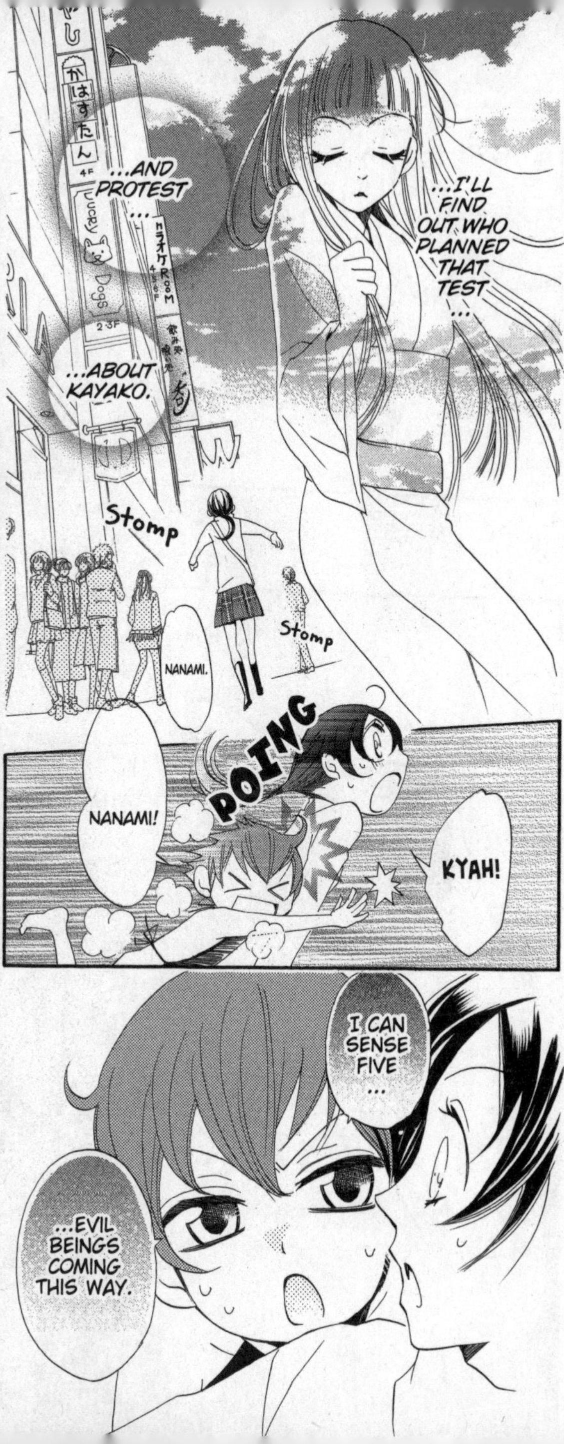
...I'LL FIND OUT WHO PLANNED THAT TEST...
...AND PROTEST...
...ABOUT KAYAKO.
Stomp
Stomp
NANAMI.
KYAH!
POING
NANAMI!
I CAN SENSE FIVE...
...EVIL BEINGS COMING THIS WAY.

③

The other day I went to France. My first France experience was sparkling and beautiful.

There were many things to look at, such as Mont Saint-Michel, Versailles, the Louvre, the Conciergerie, and Giverny, and I was impressed by how amazing the country is! But at the same time, I felt that Japan is an amazing country as well.

We can be proud of Japan's attention to details. There're lots of things I realize by venturing out of this country. Thanks to this trip, I grew to love both France and Japan!

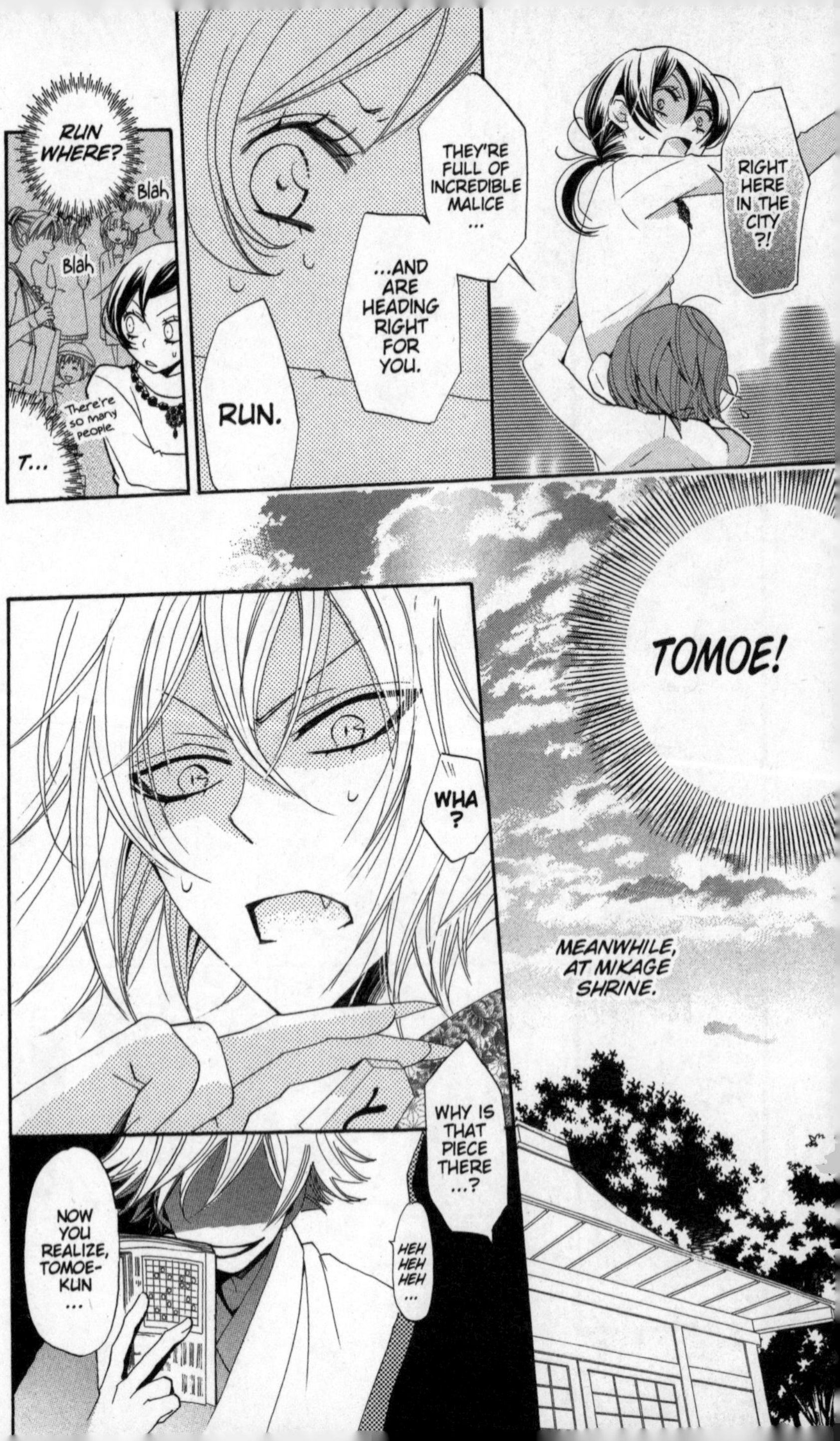
RIGHT HERE IN THE CITY ?!
THEY'RE FULL OF INCREDIBLE MALICE ...
...AND ARE HEADING RIGHT FOR YOU.
RUN.
RUN WHERE?
Blah
Blah
There're so many people
T...
TOMOE!
MEANWHILE, AT MIKAGE SHRINE.
WHA ?
WHY IS THAT PIECE THERE ...?
HEH HEH HEH ...
NOW YOU REALIZE, TOMOE-KUN ...

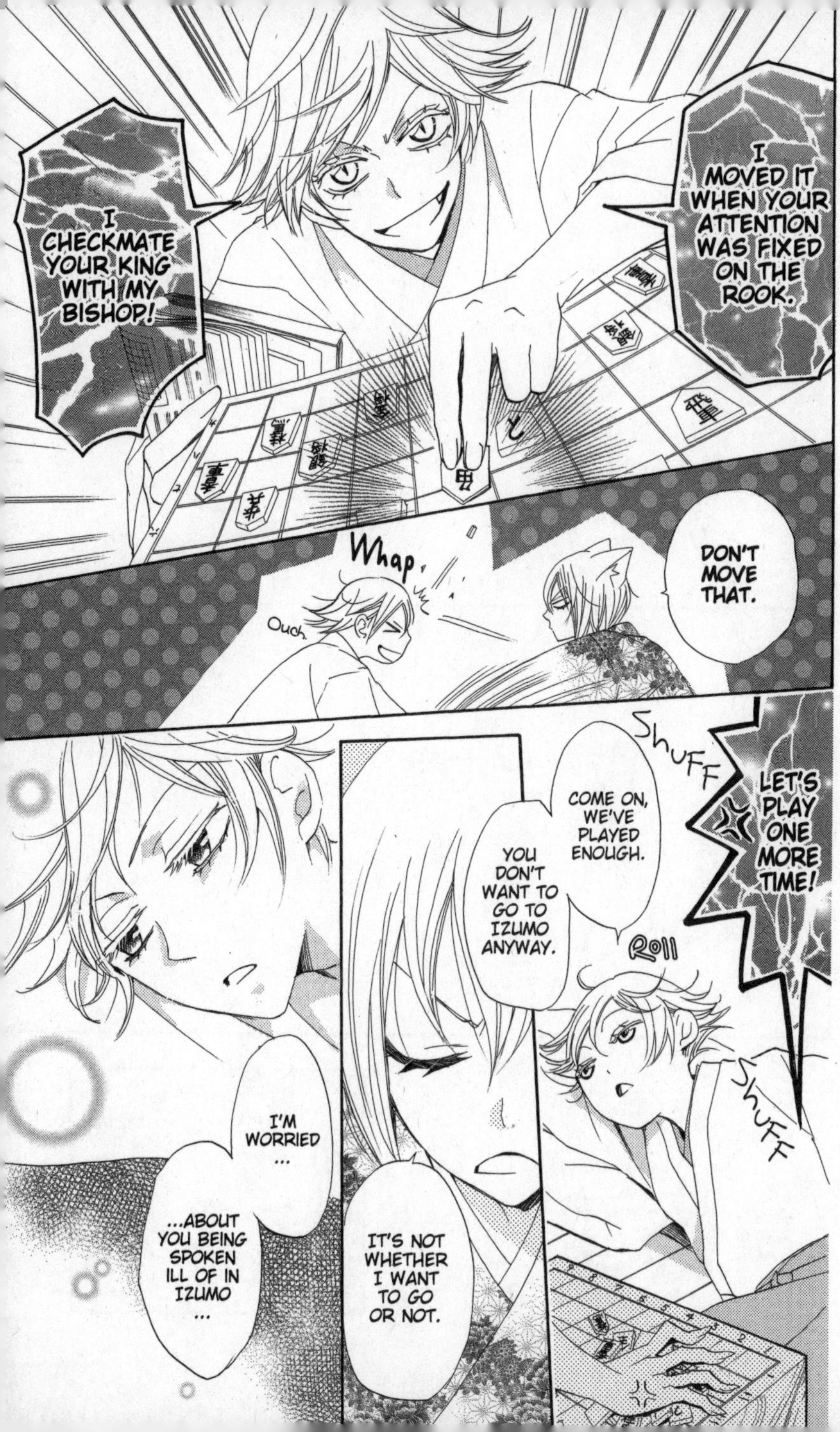
I MOVED IT WHEN YOUR ATTENTION WAS FIXED ON THE ROOK.
I CHECKMATE YOUR KING WITH MY BISHOP!
DON'T MOVE THAT.
Whap
Ouch.
SHUFF
LET'S PLAY ONE MORE TIME!
COME ON, WE'VE PLAYED ENOUGH.
YOU DON'T WANT TO GO TO IZUMO ANYWAY.
ROll
SHUFF
IT'S NOT WHETHER I WANT TO GO OR NOT.
I'M WORRIED ...
...ABOUT YOU BEING SPOKEN ILL OF IN IZUMO ...

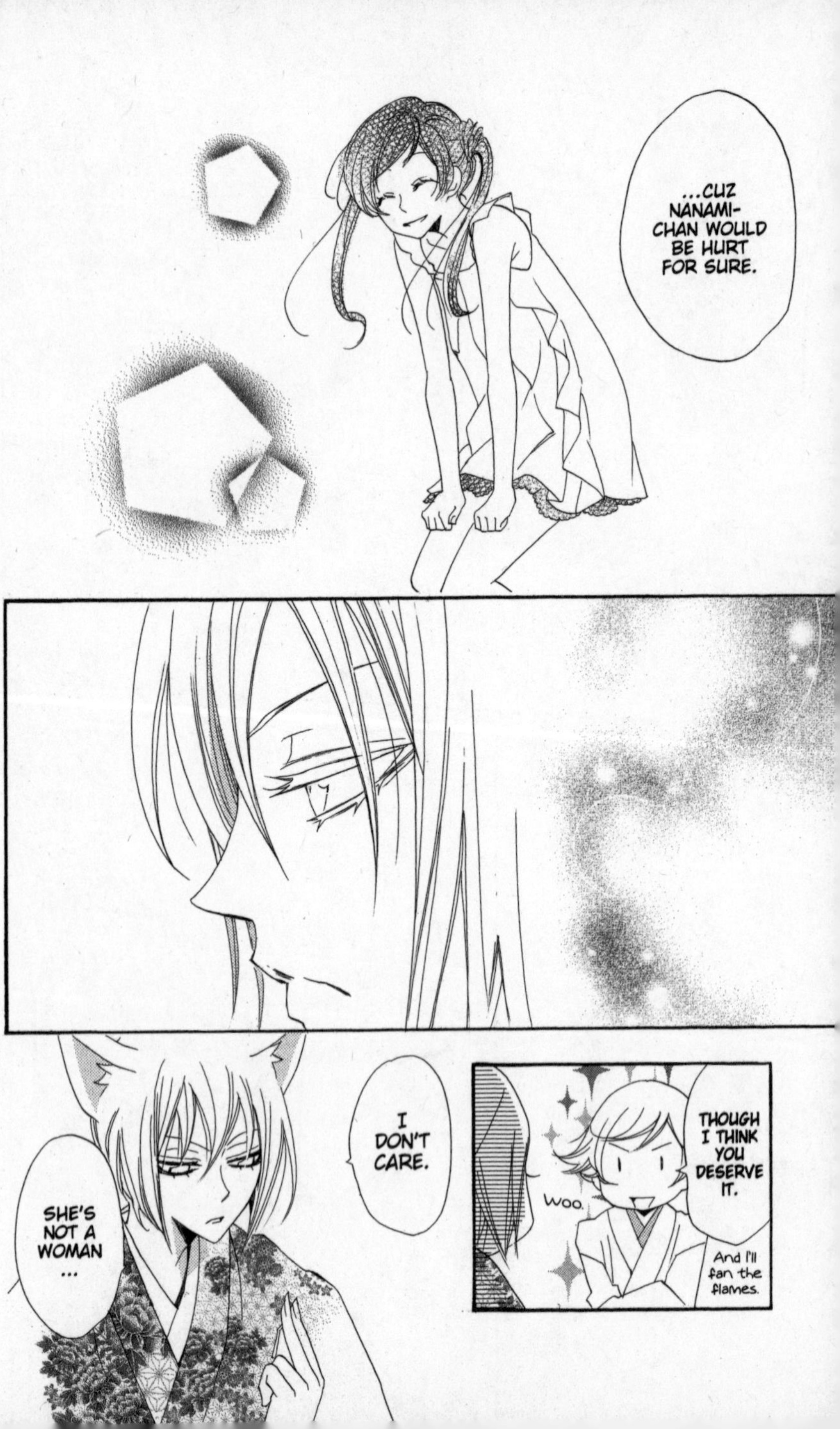
...CUZ NANAMI-CHAN WOULD BE HURT FOR SURE.
THOUGH I THINK YOU DESERVE IT.
WOO.
And I'll fan the flames.
I DON'T CARE.
SHE'S NOT A WOMAN ...

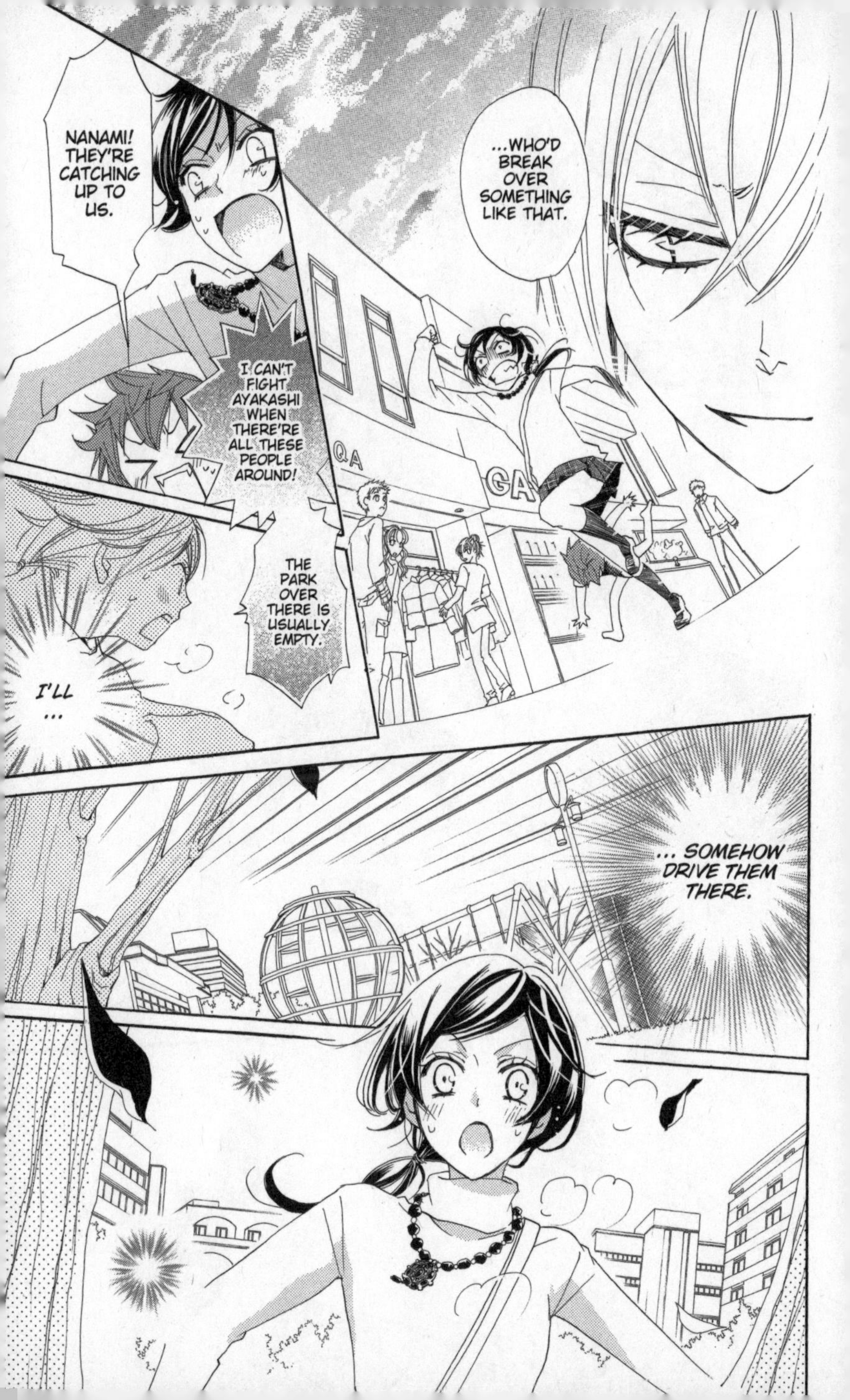
...WHO'D BREAK OVER SOMETHING LIKE THAT.
NANAMI! THEY'RE CATCHING UP TO US.
I CAN'T FIGHT AYAKASHI WHEN THERE'RE ALL THESE PEOPLE AROUND!
THE PARK OVER THERE IS USUALLY EMPTY.
I'LL ...
... SOMEHOW DRIVE THEM THERE.

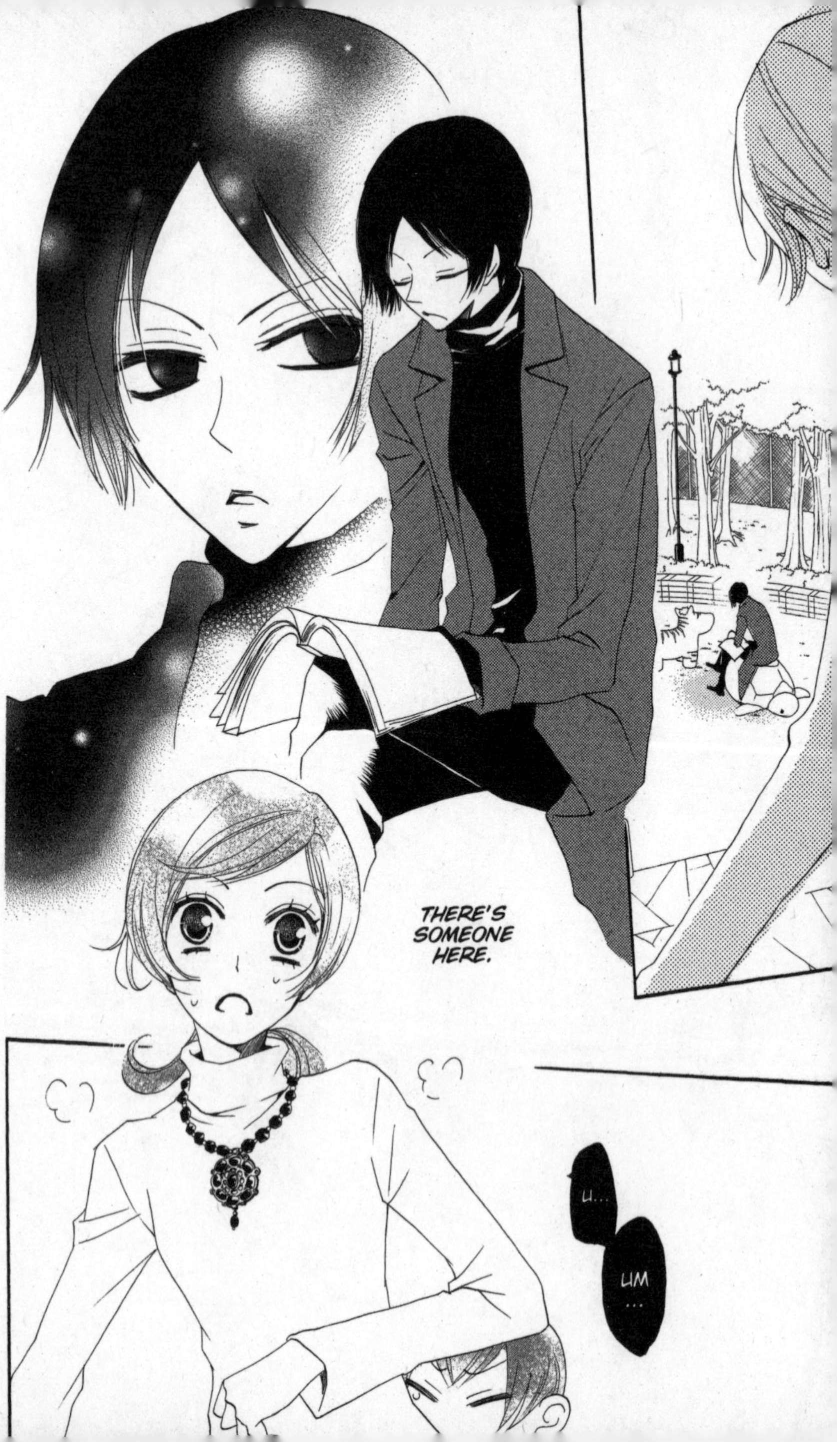
THERE'S SOMEONE HERE.
U...
UM ...

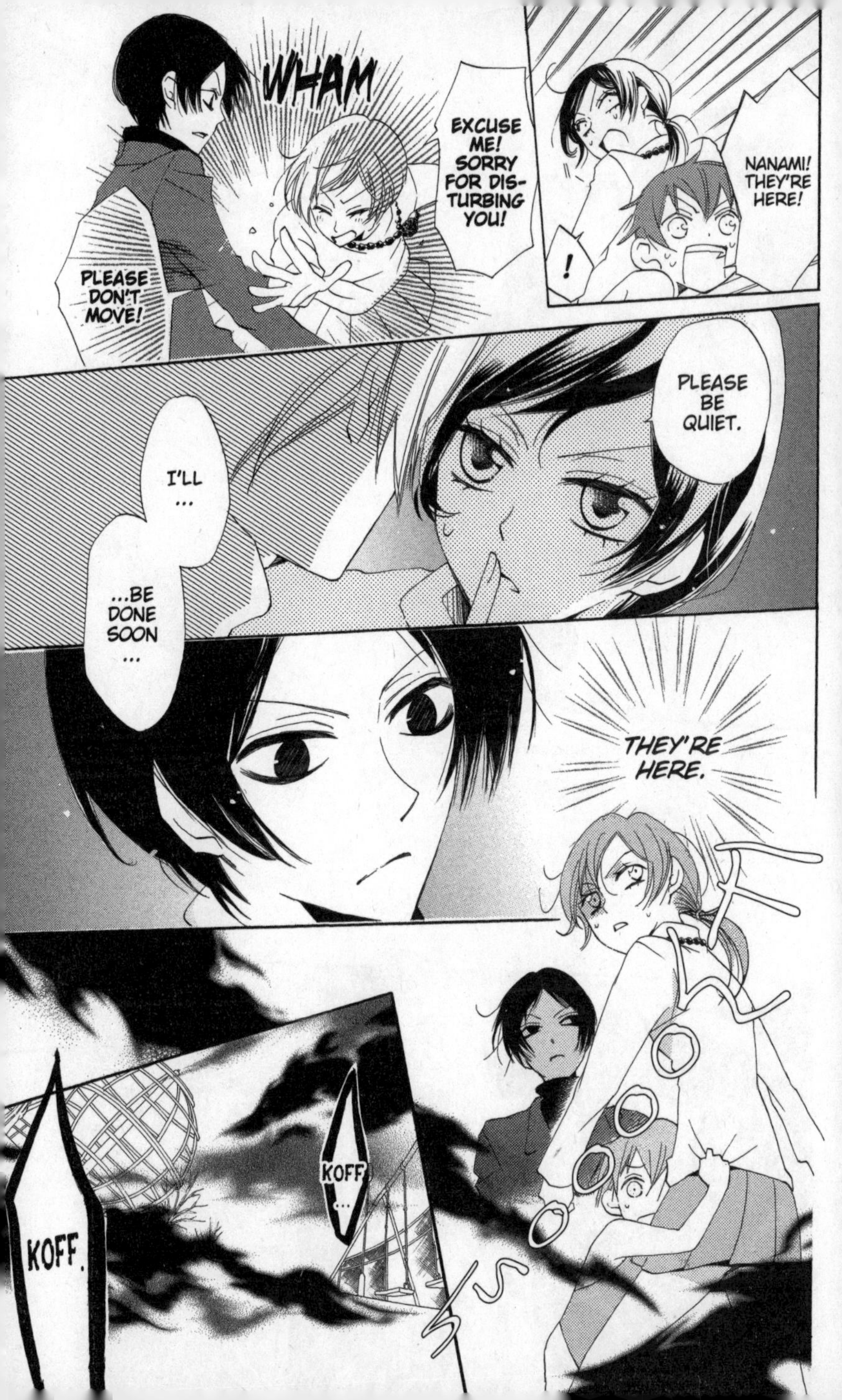
NANAMI! THEY'RE HERE!
!
WHAM
EXCUSE ME! SORRY FOR DIS-TURBING YOU!
PLEASE DON'T MOVE!
PLEASE BE QUIET.
I'LL ...
...BE DONE SOON ...
THEY'RE HERE.
KOFF ...
KOFF.

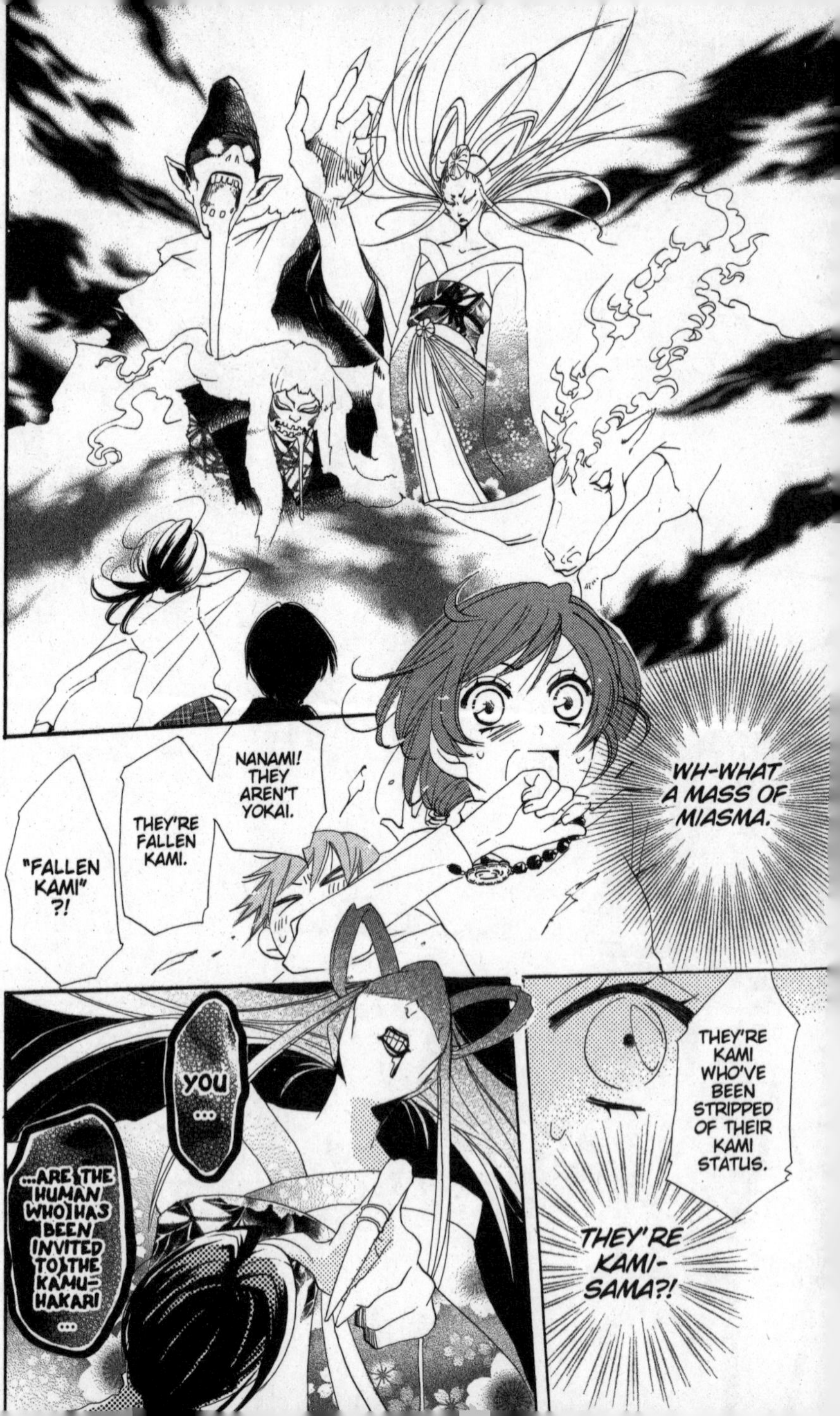
WH-WHAT A MASS OF MIASMA.
NANAMI! THEY AREN'T YOKAI.
THEY'RE FALLEN KAMI.
"FALLEN KAMI"?!
THEY'RE KAMI WHO'VE BEEN STRIPPED OF THEIR KAMI STATUS.
THEY'RE KAMI-SAMA?!
YOU...
...ARE THE HUMAN WHO HAS BEEN INVITED TO THE KAMU-HAKARI...

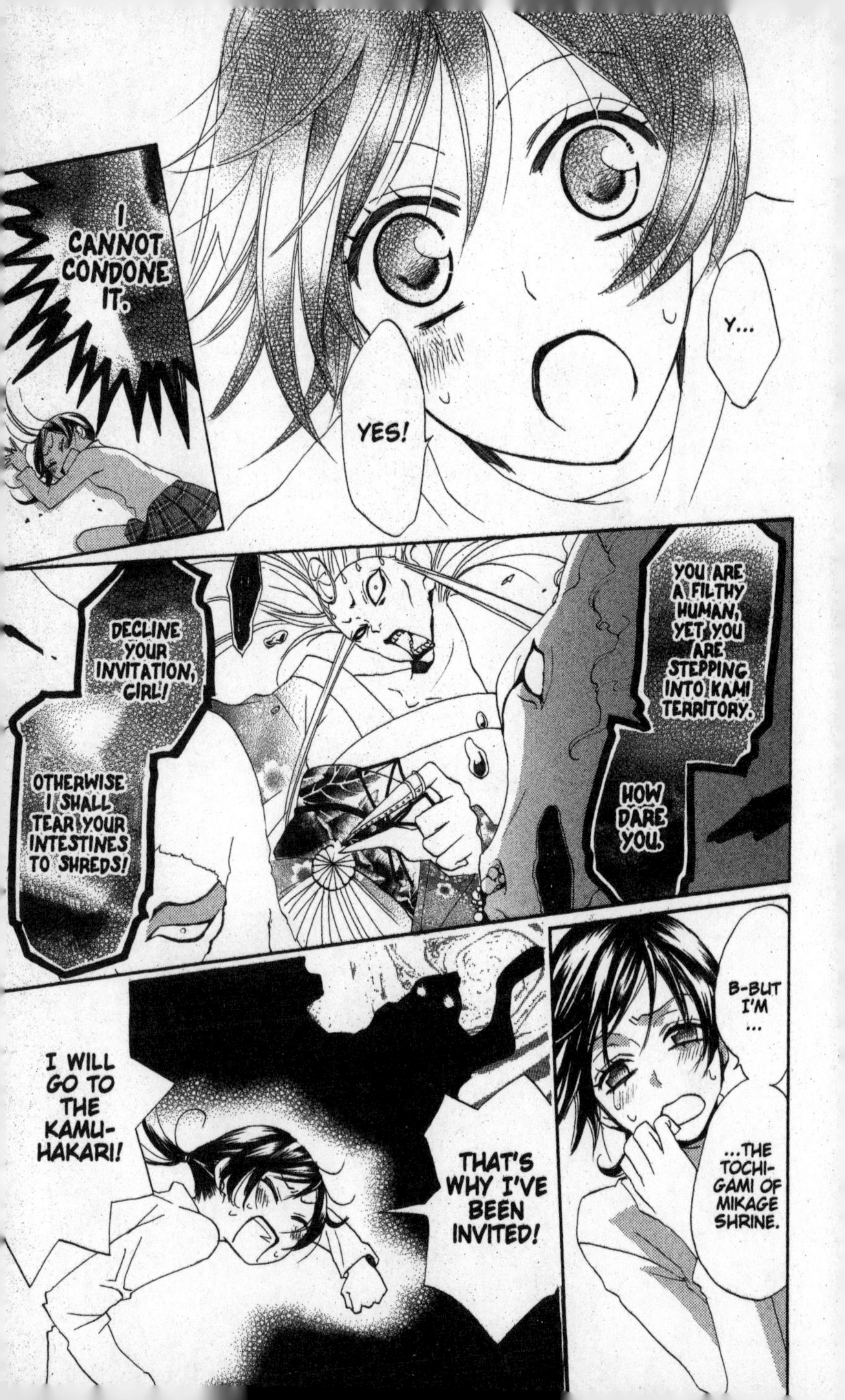
Y...
YES!
I CANNOT CONDONE IT.
YOU ARE A FILTHY HUMAN, YET YOU ARE STEPPING INTO KAMI TERRITORY.
HOW DARE YOU.
DECLINE YOUR INVITATION, GIRL!
OTHERWISE I SHALL TEAR YOUR INTESTINES TO SHREDS!
B-BUT I'M ...
...THE TOCHIGAMI OF MIKAGE SHRINE.
THAT'S WHY I'VE BEEN INVITED!
I WILL GO TO THE KAMUHAKARI!

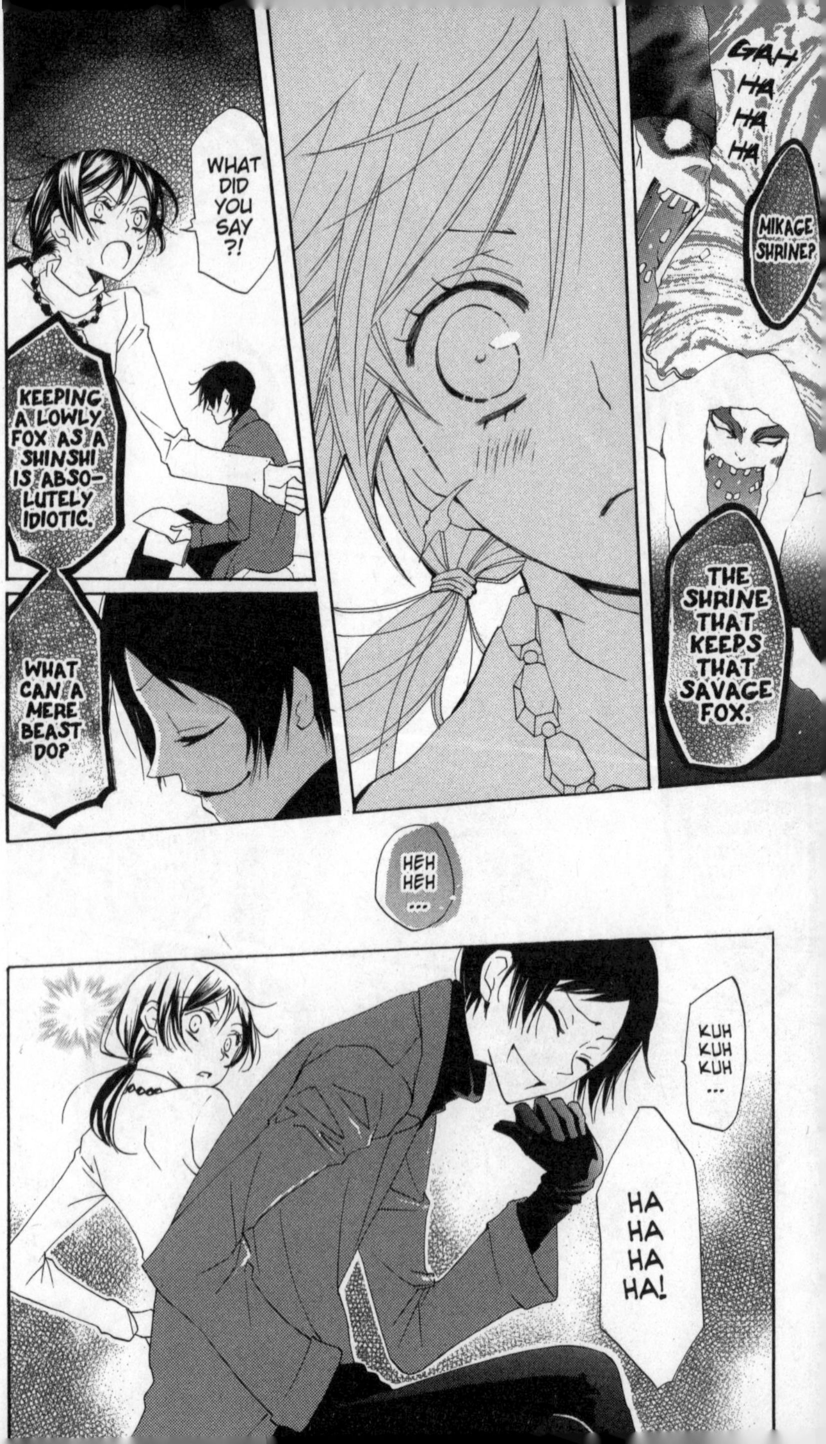
GAH HA HA HA
MIKAGE SHRINE?
THE SHRINE THAT KEEPS THAT SAVAGE FOX.
WHAT DID YOU SAY?!
KEEPING A LOWLY FOX AS A SHINSHI IS ABSOLUTELY IDIOTIC.
WHAT CAN A MERE BEAST DO?
HEH HEH ...
KUH KUH KUH ...
HA HA HA HA!

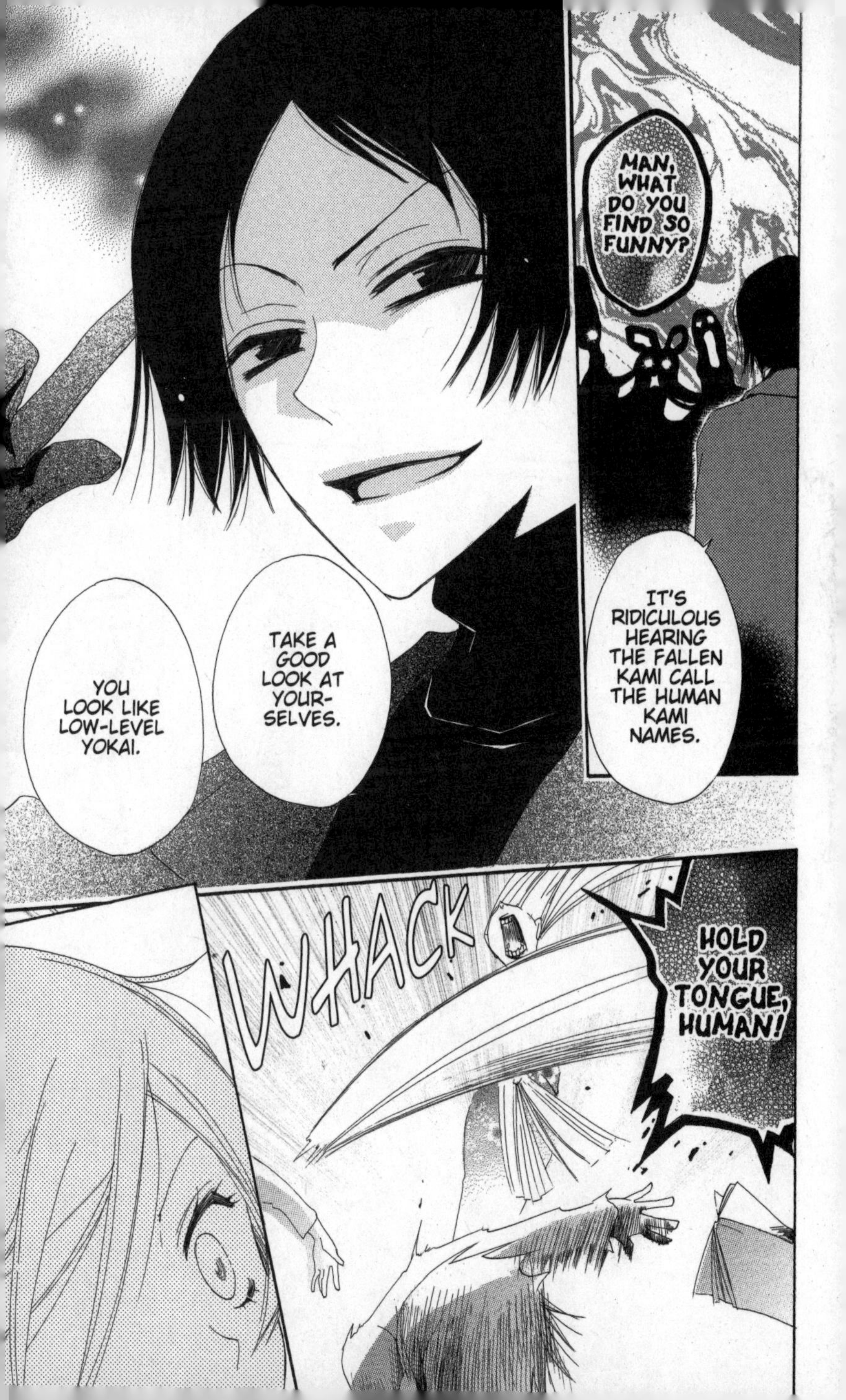
MAN, WHAT DO YOU FIND SO FUNNY?
IT'S RIDICULOUS HEARING THE FALLEN KAMI CALL THE HUMAN KAMI NAMES.
TAKE A GOOD LOOK AT YOUR-SELVES.
YOU LOOK LIKE LOW-LEVEL YOKAI.
HOLD YOUR TONGUE, HUMAN!
WHACK

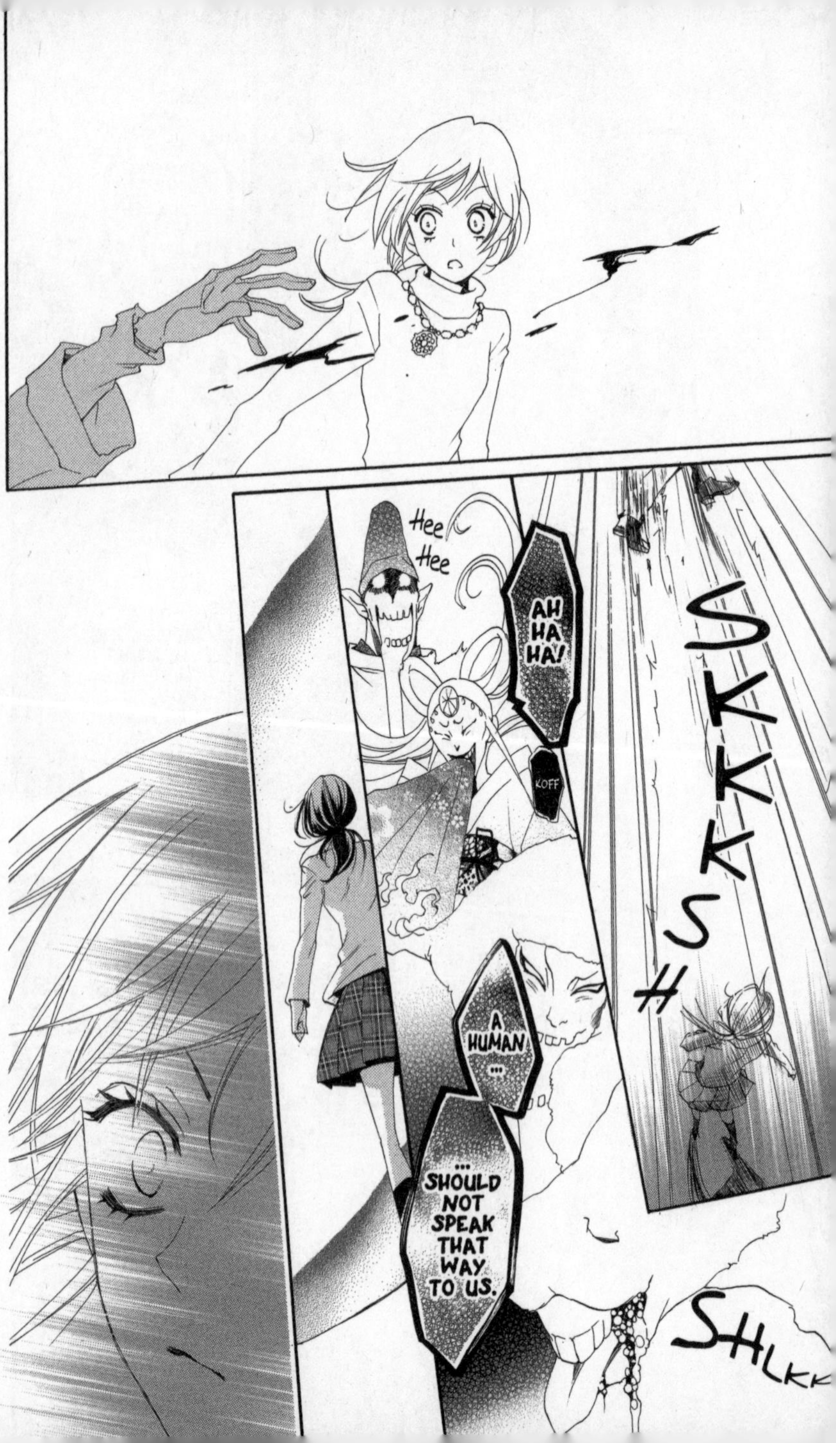
SKKKSH
Hee Hee
AH HA HA!
KOFF
A HUMAN...
...SHOULD NOT SPEAK THAT WAY TO US.
SHLKK

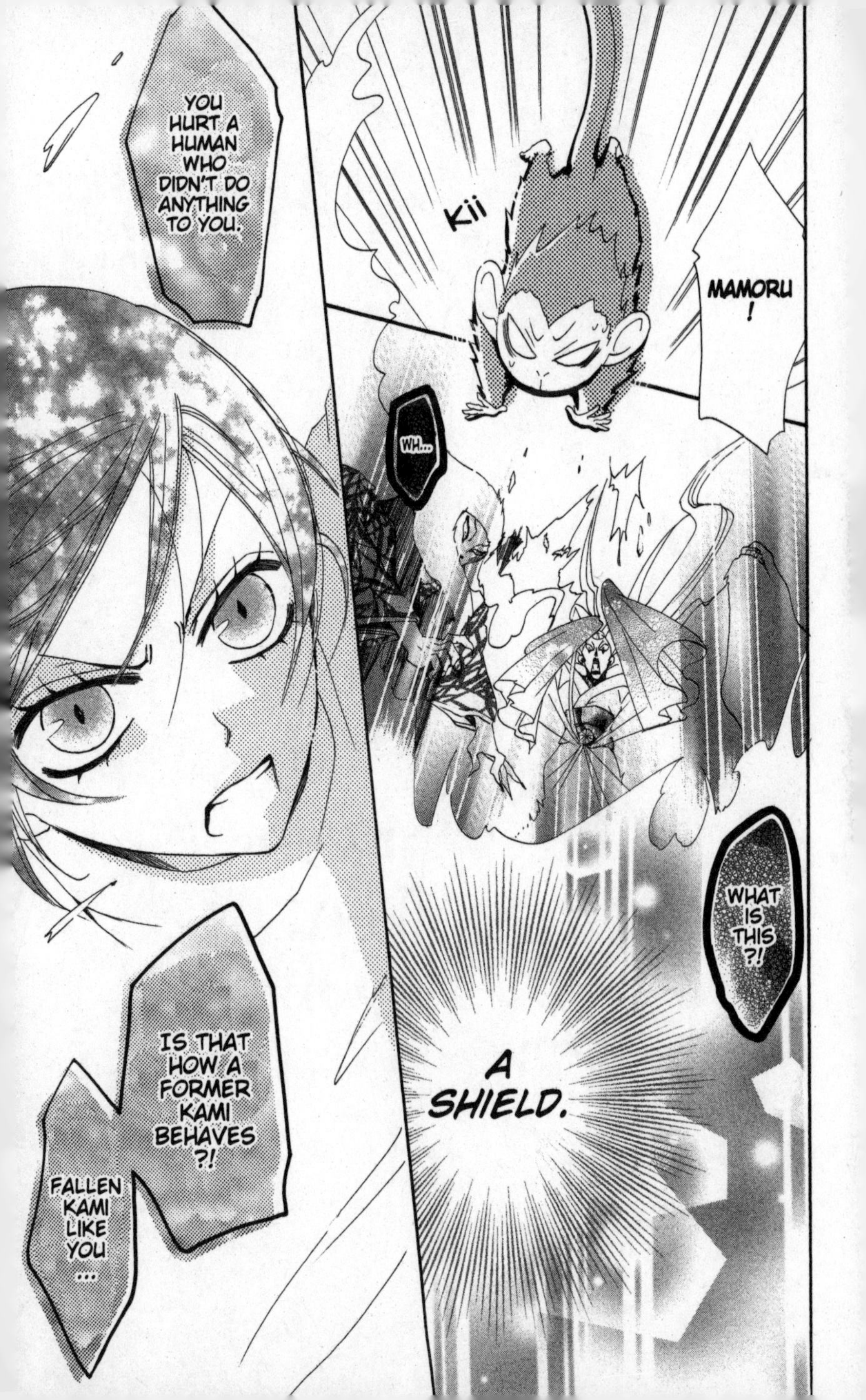
MAMORU!
Kii
WH...
WHAT IS THIS?!
A SHIELD.
YOU HURT A HUMAN WHO DIDN'T DO ANYTHING TO YOU.
IS THAT HOW A FORMER KAMI BEHAVES?!
FALLEN KAMI LIKE YOU...

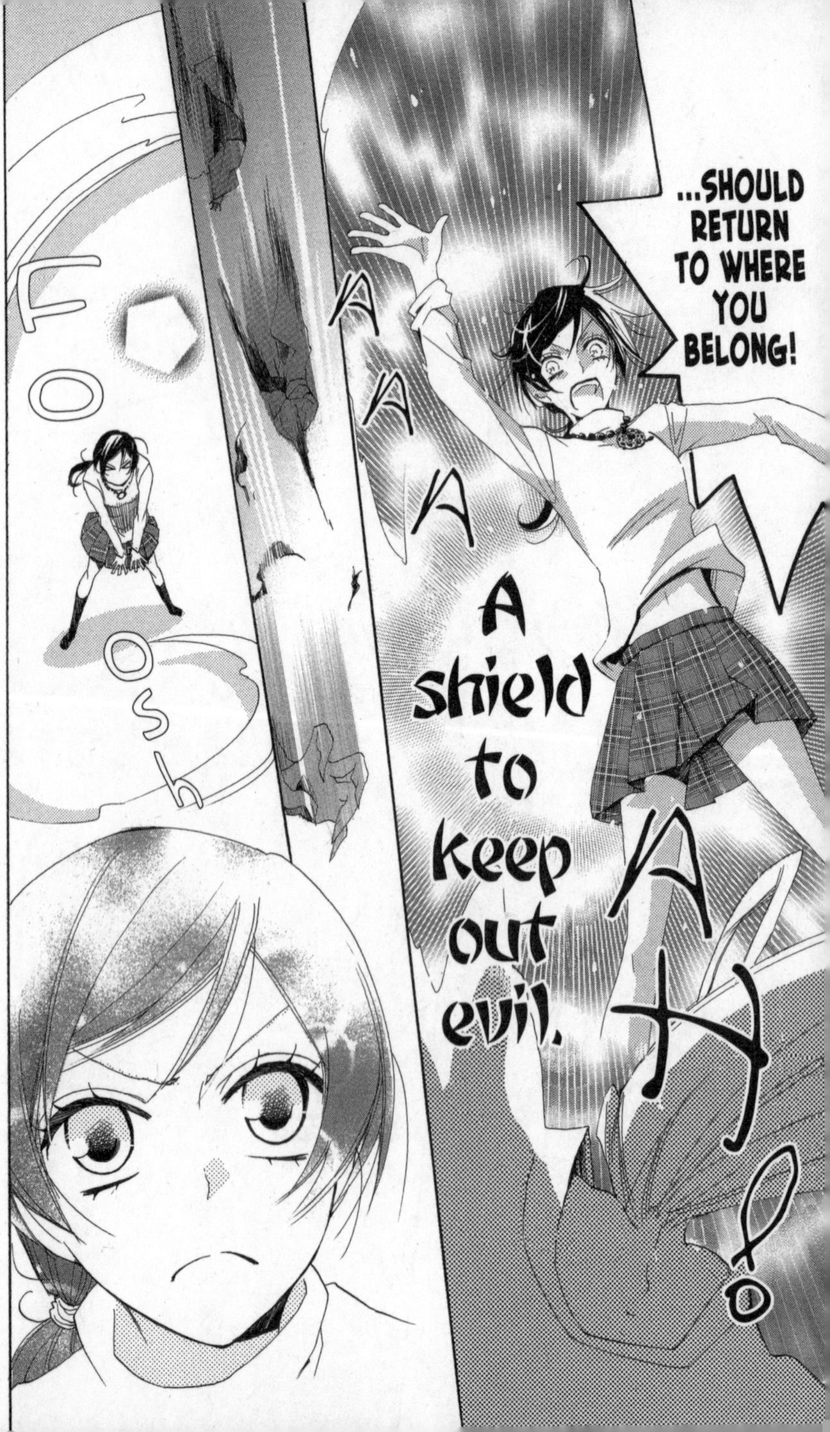
...SHOULD RETURN TO WHERE YOU BELONG!
AAAAAH!
A shield to keep out evil.
FOOSH

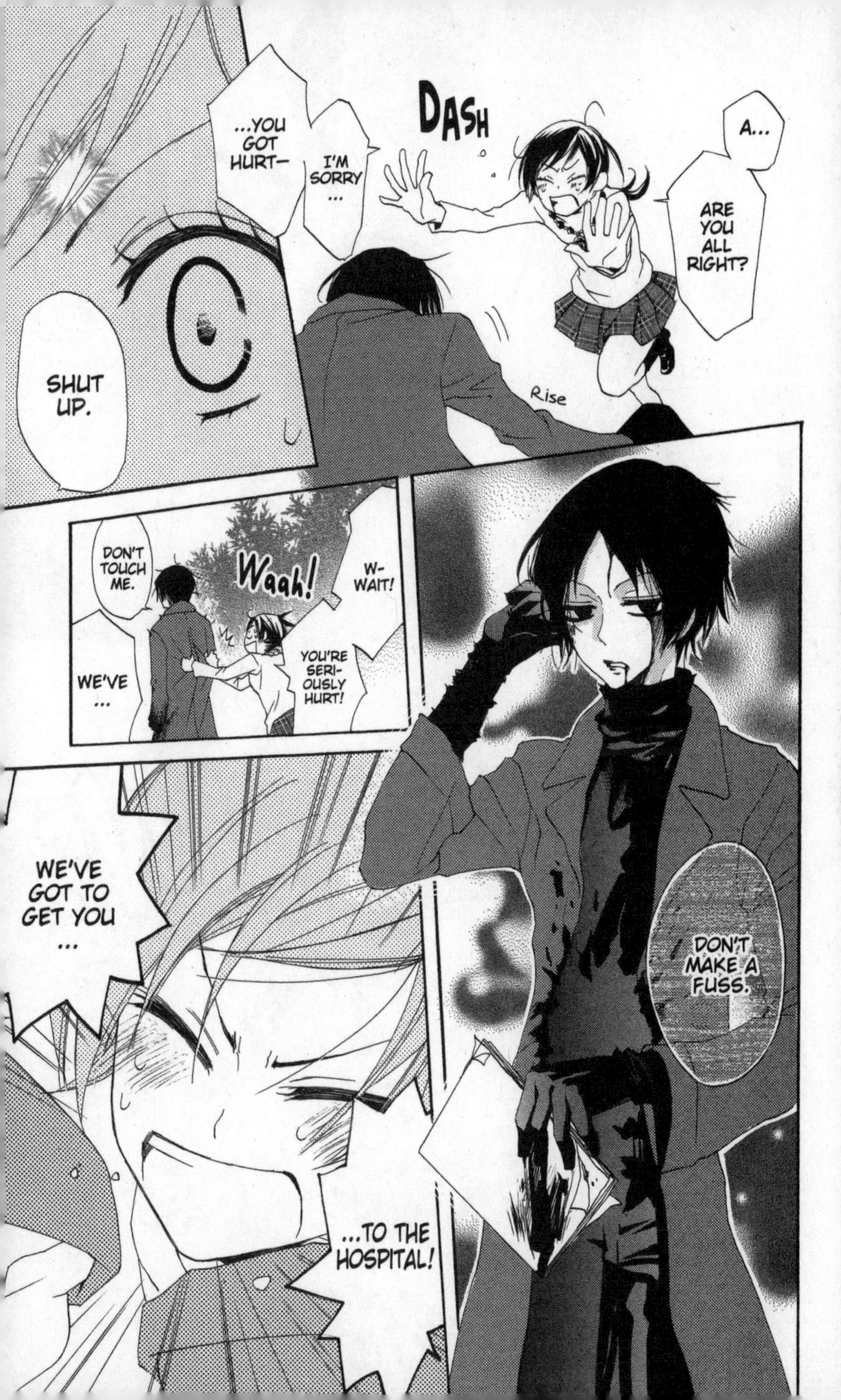

A...
ARE YOU ALL RIGHT?
DASH
I'M SORRY...
...YOU GOT HURT—
Rise
SHUT UP.
DON'T MAKE A FUSS.
W-WAIT!
YOU'RE SERIOUSLY HURT!
Waah!
DON'T TOUCH ME.
WE'VE...
WE'VE GOT TO GET YOU...
...TO THE HOSPITAL!

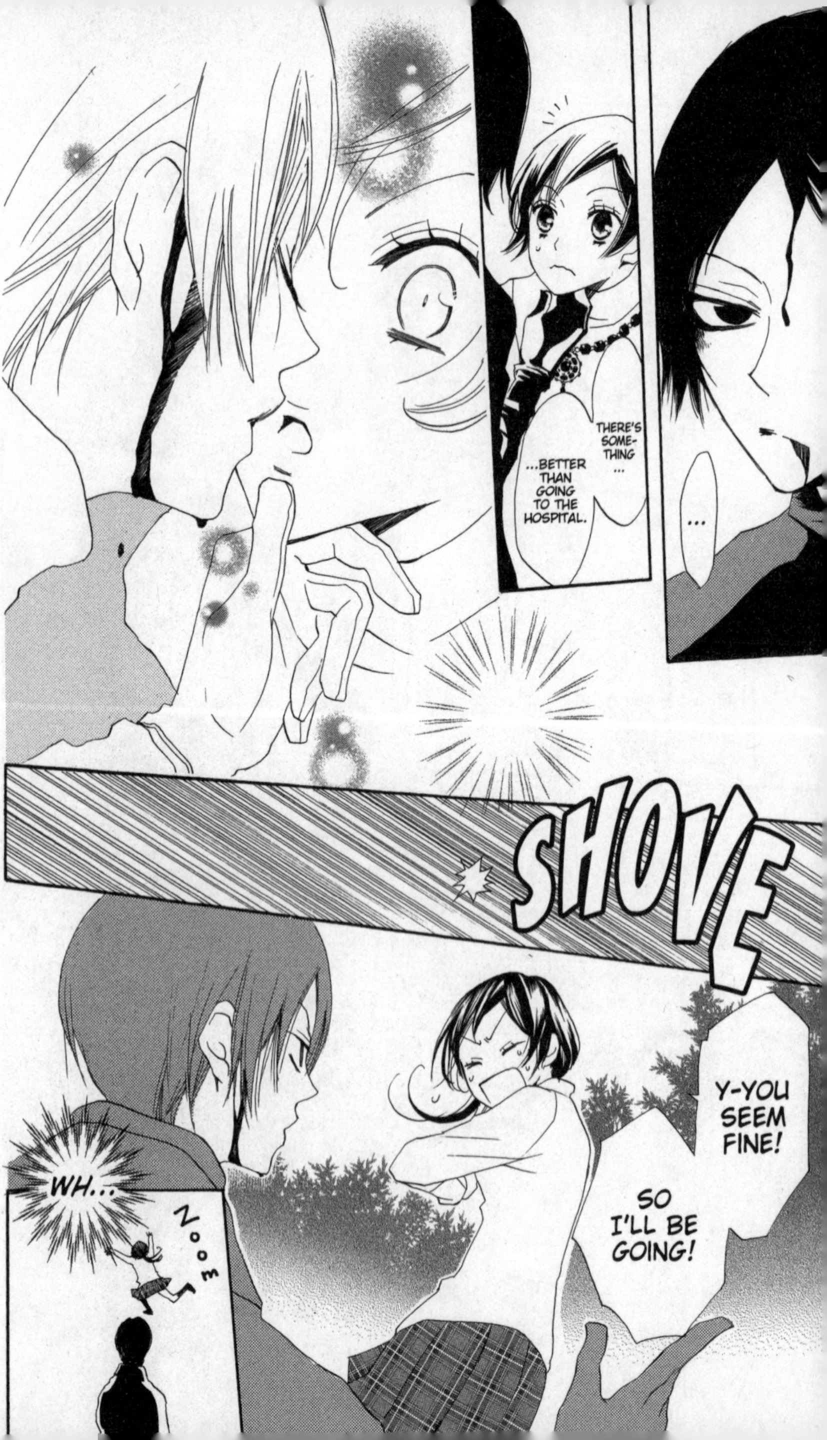
...
THERE'S SOMETHING...
...BETTER THAN GOING TO THE HOSPITAL.
SHOVE
Y-YOU SEEM FINE!
SO I'LL BE GOING!
WH...
Zoom

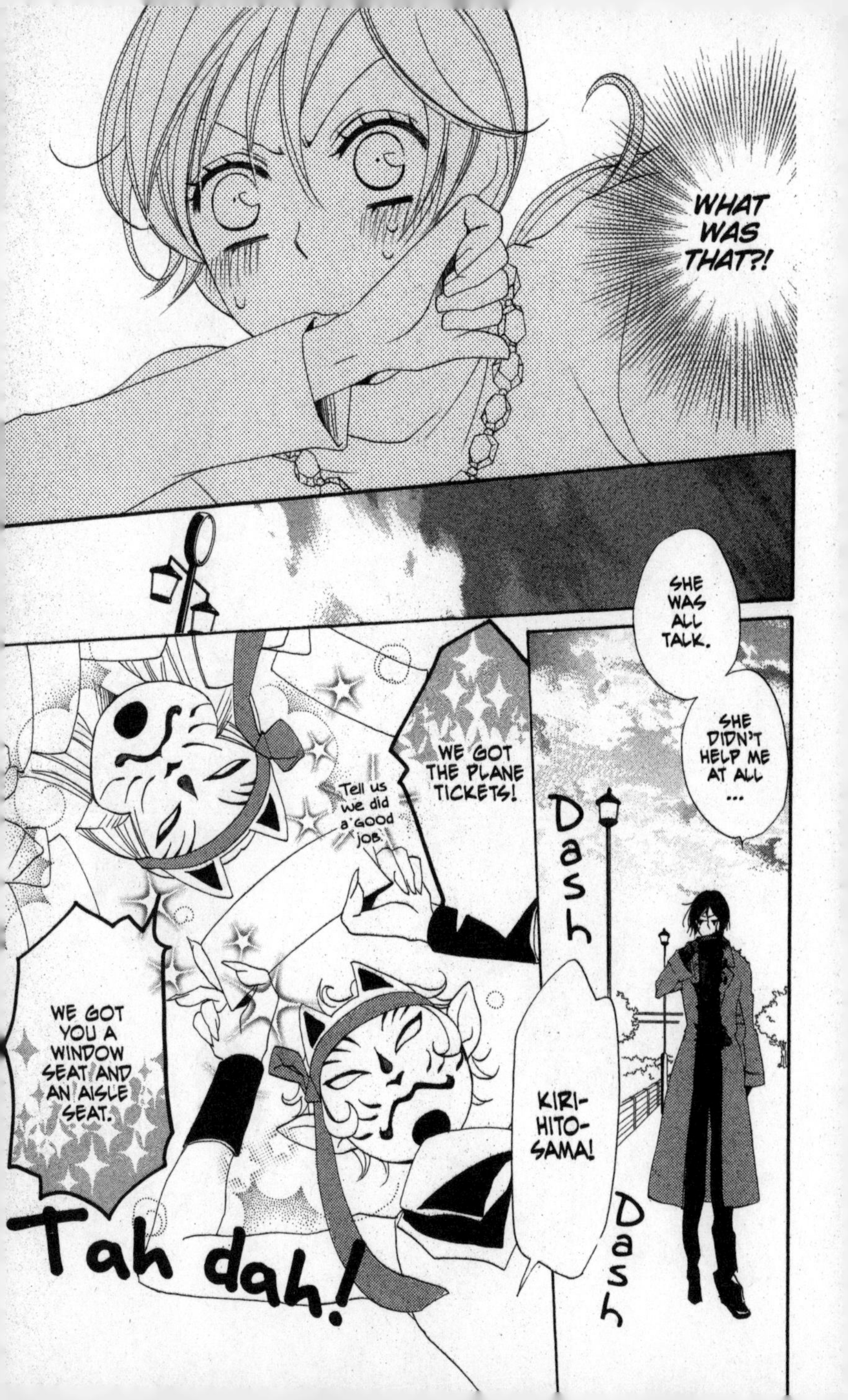
WHAT WAS THAT?!
SHE WAS ALL TALK.
SHE DIDN'T HELP ME AT ALL ...
Dash
Dash
KIRI-HITO-SAMA!
WE GOT THE PLANE TICKETS!
Tell us we did a good job.
WE GOT YOU A WINDOW SEAT AND AN AISLE SEAT.
Tah dah!

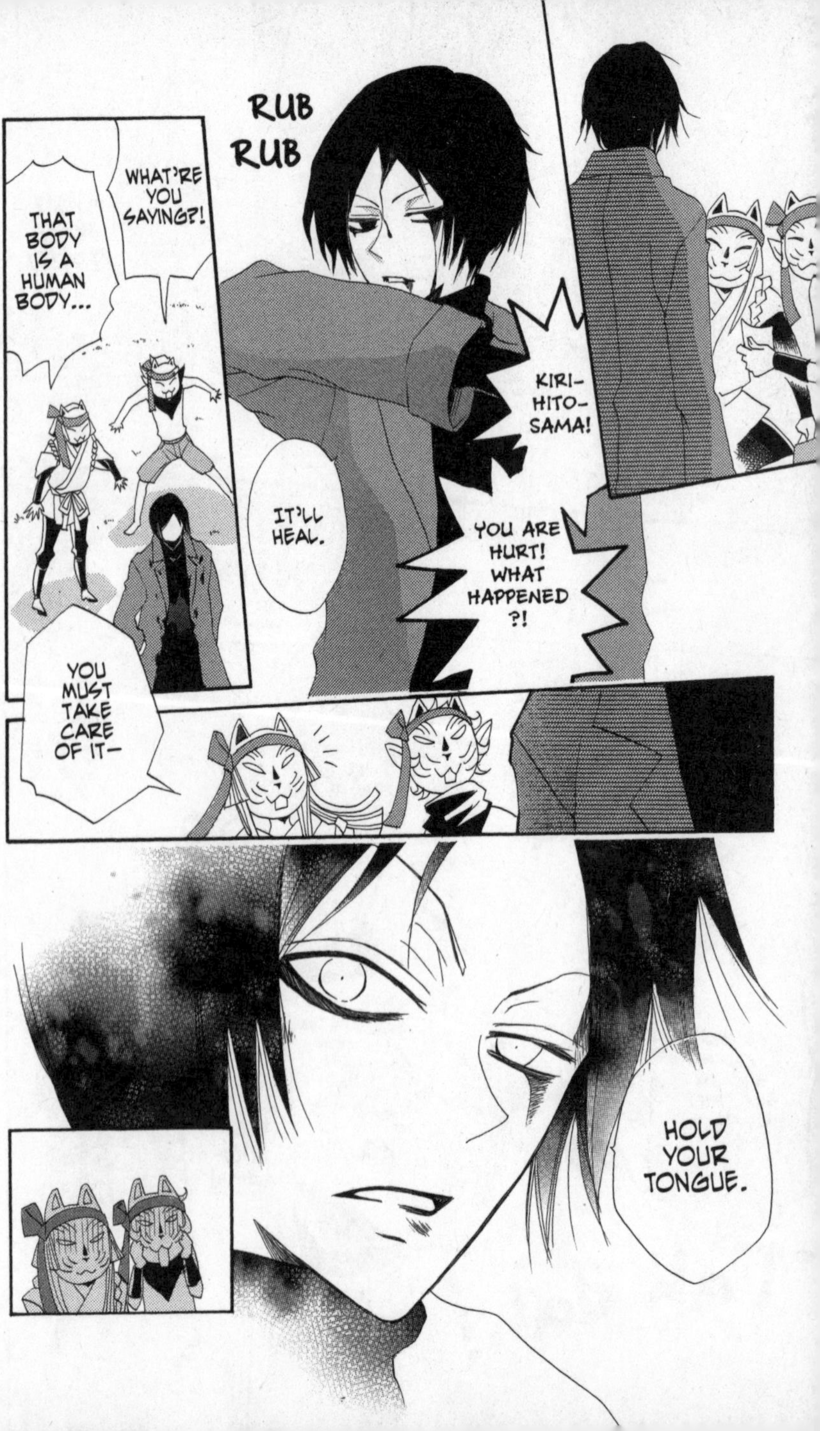
KIRI-HITO-SAMA!
YOU ARE HURT! WHAT HAPPENED?!
RUB RUB
IT'LL HEAL.
WHAT'RE YOU SAYING?!
THAT BODY IS A HUMAN BODY...
YOU MUST TAKE CARE OF IT—
HOLD YOUR TONGUE.

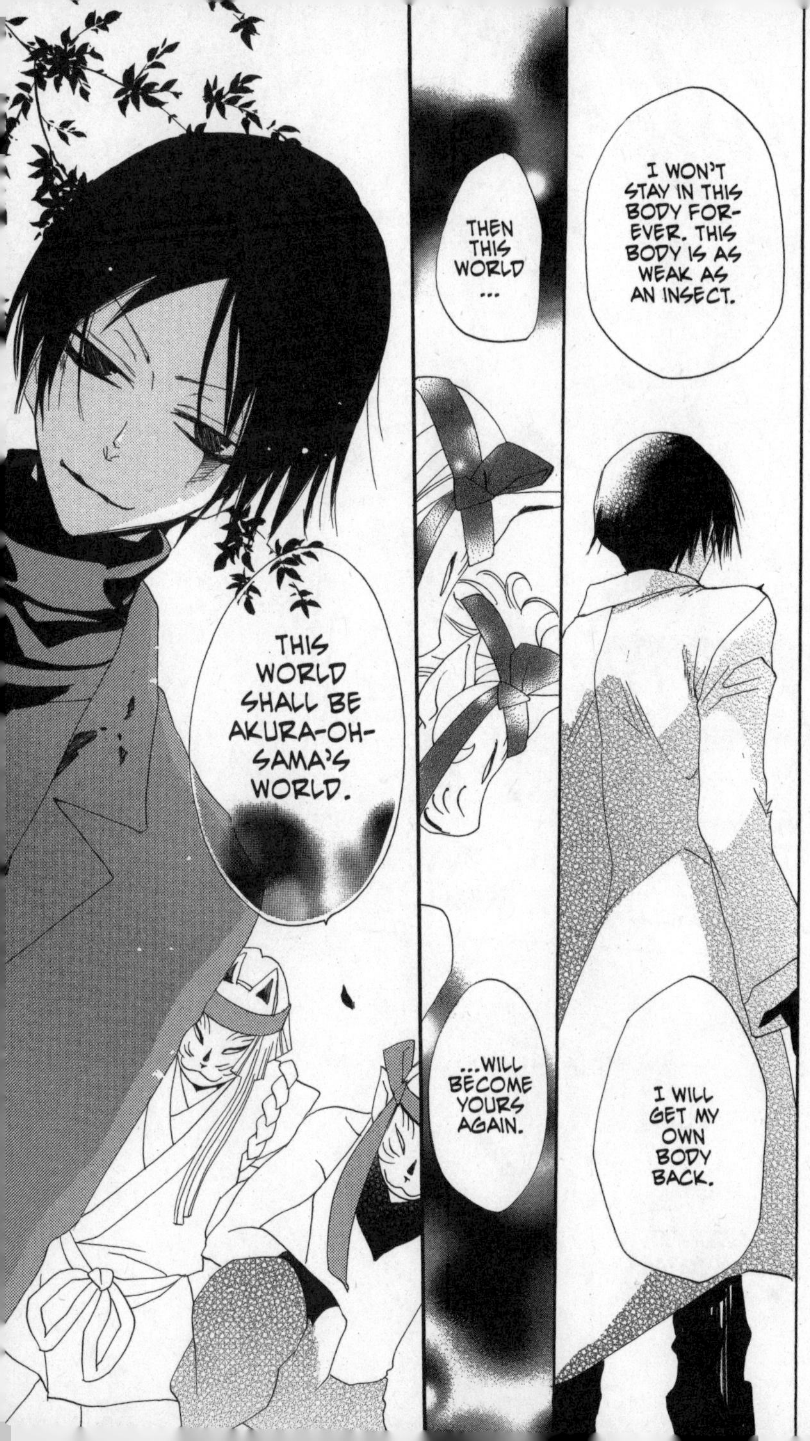
I WON'T STAY IN THIS BODY FOR-EVER. THIS BODY IS AS WEAK AS AN INSECT.
I WILL GET MY OWN BODY BACK.
THEN THIS WORLD ...
...WILL BECOME YOURS AGAIN.
THIS WORLD SHALL BE AKURA-OH-SAMA'S WORLD.

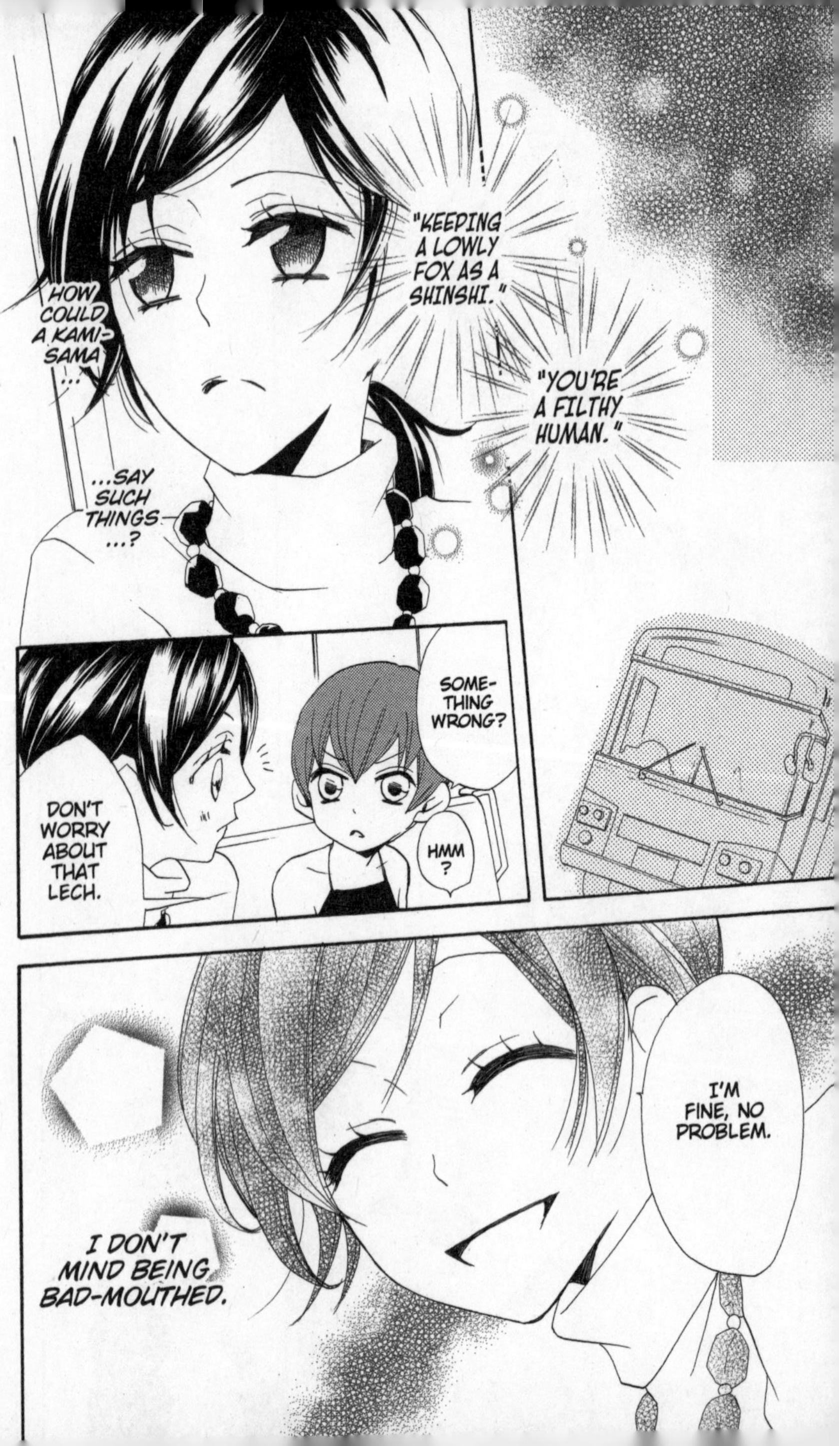
"KEEPING A LOWLY FOX AS A SHINSHI."
"YOU'RE A FILTHY HUMAN."
HOW COULD A KAMI-SAMA ...
...SAY SUCH THINGS ...?
SOME-THING WRONG?
HMM?
DON'T WORRY ABOUT THAT LECH.
I'M FINE, NO PROBLEM.
I DON'T MIND BEING BAD-MOUTHED.

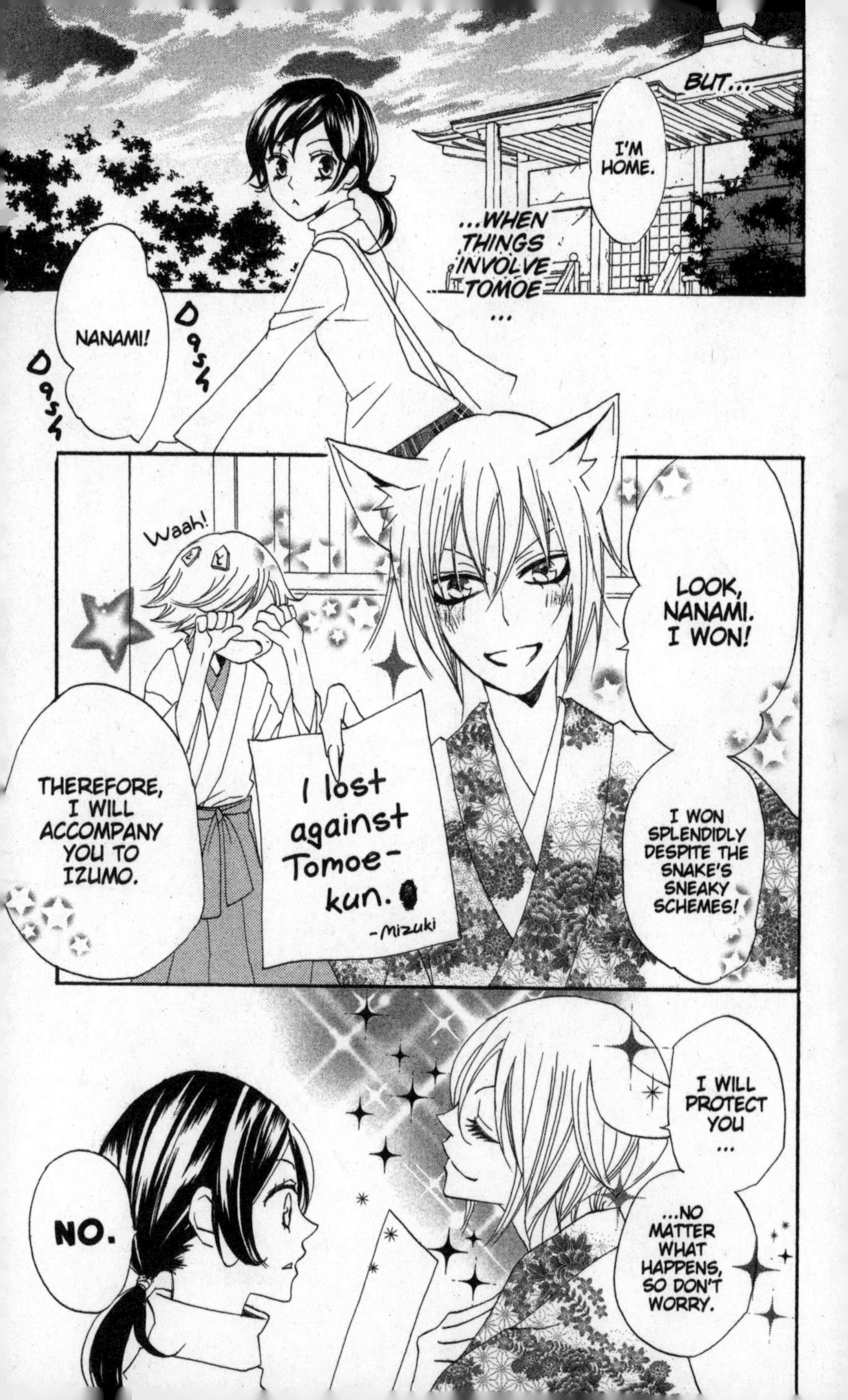
BUT...
I'M HOME.
...WHEN THINGS INVOLVE TOMOE...
NANAMI!
Dash
Dash
LOOK, NANAMI. I WON!
I WON SPLENDIDLY DESPITE THE SNAKE'S SNEAKY SCHEMES!
I lost against Tomoe-kun.
-Mizuki
Waah!
THEREFORE, I WILL ACCOMPANY YOU TO IZUMO.
I WILL PROTECT YOU...
...NO MATTER WHAT HAPPENS, SO DON'T WORRY.
NO.

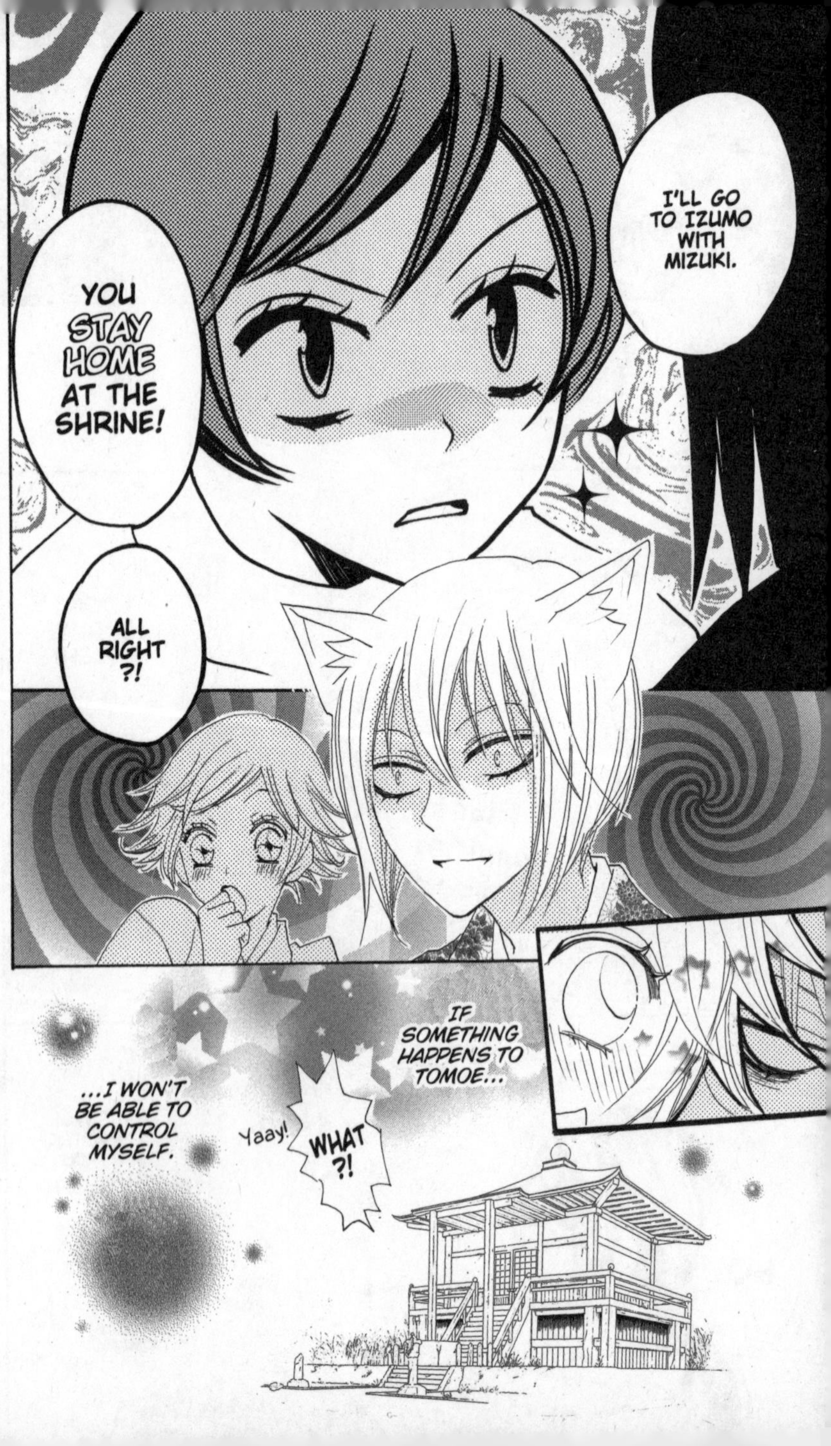

I'LL GO TO IZUMO WITH MIZUKI.
YOU STAY HOME AT THE SHRINE!
ALL RIGHT?!
IF SOMETHING HAPPENS TO TOMOE...
...I WON'T BE ABLE TO CONTROL MYSELF.
WHAT?!
Yaay!

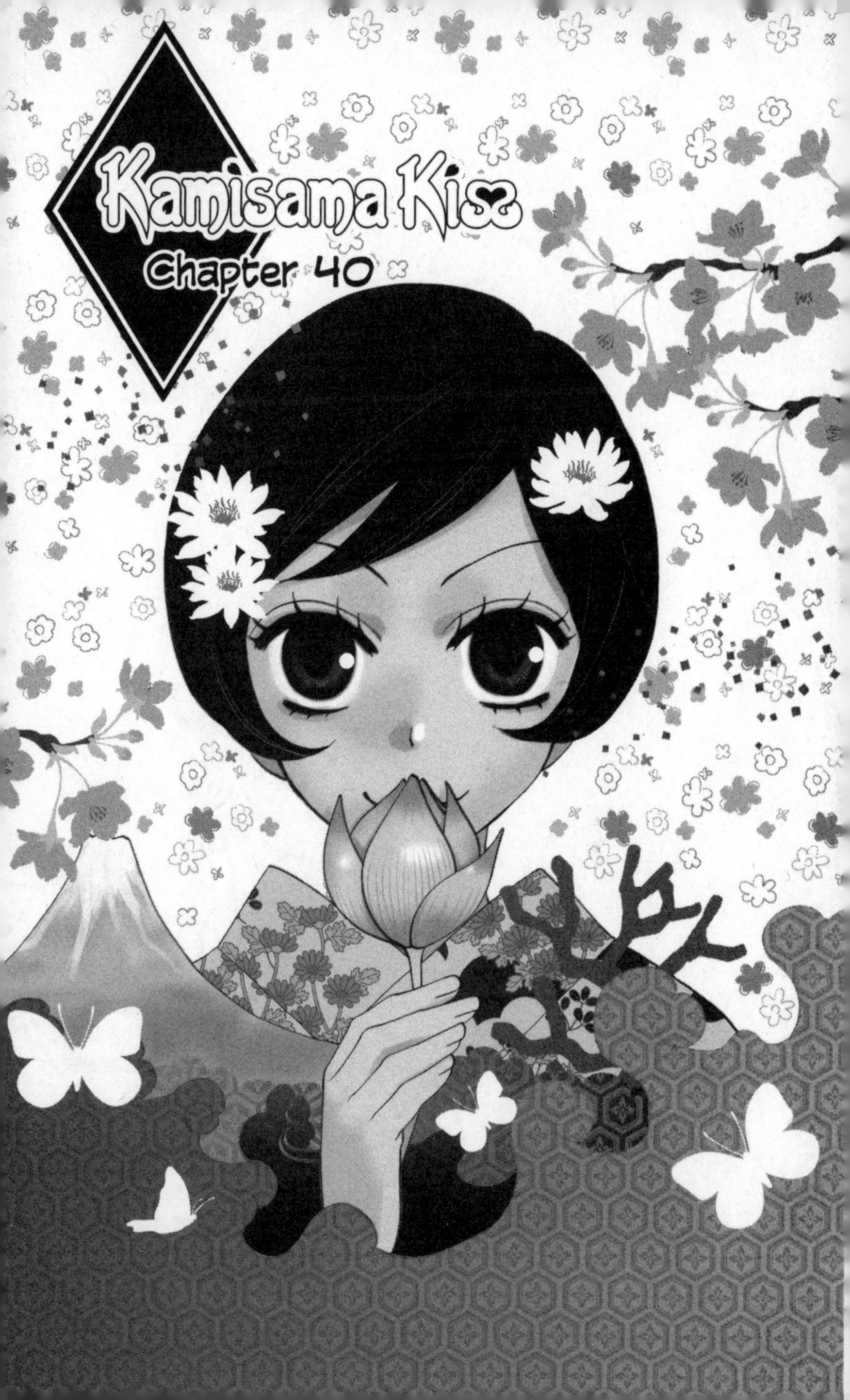
Kamisama Kiss
Chapter 40

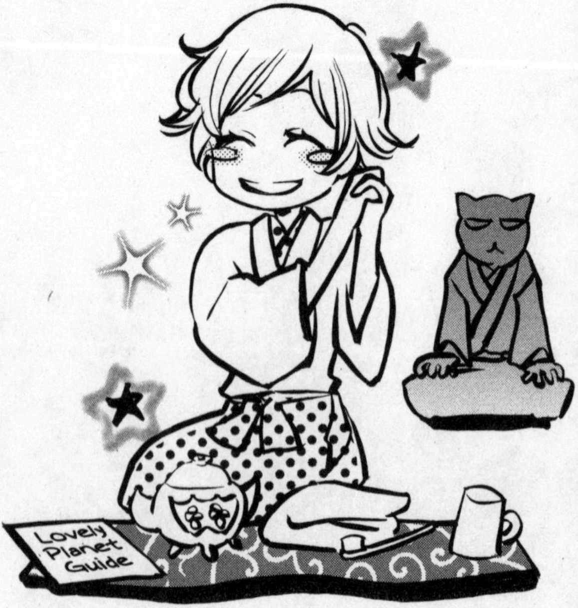
Lovely Planet Guide

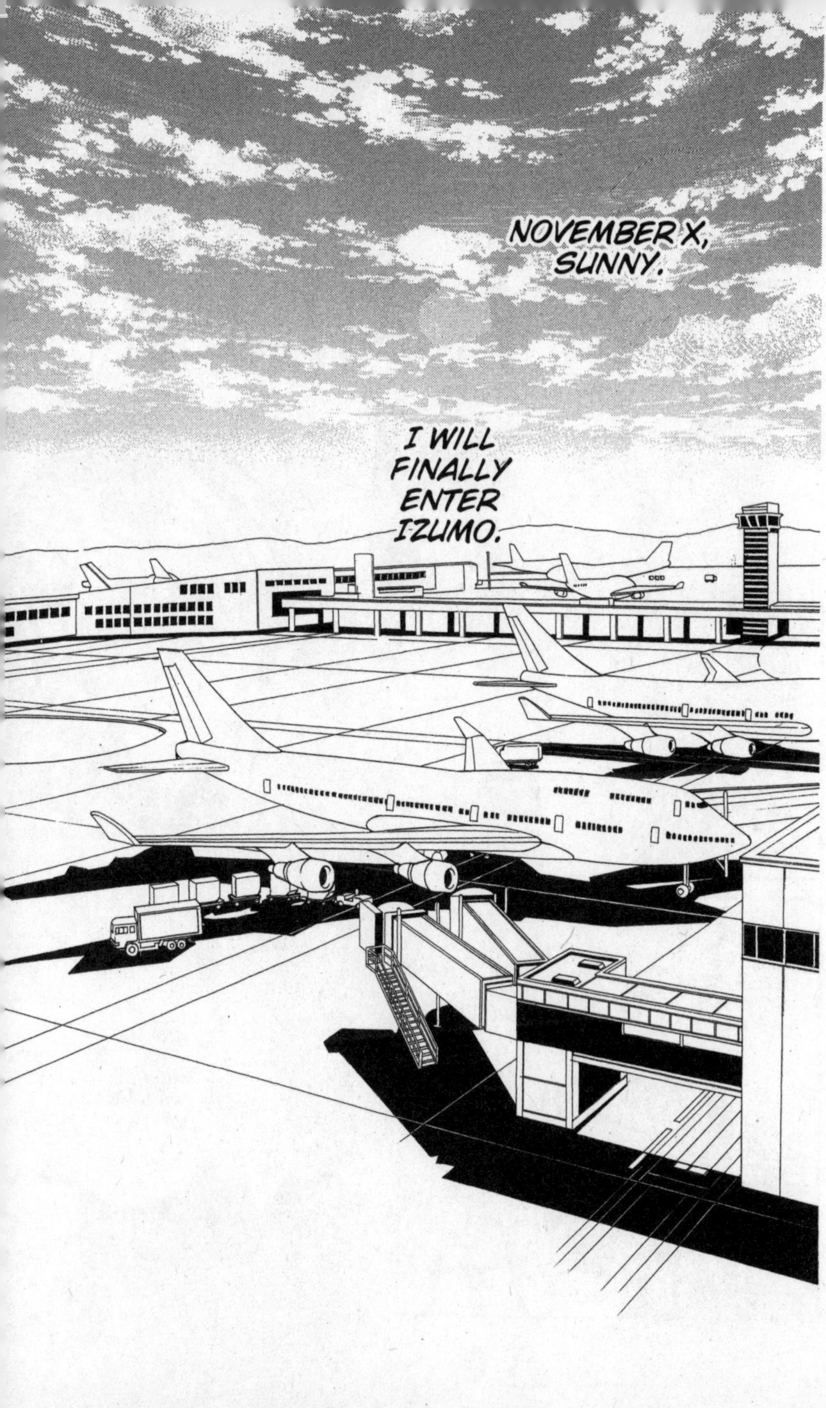
NOVEMBER X, SUNNY.
I WILL FINALLY ENTER IZUMO.

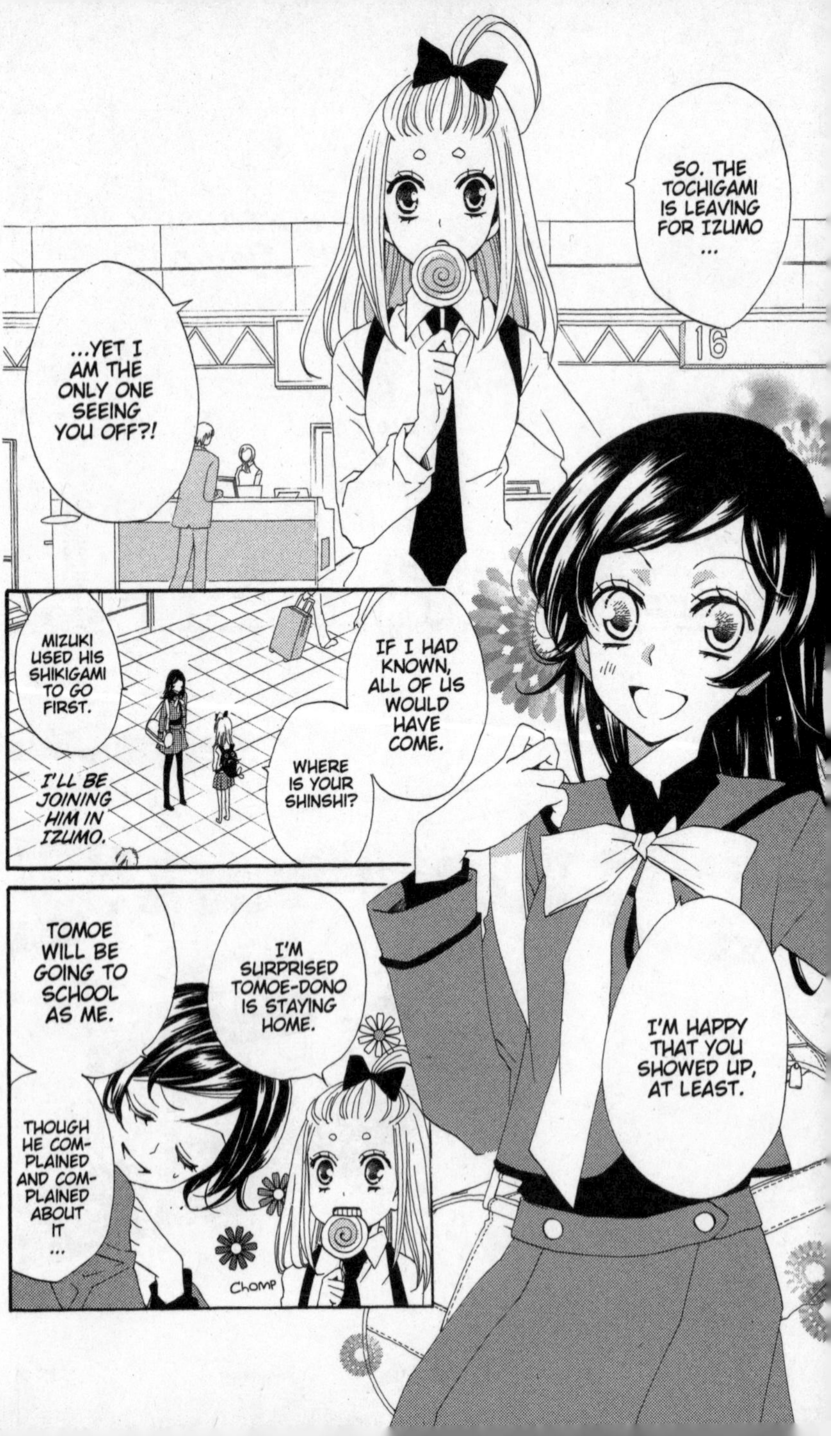
SO. THE TOCHIGAMI IS LEAVING FOR IZUMO ...
...YET I AM THE ONLY ONE SEEING YOU OFF?!
IF I HAD KNOWN, ALL OF US WOULD HAVE COME.
I'M HAPPY THAT YOU SHOWED UP, AT LEAST.
WHERE IS YOUR SHINSHI?
MIZUKI USED HIS SHIKIGAMI TO GO FIRST.
I'LL BE JOINING HIM IN IZUMO.
I'M SURPRISED TOMOE-DONO IS STAYING HOME.
TOMOE WILL BE GOING TO SCHOOL AS ME.
THOUGH HE COM-PLAINED AND COM-PLAINED ABOUT IT ...
CHOMP

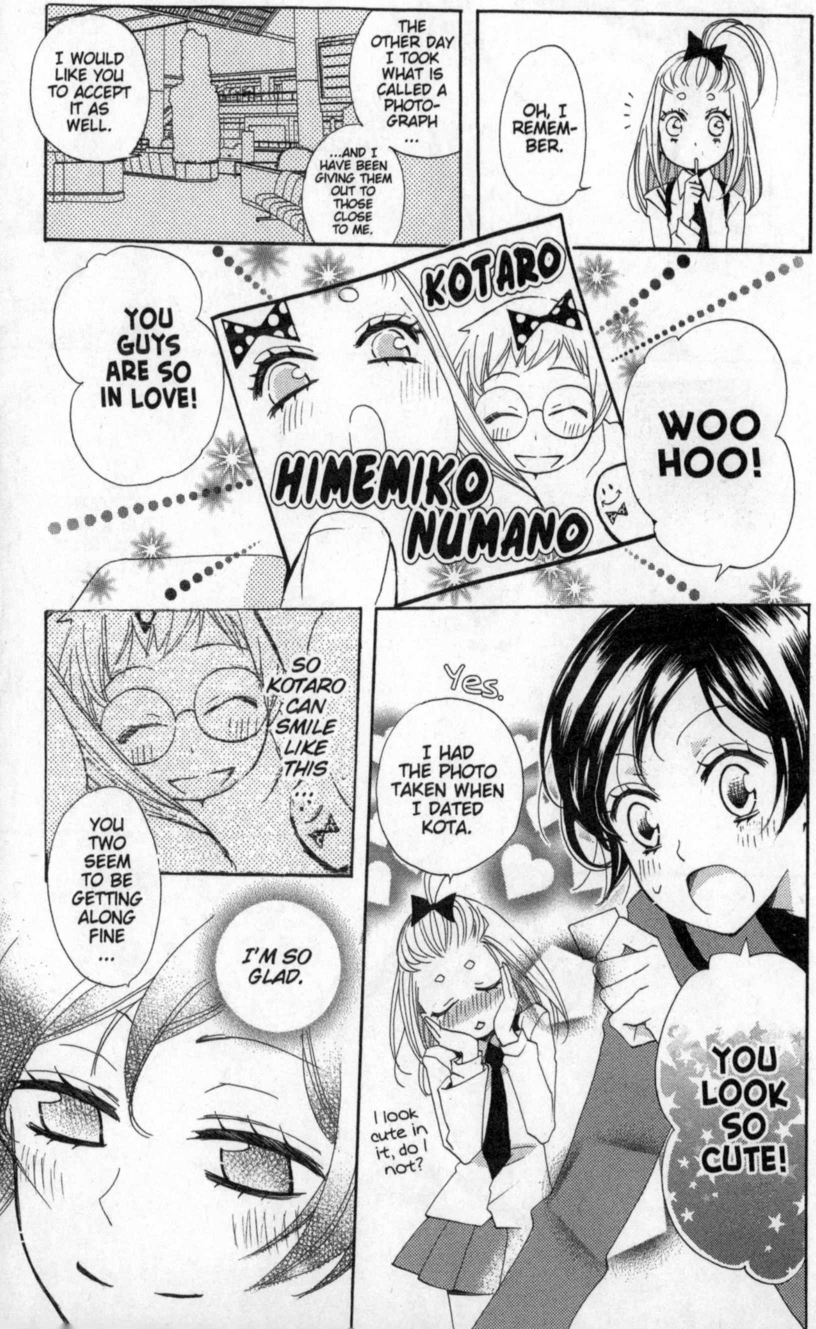
OH, I REMEMBER.
THE OTHER DAY I TOOK WHAT IS CALLED A PHOTOGRAPH...
...AND I HAVE BEEN GIVING THEM OUT TO THOSE CLOSE TO ME.
I WOULD LIKE YOU TO ACCEPT IT AS WELL.
WOO HOO!
KOTARO
HIMEMIKO NUMANO
YOU GUYS ARE SO IN LOVE!
Yes.
I HAD THE PHOTO TAKEN WHEN I DATED KOTA.
YOU LOOK SO CUTE!
I look cute in it, do I not?
SO KOTARO CAN SMILE LIKE THIS...
YOU TWO SEEM TO BE GETTING ALONG FINE...
I'M SO GLAD.

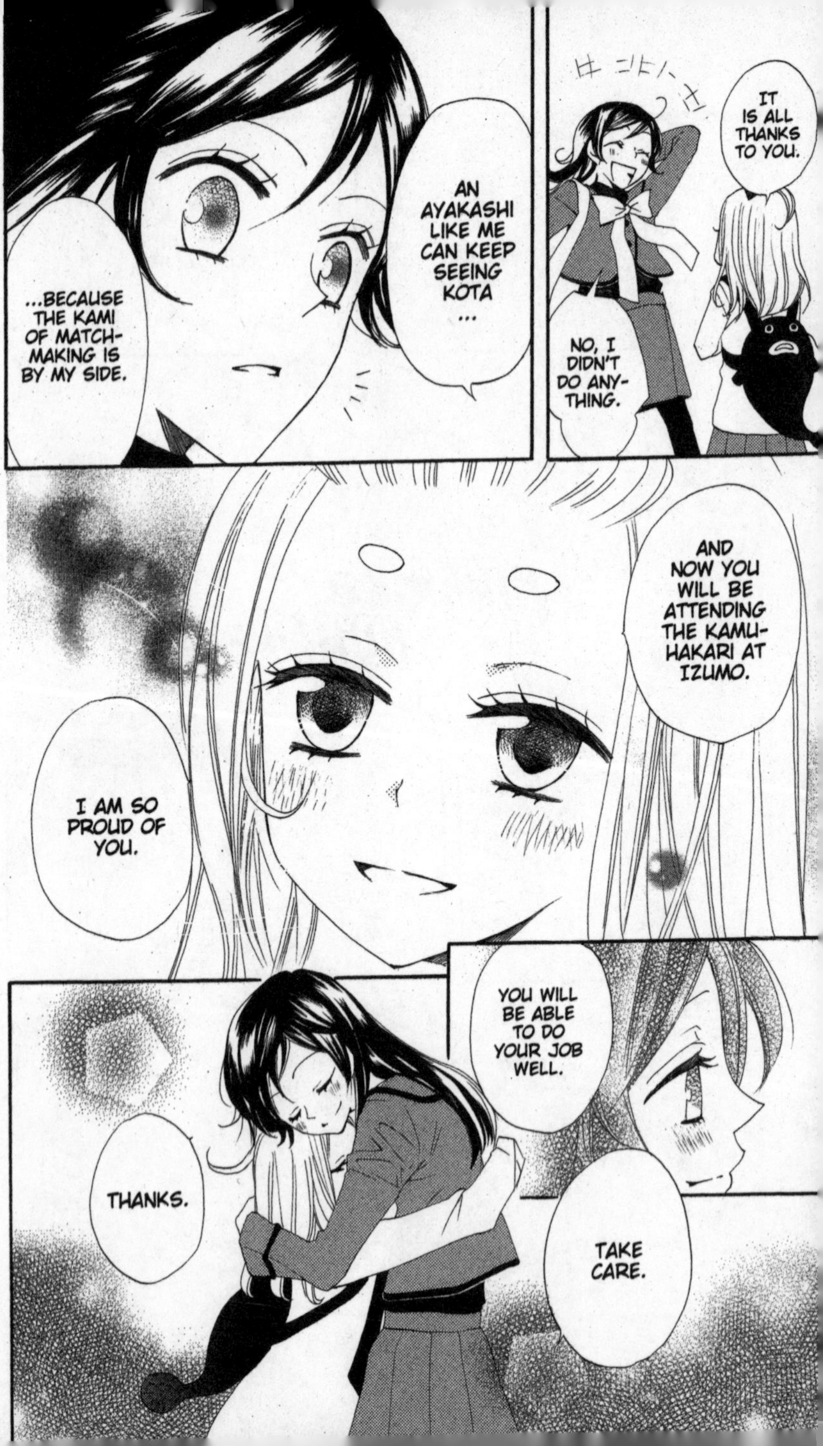

IT IS ALL THANKS TO YOU.
NO, I DIDN'T DO ANY-THING.
AN AYAKASHI LIKE ME CAN KEEP SEEING KOTA ...
...BECAUSE THE KAMI OF MATCH-MAKING IS BY MY SIDE.
AND NOW YOU WILL BE ATTENDING THE KAMU-HAKARI AT IZUMO.
I AM SO PROUD OF YOU.
YOU WILL BE ABLE TO DO YOUR JOB WELL.
TAKE CARE.
THANKS.

I'LL COME BACK WITH SOUVENIRS.

SEE YOU!

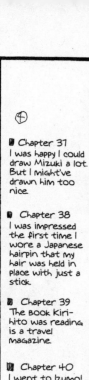

④

■ Chapter 37
I was happy I could draw Mizuki a lot. But I might've drawn him too nice.

■ Chapter 38
I was impressed the first time I wore a Japanese hairpin that my hair was held in place with just a stick.

■ Chapter 39
The book Kirihito was reading is a travel magazine.

■ Chapter 40
I went to Izumo!

■ Chapter 41
My editor liked Tetsukimaru, and I was happy.

■ Chapter 42
Drawing the raccoons was a chore. There were so many... And for the first time, the story arc continues to the next volume.

I hope you read Volume 8 as well!

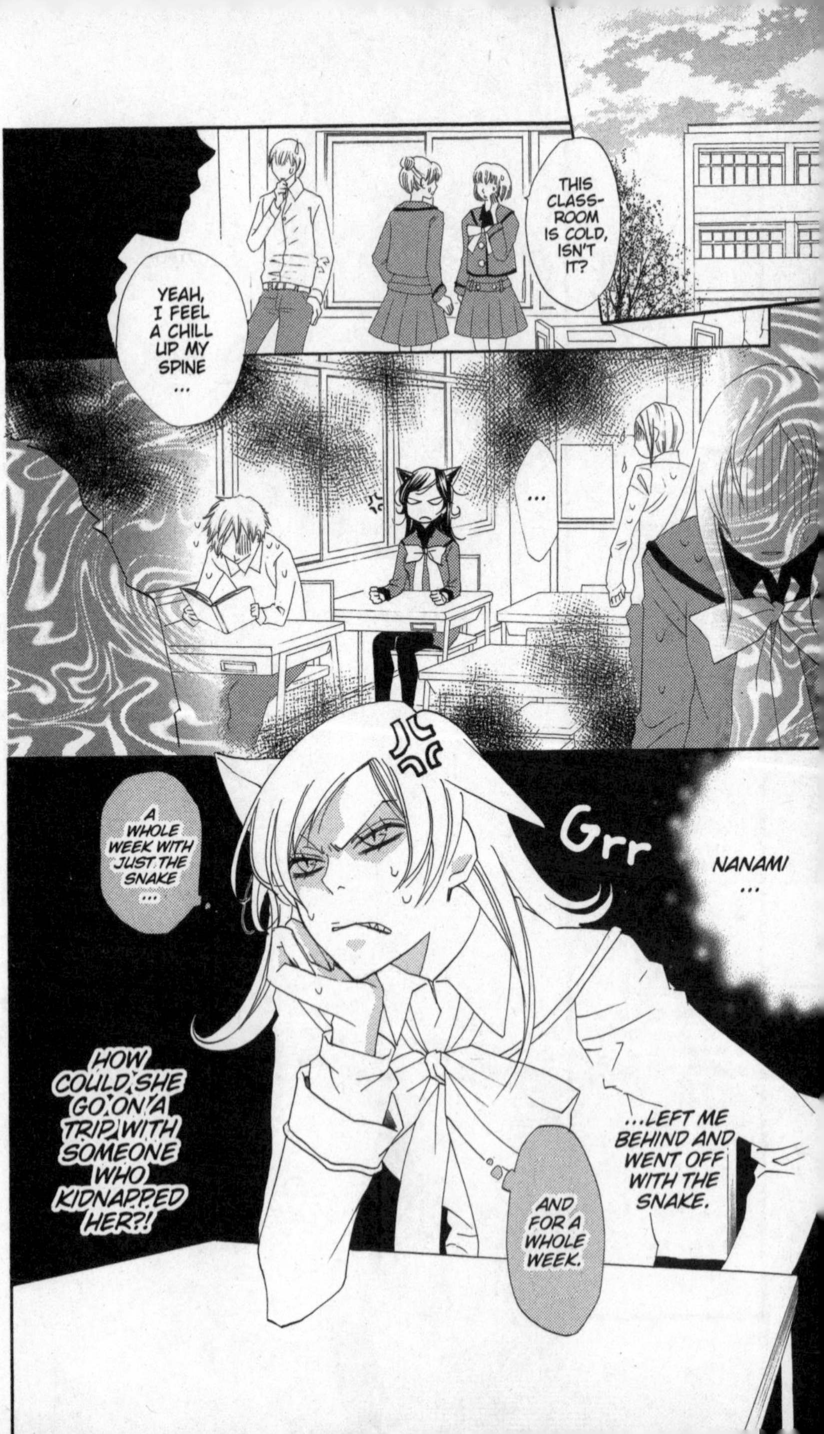
THIS CLASSROOM IS COLD, ISN'T IT?
YEAH, I FEEL A CHILL UP MY SPINE...
...
NANAMI...
...LEFT ME BEHIND AND WENT OFF WITH THE SNAKE.
Grr
AND FOR A WHOLE WEEK.
A WHOLE WEEK WITH JUST THE SNAKE...
HOW COULD SHE GO ON A TRIP WITH SOMEONE WHO KIDNAPPED HER?!

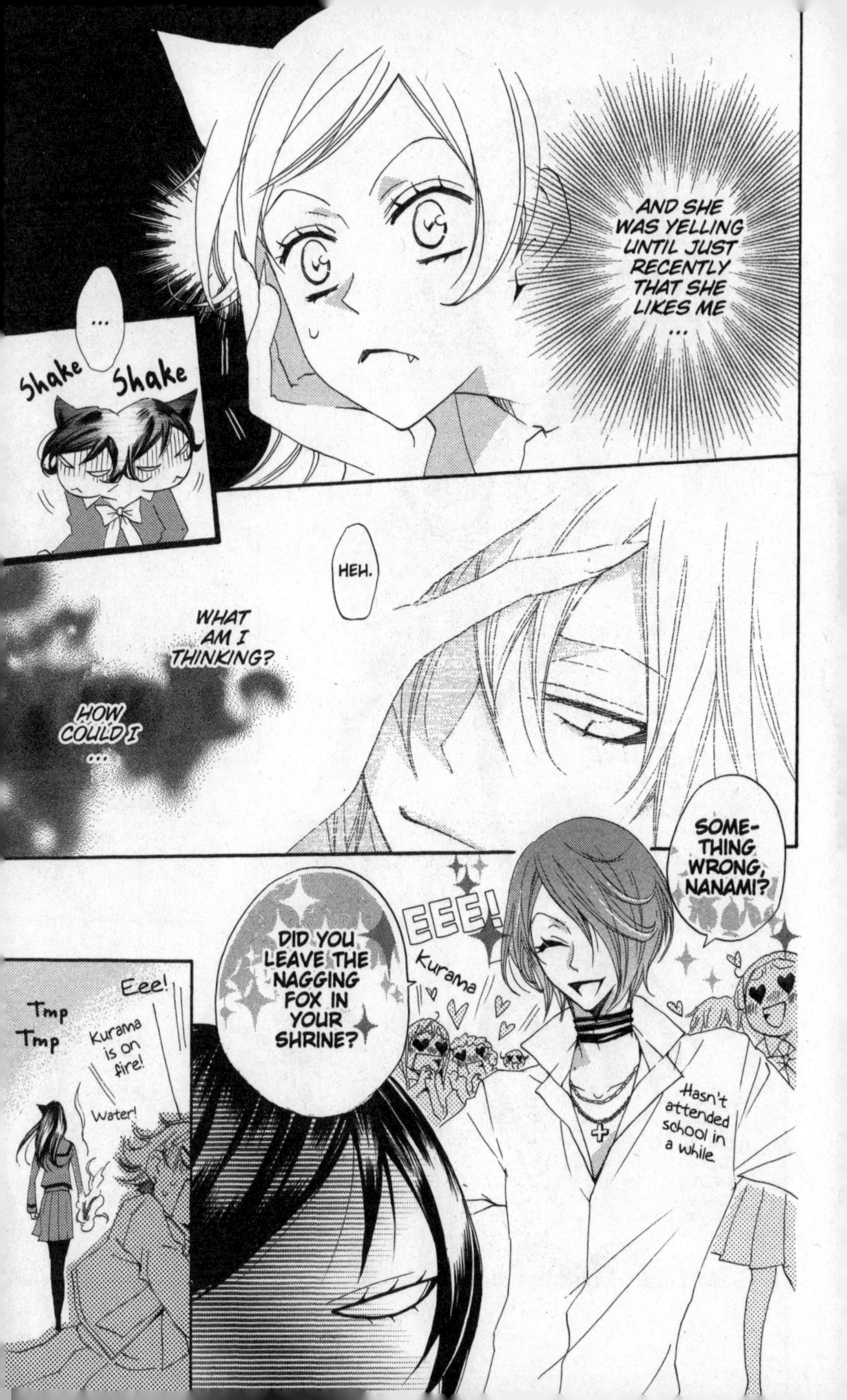
AND SHE WAS YELLING UNTIL JUST RECENTLY THAT SHE LIKES ME ...
...
Shake Shake
HEH.
WHAT AM I THINKING?
HOW COULD I ...
SOME-THING WRONG, NANAMI?
EEE!
Kurama
Hasn't attended school in a while
DID YOU LEAVE THE NAGGING FOX IN YOUR SHRINE?
Eee!
Kurama is on fire!
Tmp Tmp
Water!

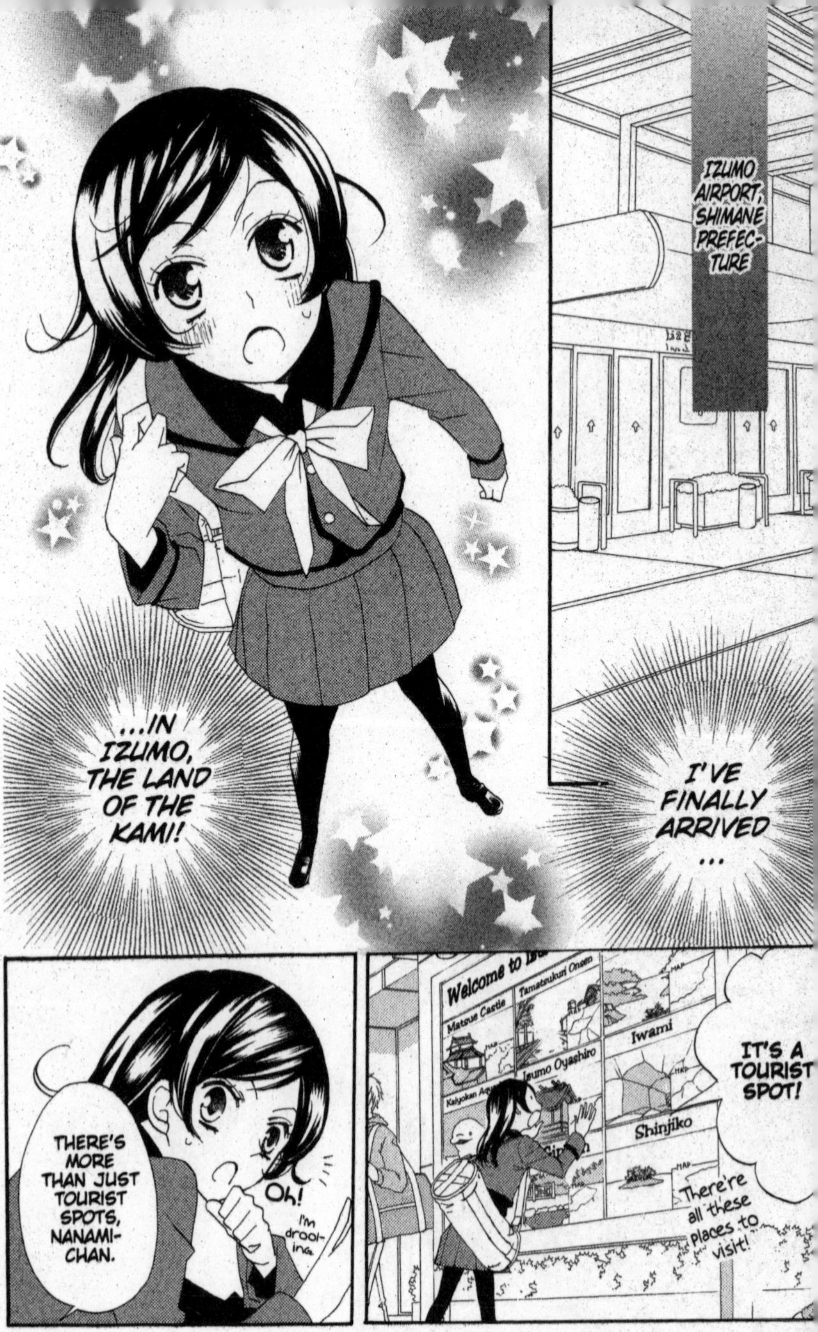
IZUMO AIRPORT, SHIMANE PREFECTURE
I'VE FINALLY ARRIVED...
...IN IZUMO, THE LAND OF THE KAMI!
IT'S A TOURIST SPOT!
Tamatsukuri Onsen
Matsue Castle
Iwami
Izumo Oyashiro
Shinjiko
There're all these places to visit!
Oh!
I'm drooling.
THERE'S MORE THAN JUST TOURIST SPOTS, NANAMI-CHAN.

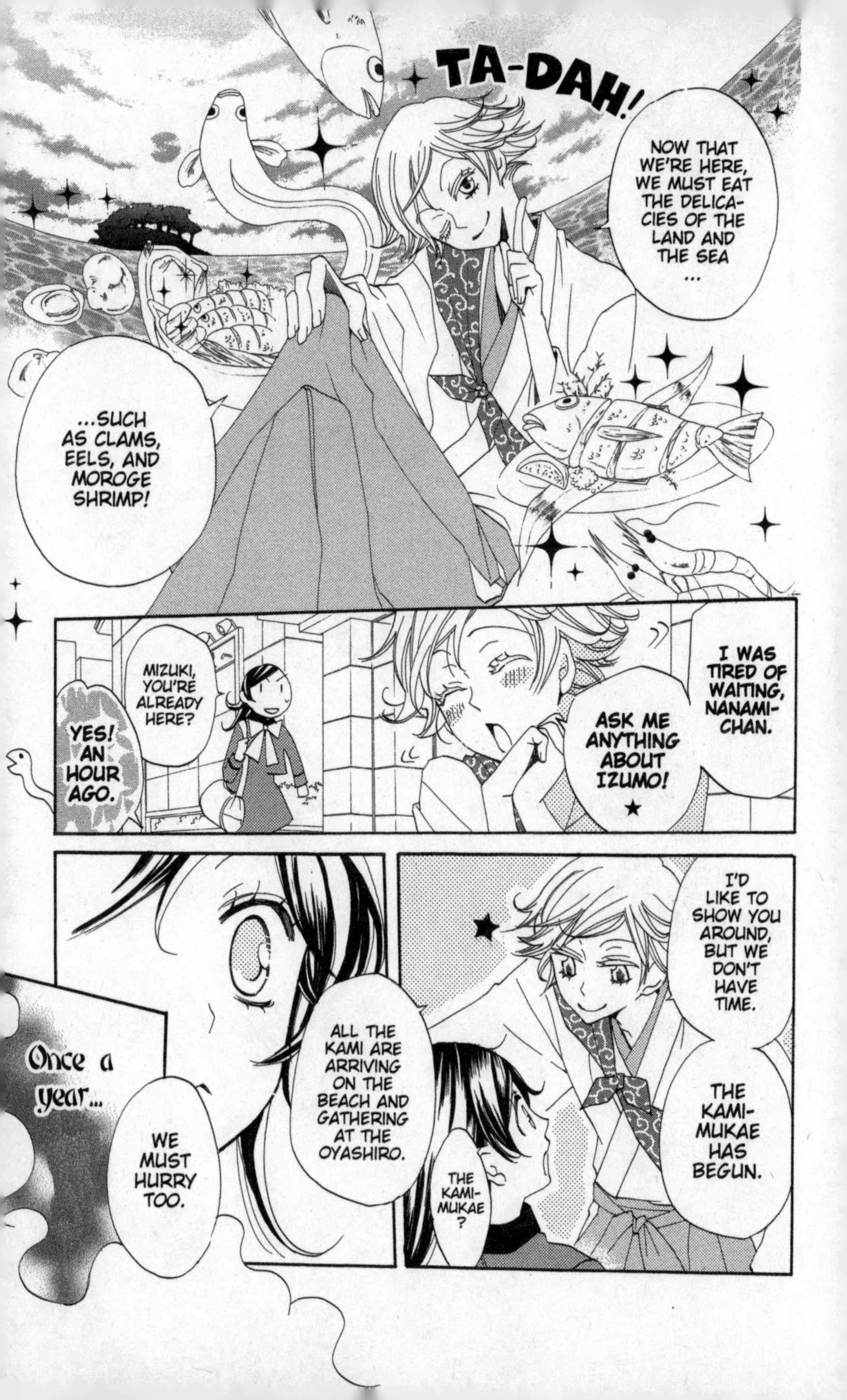
TA-DAH!
NOW THAT WE'RE HERE, WE MUST EAT THE DELICACIES OF THE LAND AND THE SEA ...
...SUCH AS CLAMS, EELS, AND MOROGE SHRIMP!
I WAS TIRED OF WAITING, NANAMI-CHAN.
ASK ME ANYTHING ABOUT IZUMO! ★
MIZUKI, YOU'RE ALREADY HERE?
YES! AN HOUR AGO.
I'D LIKE TO SHOW YOU AROUND, BUT WE DON'T HAVE TIME.
THE KAMI-MUKAE HAS BEGUN.
THE KAMI-MUKAE?
ALL THE KAMI ARE ARRIVING ON THE BEACH AND GATHERING AT THE OYASHIRO.
WE MUST HURRY TOO.
Once a year...

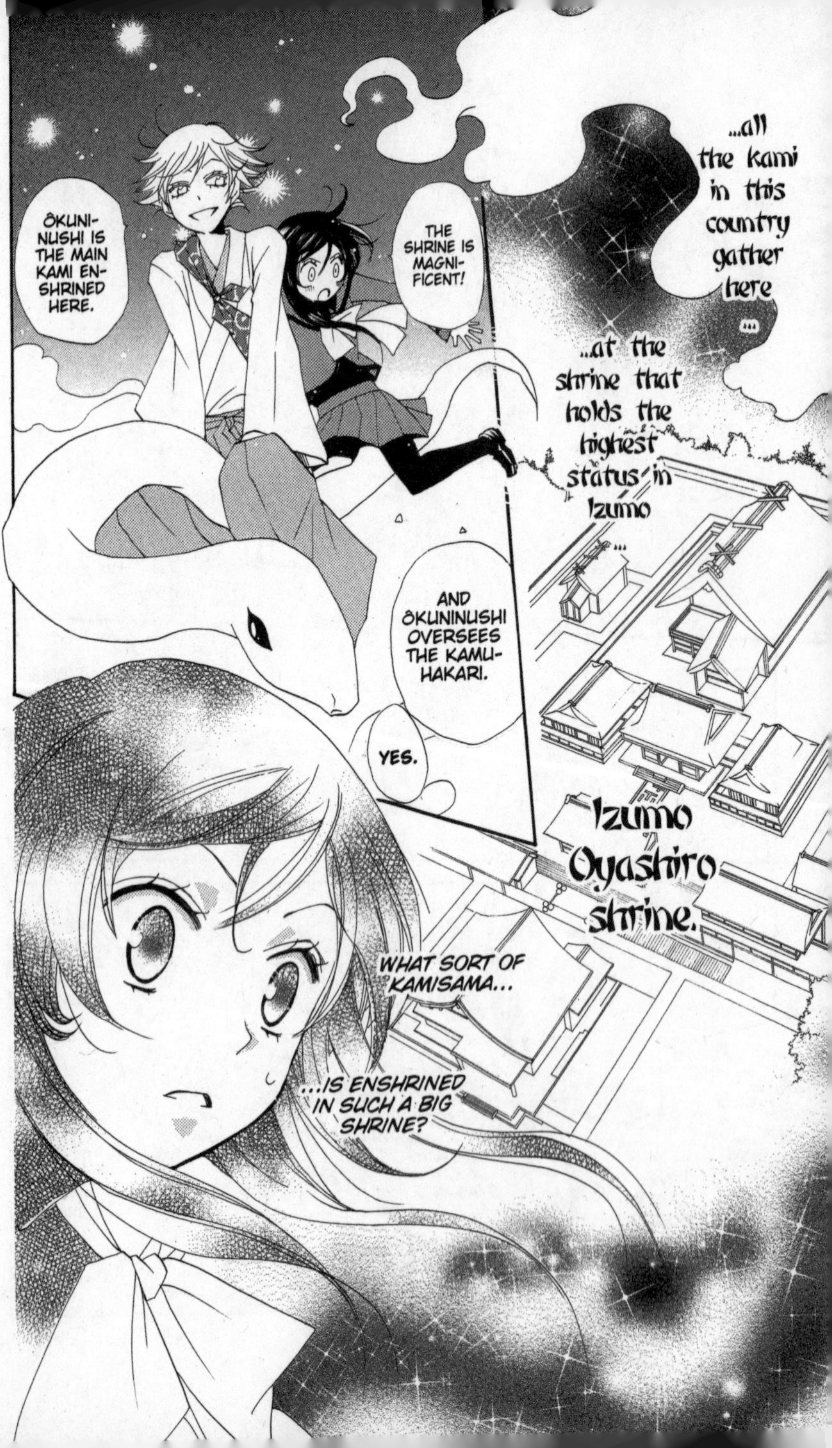
...all the kami in this country gather here...
...at the shrine that holds the highest status in Izumo...
Izumo Oyashiro shrine.
THE SHRINE IS MAGNIFICENT!
ÔKUNINUSHI IS THE MAIN KAMI ENSHRINED HERE.
AND ÔKUNINUSHI OVERSEES THE KAMUHAKARI.
YES.
WHAT SORT OF KAMISAMA...
...IS ENSHRINED IN SUCH A BIG SHRINE?

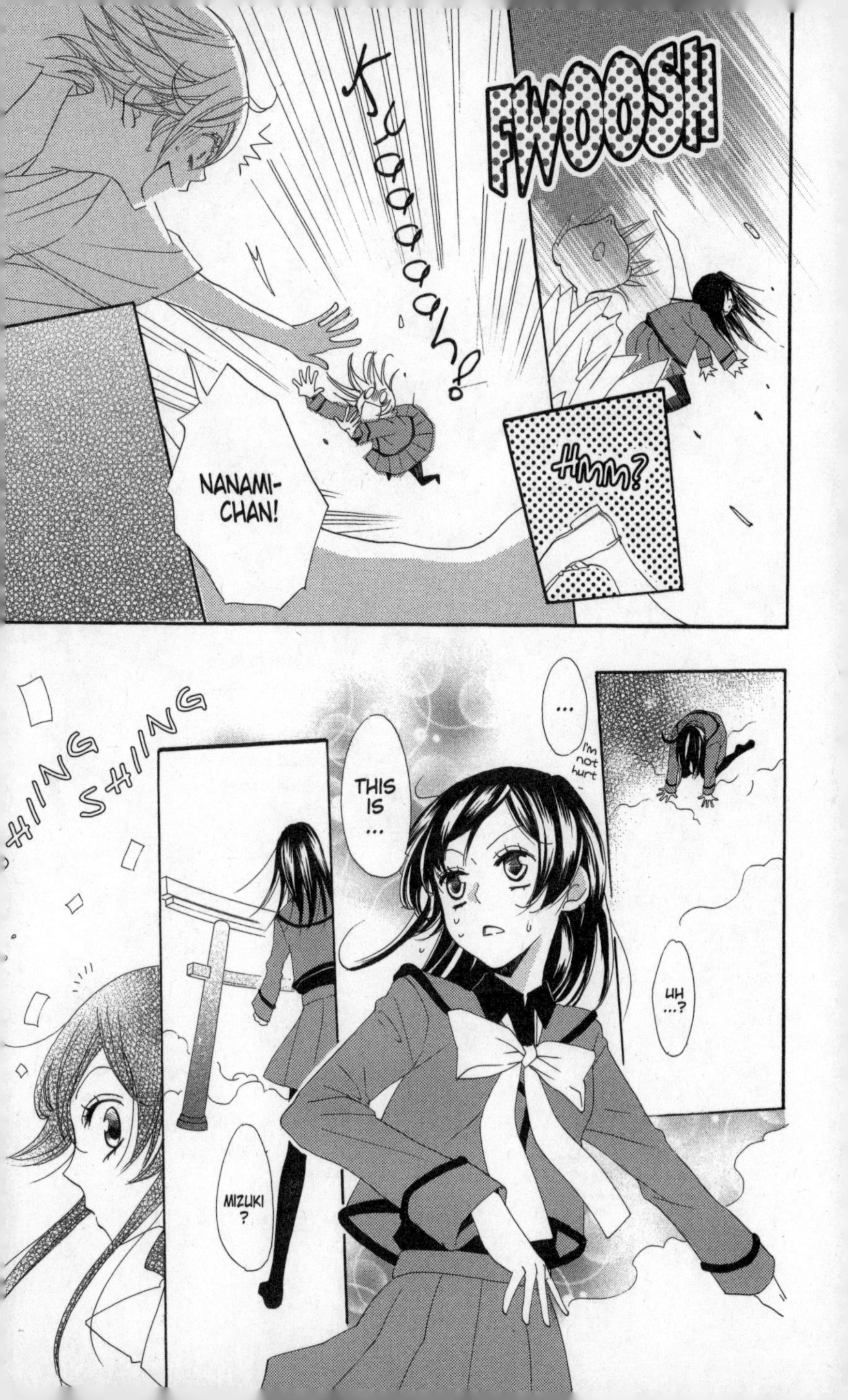
FWOOSH
Hmm?
Kyaaaaah!
NANAMI-CHAN!
...
I'm not hurt
UH ...?
THIS IS ...
SHING SHING
MIZUKI ?

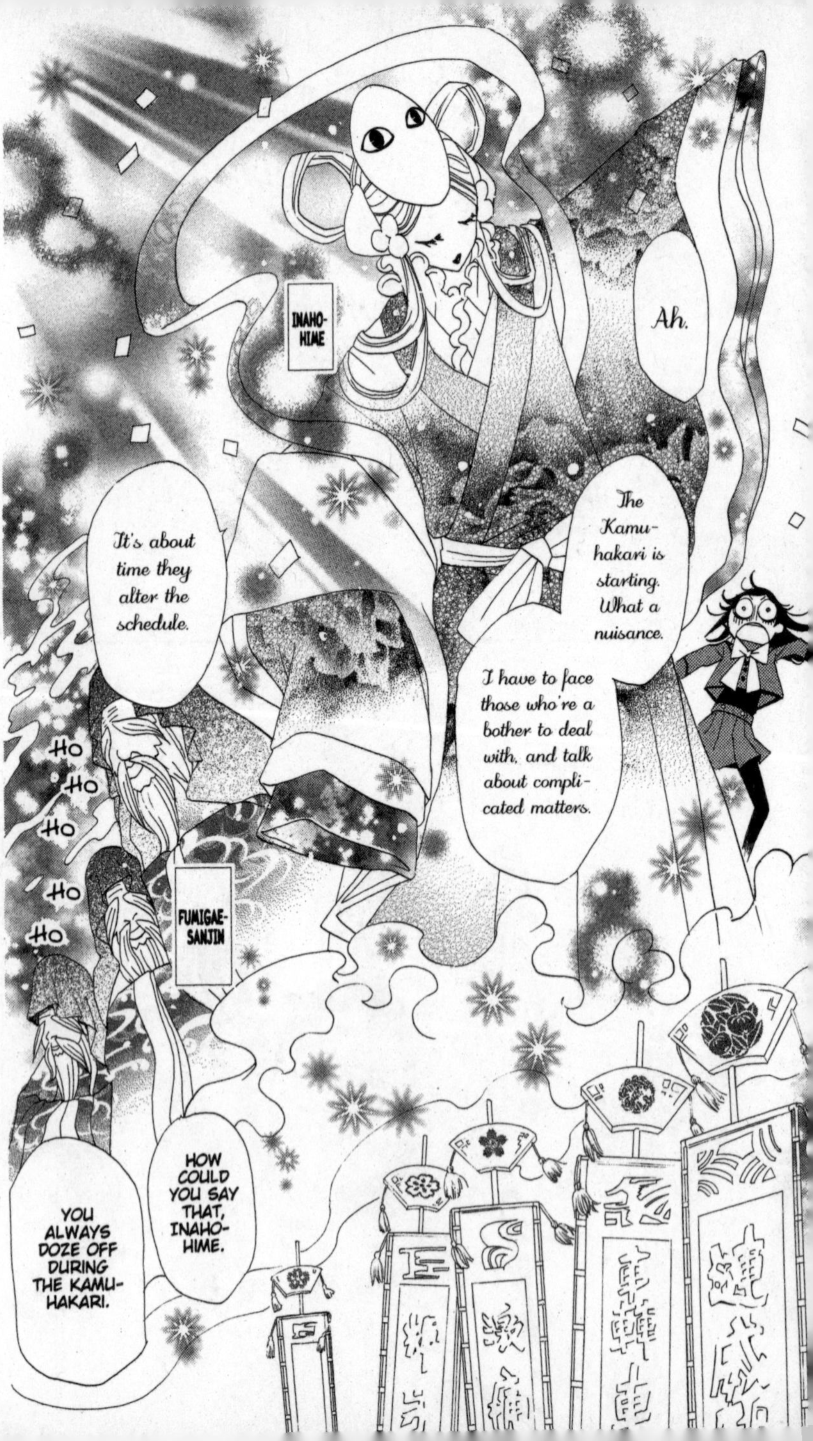
Ah.
INAHO-HIME
The Kamu-hakari is starting. What a nuisance.
It's about time they alter the schedule.
I have to face those who're a bother to deal with, and talk about compli-cated matters.
Ho Ho Ho Ho Ho
FUMIGAE-SANJIN
HOW COULD YOU SAY THAT, INAHO-HIME.
YOU ALWAYS DOZE OFF DURING THE KAMU-HAKARI.

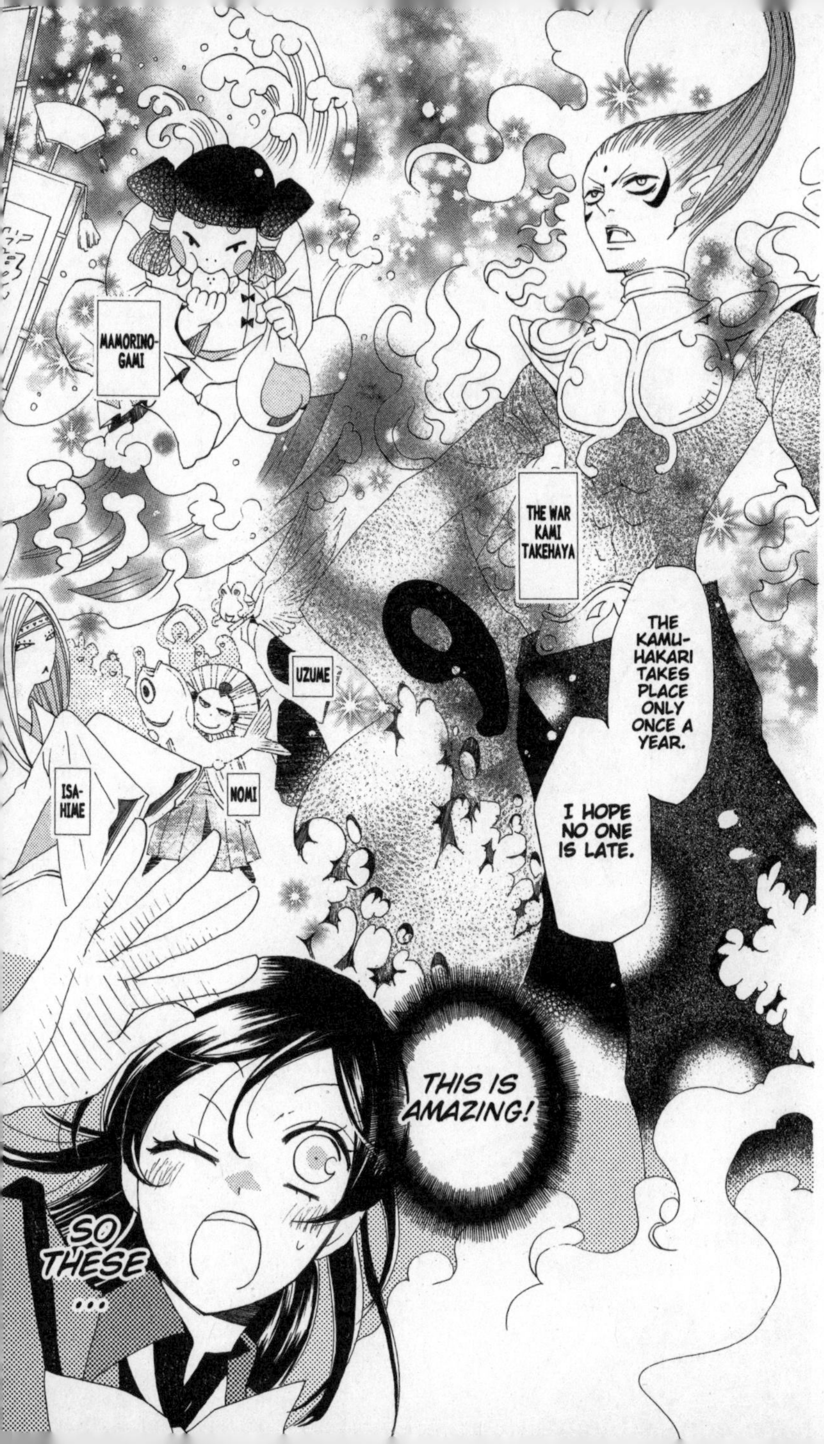
THE WAR KAMI TAKEHAYA
THE KAMU-HAKARI TAKES PLACE ONLY ONCE A YEAR.
I HOPE NO ONE IS LATE.
MAMORINO-GAMI
UZUME
NOMI
ISA-HIME
THIS IS AMAZING!
SO THESE...

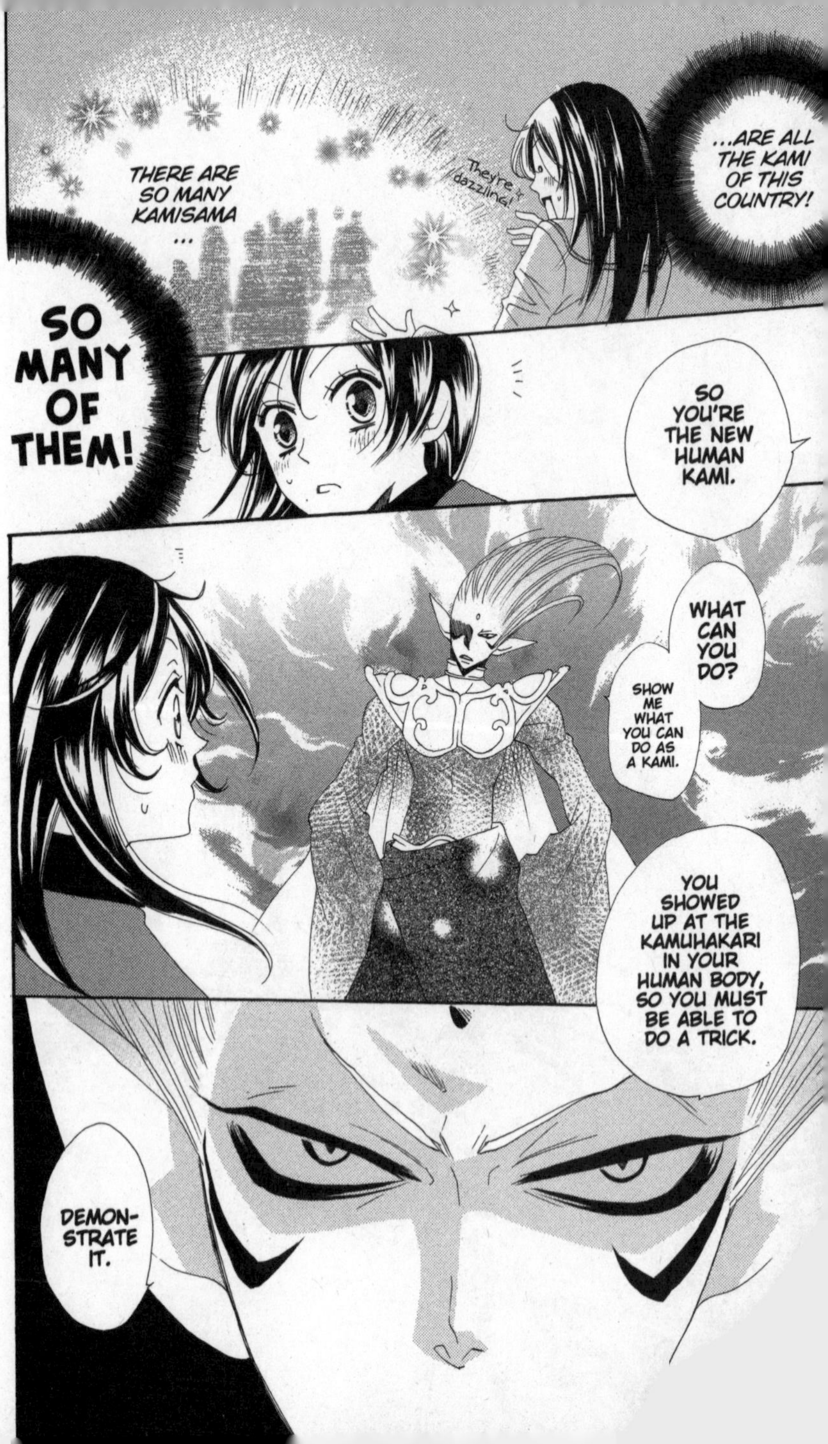
...ARE ALL THE KAMI OF THIS COUNTRY!
They're dazzling!
THERE ARE SO MANY KAMISAMA ...
SO MANY OF THEM!
SO YOU'RE THE NEW HUMAN KAMI.
WHAT CAN YOU DO?
SHOW ME WHAT YOU CAN DO AS A KAMI.
YOU SHOWED UP AT THE KAMUHAKARI IN YOUR HUMAN BODY, SO YOU MUST BE ABLE TO DO A TRICK.
DEMON-STRATE IT.

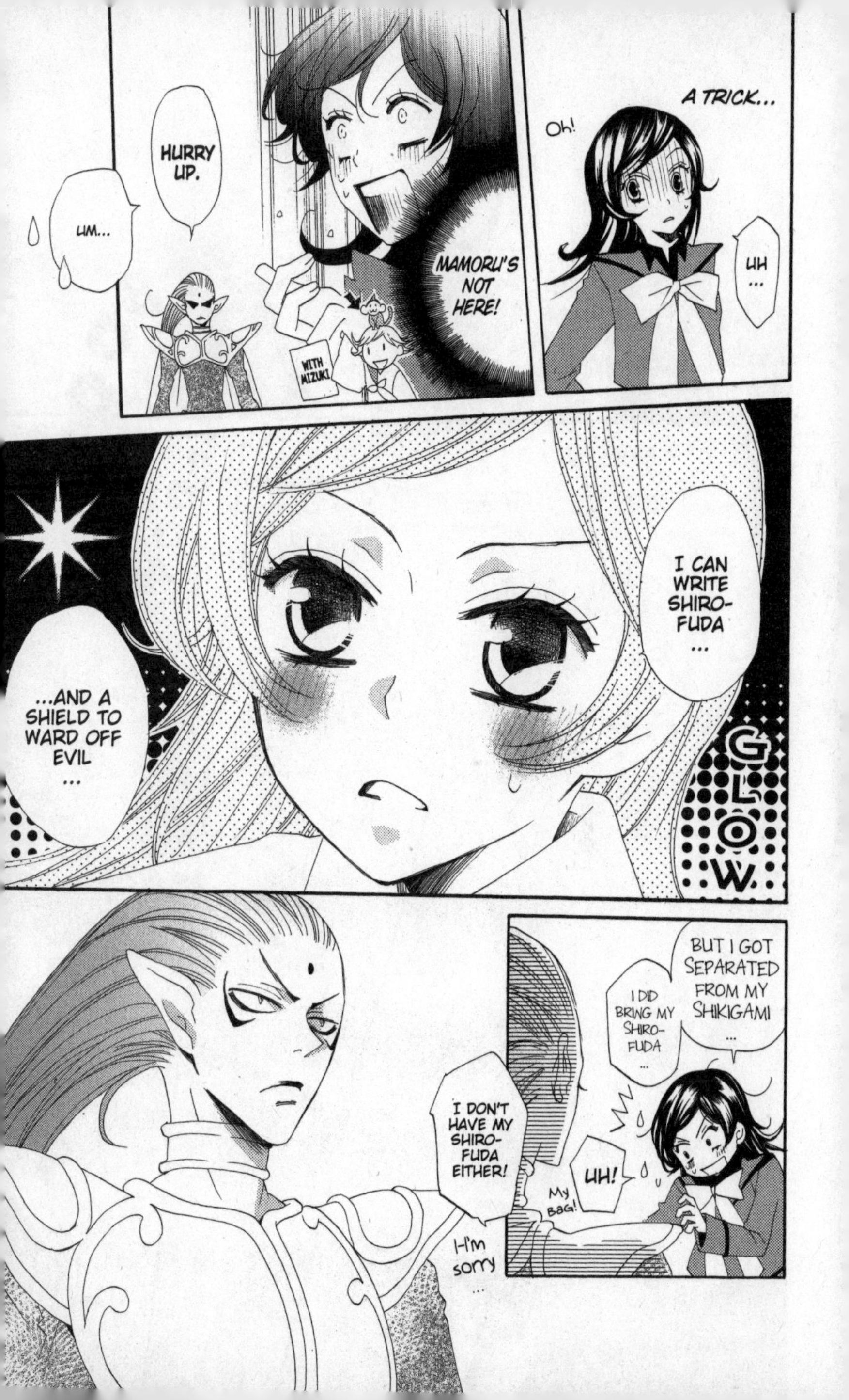
A TRICK...
Oh!
UH ...
MAMORU'S NOT HERE!
WITH MIZUKI
HURRY UP.
UM...
I CAN WRITE SHIRO-FUDA ...
GLOW
...AND A SHIELD TO WARD OFF EVIL ...
BUT I GOT SEPARATED FROM MY SHIKIGAMI ...
I DID BRING MY SHIRO-FUDA ...
UH!
My bag!
I DON'T HAVE MY SHIRO-FUDA EITHER!
I-I'm sorry ...

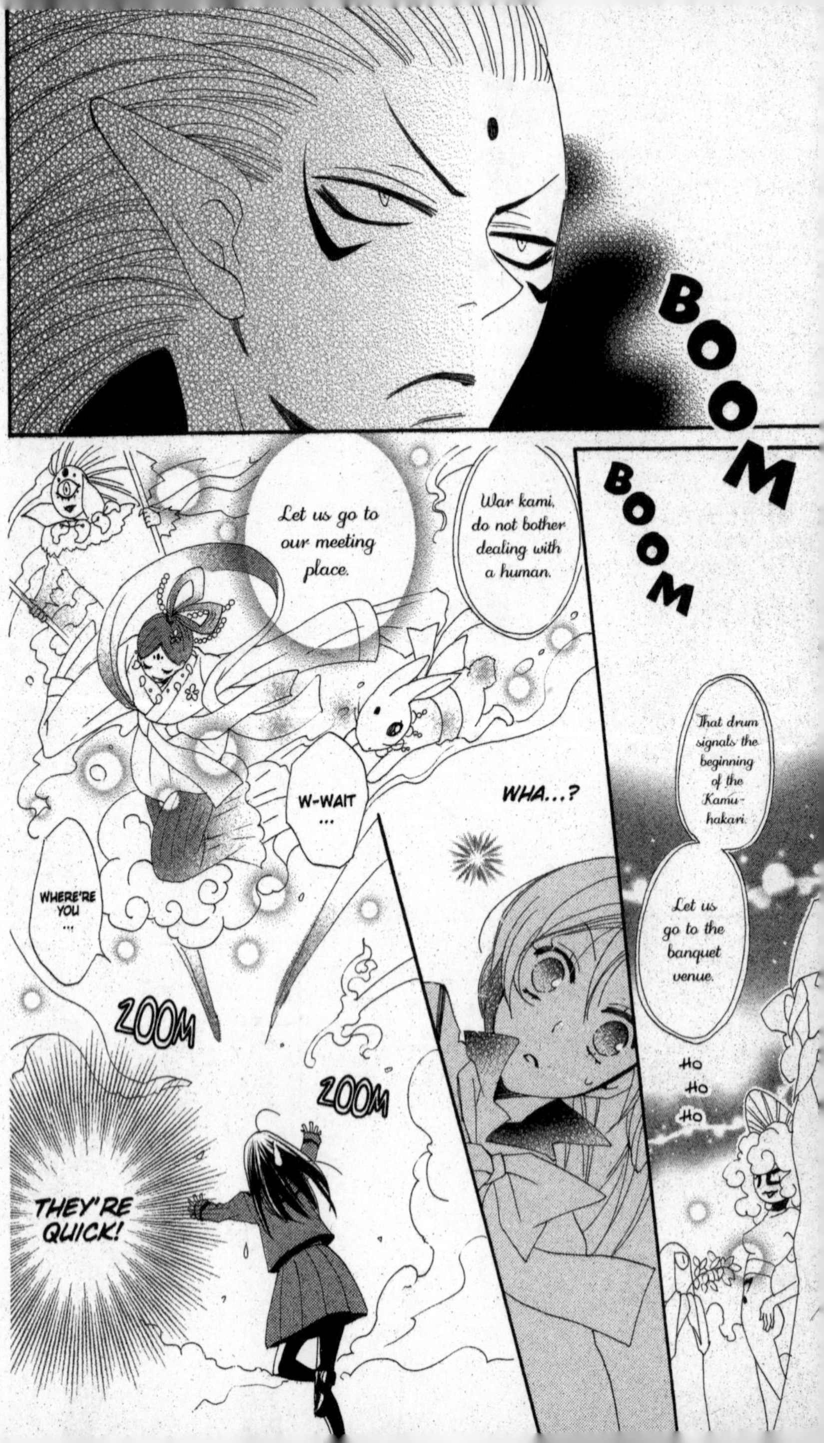
BOOM
BOOM
That drum signals the beginning of the Kamu-hakari.
Let us go to the banquet venue.
HO HO HO
WHA...?
War kami, do not bother dealing with a human.
Let us go to our meeting place.
W-WAIT...
WHERE'RE YOU...
ZOOM
ZOOM
THEY'RE QUICK!

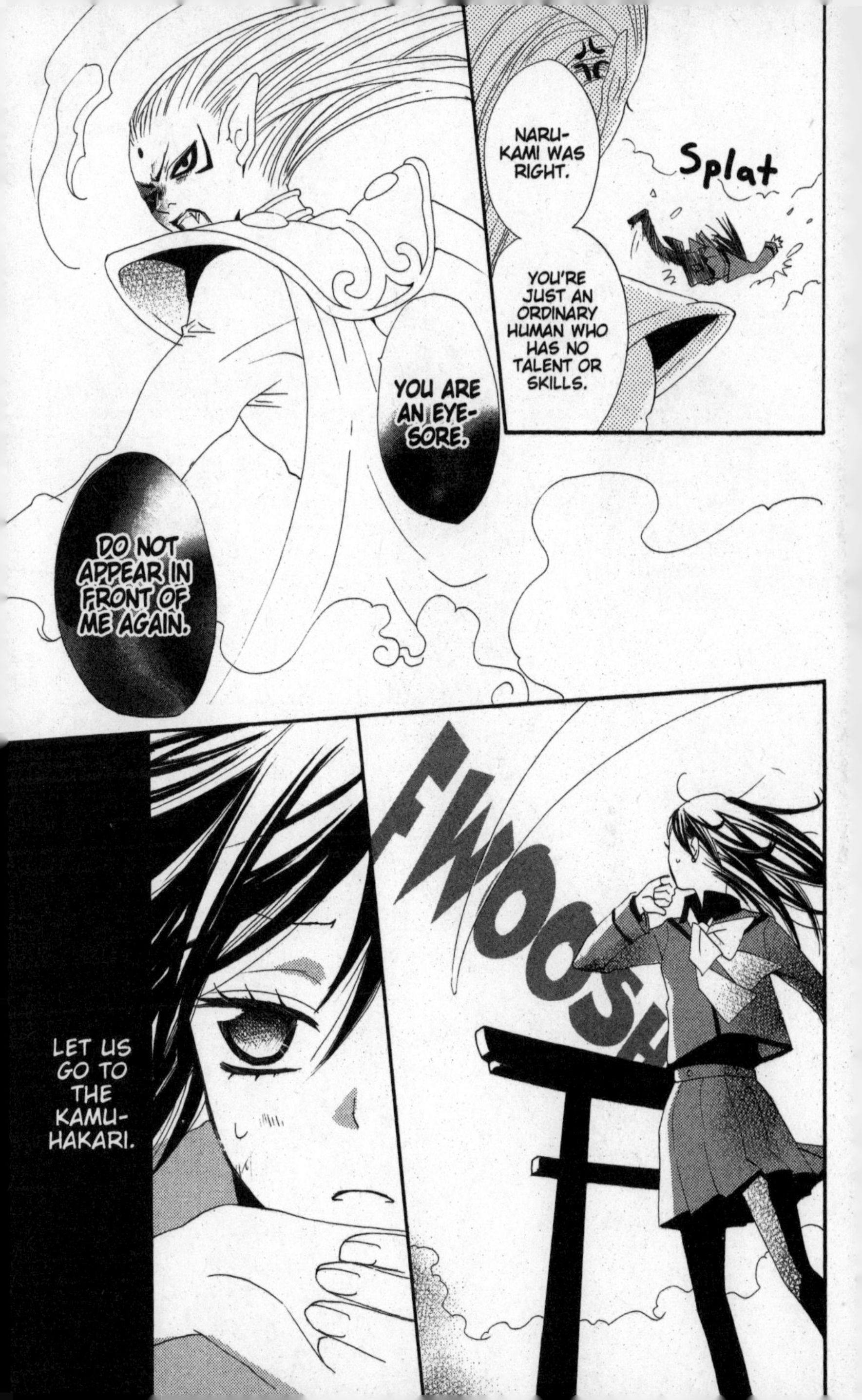

Splat
NARU-KAMI WAS RIGHT.
YOU'RE JUST AN ORDINARY HUMAN WHO HAS NO TALENT OR SKILLS.
YOU ARE AN EYE-SORE.
DO NOT APPEAR IN FRONT OF ME AGAIN.
FWOOSH
LET US GO TO THE KAMU-HAKARI.

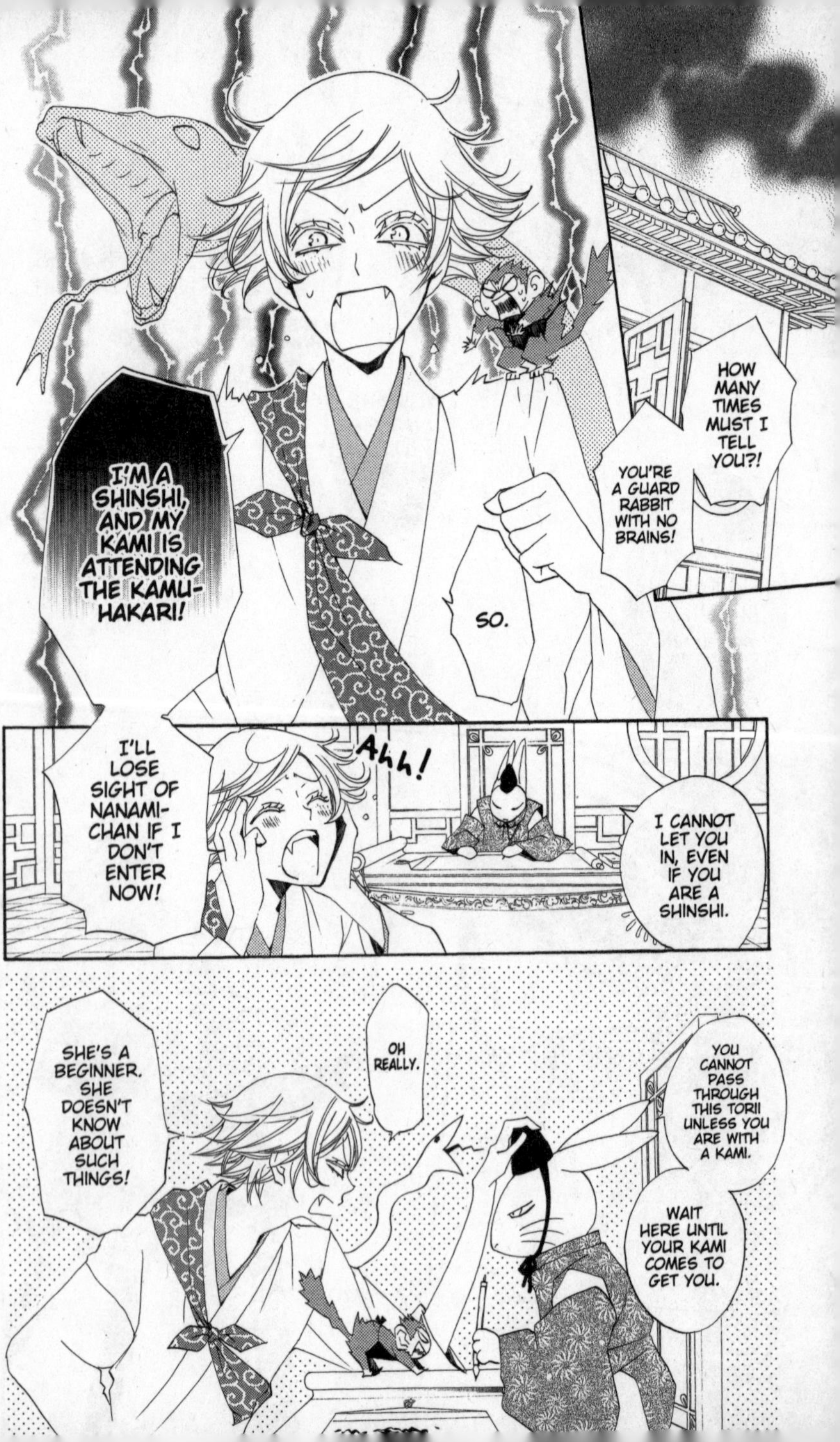
HOW MANY TIMES MUST I TELL YOU?!
YOU'RE A GUARD RABBIT WITH NO BRAINS!
SO.
I'M A SHINSHI, AND MY KAMI IS ATTENDING THE KAMU-HAKARI!
I CANNOT LET YOU IN, EVEN IF YOU ARE A SHINSHI.
Ahh!
I'LL LOSE SIGHT OF NANAMI-CHAN IF I DON'T ENTER NOW!
YOU CANNOT PASS THROUGH THIS TORII UNLESS YOU ARE WITH A KAMI.
WAIT HERE UNTIL YOUR KAMI COMES TO GET YOU.
OH REALLY.
SHE'S A BEGINNER. SHE DOESN'T KNOW ABOUT SUCH THINGS!

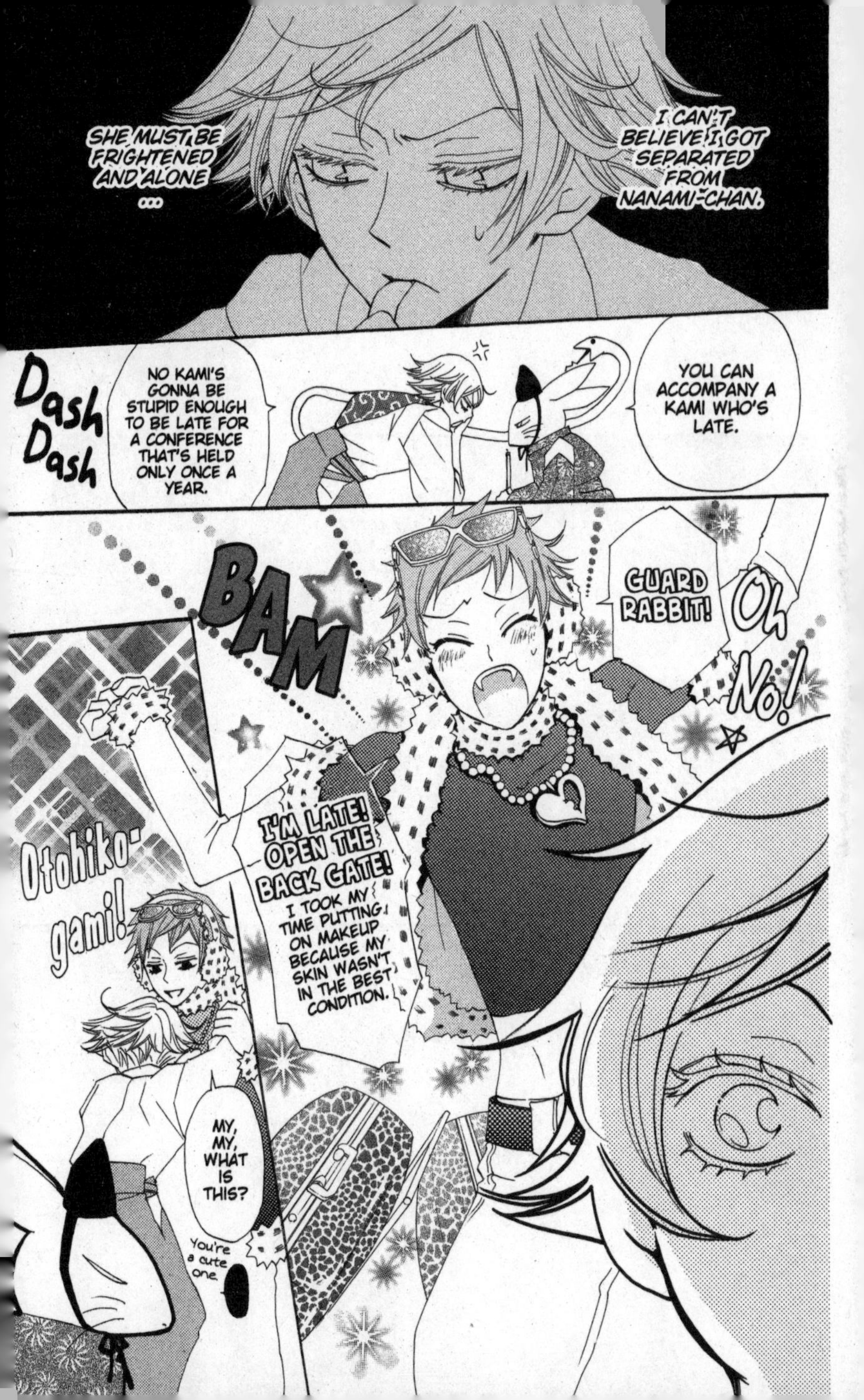

I CAN'T BELIEVE I GOT SEPARATED FROM NANAMI-CHAN.
SHE MUST BE FRIGHTENED AND ALONE...
YOU CAN ACCOMPANY A KAMI WHO'S LATE.
NO KAMI'S GONNA BE STUPID ENOUGH TO BE LATE FOR A CONFERENCE THAT'S HELD ONLY ONCE A YEAR.
Dash Dash
GUARD RABBIT!
Oh No!
BAM
I'M LATE! OPEN THE BACK GATE!
I TOOK MY TIME PUTTING ON MAKEUP BECAUSE MY SKIN WASN'T IN THE BEST CONDITION.
Otohiko-gami!
MY, MY, WHAT IS THIS?
You're a cute one.

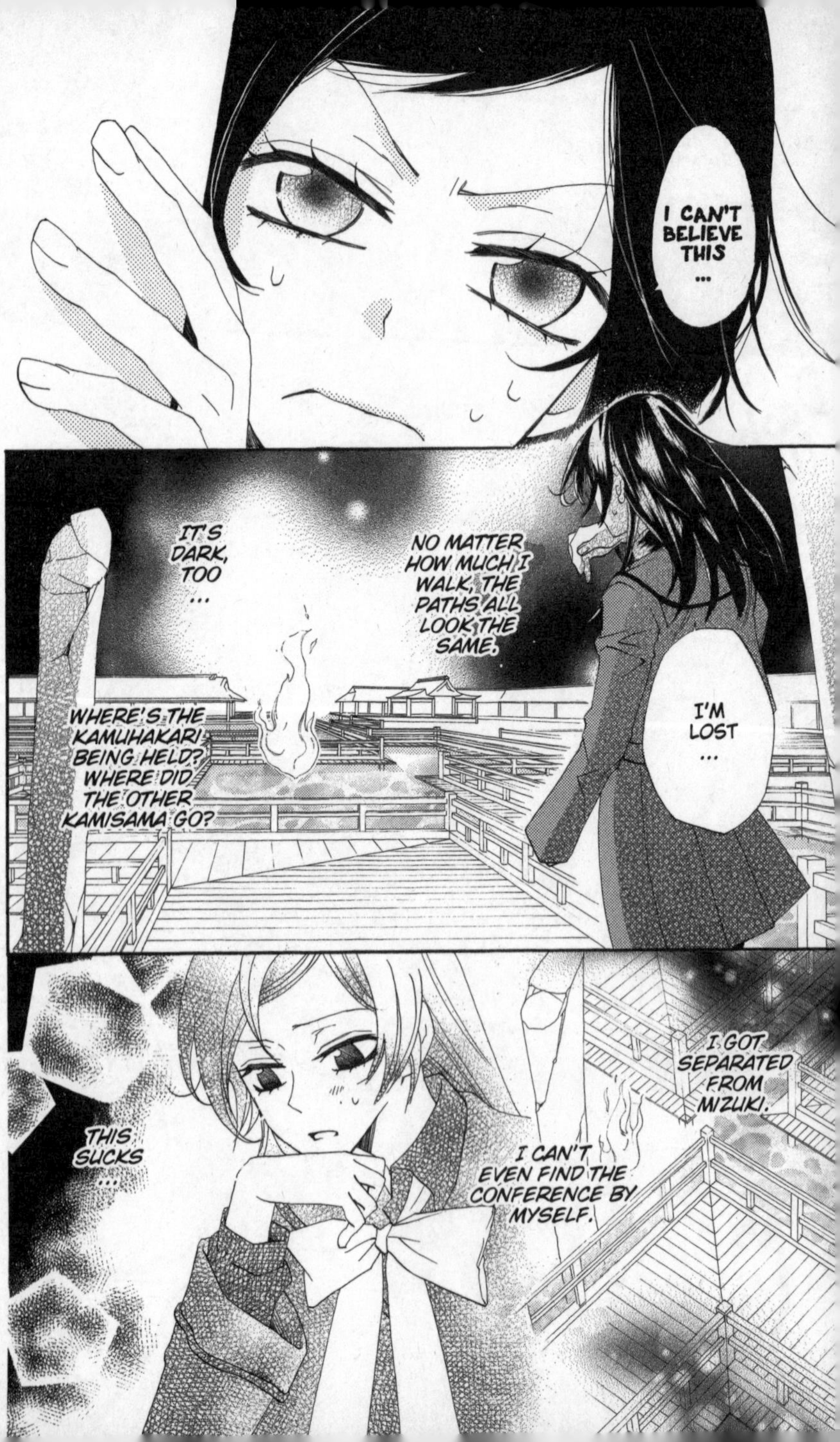
I CAN'T BELIEVE THIS ...
I'M LOST ...
NO MATTER HOW MUCH I WALK, THE PATHS ALL LOOK THE SAME.
IT'S DARK, TOO ...
WHERE'S THE KAMUHAKARI BEING HELD? WHERE DID THE OTHER KAMISAMA GO?
I GOT SEPARATED FROM MIZUKI.
I CAN'T EVEN FIND THE CONFERENCE BY MYSELF.
THIS SUCKS ...

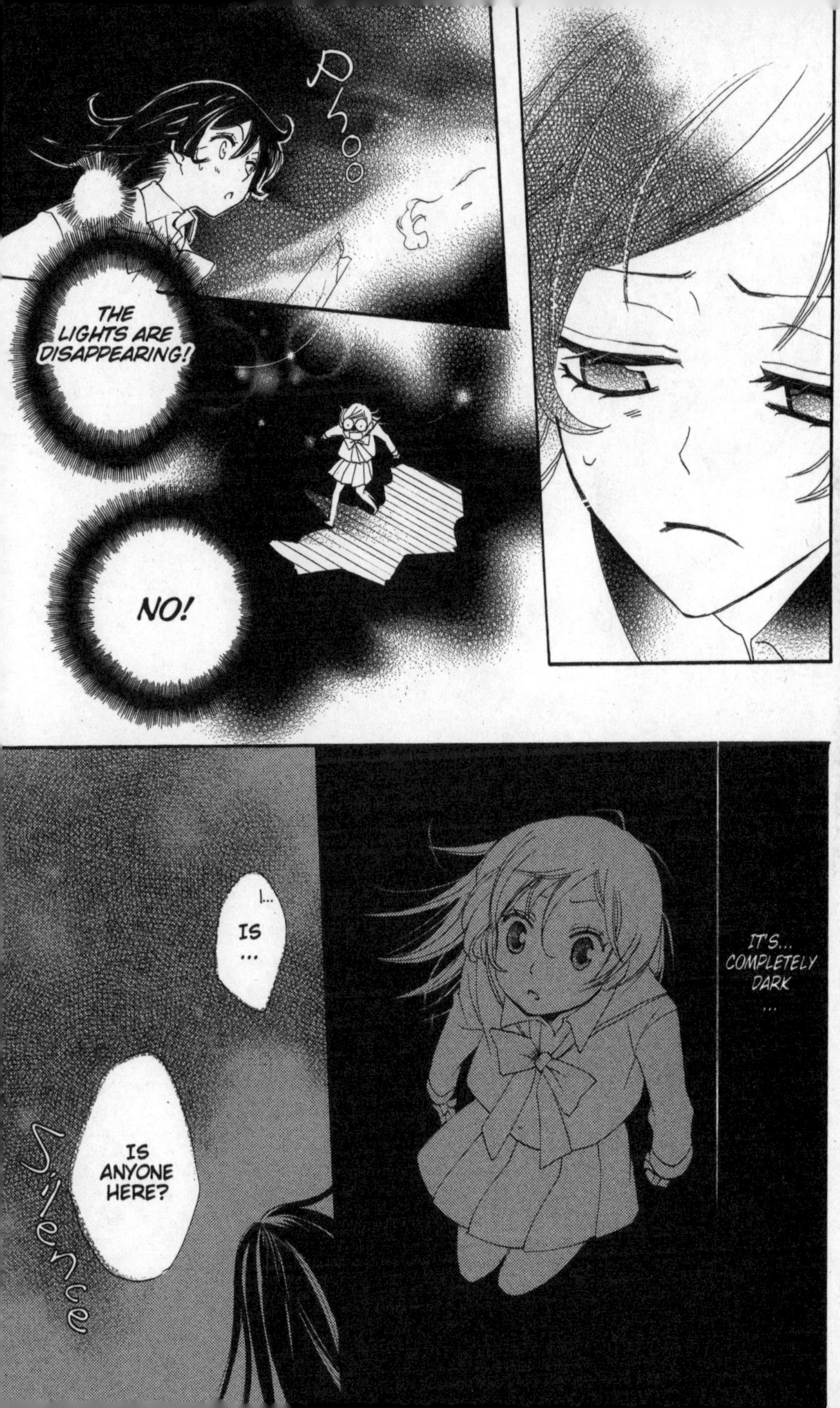
Phoo
THE LIGHTS ARE DISAPPEARING!
NO!
IT'S... COMPLETELY DARK ...
I... IS ...
IS ANYONE HERE?
Silence

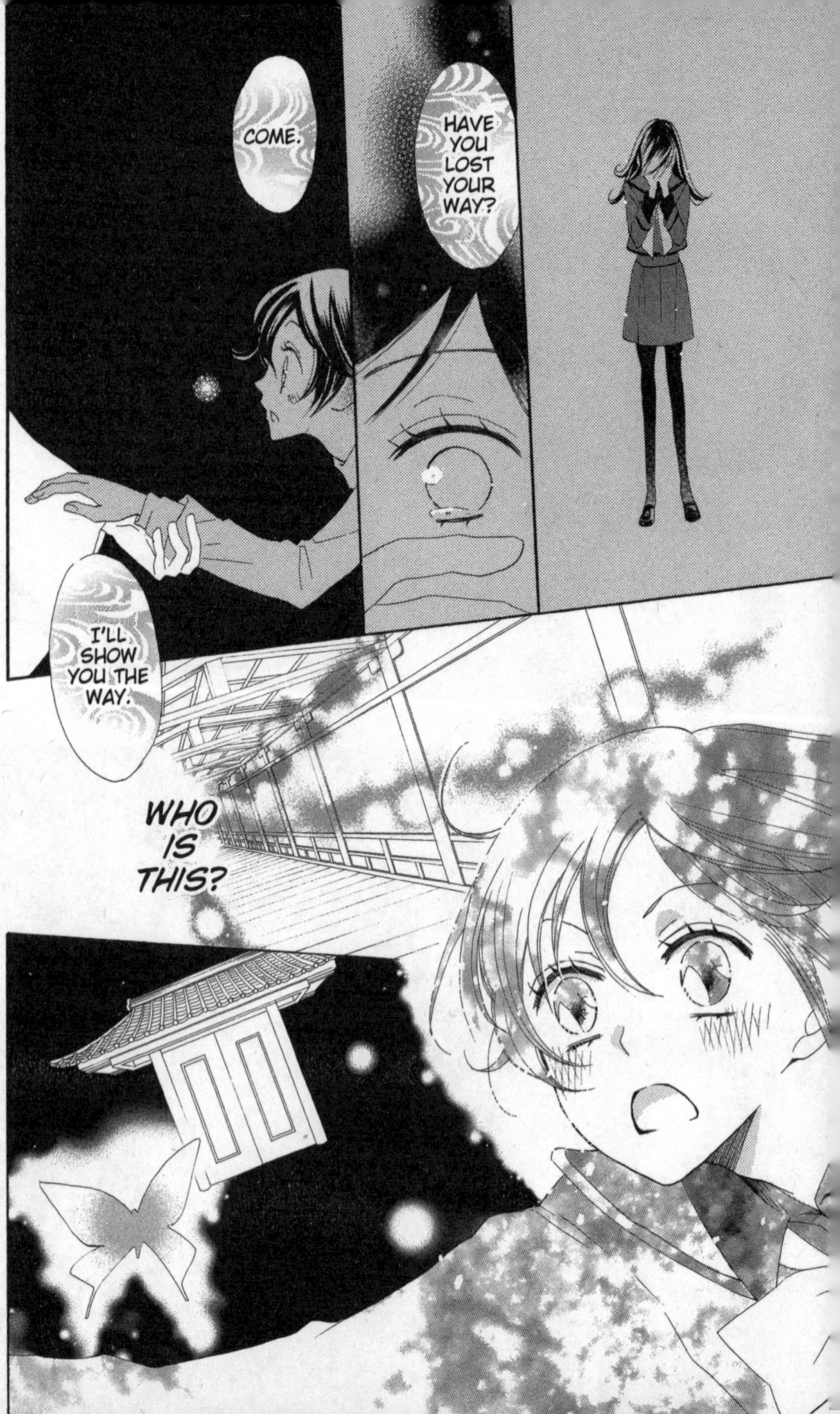
HAVE YOU LOST YOUR WAY?
COME.
I'LL SHOW YOU THE WAY.
WHO IS THIS?

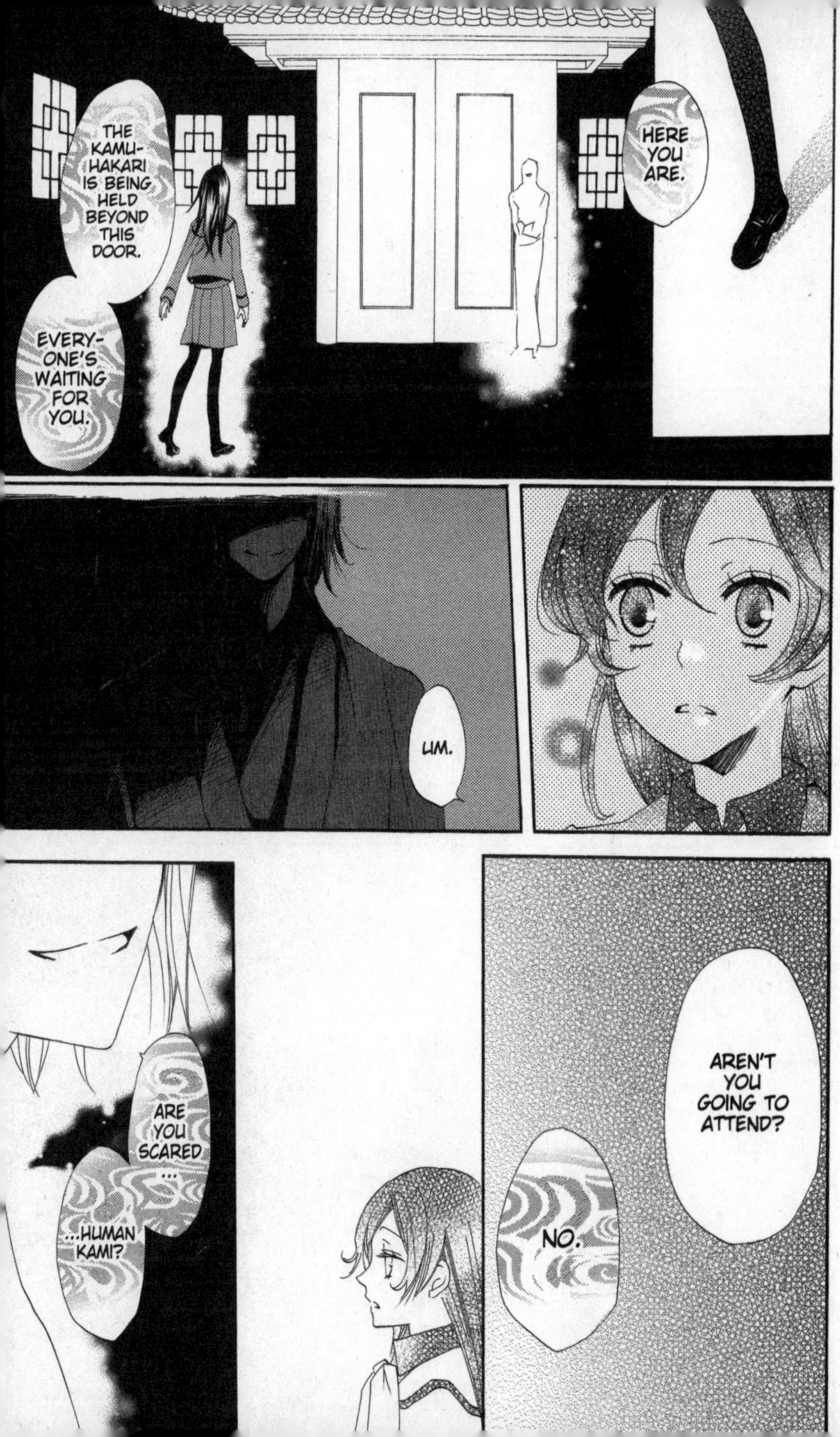
HERE YOU ARE.
THE KAMU-HAKARI IS BEING HELD BEYOND THIS DOOR.
EVERY-ONE'S WAITING FOR YOU.
UM.
AREN'T YOU GOING TO ATTEND?
NO.
ARE YOU SCARED...
...HUMAN KAMI?

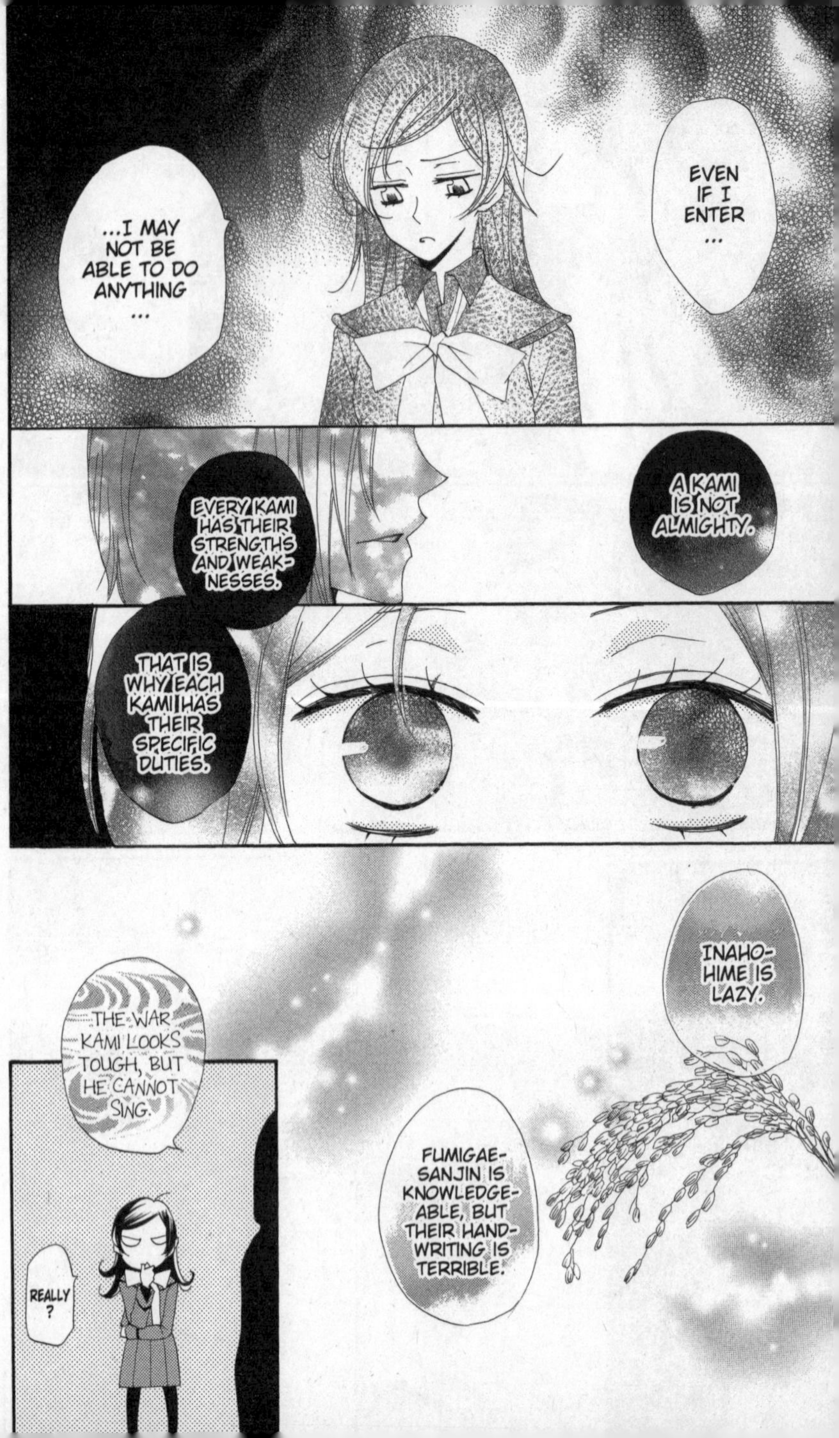
EVEN IF I ENTER ...
...I MAY NOT BE ABLE TO DO ANYTHING ...
A KAMI IS NOT ALMIGHTY.
EVERY KAMI HAS THEIR STRENGTHS AND WEAK-NESSES.
THAT IS WHY EACH KAMI HAS THEIR SPECIFIC DUTIES.
INAHO-HIME IS LAZY.
FUMIGAE-SANJIN IS KNOWLEDGE-ABLE, BUT THEIR HAND-WRITING IS TERRIBLE.
THE WAR KAMI LOOKS TOUGH, BUT HE CANNOT SING.
REALLY ?

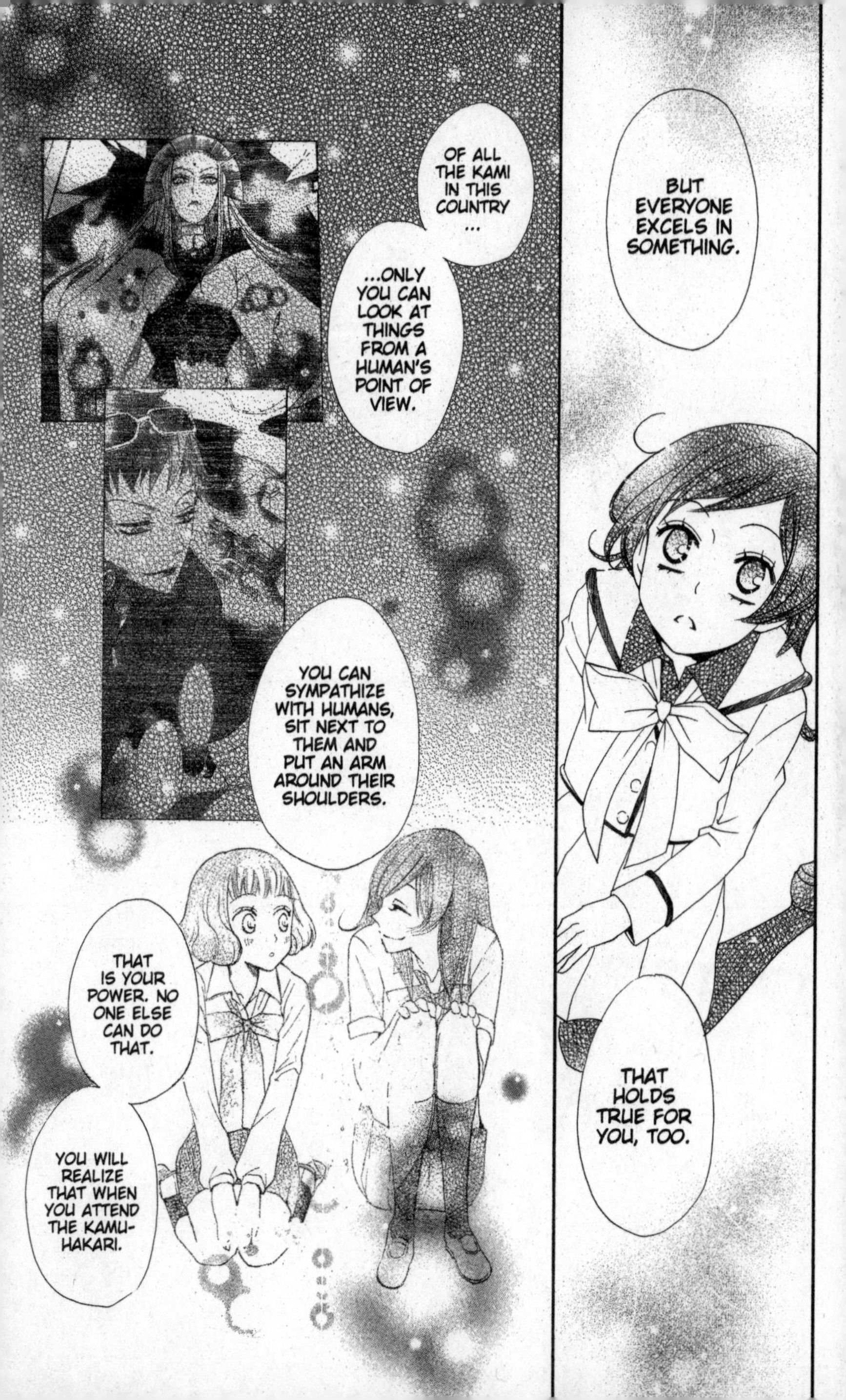
BUT EVERYONE EXCELS IN SOMETHING.
THAT HOLDS TRUE FOR YOU, TOO.
OF ALL THE KAMI IN THIS COUNTRY ...
...ONLY YOU CAN LOOK AT THINGS FROM A HUMAN'S POINT OF VIEW.
YOU CAN SYMPATHIZE WITH HUMANS, SIT NEXT TO THEM AND PUT AN ARM AROUND THEIR SHOULDERS.
THAT IS YOUR POWER. NO ONE ELSE CAN DO THAT.
YOU WILL REALIZE THAT WHEN YOU ATTEND THE KAMU-HAKARI.

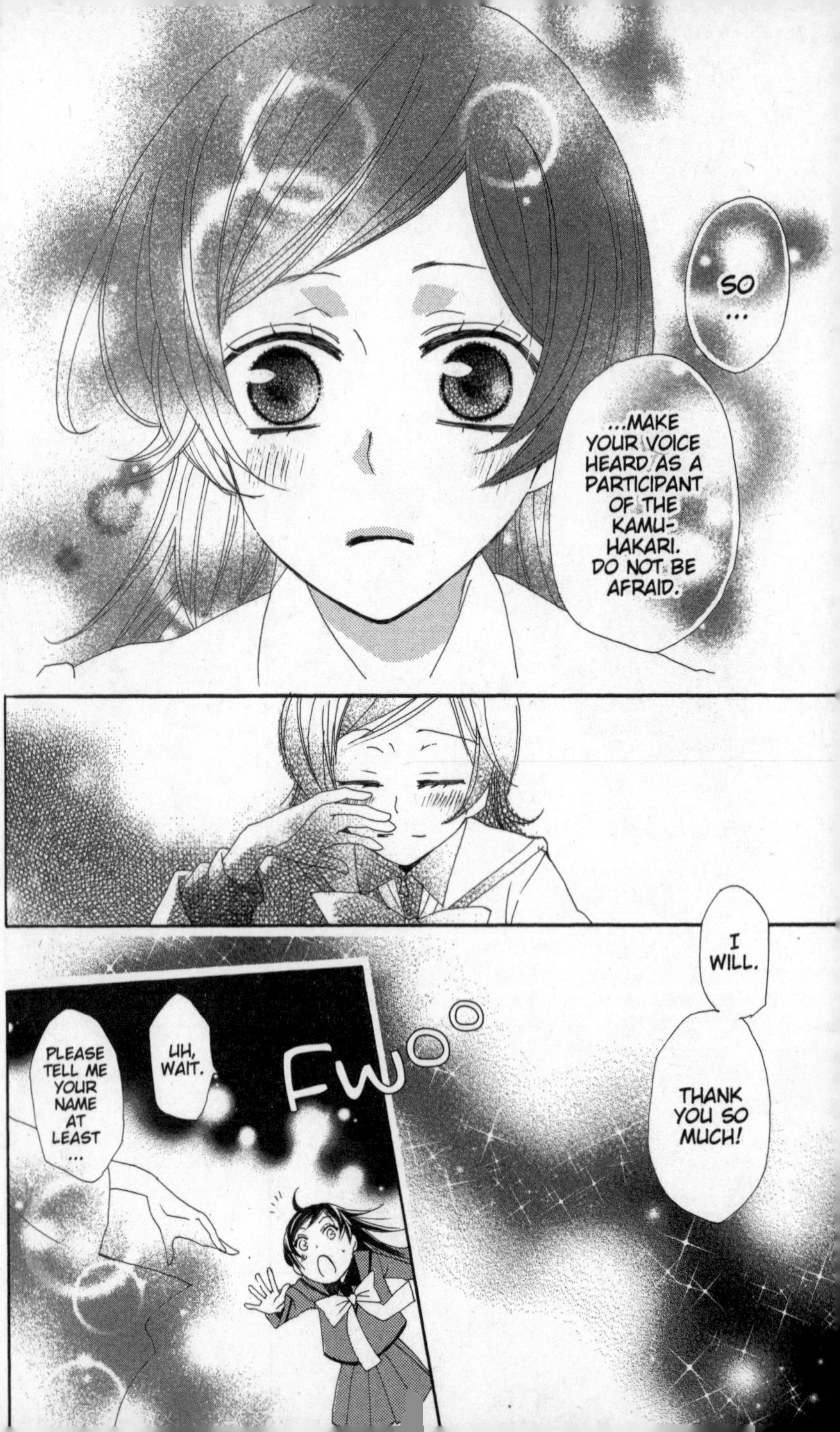
SO...
...MAKE YOUR VOICE HEARD AS A PARTICIPANT OF THE KAMU-HAKARI. DO NOT BE AFRAID.
I WILL.
THANK YOU SO MUCH!
FWOOO
UH, WAIT.
PLEASE TELL ME YOUR NAME AT LEAST...

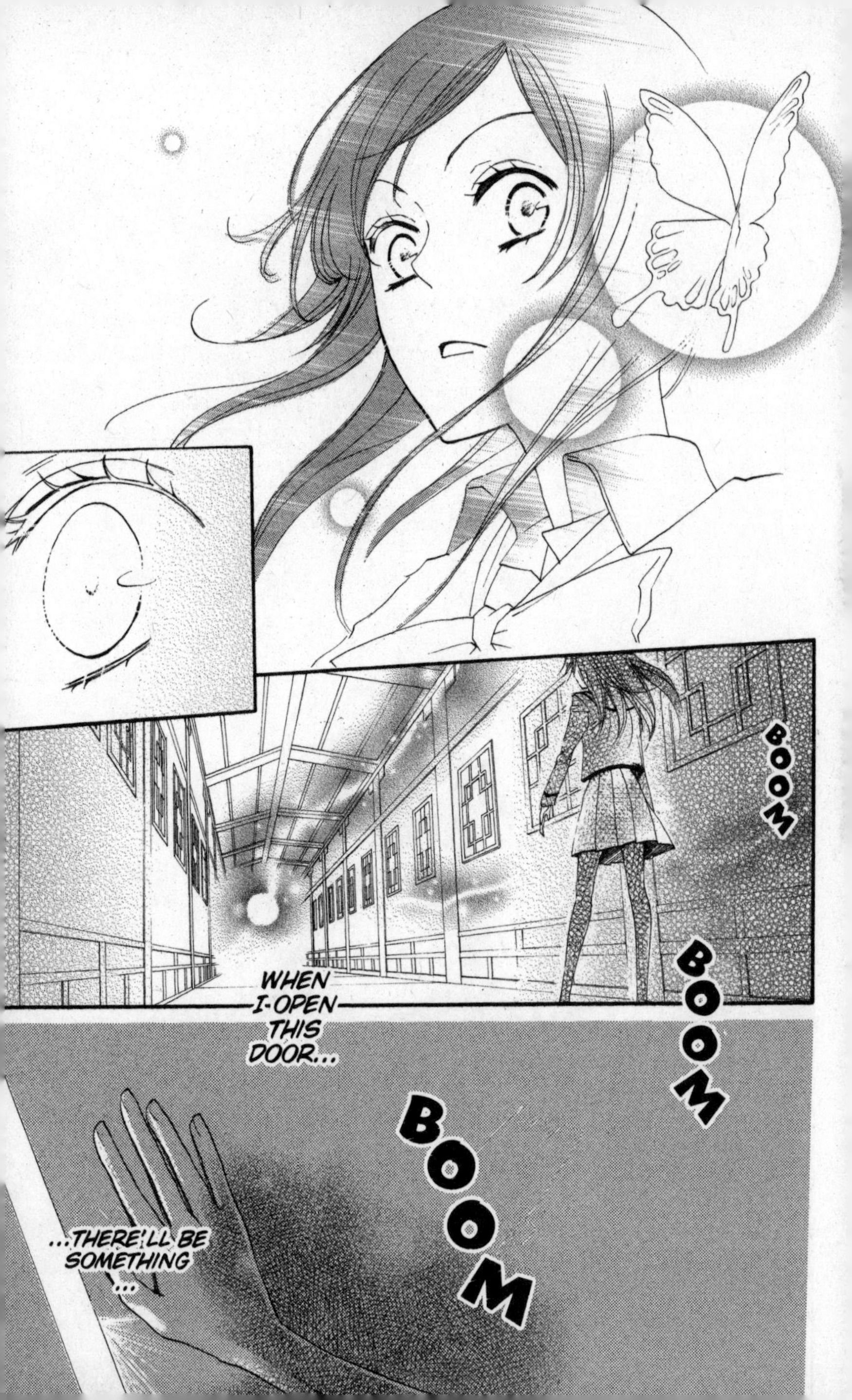
BOOM
BOOM
WHEN I-OPEN THIS DOOR...
BOOM
...THERE'LL BE SOMETHING ...

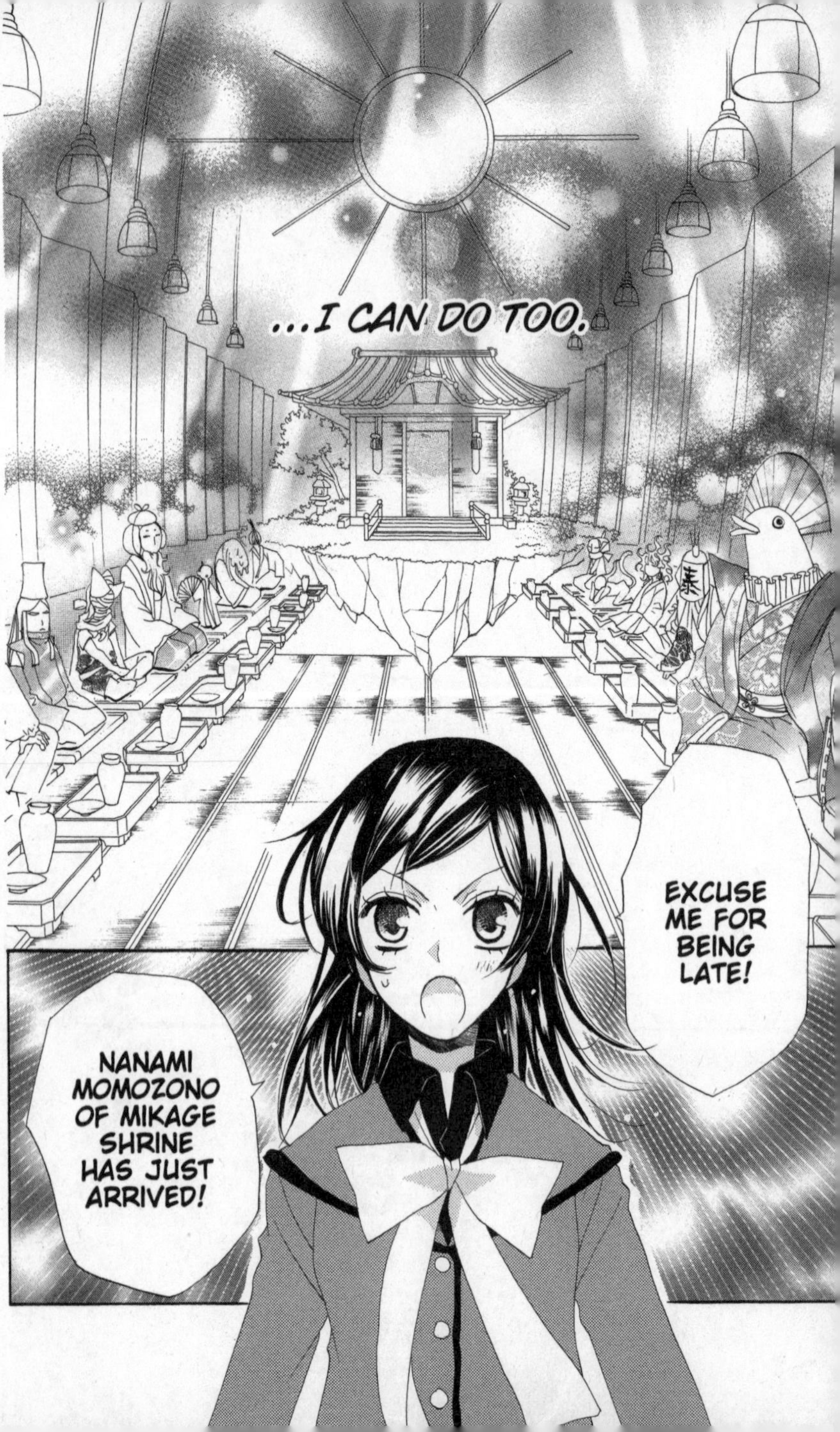
...I CAN DO TOO.
EXCUSE ME FOR BEING LATE!
NANAMI MOMOZONO OF MIKAGE SHRINE HAS JUST ARRIVED!

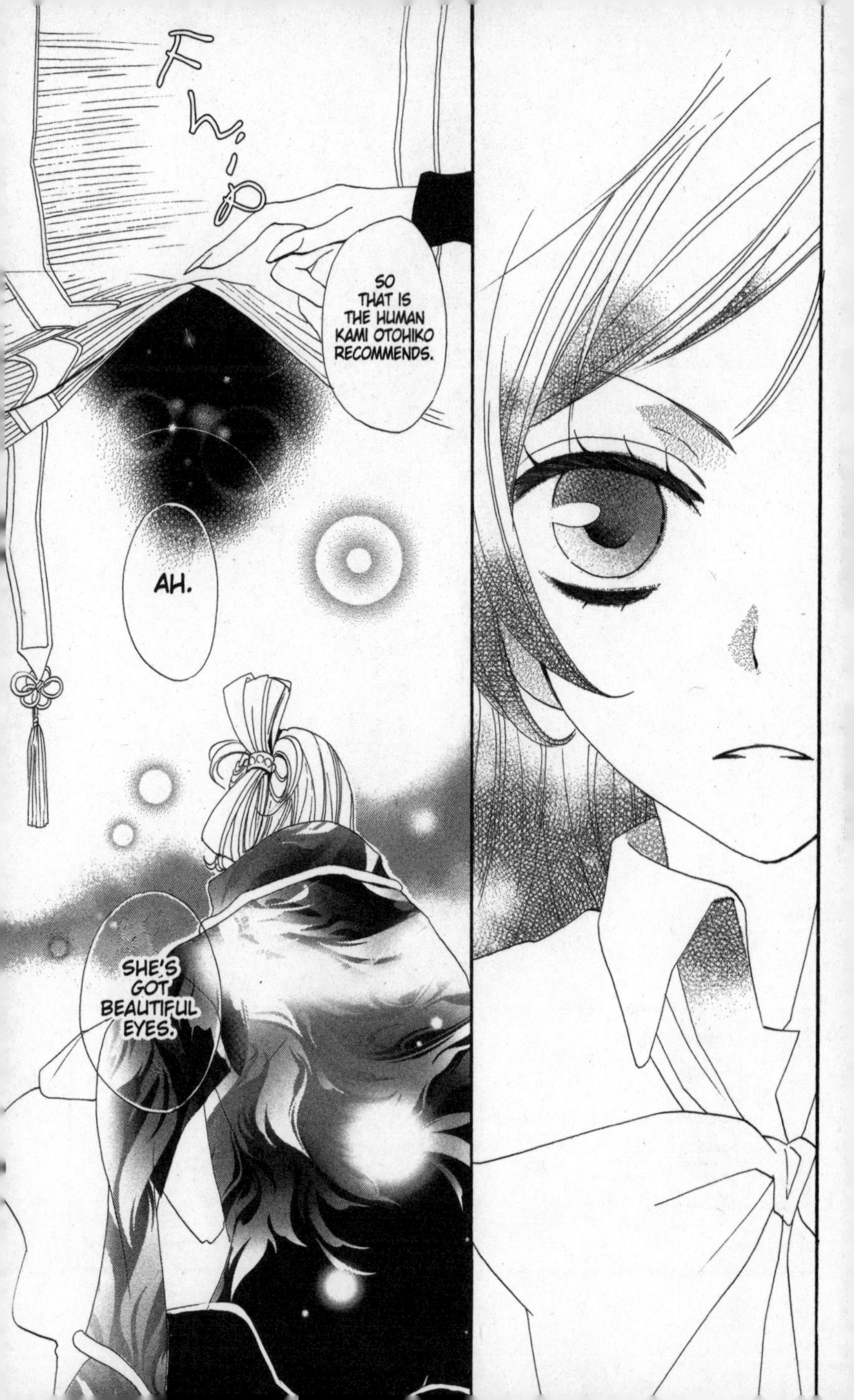
Flip
SO THAT IS THE HUMAN KAMI OTOHIKO RECOMMENDS.
AH.
SHE'S GOT BEAUTIFUL EYES.

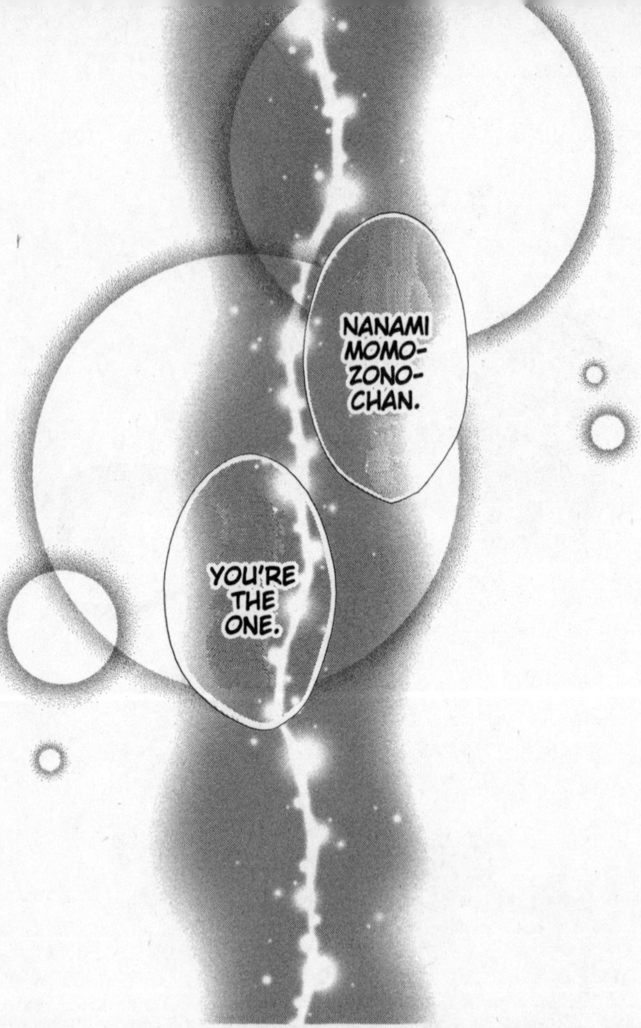
NANAMI MOMO-ZONO-CHAN.
YOU'RE THE ONE.

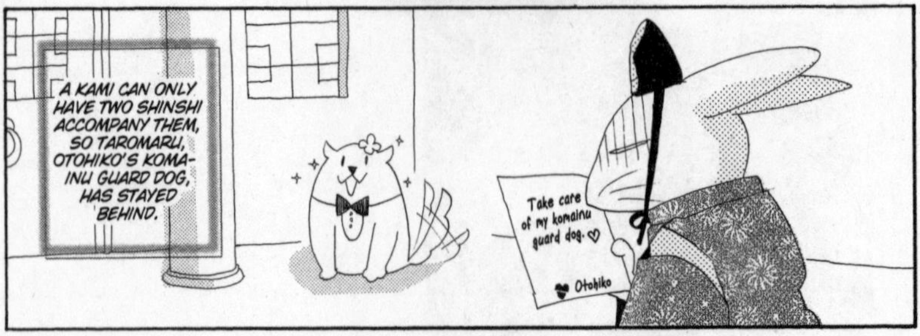
Take care of my komainu guard dog. ♡
Otohiko
A KAMI CAN ONLY HAVE TWO SHINSHI ACCOMPANY THEM, SO TAROMARU, OTOHIKO'S KOMA-INU GUARD DOG, HAS STAYED BEHIND.

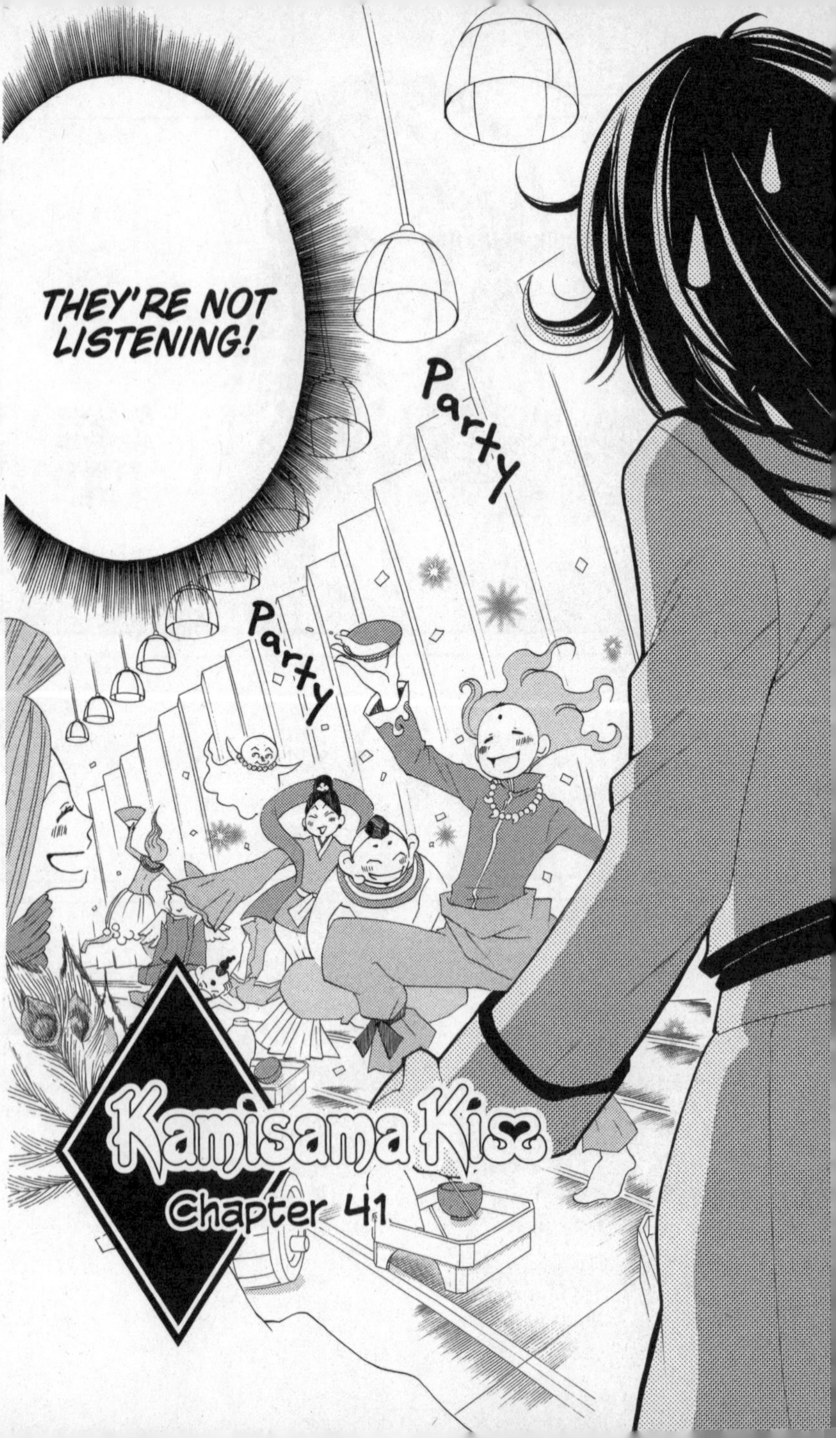
THEY'RE NOT LISTENING!
Party
Party
Kamisama Kiss
Chapter 41

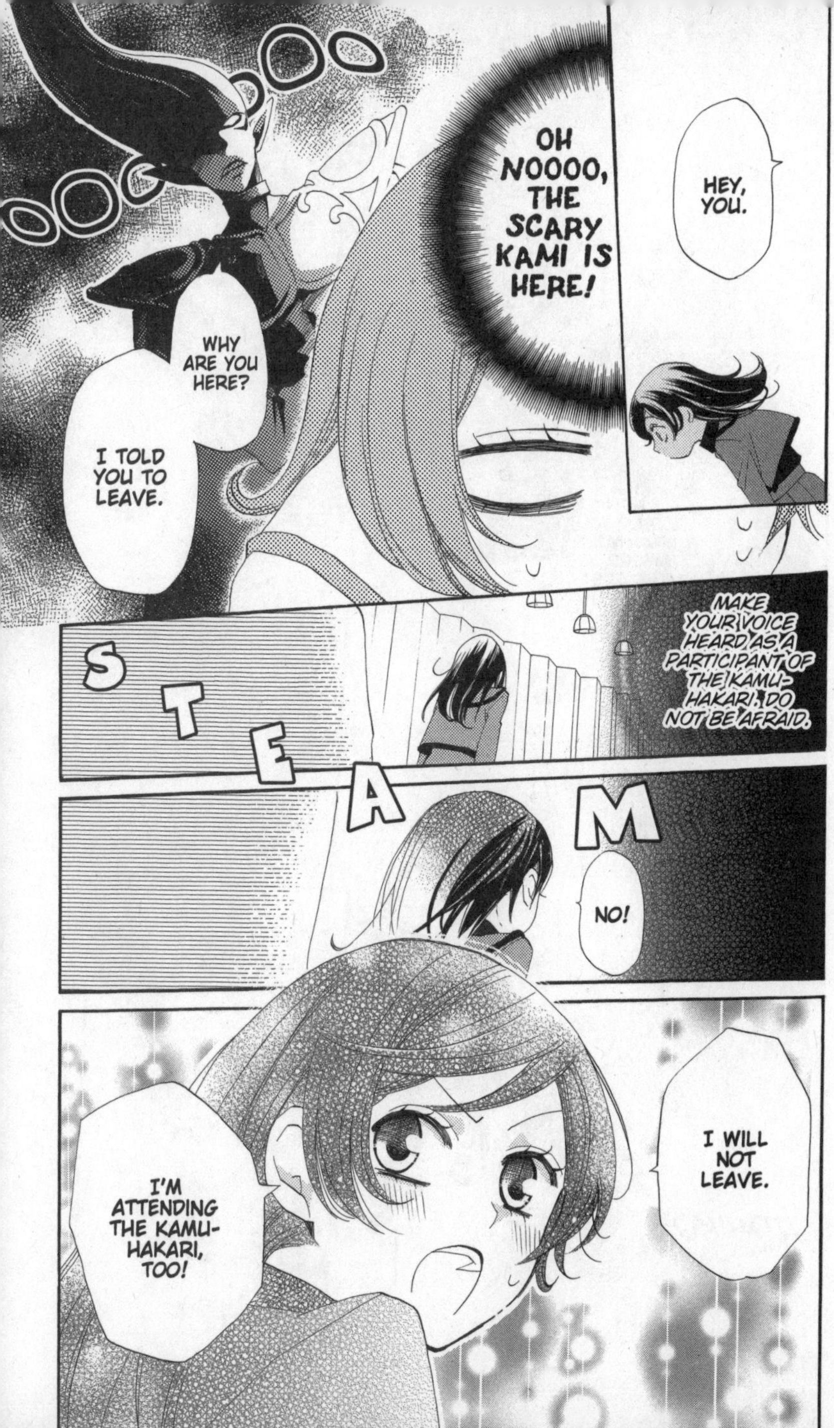
HEY, YOU.
OH NOOOO, THE SCARY KAMI IS HERE!
WHY ARE YOU HERE?
I TOLD YOU TO LEAVE.
MAKE YOUR VOICE HEARD AS A PARTICIPANT OF THE KAMU-HAKARI. DO NOT BE AFRAID.
STEAM
NO!
I WILL NOT LEAVE.
I'M ATTENDING THE KAMU-HAKARI, TOO!

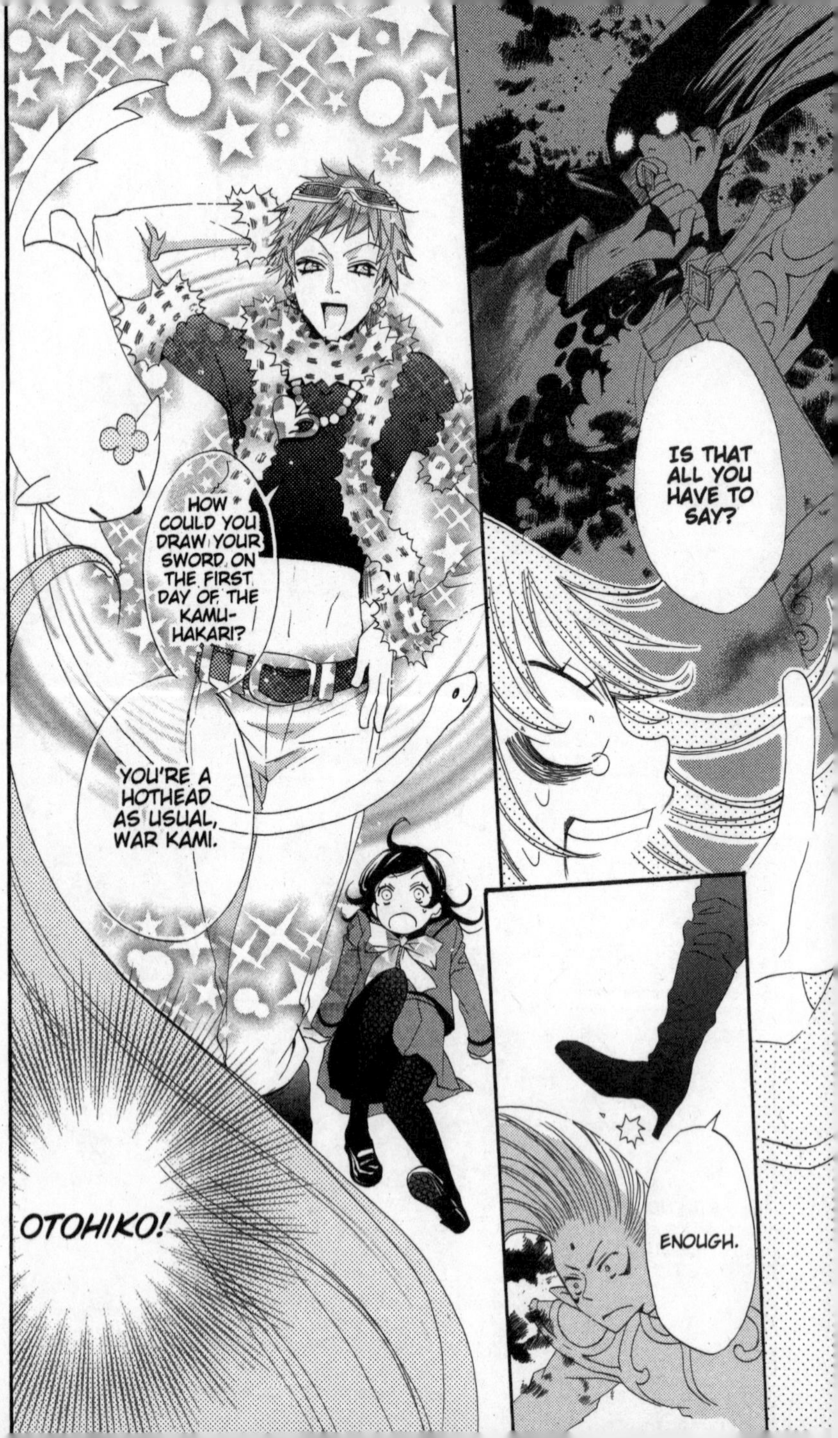
IS THAT ALL YOU HAVE TO SAY?
ENOUGH.
HOW COULD YOU DRAW YOUR SWORD ON THE FIRST DAY OF THE KAMU-HAKARI?
YOU'RE A HOTHEAD AS USUAL, WAR KAMI.
OTOHIKO!

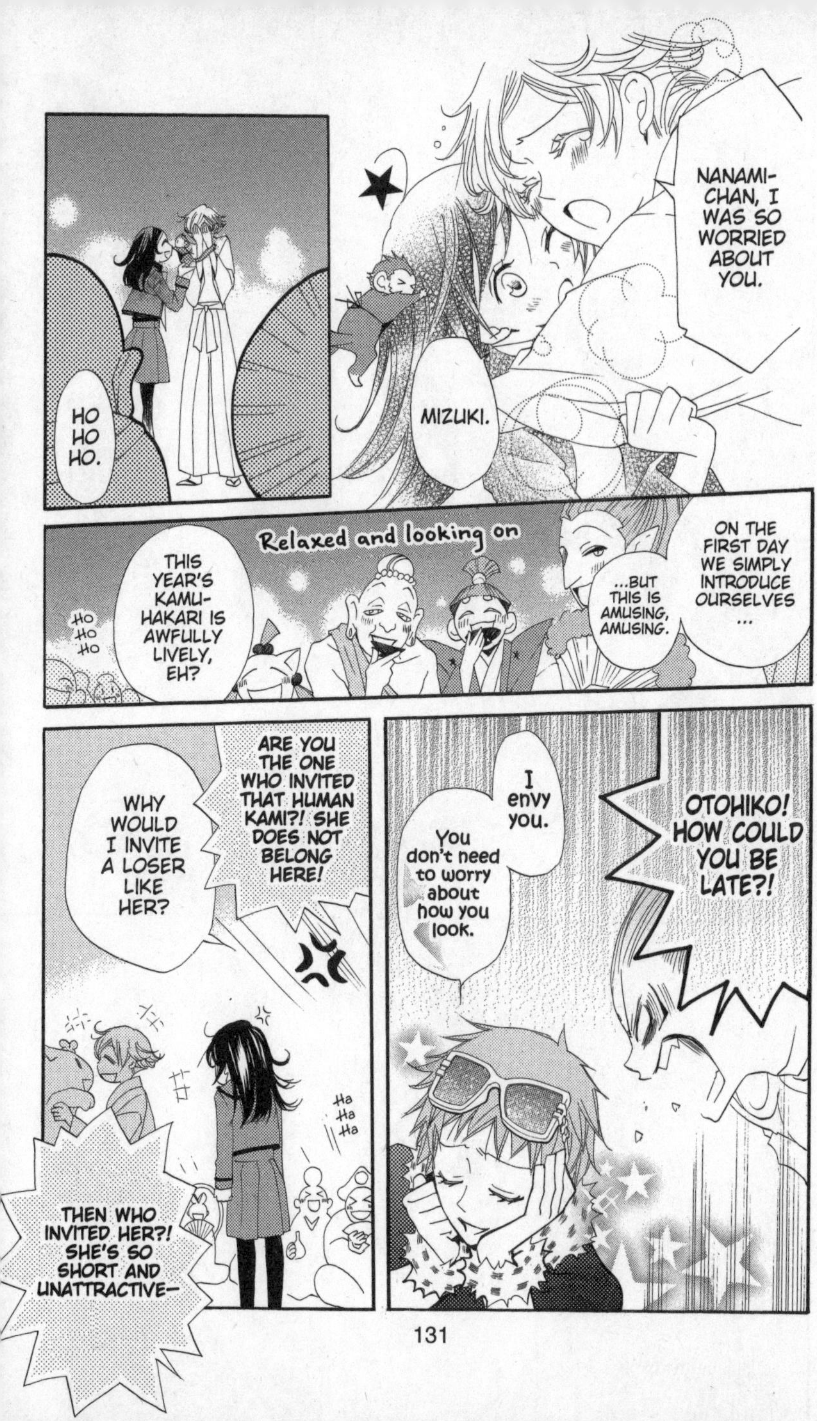
NANAMI-CHAN, I WAS SO WORRIED ABOUT YOU.
MIZUKI.
HO HO HO.
Relaxed and looking on
ON THE FIRST DAY WE SIMPLY INTRODUCE OURSELVES ...
...BUT THIS IS AMUSING, AMUSING.
THIS YEAR'S KAMU-HAKARI IS AWFULLY LIVELY, EH?
HO HO HO
OTOHIKO! HOW COULD YOU BE LATE?!
I envy you.
You don't need to worry about how you look.
ARE YOU THE ONE WHO INVITED THAT HUMAN KAMI?! SHE DOES NOT BELONG HERE!
WHY WOULD I INVITE A LOSER LIKE HER?
Ha Ha Ha
THEN WHO INVITED HER?! SHE'S SO SHORT AND UNATTRACTIVE—

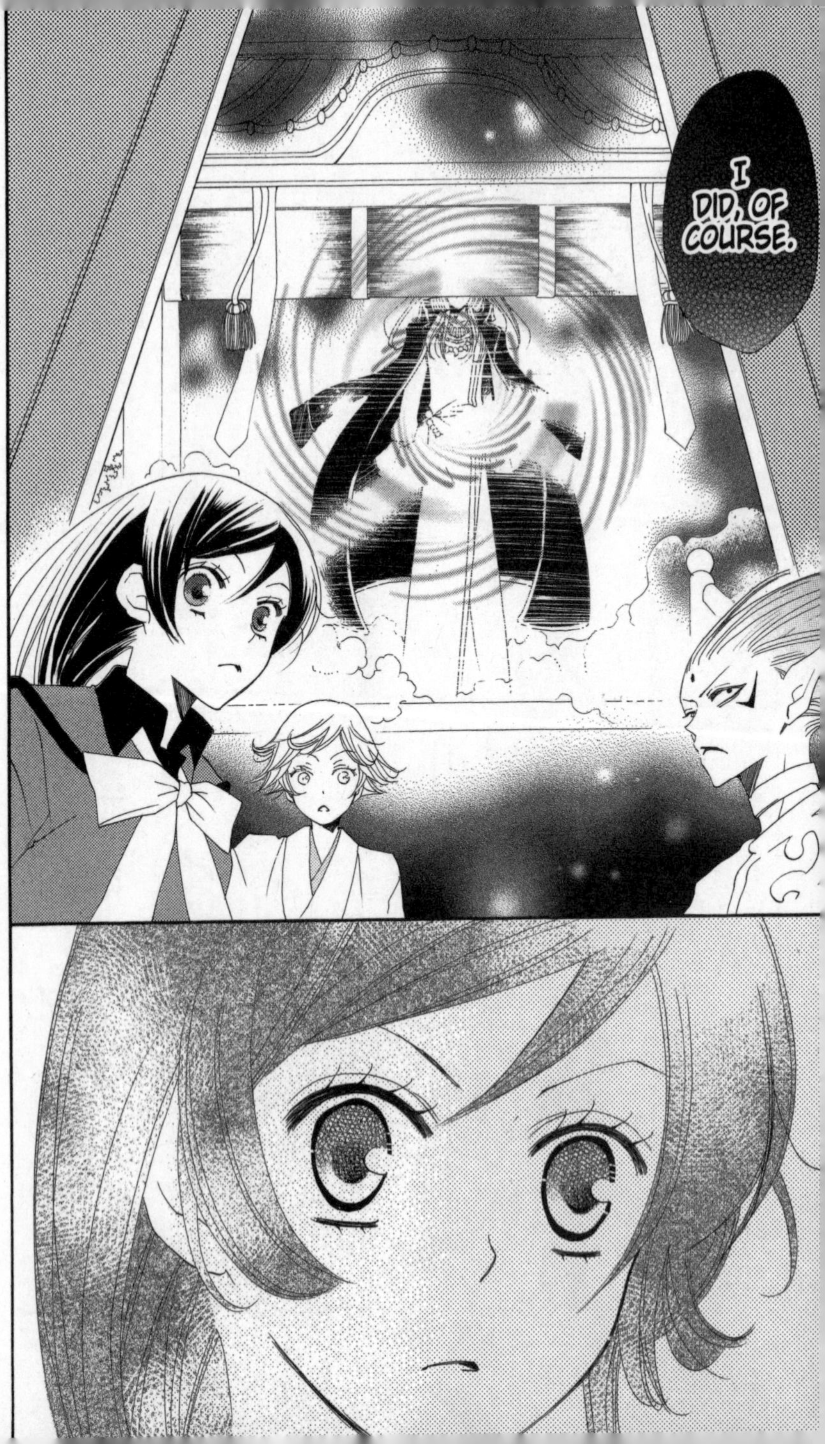
I DID, OF COURSE.

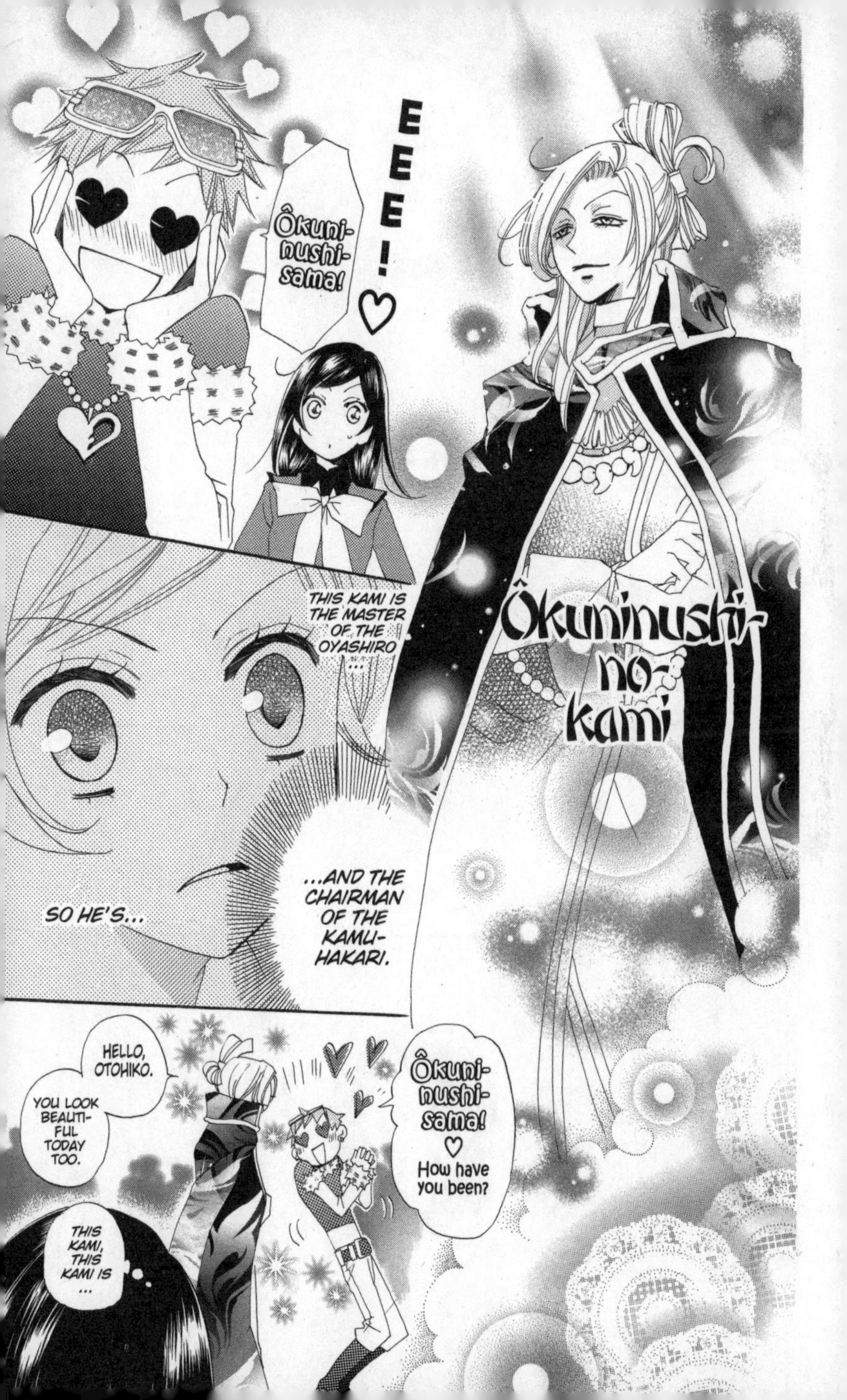
Ôkuninushi-no-kami
EEE! ♡
Ôkuni-nushi-sama!
THIS KAMI IS THE MASTER OF THE OYASHIRO...
...AND THE CHAIRMAN OF THE KAMU-HAKARI.
SO HE'S...
Ôkuni-nushi-sama! ♡ How have you been?
HELLO, OTOHIKO.
YOU LOOK BEAUTI-FUL TODAY TOO.
THIS KAMI, THIS KAMI IS ...

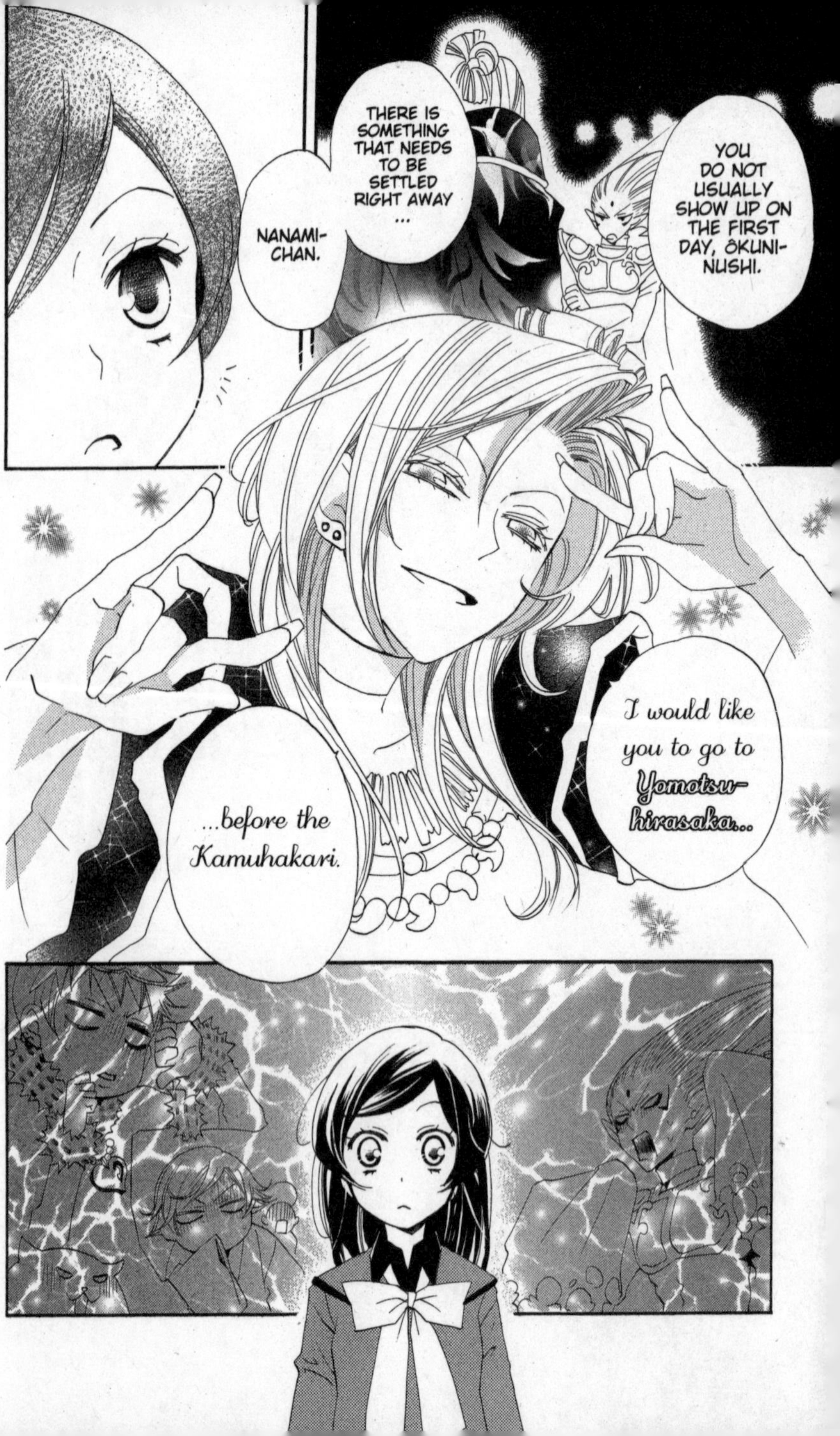
YOU DO NOT USUALLY SHOW UP ON THE FIRST DAY, ŌKUNI-NUSHI.
THERE IS SOMETHING THAT NEEDS TO BE SETTLED RIGHT AWAY ...
NANAMI-CHAN.
I would like you to go to Yomotsu-hirasaka...
...before the Kamuhakari.

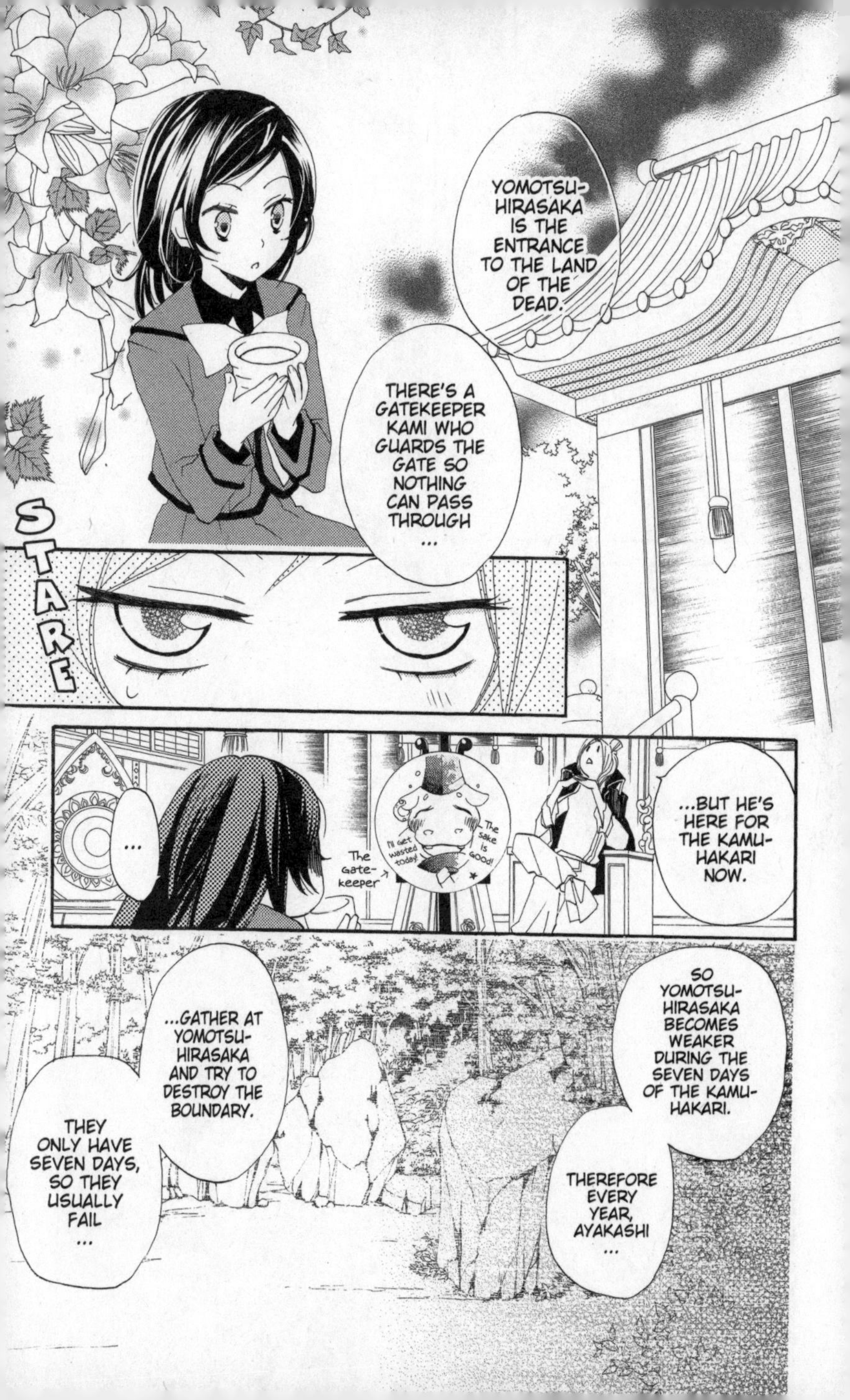
YOMOTSU-HIRASAKA IS THE ENTRANCE TO THE LAND OF THE DEAD.
THERE'S A GATEKEEPER KAMI WHO GUARDS THE GATE SO NOTHING CAN PASS THROUGH...
STARE
...BUT HE'S HERE FOR THE KAMU-HAKARI NOW.
The sake is good!
I'll get wasted today!
The Gate-keeper
...
SO YOMOTSU-HIRASAKA BECOMES WEAKER DURING THE SEVEN DAYS OF THE KAMU-HAKARI.
THEREFORE EVERY YEAR, AYAKASHI...
...GATHER AT YOMOTSU-HIRASAKA AND TRY TO DESTROY THE BOUNDARY.
THEY ONLY HAVE SEVEN DAYS, SO THEY USUALLY FAIL...

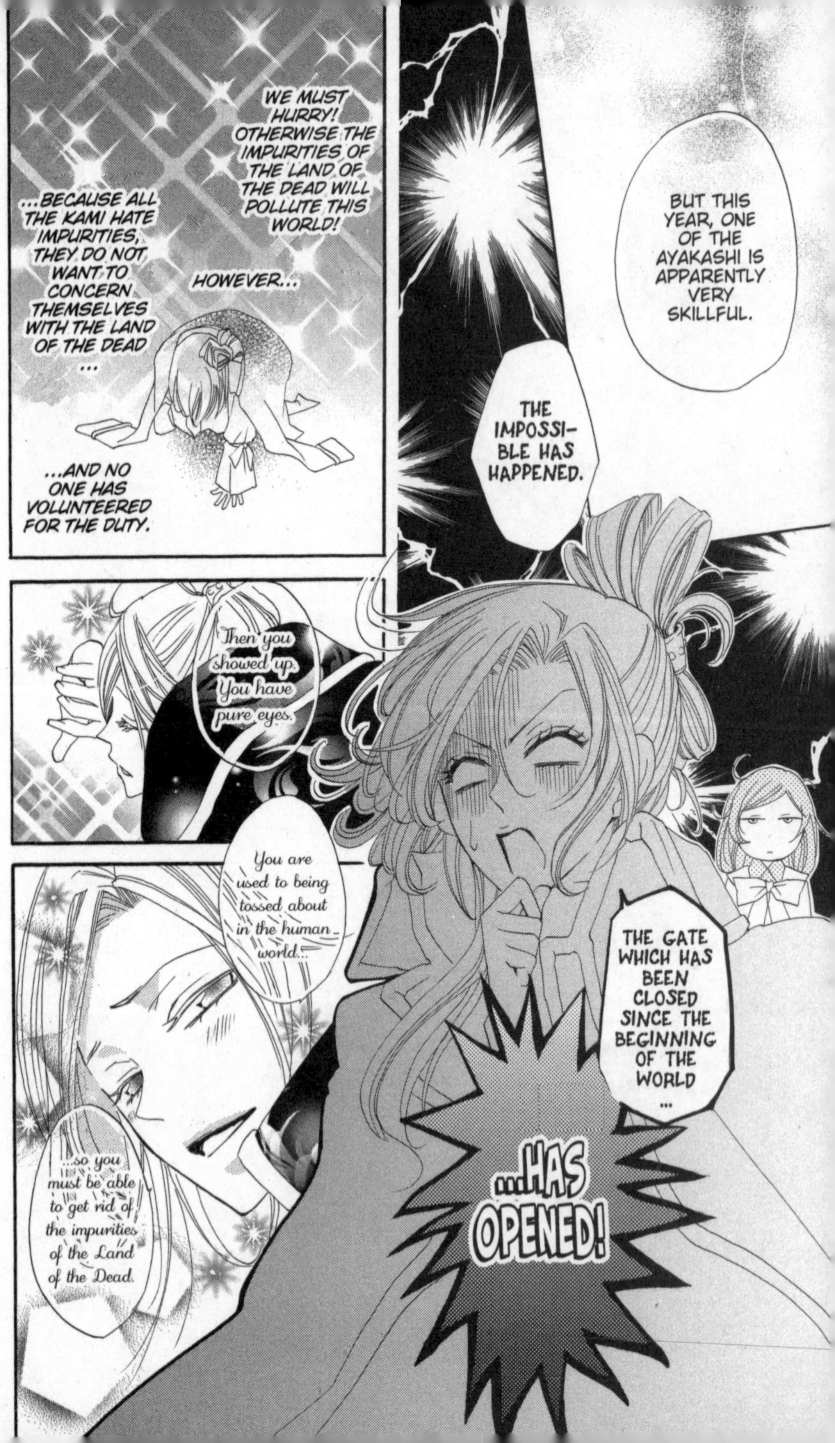
BUT THIS YEAR, ONE OF THE AYAKASHI IS APPARENTLY VERY SKILLFUL.
THE IMPOSSIBLE HAS HAPPENED.
THE GATE WHICH HAS BEEN CLOSED SINCE THE BEGINNING OF THE WORLD...
...HAS OPENED!
WE MUST HURRY! OTHERWISE THE IMPURITIES OF THE LAND OF THE DEAD WILL POLLUTE THIS WORLD!
...BECAUSE ALL THE KAMI HATE IMPURITIES, THEY DO NOT WANT TO CONCERN THEMSELVES WITH THE LAND OF THE DEAD...
HOWEVER...
...AND NO ONE HAS VOLUNTEERED FOR THE DUTY.
Then you showed up. You have pure eyes.
You are used to being tossed about in the human world...
...so you must be able to get rid of the impurities of the Land of the Dead.

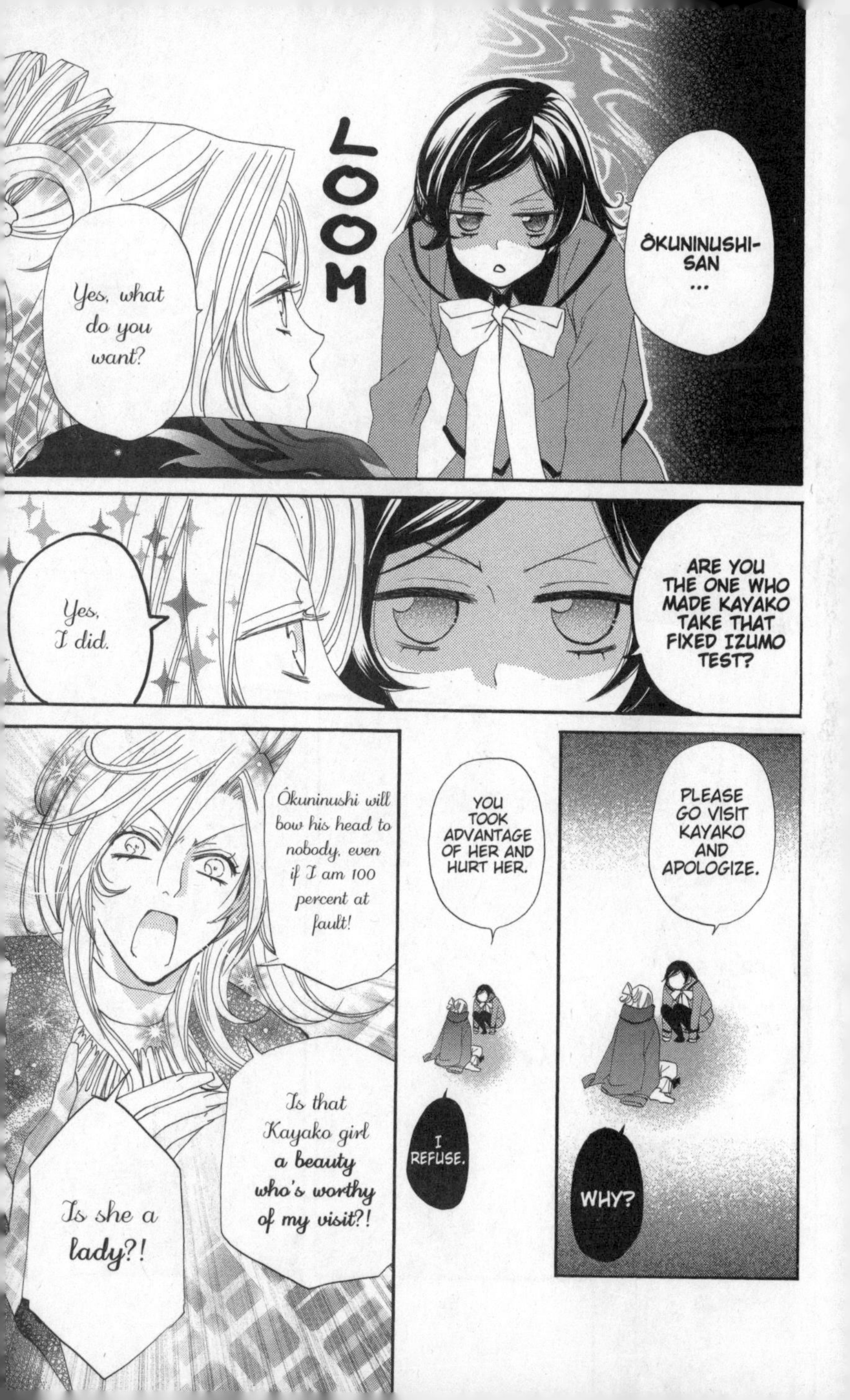
ŌKUNINUSHI-SAN ...
LOOM
Yes, what do you want?
ARE YOU THE ONE WHO MADE KAYAKO TAKE THAT FIXED IZUMO TEST?
Yes, I did.
PLEASE GO VISIT KAYAKO AND APOLOGIZE.
WHY?
YOU TOOK ADVANTAGE OF HER AND HURT HER.
I REFUSE.
Ôkuninushi will bow his head to nobody, even if I am 100 percent at fault!
Is that Kayako girl a beauty who's worthy of my visit?!
Is she a lady?!

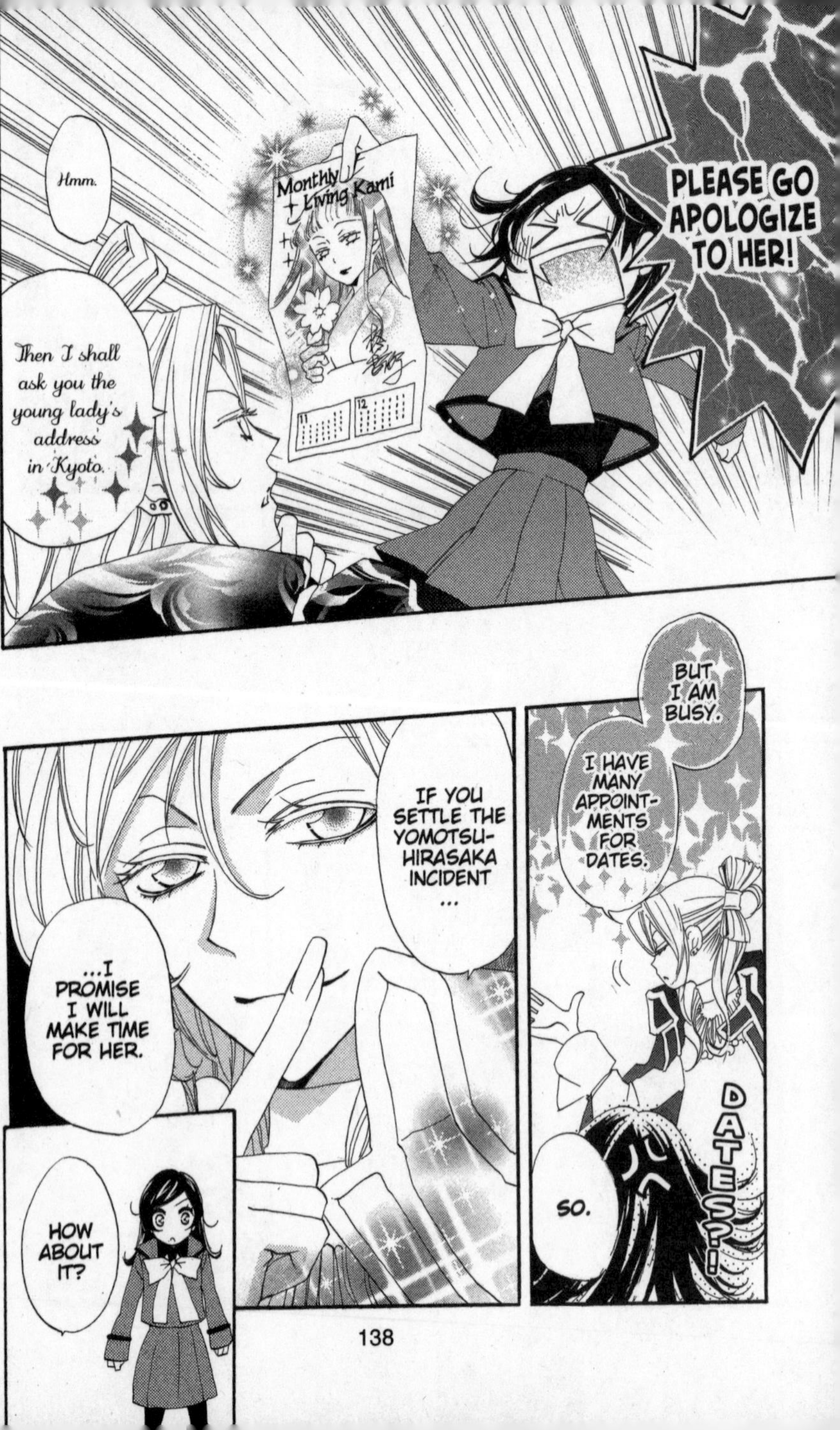

PLEASE GO APOLOGIZE TO HER!
Monthly Living Kami
Hmm.
Then I shall ask you the young lady's address in Kyoto.
BUT I AM BUSY.
I HAVE MANY APPOINTMENTS FOR DATES.
DATES?!
SO.
IF YOU SETTLE THE YOMOTSU-HIRASAKA INCIDENT...
...I PROMISE I WILL MAKE TIME FOR HER.
HOW ABOUT IT?

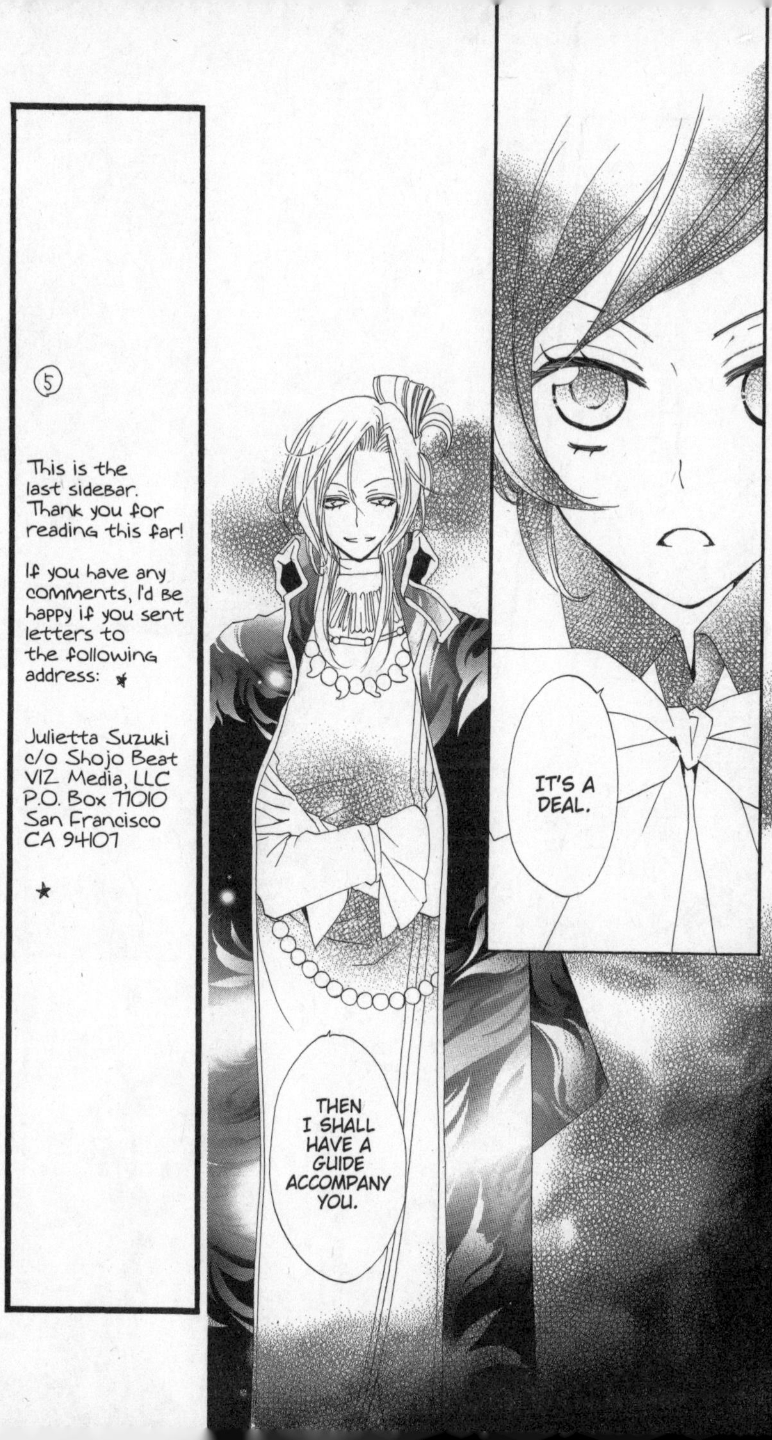
IT'S A DEAL.
THEN I SHALL HAVE A GUIDE ACCOMPANY YOU.

⑤

This is the last sidebar. Thank you for reading this far!

If you have any comments, I'd be happy if you sent letters to the following address: ★

Julietta Suzuki
c/o Shojo Beat
VIZ Media, LLC
P.O. Box 77010
San Francisco
CA 94107

★

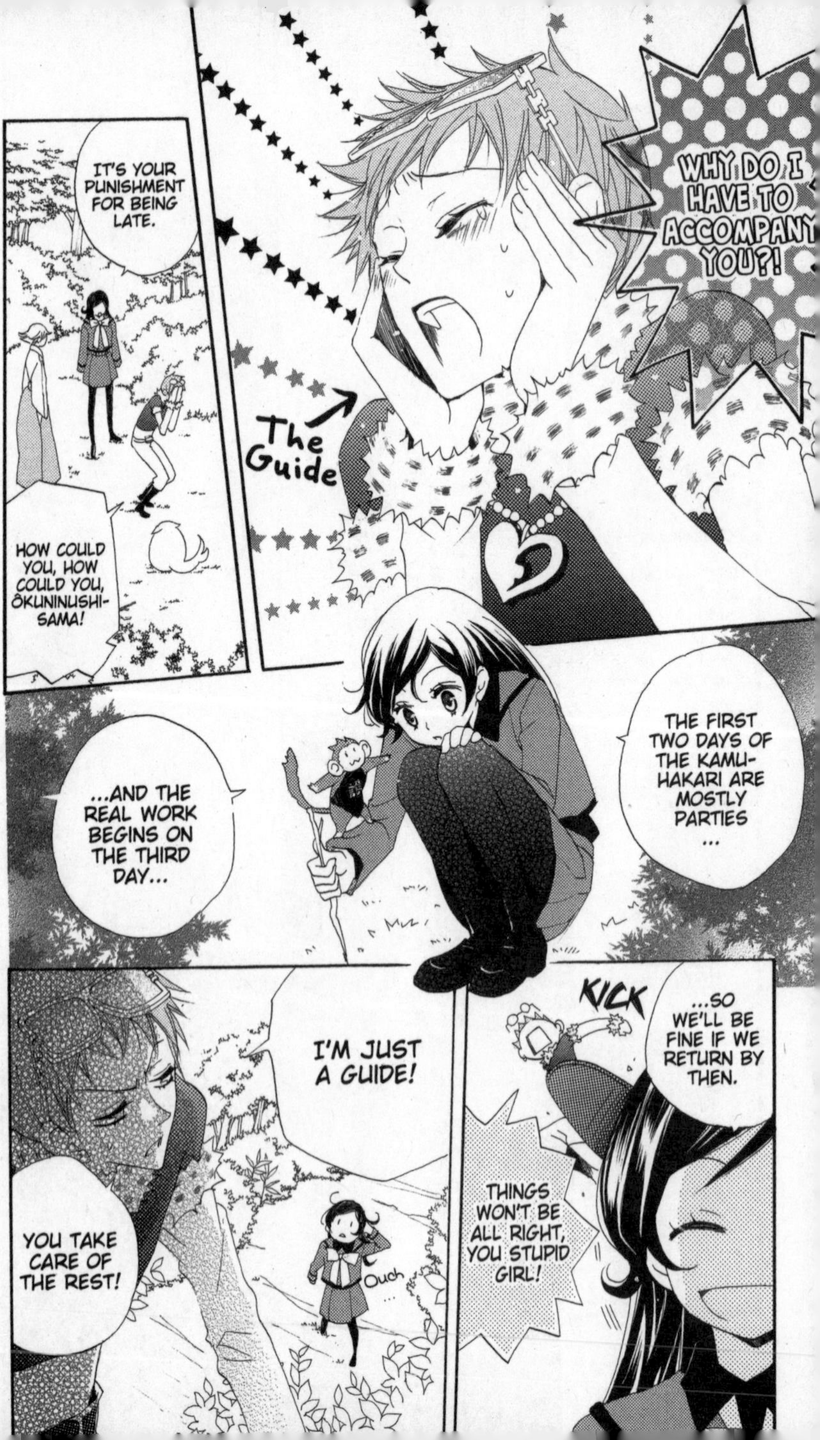
WHY DO I HAVE TO ACCOMPANY YOU?!
The Guide
IT'S YOUR PUNISHMENT FOR BEING LATE.
HOW COULD YOU, HOW COULD YOU, ŌKUNINUSHI-SAMA!
THE FIRST TWO DAYS OF THE KAMU-HAKARI ARE MOSTLY PARTIES ...
...AND THE REAL WORK BEGINS ON THE THIRD DAY...
...SO WE'LL BE FINE IF WE RETURN BY THEN.
KICK
THINGS WON'T BE ALL RIGHT, YOU STUPID GIRL!
I'M JUST A GUIDE!
YOU TAKE CARE OF THE REST!
Ouch ...

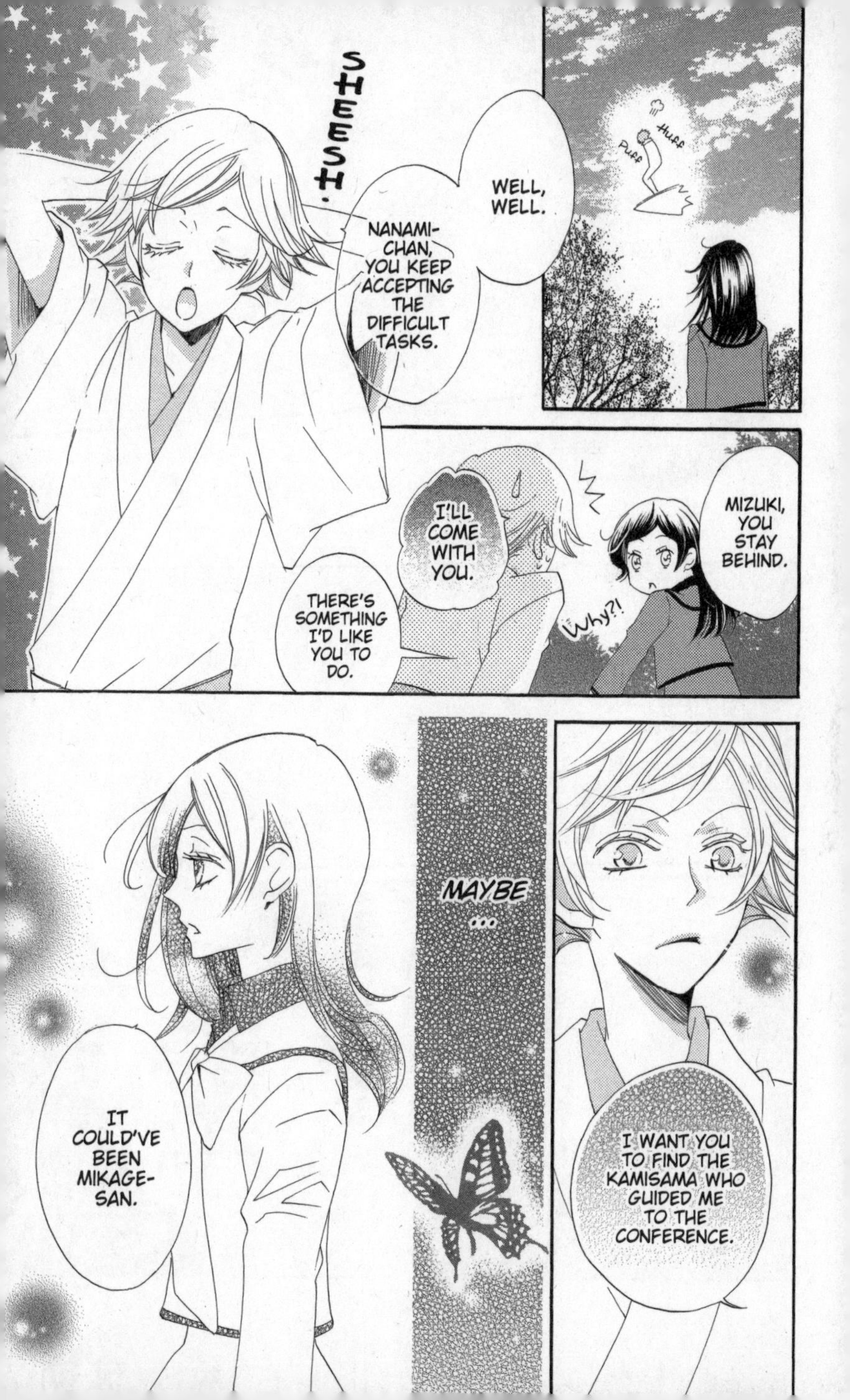
Huff
Puff
WELL, WELL.
NANAMI-CHAN, YOU KEEP ACCEPTING THE DIFFICULT TASKS.
SHEESH.
I'LL COME WITH YOU.
MIZUKI, YOU STAY BEHIND.
Why?!
THERE'S SOMETHING I'D LIKE YOU TO DO.
I WANT YOU TO FIND THE KAMISAMA WHO GUIDED ME TO THE CONFERENCE.
MAYBE...
IT COULD'VE BEEN MIKAGE-SAN.

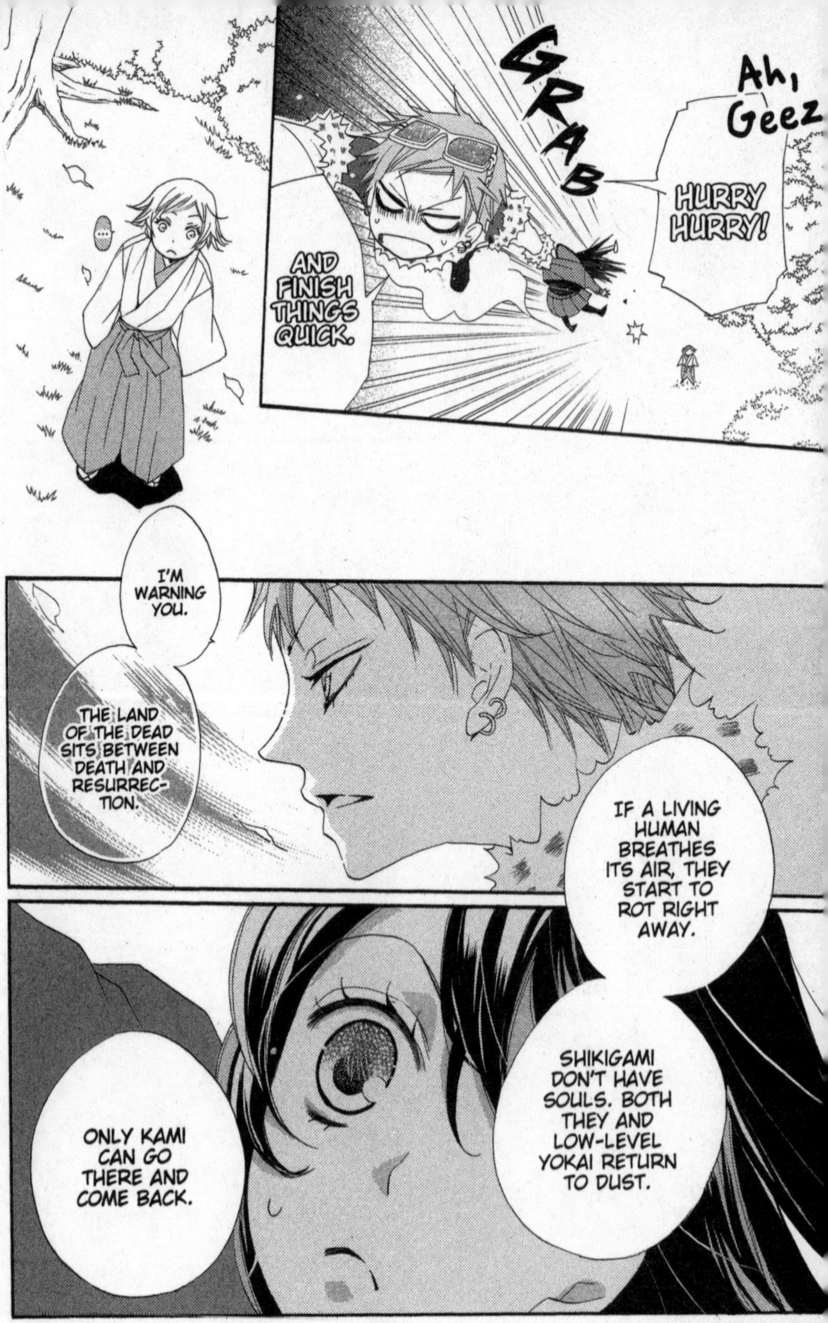
Ah, Geez
GRAB
HURRY HURRY!
AND FINISH THINGS QUICK.
...
I'M WARNING YOU.
THE LAND OF THE DEAD SITS BETWEEN DEATH AND RESURREC-TION.
IF A LIVING HUMAN BREATHES ITS AIR, THEY START TO ROT RIGHT AWAY.
SHIKIGAMI DON'T HAVE SOULS. BOTH THEY AND LOW-LEVEL YOKAI RETURN TO DUST.
ONLY KAMI CAN GO THERE AND COME BACK.

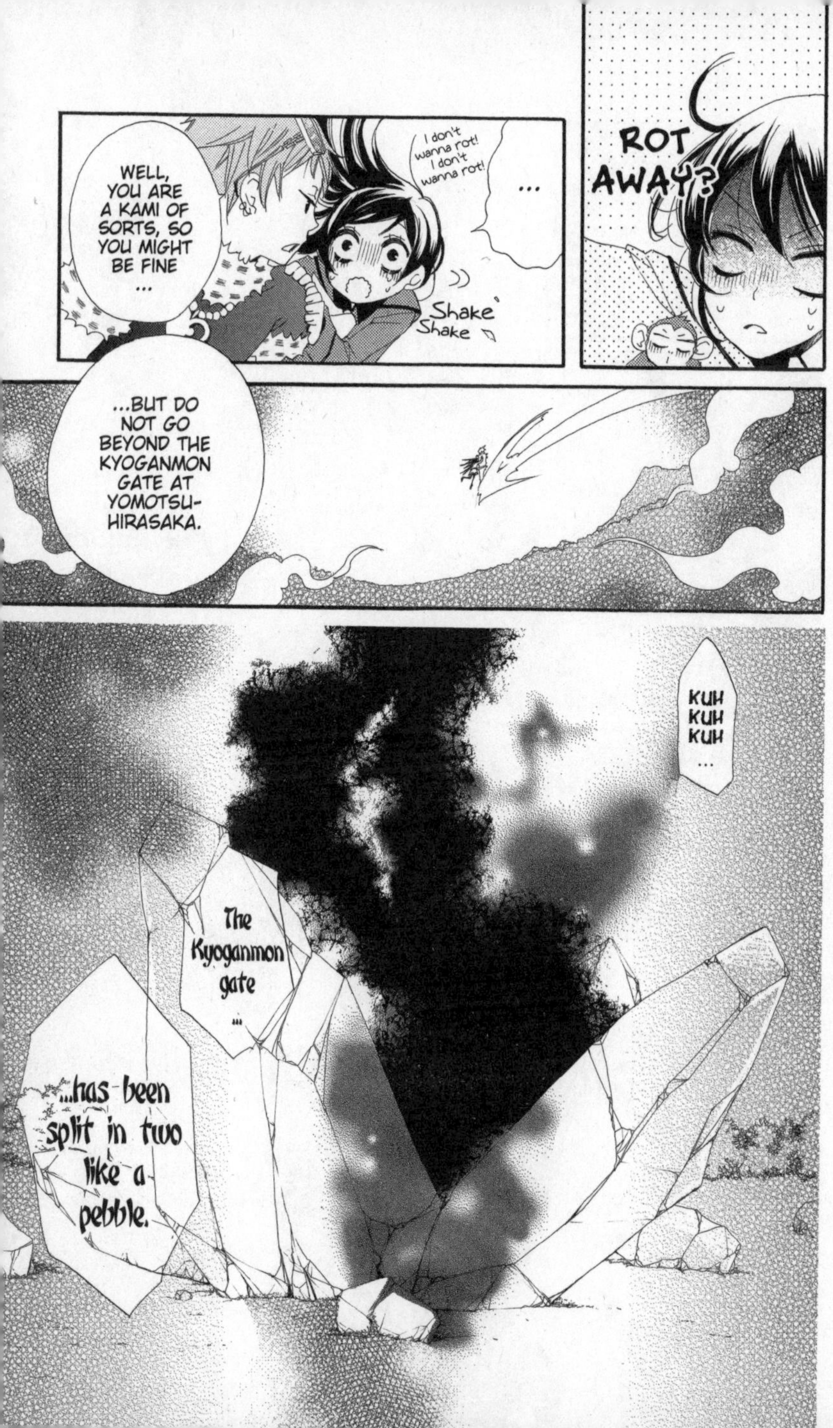
ROT AWAY?
...
I don't wanna rot! I don't wanna rot!
WELL, YOU ARE A KAMI OF SORTS, SO YOU MIGHT BE FINE ...
Shake Shake
...BUT DO NOT GO BEYOND THE KYOGANMON GATE AT YOMOTSU-HIRASAKA.
KUH KUH KUH ...
The Kyoganmon gate ...
...has been split in two like a pebble.

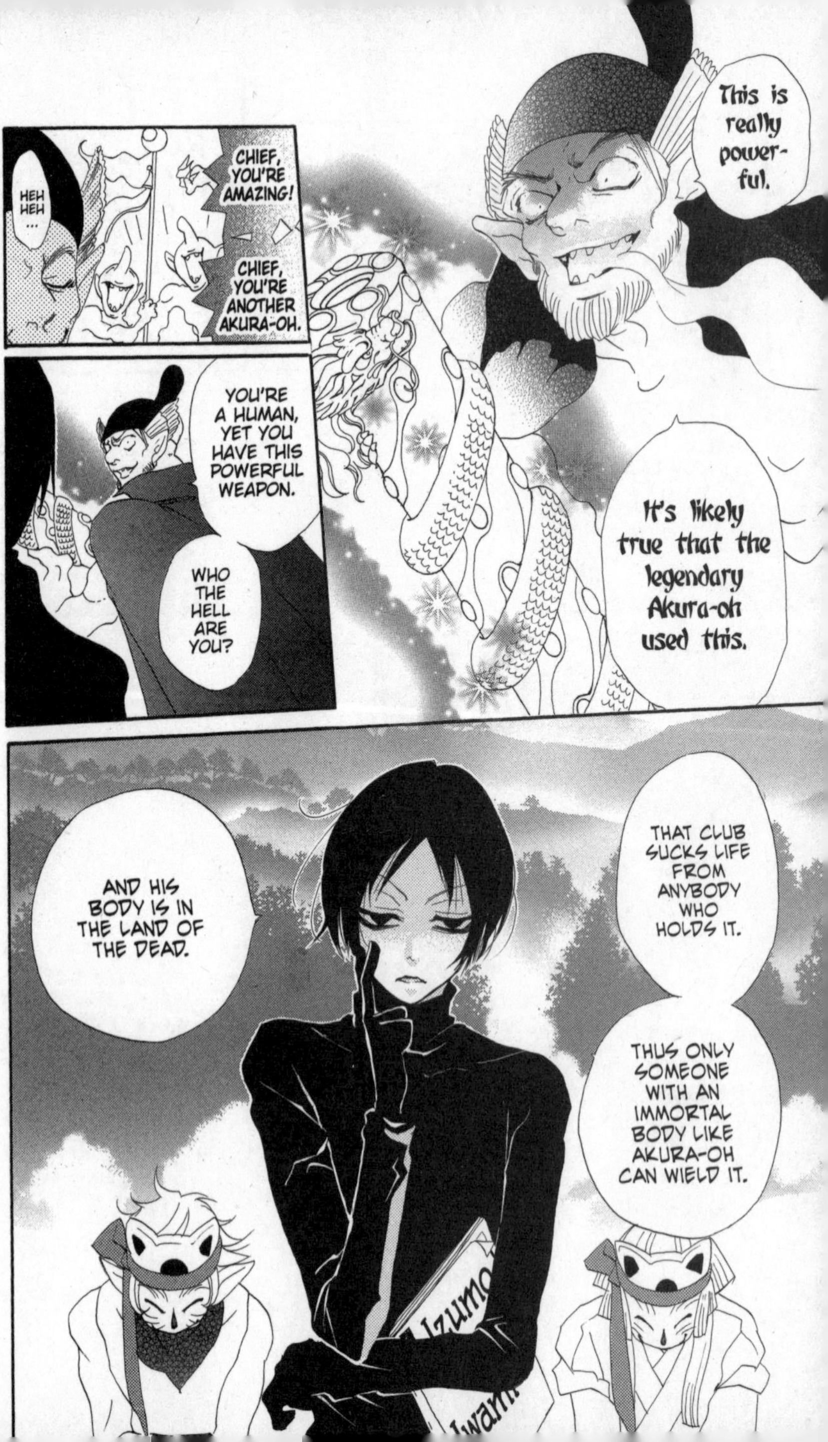
This is really powerful.
It's likely true that the legendary Akura-oh used this.
CHIEF, YOU'RE AMAZING!
CHIEF, YOU'RE ANOTHER AKURA-OH.
HEH HEH ...
YOU'RE A HUMAN, YET YOU HAVE THIS POWERFUL WEAPON.
WHO THE HELL ARE YOU?
THAT CLUB SUCKS LIFE FROM ANYBODY WHO HOLDS IT.
THUS ONLY SOMEONE WITH AN IMMORTAL BODY LIKE AKURA-OH CAN WIELD IT.
AND HIS BODY IS IN THE LAND OF THE DEAD.

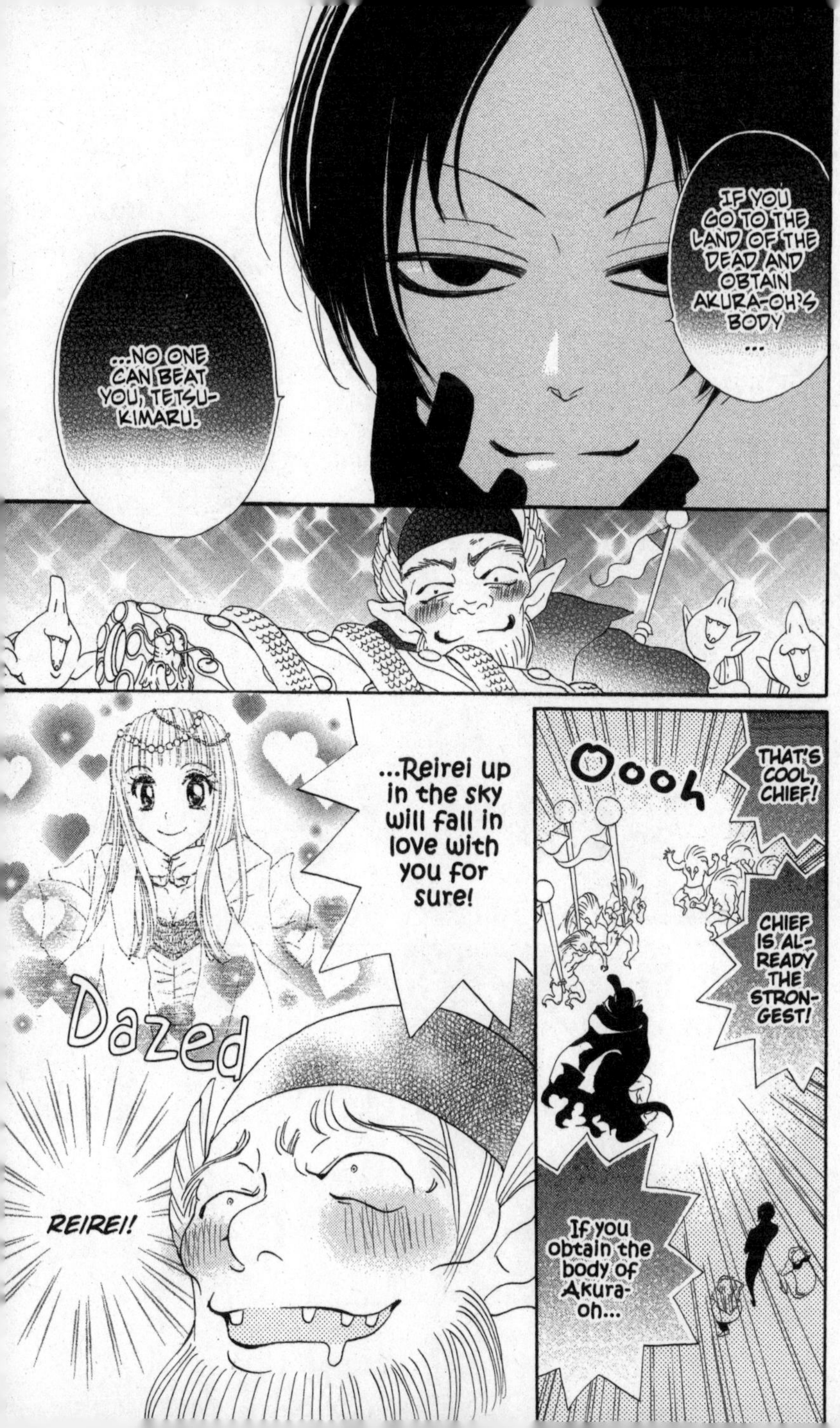
IF YOU GO TO THE LAND OF THE DEAD AND OBTAIN AKURA-OH'S BODY ...
...NO ONE CAN BEAT YOU, TETSU-KIMARU.
Oooh
THAT'S COOL, CHIEF!
CHIEF IS AL-READY THE STRON-GEST!
If you obtain the body of Akura-oh...
...Reirei up in the sky will fall in love with you for sure!
Dazed
REIREI!

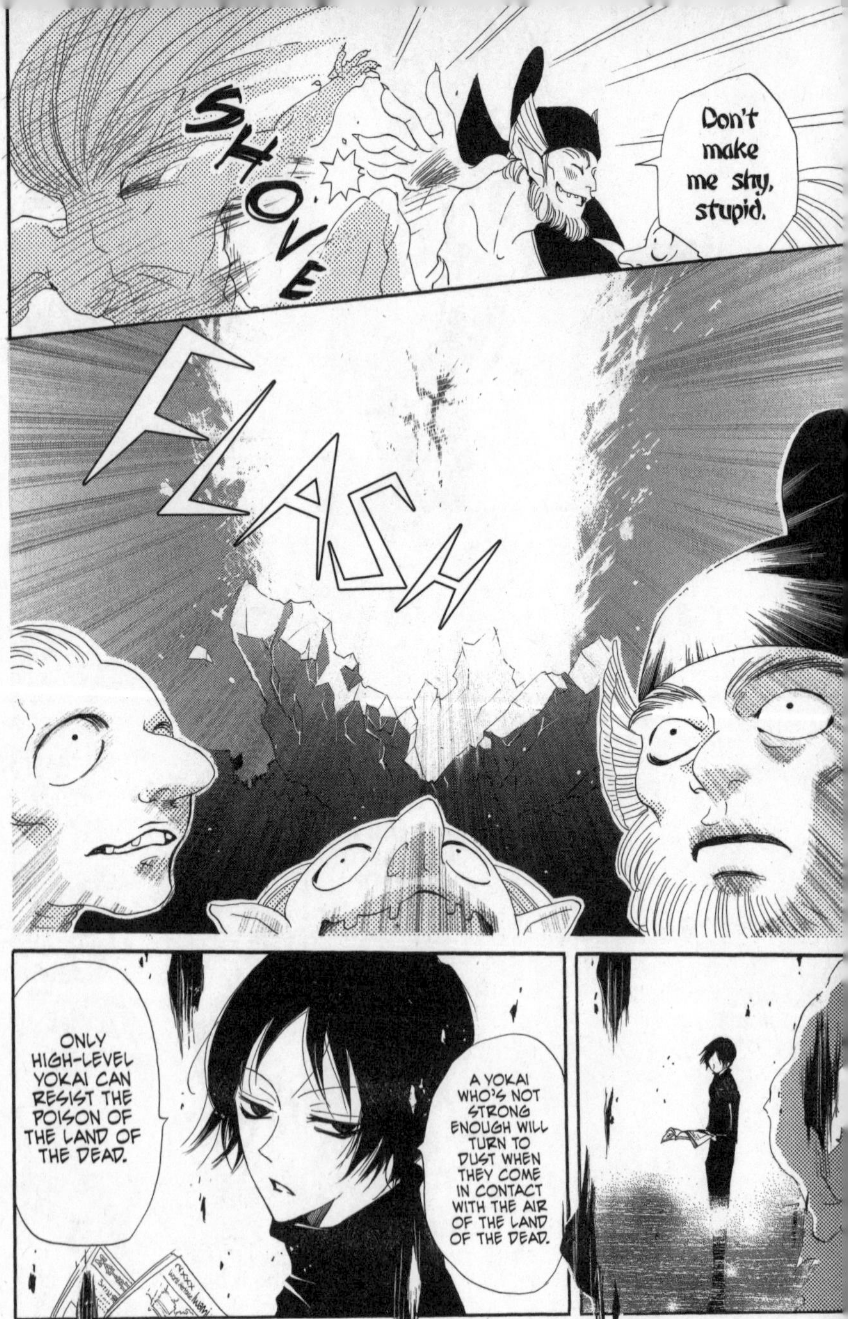

Don't make me shy, stupid.
SHOVE
FLASH
A YOKAI WHO'S NOT STRONG ENOUGH WILL TURN TO DUST WHEN THEY COME IN CONTACT WITH THE AIR OF THE LAND OF THE DEAD.
ONLY HIGH-LEVEL YOKAI CAN RESIST THE POISON OF THE LAND OF THE DEAD.

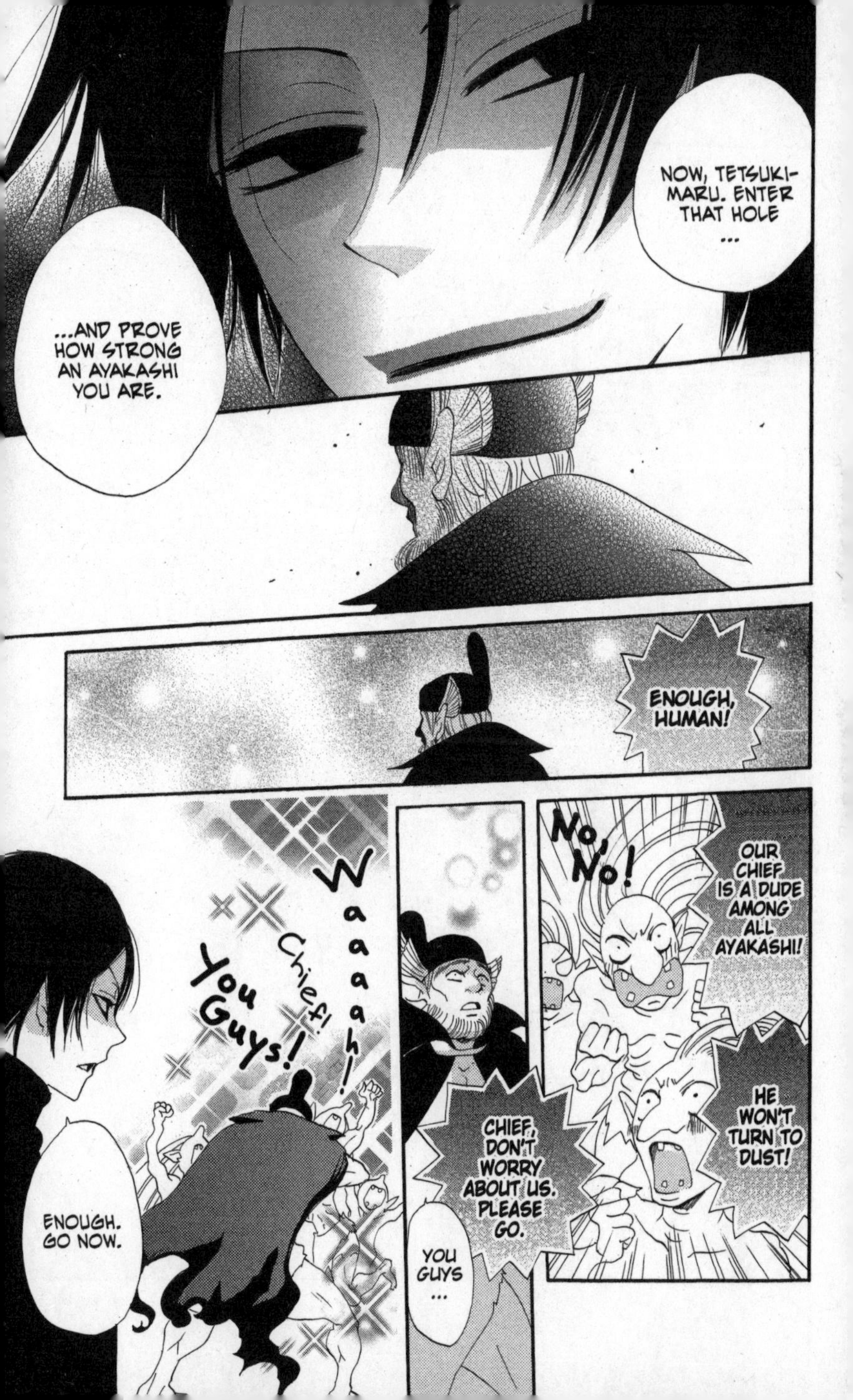
NOW, TETSUKI-MARU. ENTER THAT HOLE ...
...AND PROVE HOW STRONG AN AYAKASHI YOU ARE.
ENOUGH, HUMAN!
No, No!
OUR CHIEF IS A DUDE AMONG ALL AYAKASHI!
HE WON'T TURN TO DUST!
CHIEF, DON'T WORRY ABOUT US. PLEASE GO.
YOU GUYS ...
Waaaah!
Chief!
You Guys!
ENOUGH. GO NOW.

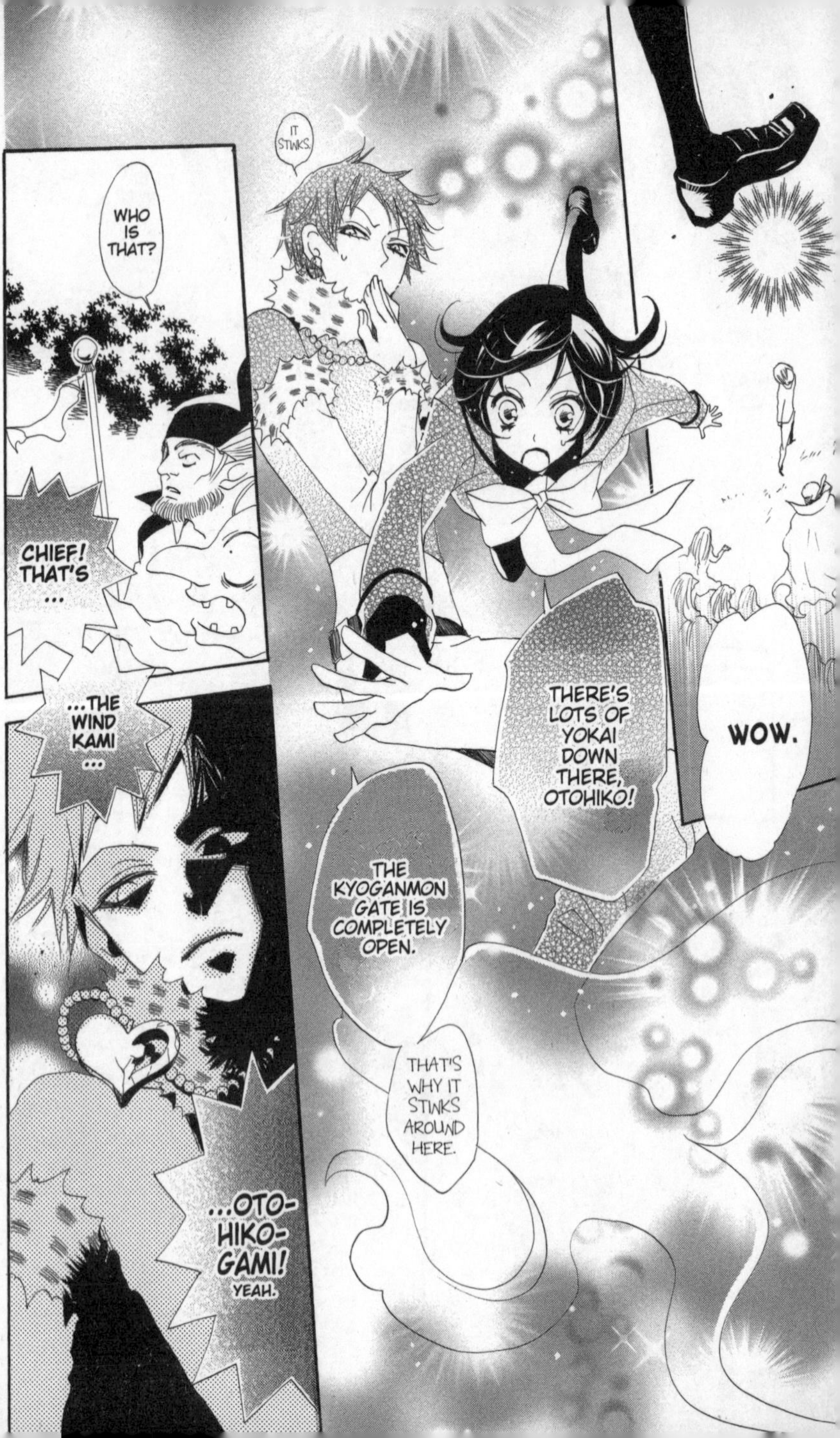
IT STINKS.
WOW.
THERE'S LOTS OF YOKAI DOWN THERE, OTOHIKO!
THE KYOGANMON GATE IS COMPLETELY OPEN.
THAT'S WHY IT STINKS AROUND HERE.
WHO IS THAT?
CHIEF! THAT'S...
...THE WIND KAMI...
...OTO-HIKO-GAMI!
YEAH.

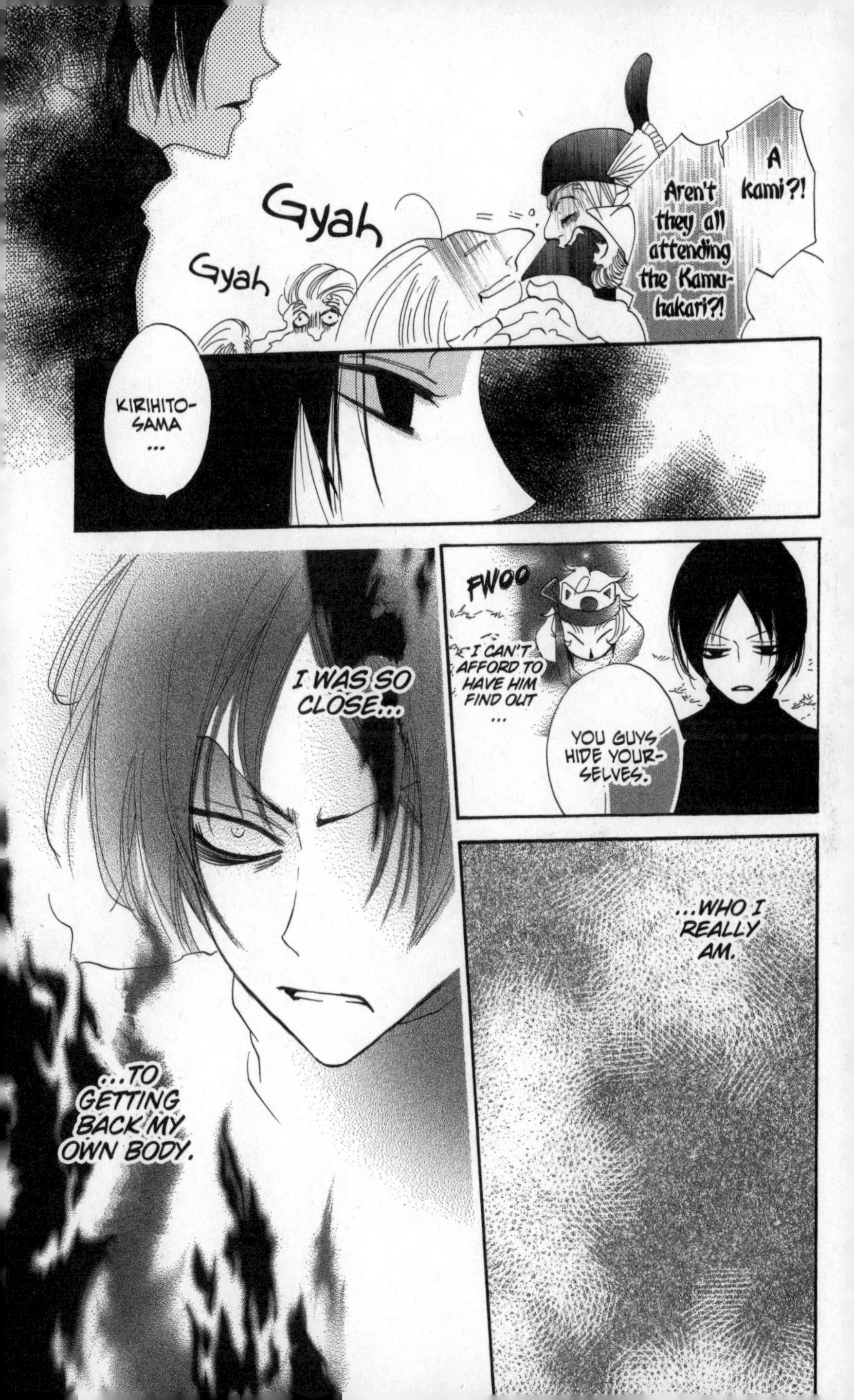
A kami?!
Aren't they all attending the Kamu-hakari?!
Gyah
Gyah
Kirihito-sama ...
FWOO
YOU GUYS HIDE YOUR-SELVES.
I CAN'T AFFORD TO HAVE HIM FIND OUT ...
...WHO I REALLY AM.
I WAS SO CLOSE...
...TO GETTING BACK MY OWN BODY.

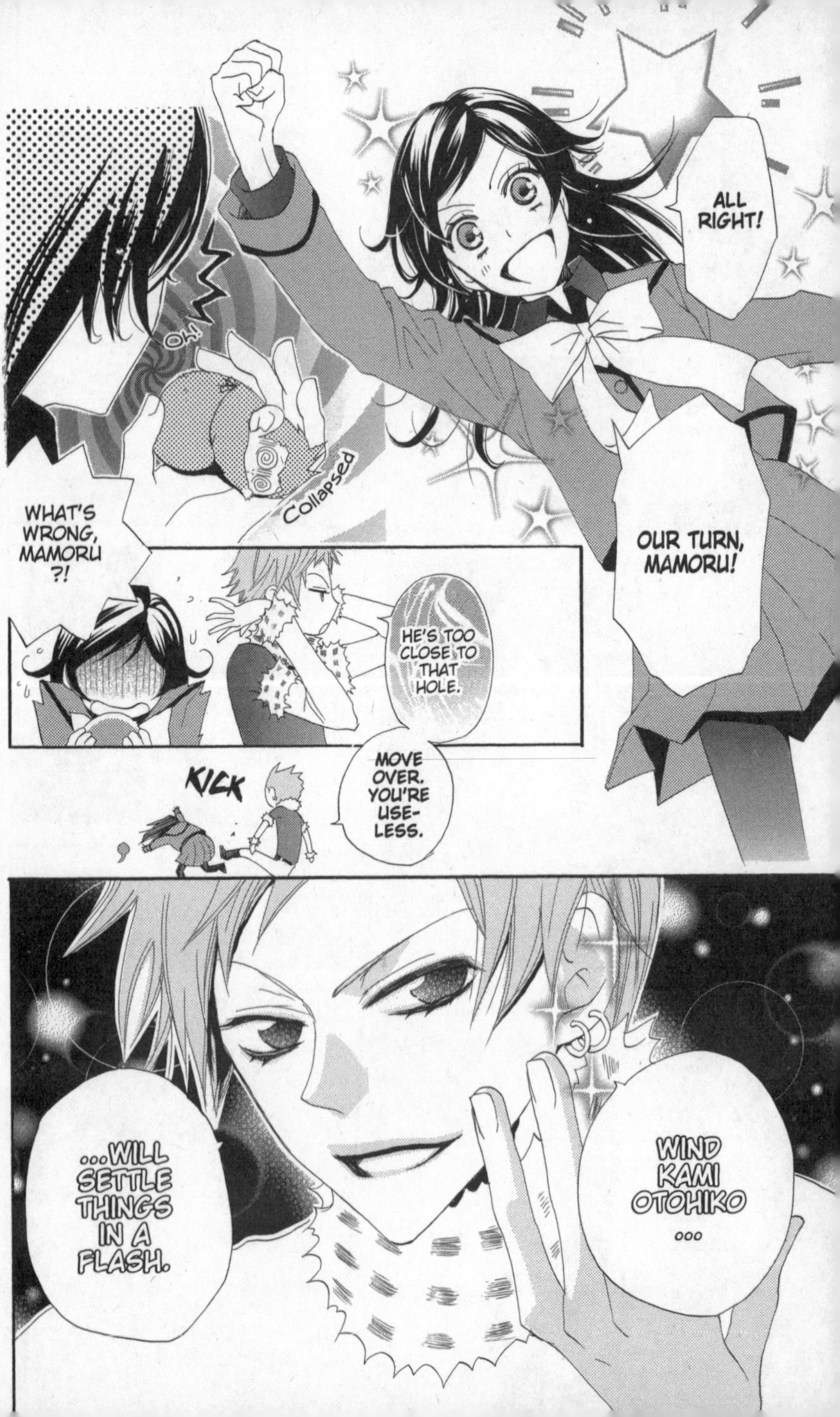
ALL RIGHT!
OUR TURN, MAMORU!
Oh!
Collapsed
WHAT'S WRONG, MAMORU?!
HE'S TOO CLOSE TO THAT HOLE.
MOVE OVER. YOU'RE USELESS.
KICK
WIND KAMI OTOHIKO...
...WILL SETTLE THINGS IN A FLASH.

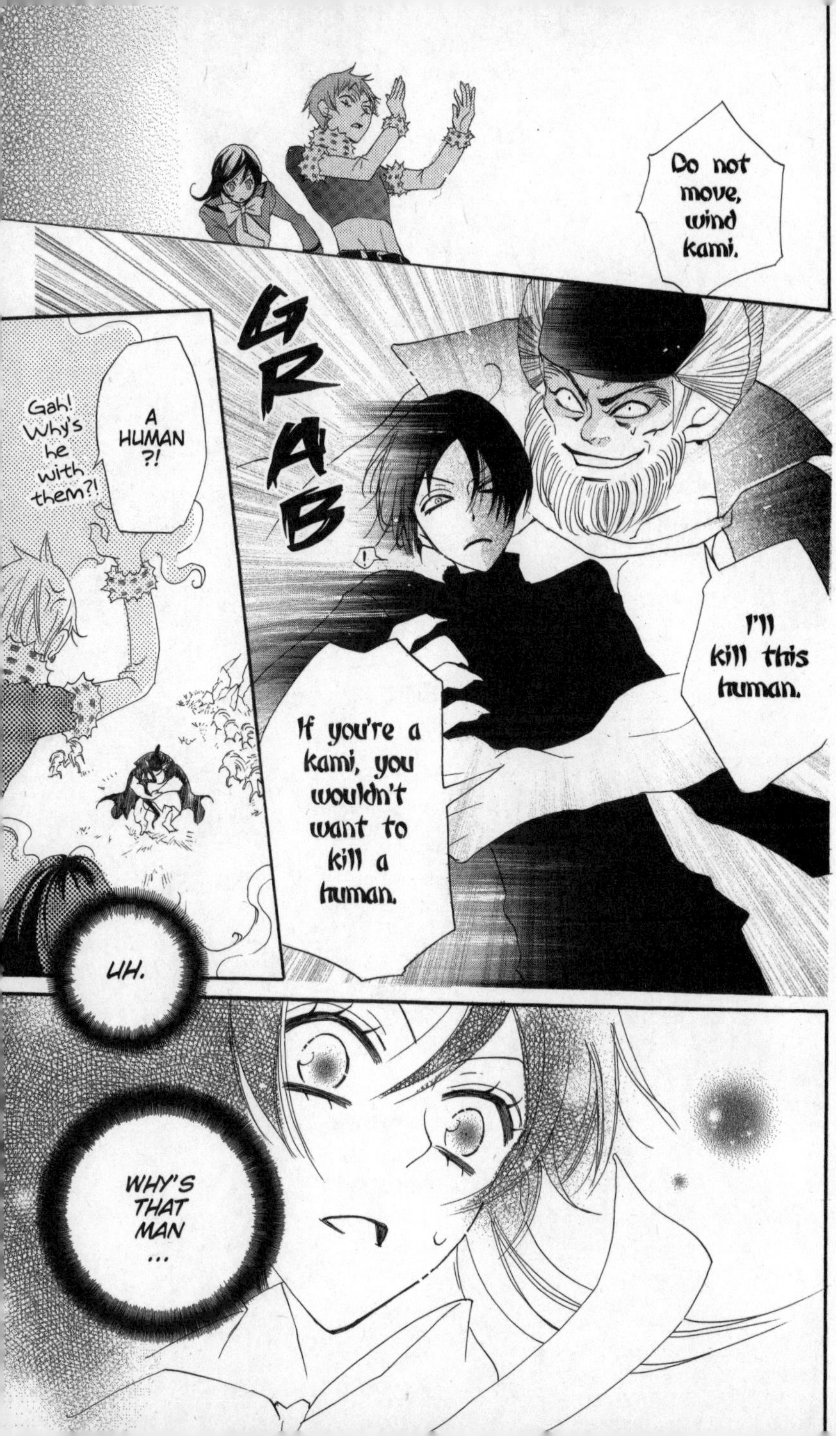
Do not move, wind kami.
GRAB
I'll kill this human.
If you're a kami, you wouldn't want to kill a human.
!
A HUMAN?!
Gah! Why's he with them?!
UH.
WHY'S THAT MAN ...

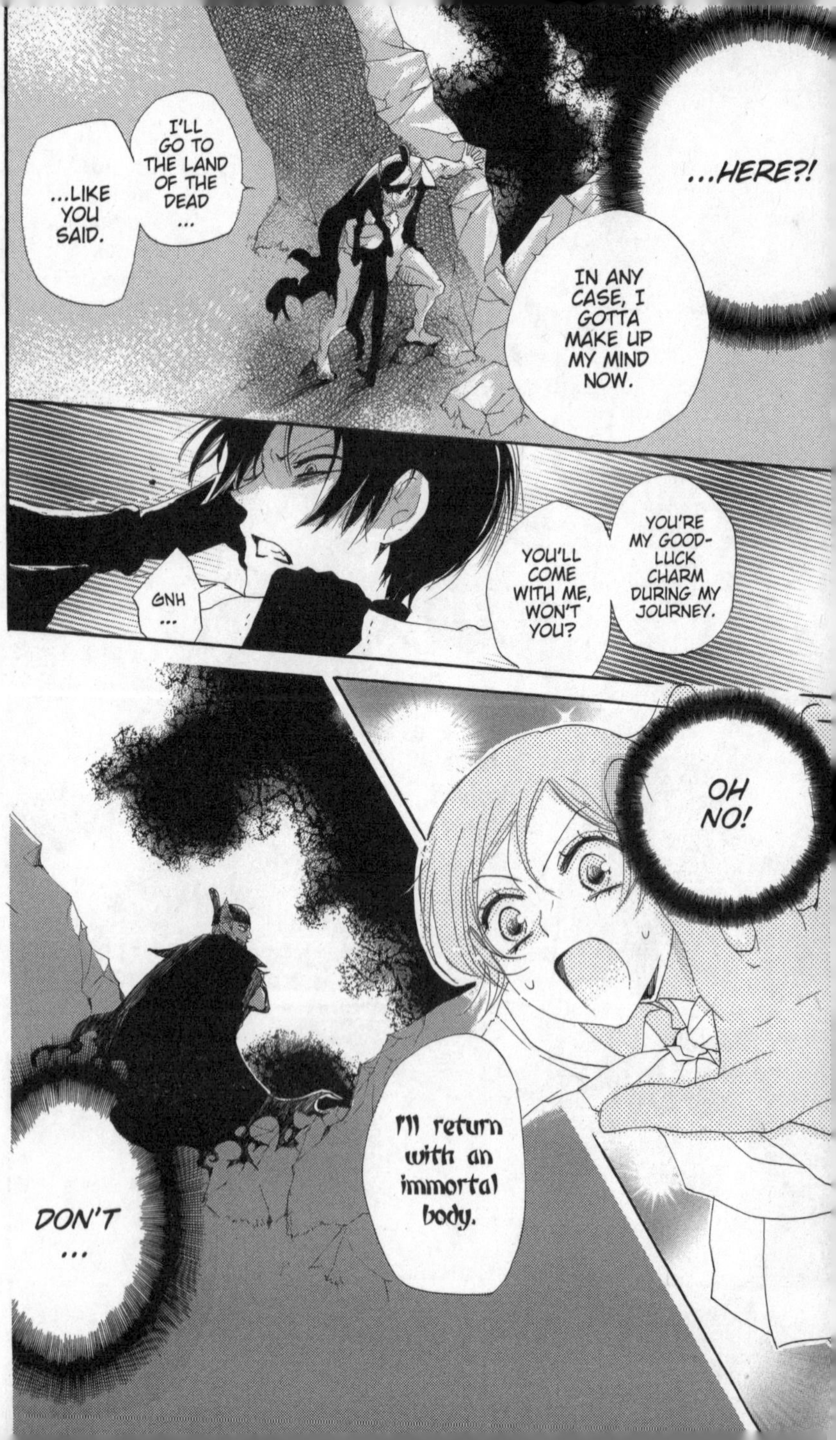
...HERE?!
IN ANY CASE, I GOTTA MAKE UP MY MIND NOW.
I'LL GO TO THE LAND OF THE DEAD...
...LIKE YOU SAID.
YOU'RE MY GOOD-LUCK CHARM DURING MY JOURNEY.
YOU'LL COME WITH ME, WON'T YOU?
GNH...
OH NO!
I'll return with an immortal body.
DON'T...

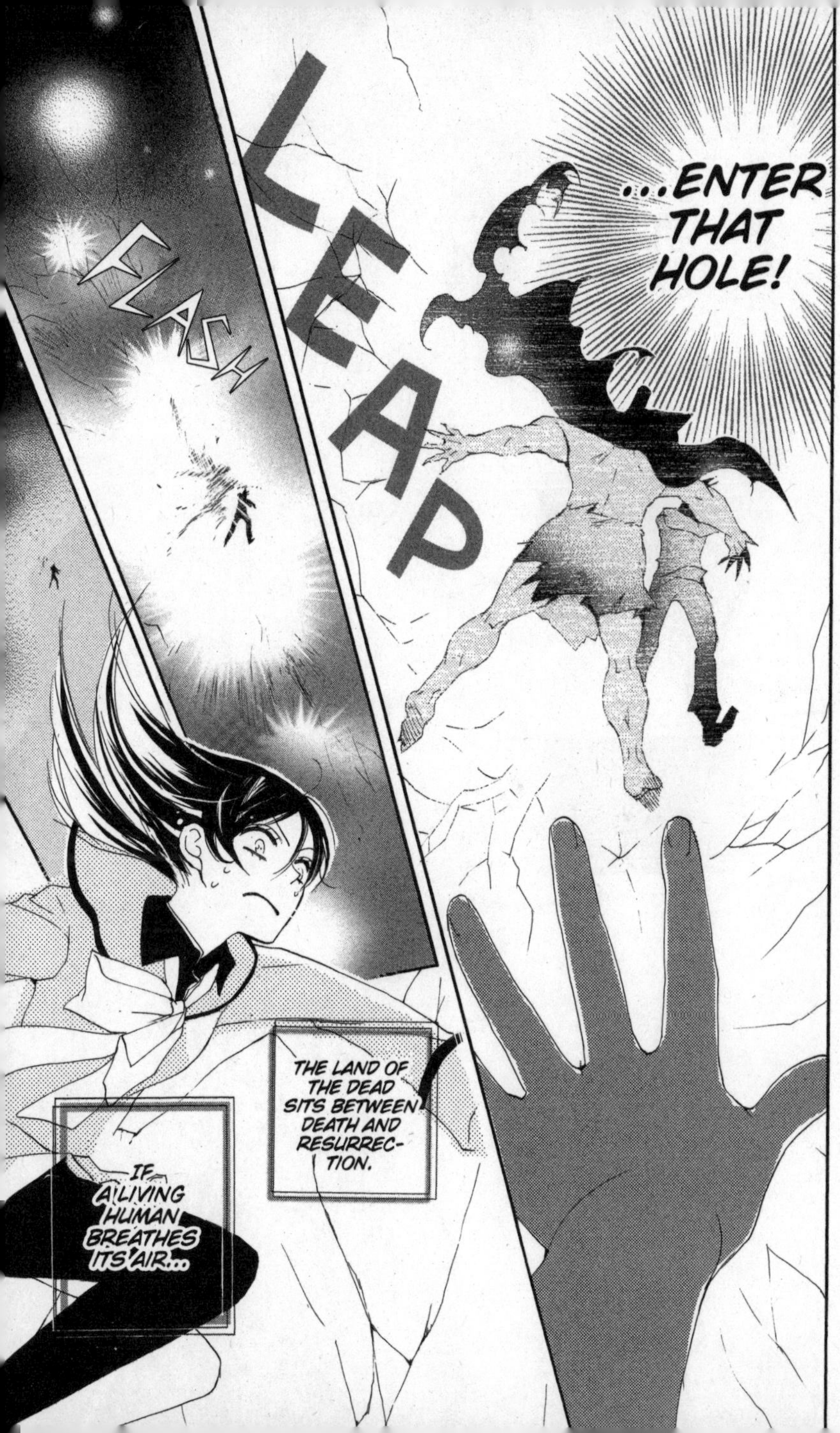
...ENTER THAT HOLE!
LEAP
FLASH
THE LAND OF THE DEAD SITS BETWEEN DEATH AND RESURREC-TION.
IF A LIVING HUMAN BREATHES ITS AIR...

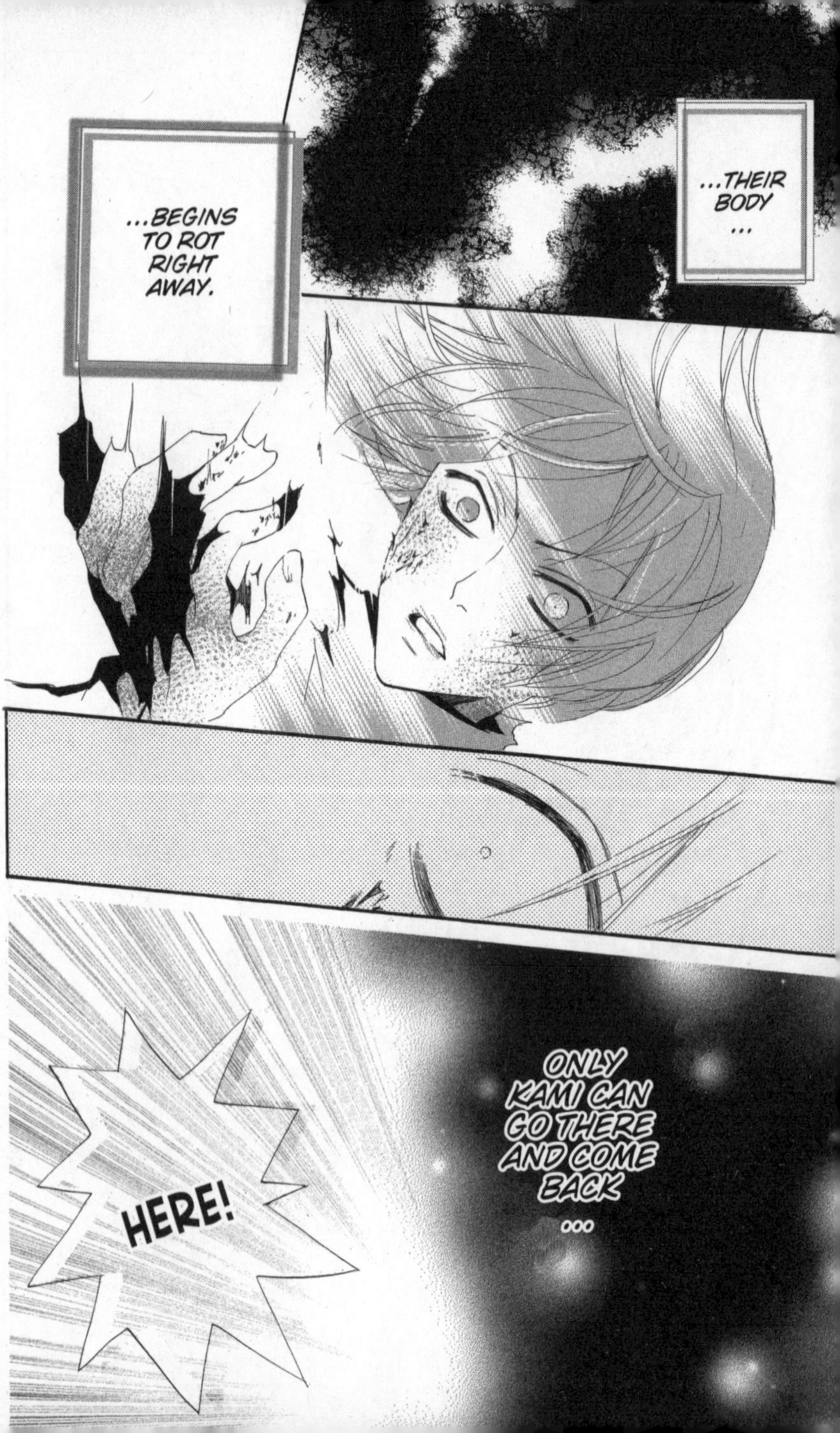
...THEIR BODY ...
...BEGINS TO ROT RIGHT AWAY.
ONLY KAMI CAN GO THERE AND COME BACK ...
HERE!

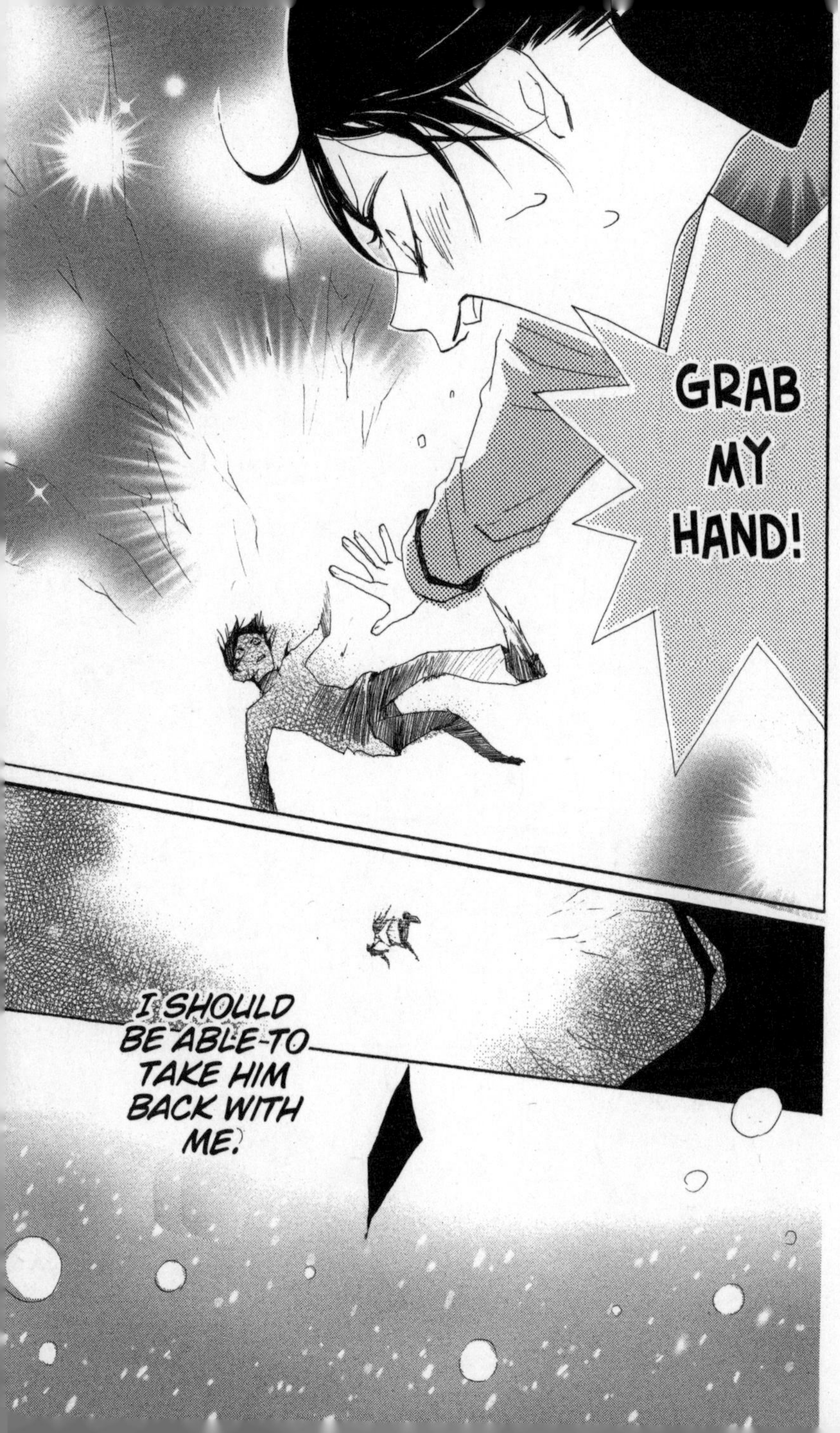
GRAB MY HAND!
I SHOULD BE ABLE TO TAKE HIM BACK WITH ME.

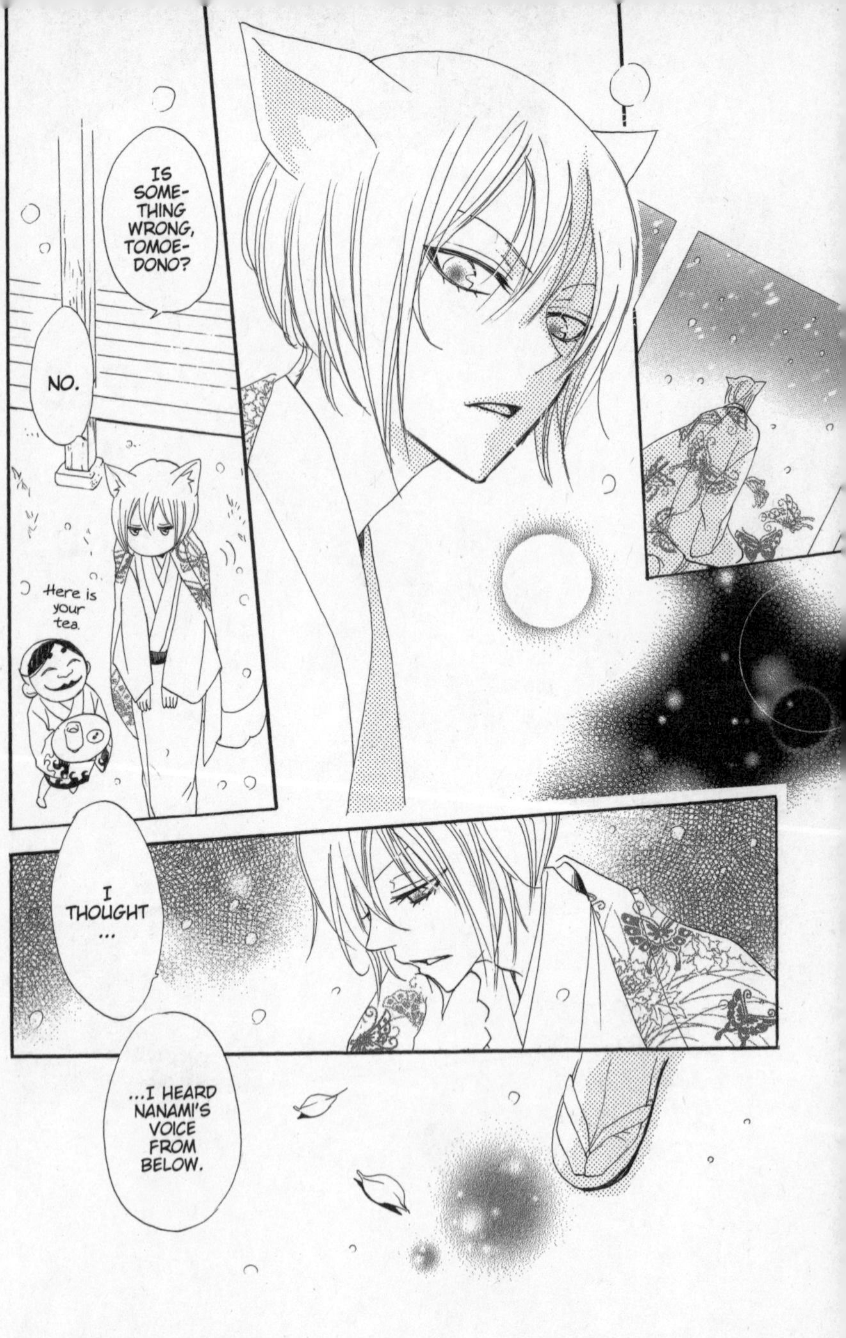
IS SOMETHING WRONG, TOMOE-DONO?
NO.
Here is your tea.
I THOUGHT...
...I HEARD NANAMI'S VOICE FROM BELOW.

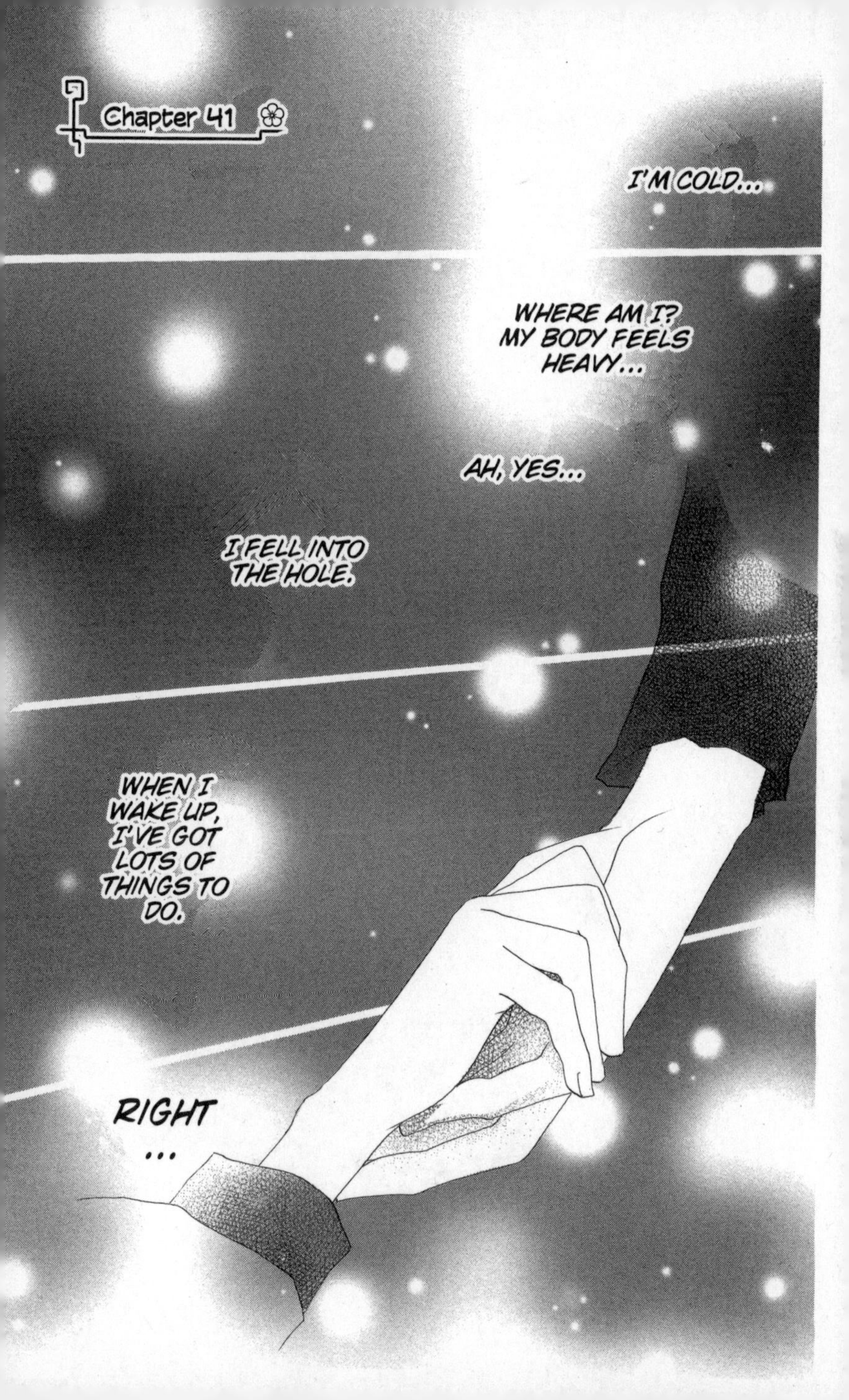
Chapter 41
I'M COLD...
WHERE AM I? MY BODY FEELS HEAVY...
AH, YES...
I FELL INTO THE HOLE.
WHEN I WAKE UP, I'VE GOT LOTS OF THINGS TO DO.
RIGHT ...

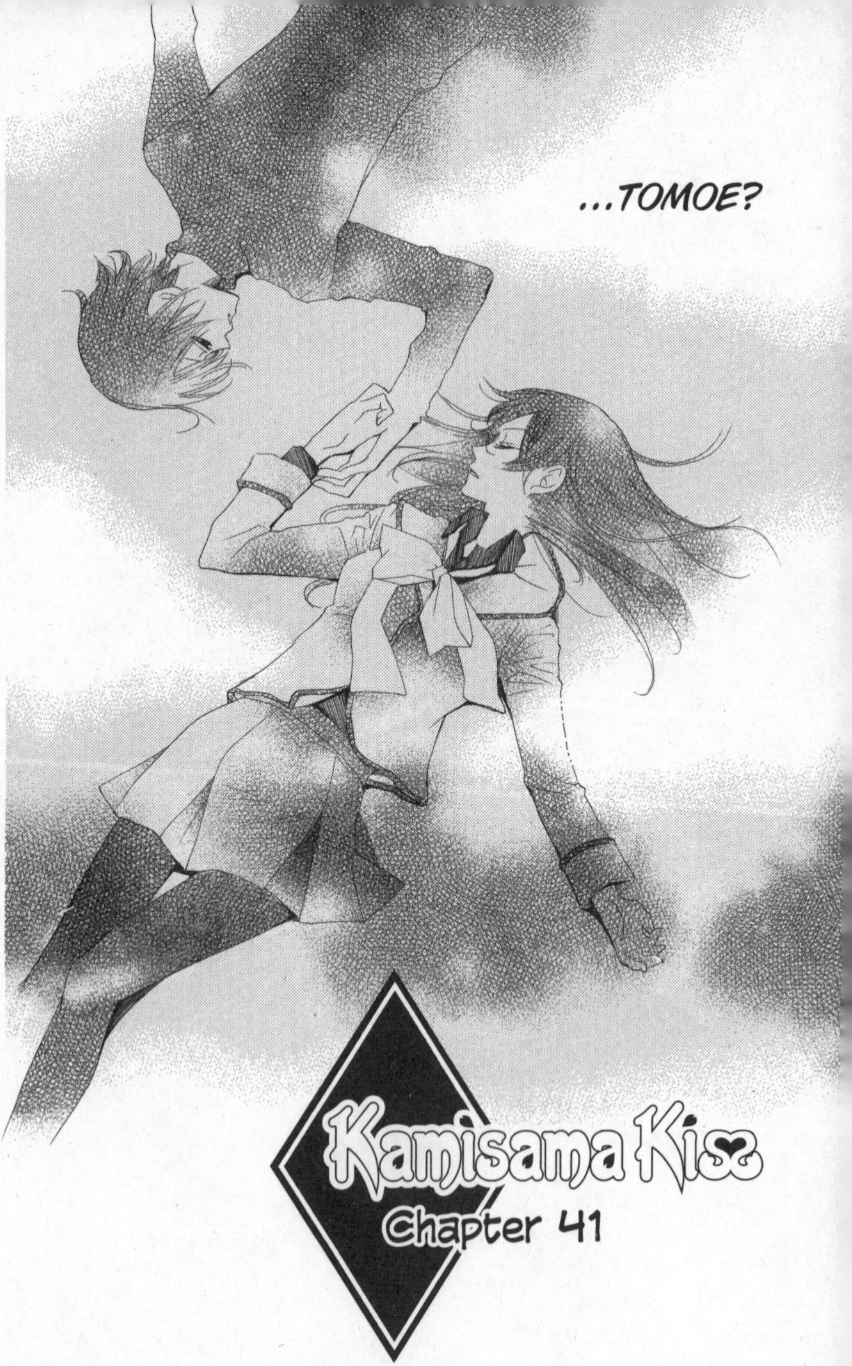
...TOMOE?
Kamisama Kiss
Chapter 41

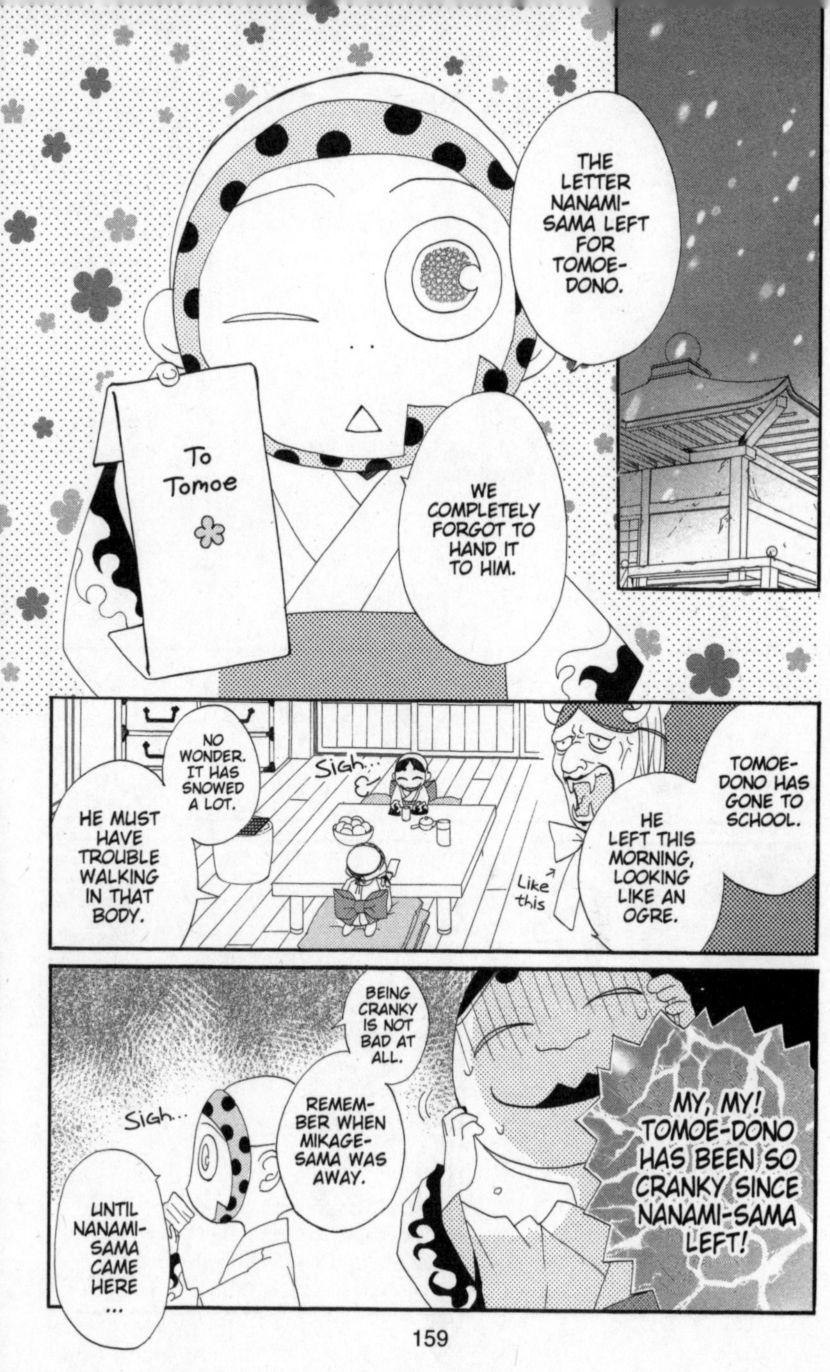
THE LETTER NANAMI-SAMA LEFT FOR TOMOE-DONO.
WE COMPLETELY FORGOT TO HAND IT TO HIM.
To Tomoe
TOMOE-DONO HAS GONE TO SCHOOL.
HE LEFT THIS MORNING, LOOKING LIKE AN OGRE.
Like this
Sigh...
NO WONDER. IT HAS SNOWED A LOT.
HE MUST HAVE TROUBLE WALKING IN THAT BODY.
MY, MY! TOMOE-DONO HAS BEEN SO CRANKY SINCE NANAMI-SAMA LEFT!
BEING CRANKY IS NOT BAD AT ALL.
REMEMBER WHEN MIKAGE-SAMA WAS AWAY.
Sigh...
UNTIL NANAMI-SAMA CAME HERE ...

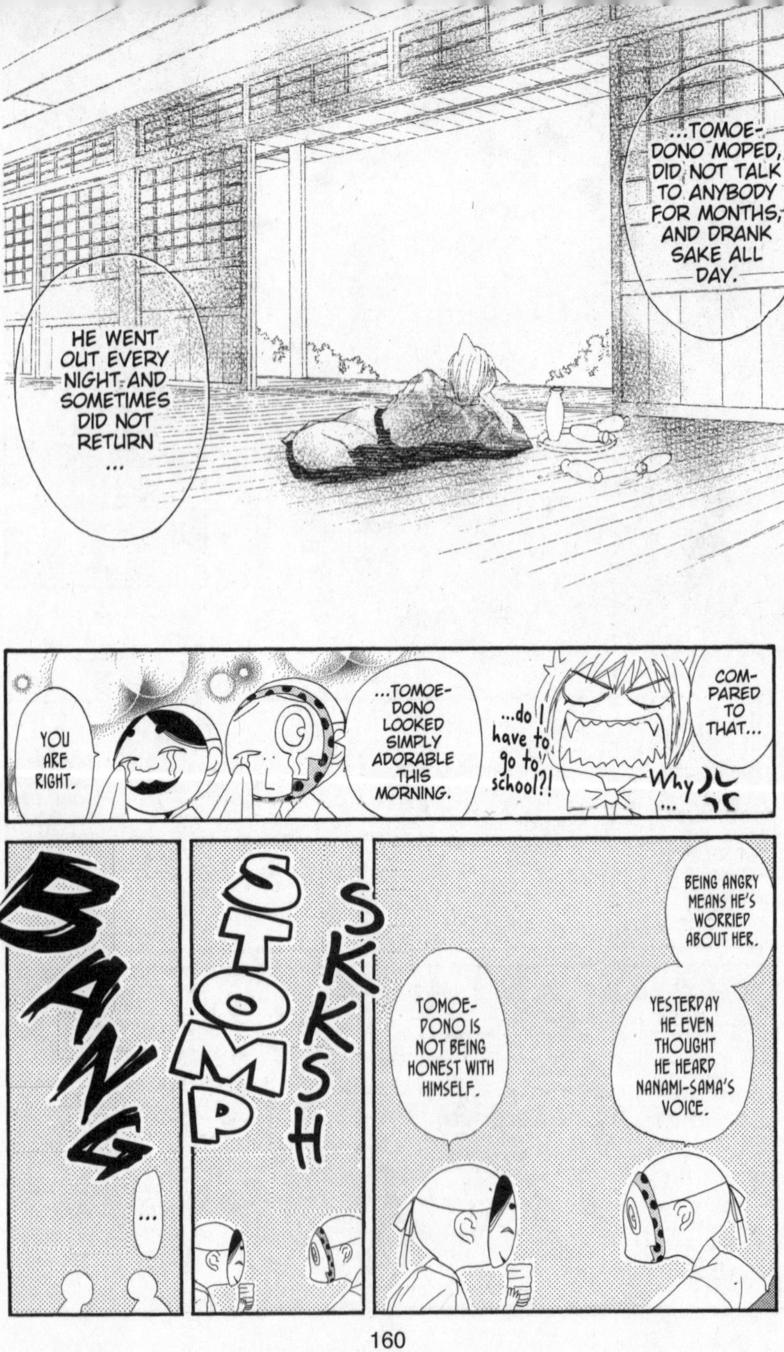
...TOMOE-DONO MOPED, DID NOT TALK TO ANYBODY FOR MONTHS, AND DRANK SAKE ALL DAY.
HE WENT OUT EVERY NIGHT AND SOMETIMES DID NOT RETURN ...
COMPARED TO THAT...
Why ... do I have to go to school?!
...TOMOE-DONO LOOKED SIMPLY ADORABLE THIS MORNING.
YOU ARE RIGHT.
BEING ANGRY MEANS HE'S WORRIED ABOUT HER.
YESTERDAY HE EVEN THOUGHT HE HEARD NANAMI-SAMA'S VOICE.
TOMOE-DONO IS NOT BEING HONEST WITH HIMSELF.
SKKSH
STOMP
BANG
...

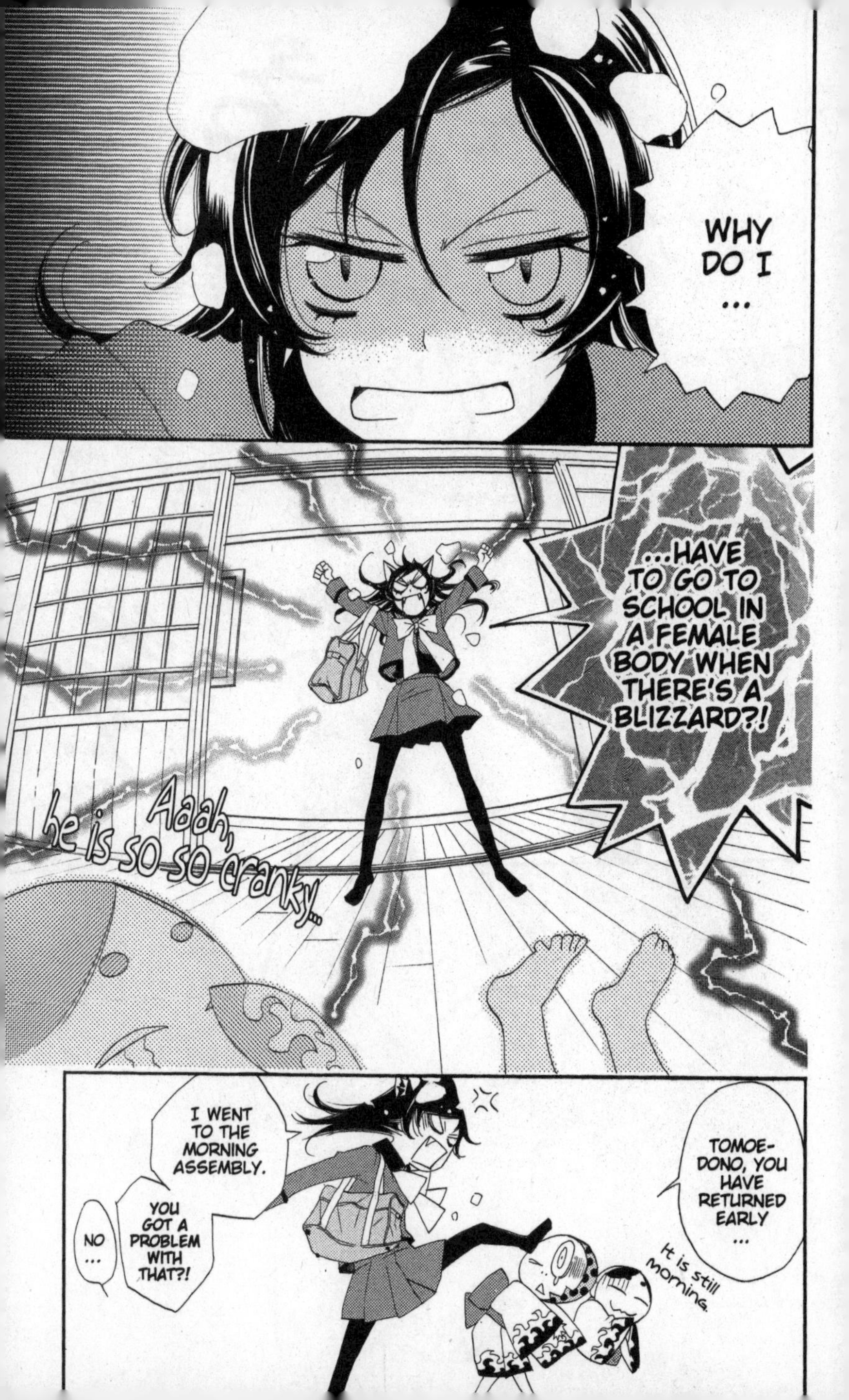
WHY DO I ...
...HAVE TO GO TO SCHOOL IN A FEMALE BODY WHEN THERE'S A BLIZZARD?!
Aaah, he is so so cranky...
TOMOE-DONO, YOU HAVE RETURNED EARLY ...
It is still morning.
I WENT TO THE MORNING ASSEMBLY.
YOU GOT A PROBLEM WITH THAT?!
NO ...

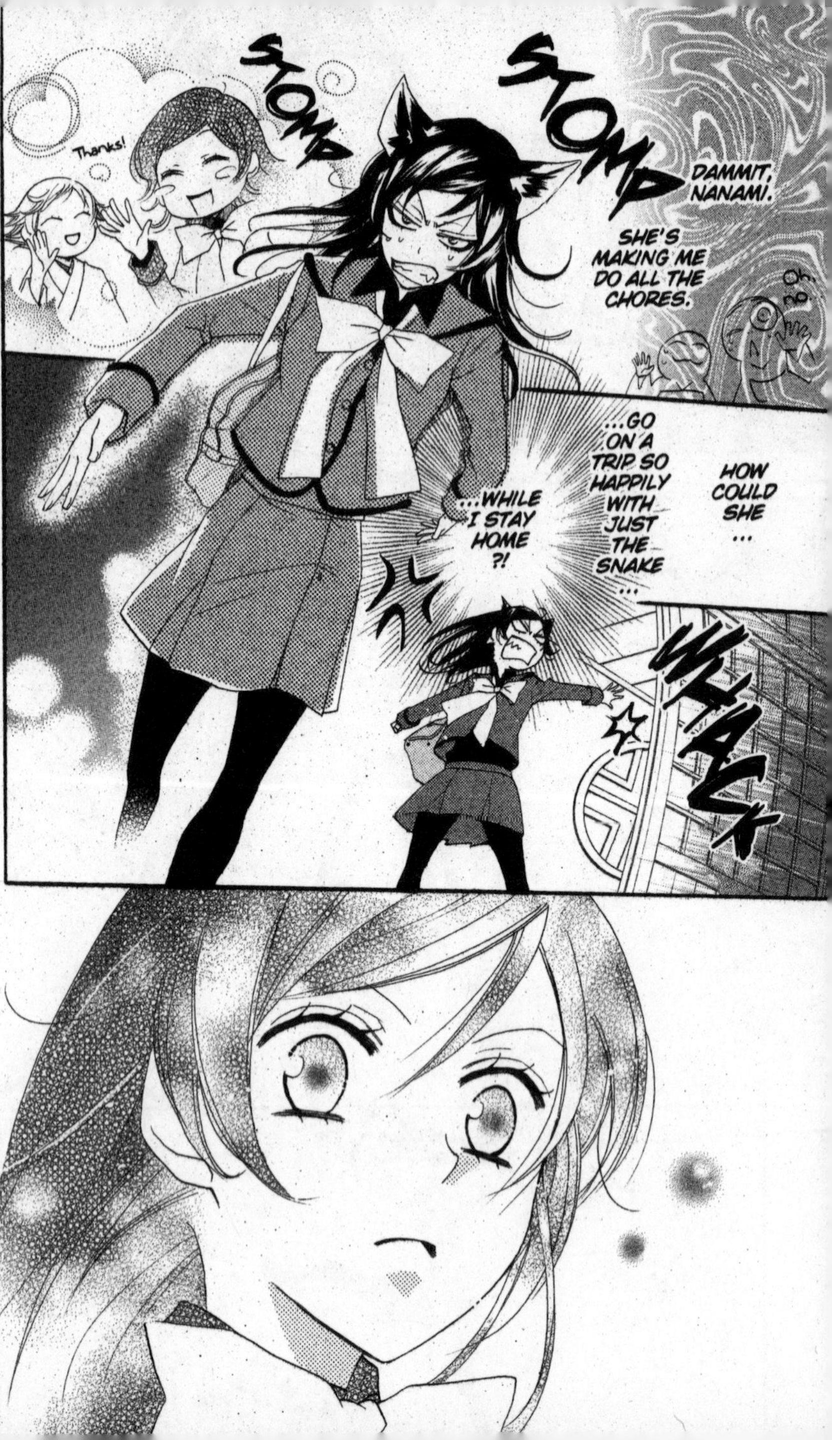
STOMP
STOMP
DAMMIT, NANAMI.
SHE'S MAKING ME DO ALL THE CHORES.
Oh, no.
Thanks!
HOW COULD SHE ...
...GO ON A TRIP SO HAPPILY WITH JUST THE SNAKE ...
...WHILE I STAY HOME ?!
WHACK

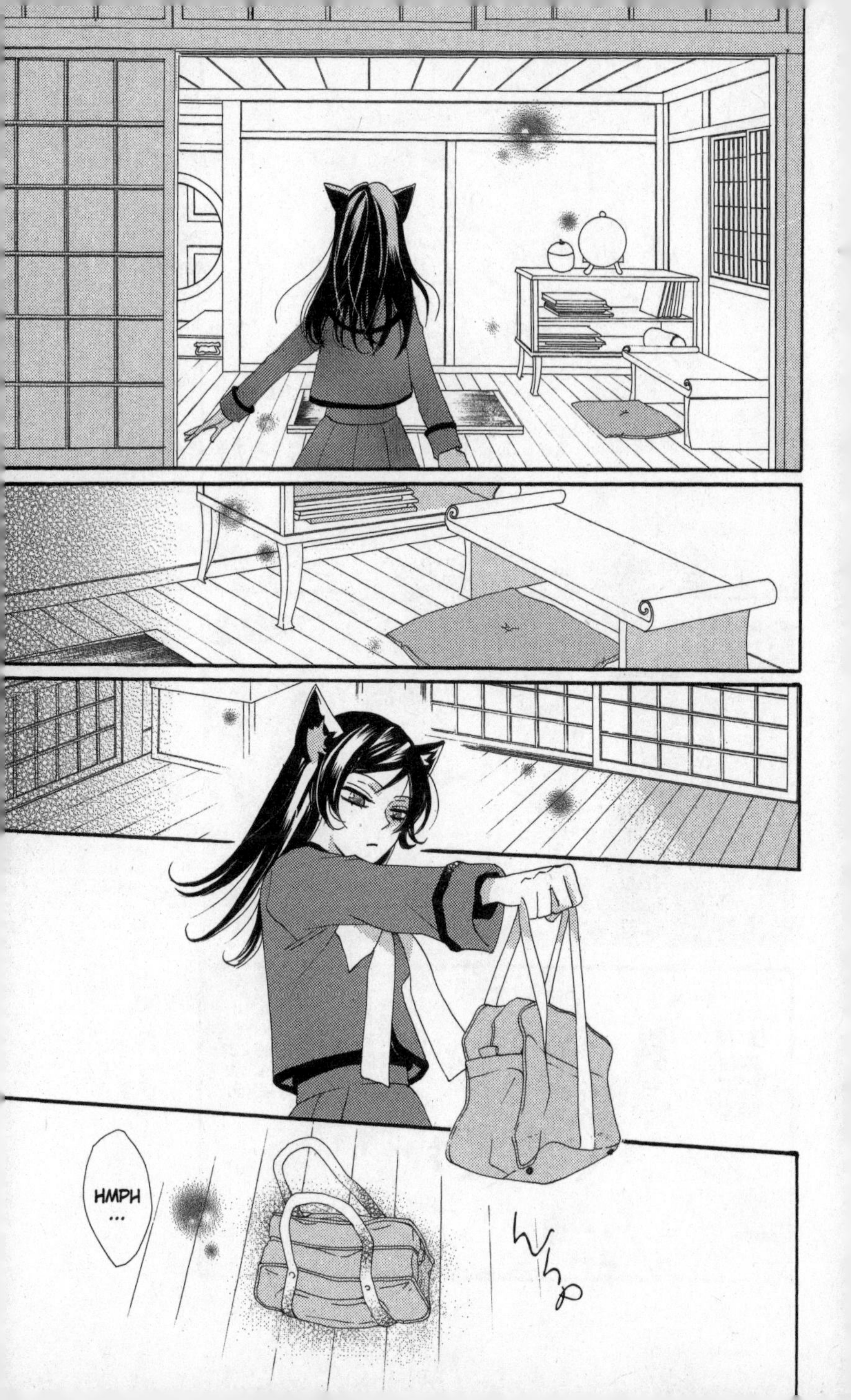
HMPH
...
WHP

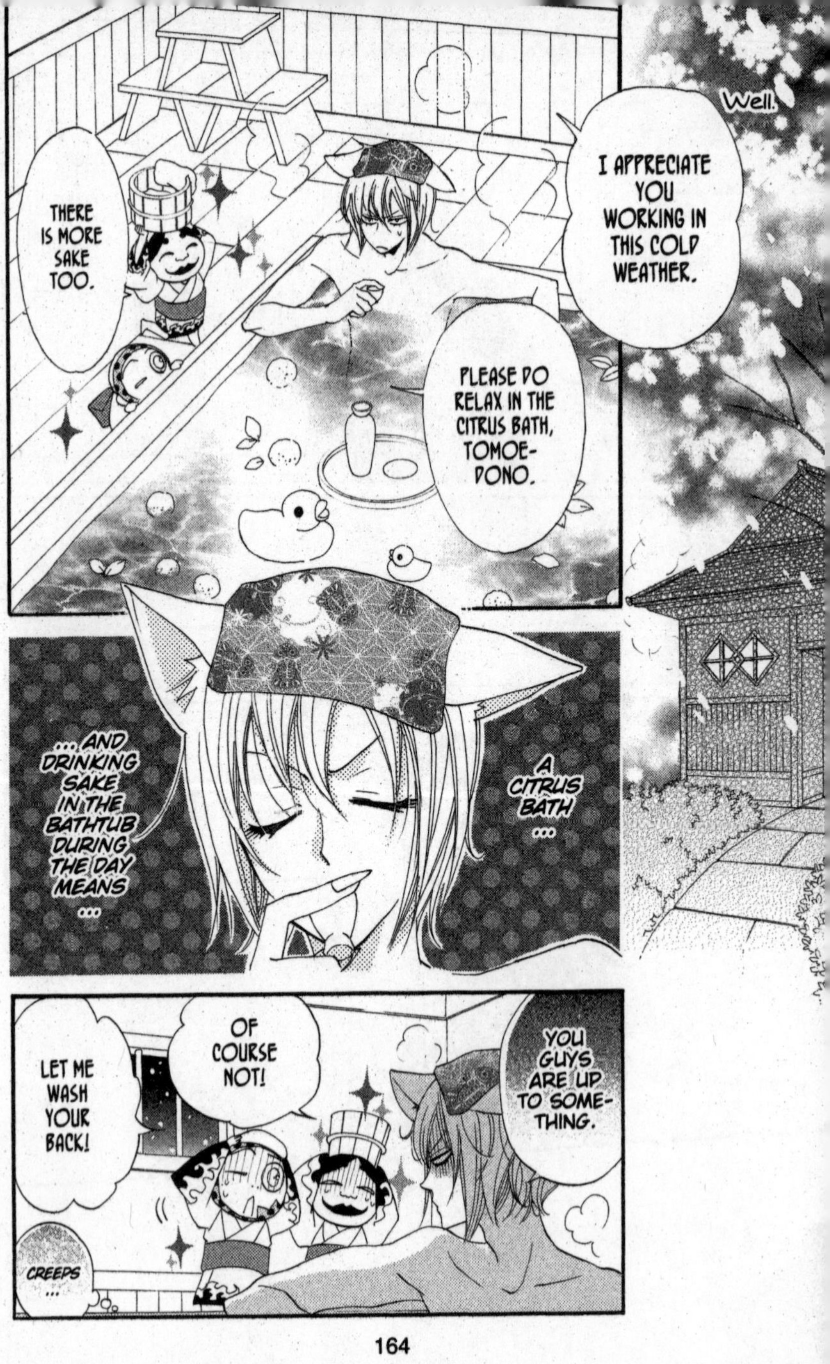
Well.
I APPRECIATE YOU WORKING IN THIS COLD WEATHER.
PLEASE DO RELAX IN THE CITRUS BATH, TOMOE-DONO.
THERE IS MORE SAKE TOO.
A CITRUS BATH ...
... AND DRINKING SAKE IN THE BATHTUB DURING THE DAY MEANS ...
YOU GUYS ARE UP TO SOME-THING.
OF COURSE NOT!
LET ME WASH YOUR BACK!
CREEPS ...

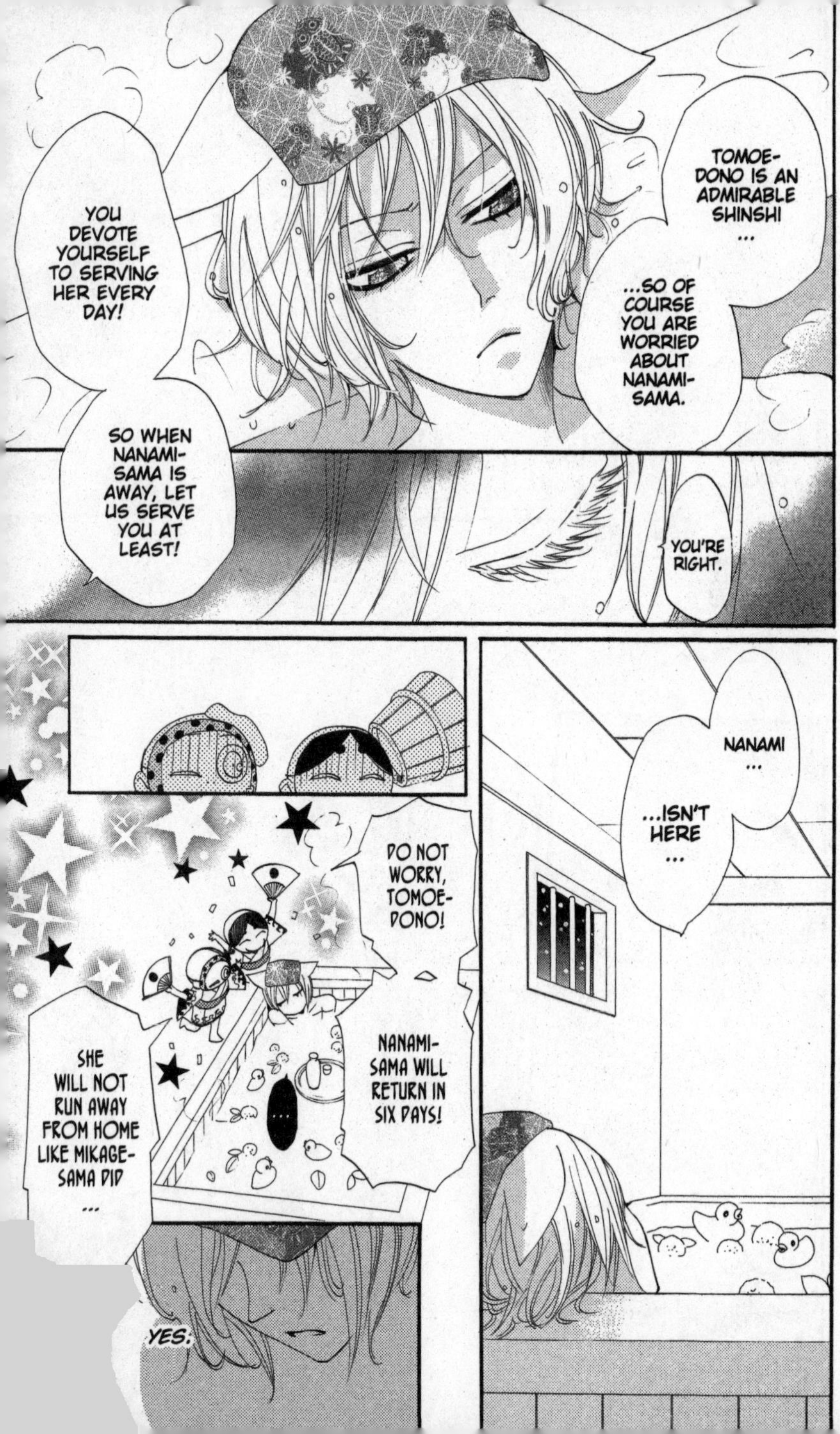
TOMOE-DONO IS AN ADMIRABLE SHINSHI ...
...SO OF COURSE YOU ARE WORRIED ABOUT NANAMI-SAMA.
YOU DEVOTE YOURSELF TO SERVING HER EVERY DAY!
SO WHEN NANAMI-SAMA IS AWAY, LET US SERVE YOU AT LEAST!
YOU'RE RIGHT.
NANAMI ...
...ISN'T HERE ...
DO NOT WORRY, TOMOE-DONO!
NANAMI-SAMA WILL RETURN IN SIX DAYS!
...
SHE WILL NOT RUN AWAY FROM HOME LIKE MIKAGE-SAMA DID ...
YES.

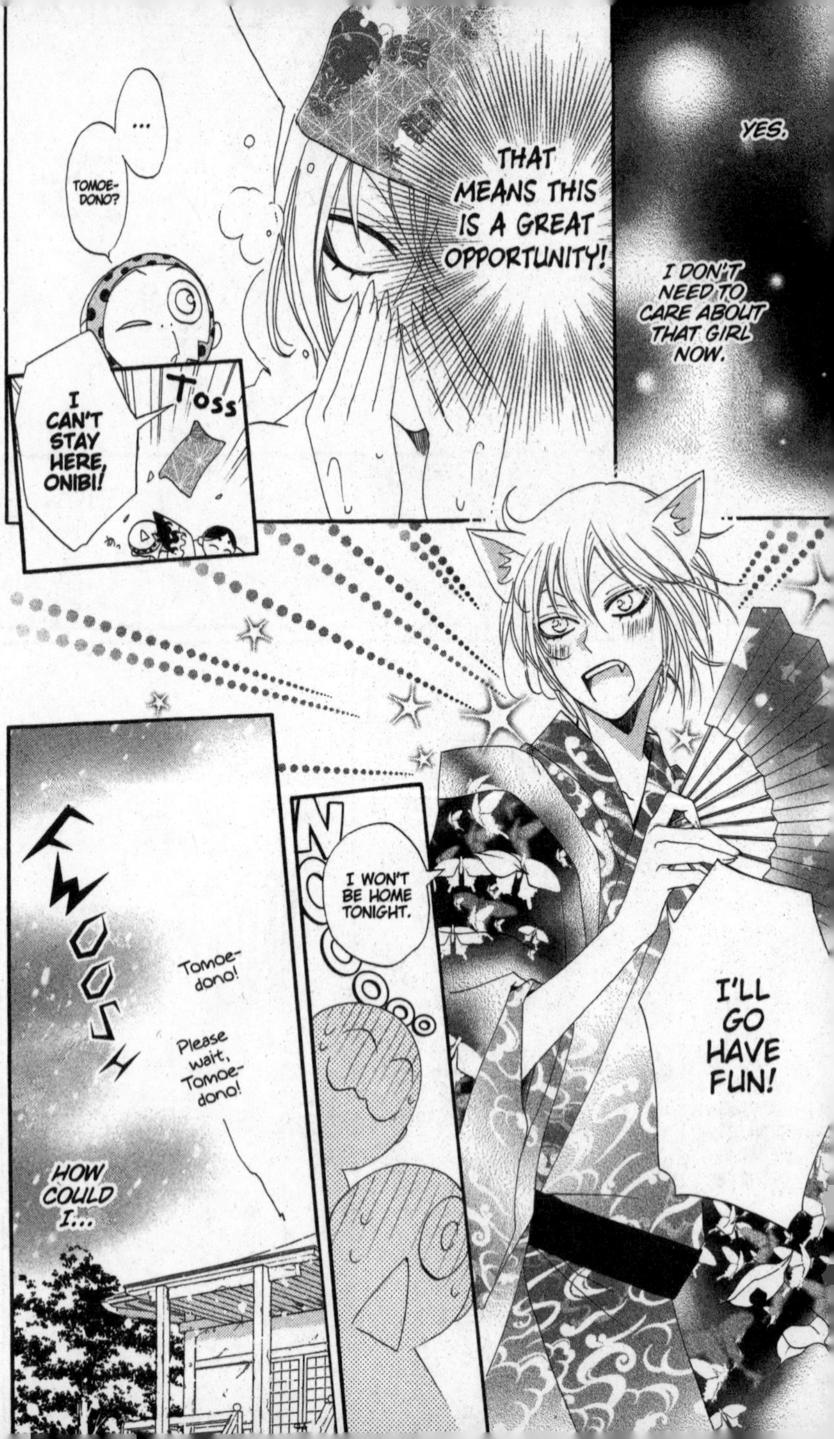
YES.
I DON'T NEED TO CARE ABOUT THAT GIRL NOW.
THAT MEANS THIS IS A GREAT OPPORTUNITY!
...
TOMOE-DONO?
I CAN'T STAY HERE, ONIBI!
TOSS
I'LL GO HAVE FUN!
I WON'T BE HOME TONIGHT.
NOOOOOO
FWOOSH
Tomoe-dono!
Please wait, Tomoe-dono!
HOW COULD I...

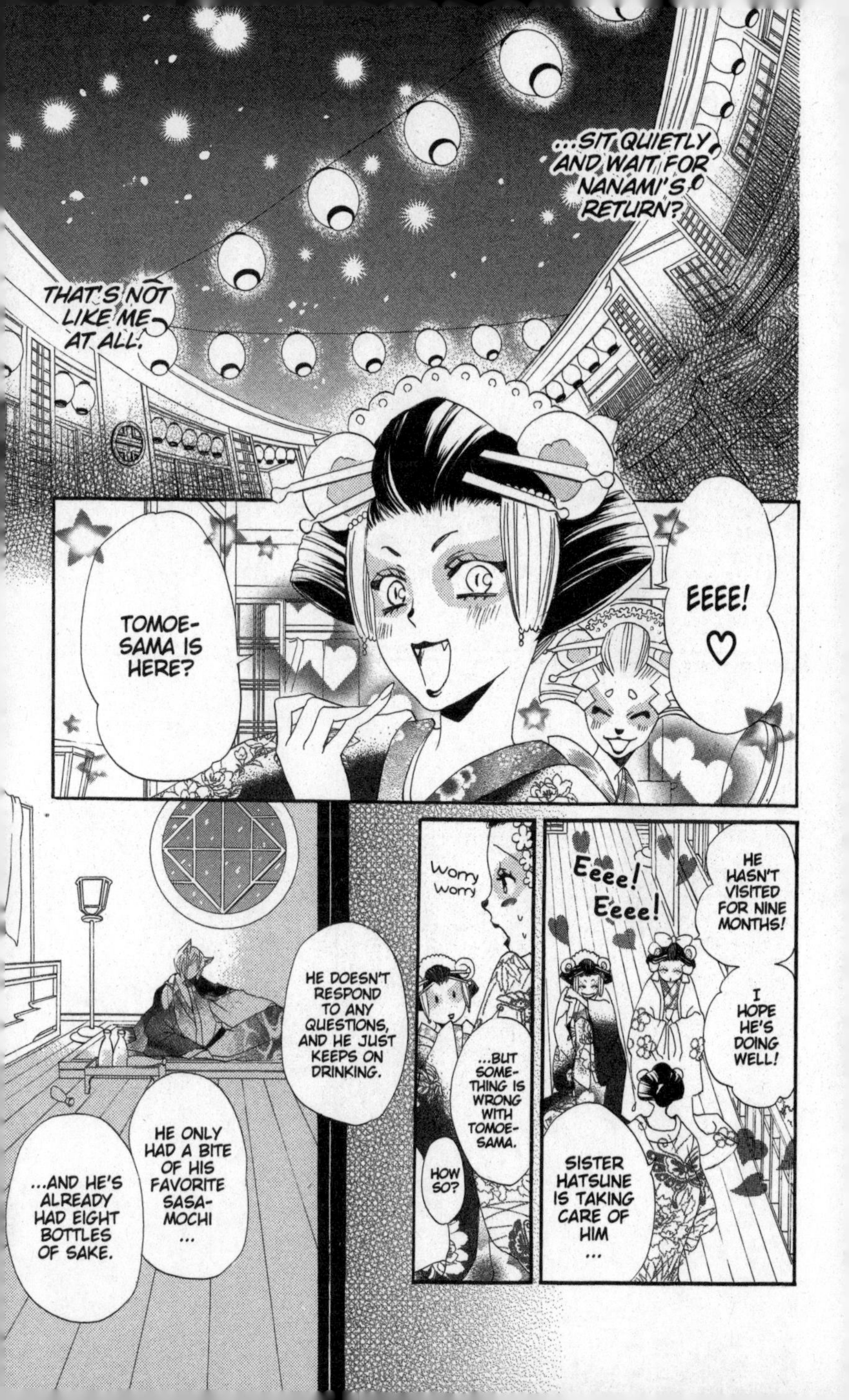
...SIT QUIETLY AND WAIT FOR NANAMI'S RETURN?
THAT'S NOT LIKE ME AT ALL.
EEEE! ♥
TOMOE-SAMA IS HERE?
Eeee! Eeee!
HE HASN'T VISITED FOR NINE MONTHS!
I HOPE HE'S DOING WELL!
SISTER HATSUNE IS TAKING CARE OF HIM ...
Worry worry
...BUT SOMETHING IS WRONG WITH TOMOE-SAMA.
HOW SO?
HE DOESN'T RESPOND TO ANY QUESTIONS, AND HE JUST KEEPS ON DRINKING.
HE ONLY HAD A BITE OF HIS FAVORITE SASA-MOCHI ...
...AND HE'S ALREADY HAD EIGHT BOTTLES OF SAKE.

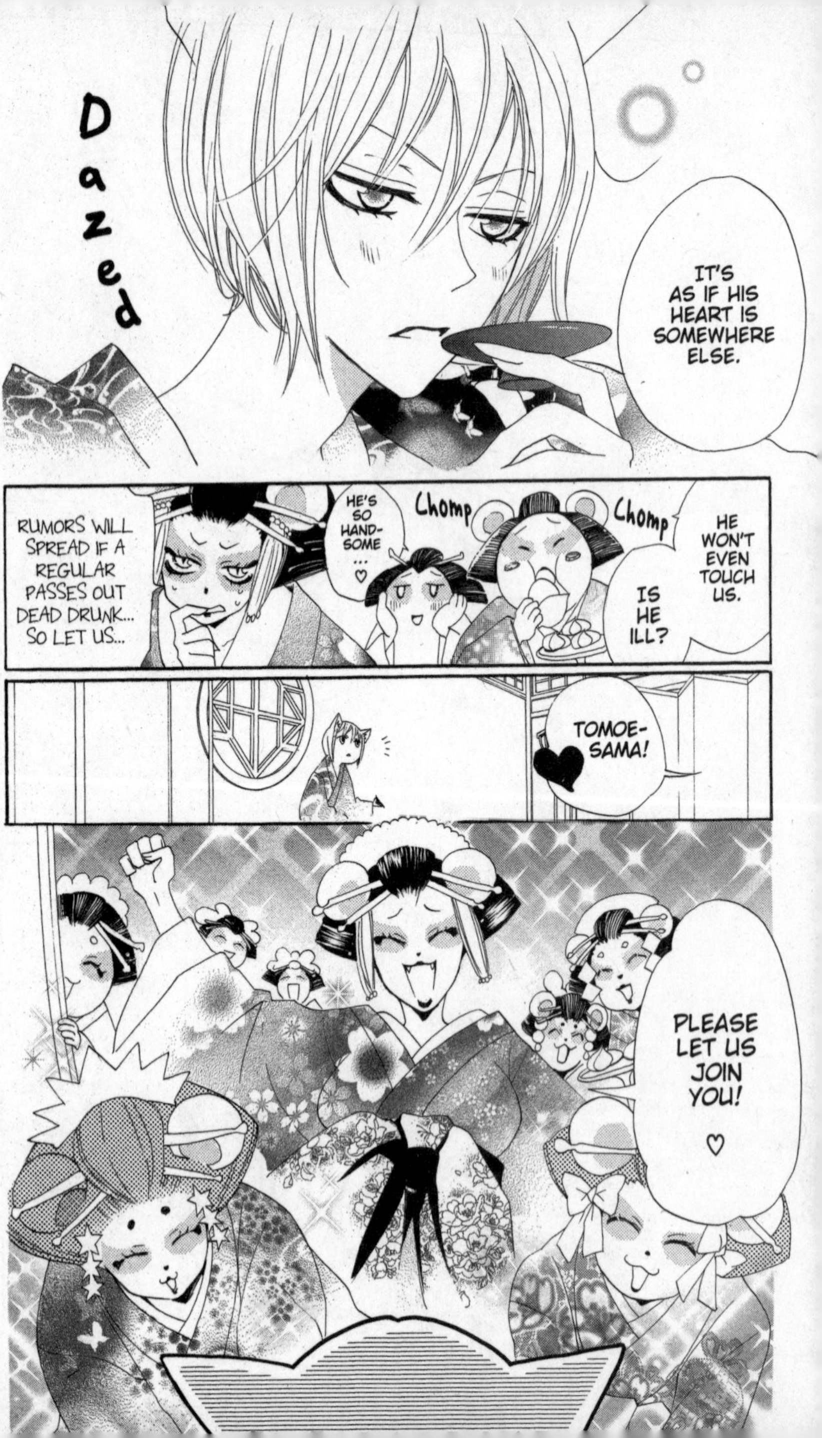
IT'S AS IF HIS HEART IS SOMEWHERE ELSE.
Dazed
HE WON'T EVEN TOUCH US.
IS HE ILL?
Chomp
Chomp
HE'S SO HAND-SOME... ♡
RUMORS WILL SPREAD IF A REGULAR PASSES OUT DEAD DRUNK... SO LET US...
TOMOE-SAMA!
PLEASE LET US JOIN YOU! ♡

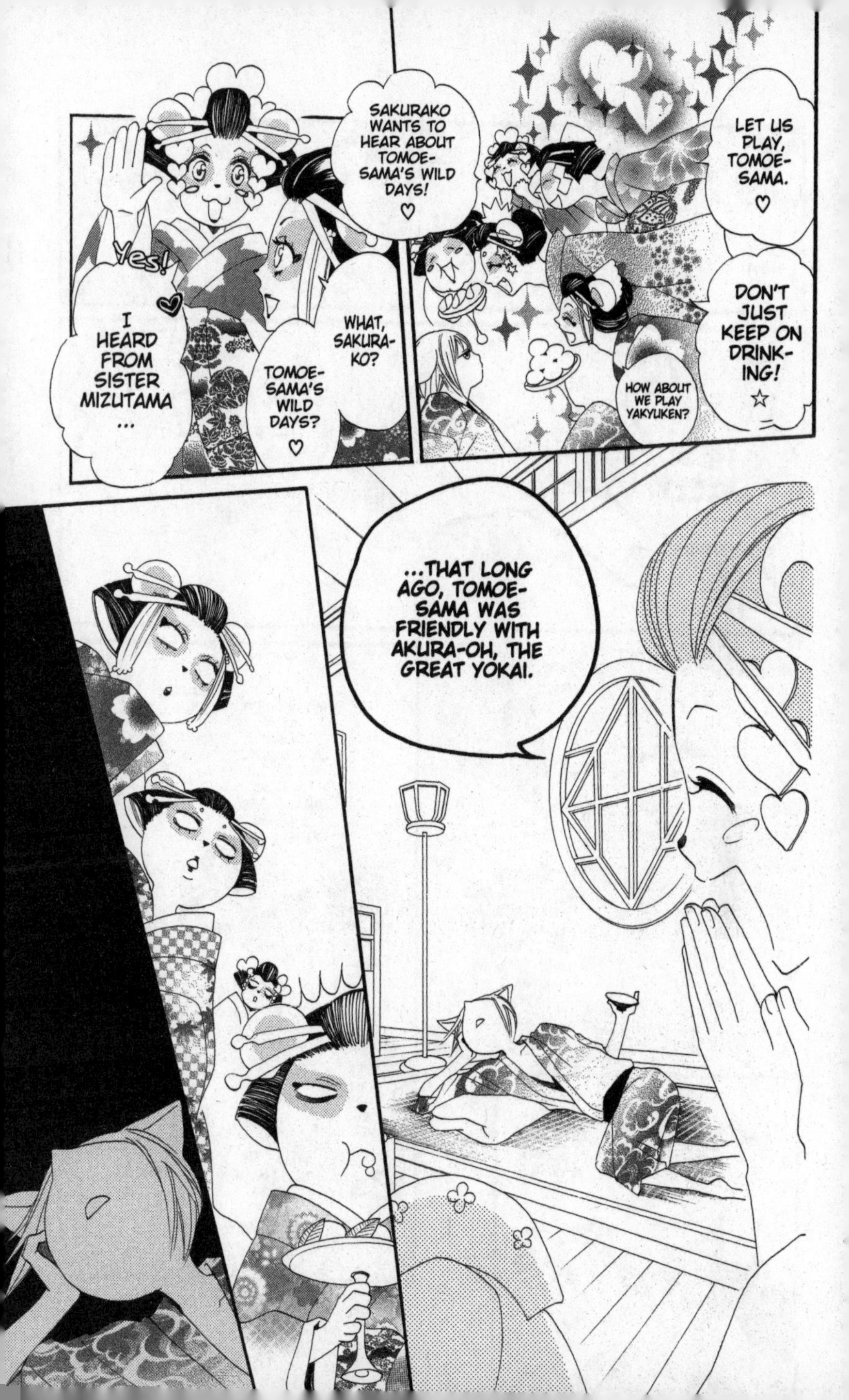
LET US PLAY, TOMOE-SAMA. ♡
DON'T JUST KEEP ON DRINK-ING! ☆
HOW ABOUT WE PLAY YAKYUKEN?
SAKURAKO WANTS TO HEAR ABOUT TOMOE-SAMA'S WILD DAYS! ♡
WHAT, SAKURA-KO?
TOMOE-SAMA'S WILD DAYS? ♡
Yes!
I HEARD FROM SISTER MIZUTAMA ...
...THAT LONG AGO, TOMOE-SAMA WAS FRIENDLY WITH AKURA-OH, THE GREAT YOKAI.

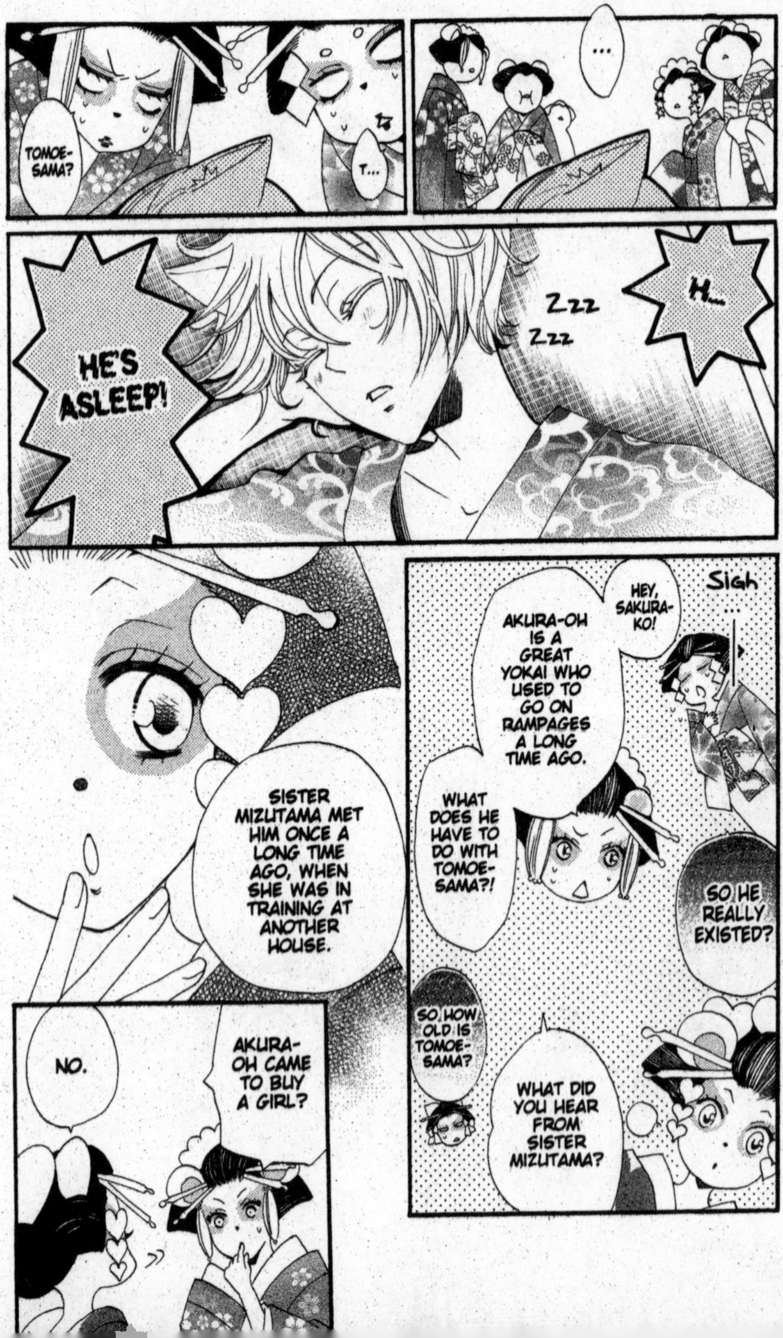
...
T...
TOMOE-SAMA?
H...
Zzz
Zzz
HE'S ASLEEP!
Sigh...
HEY, SAKURAKO!
AKURA-OH IS A GREAT YOKAI WHO USED TO GO ON RAMPAGES A LONG TIME AGO.
WHAT DOES HE HAVE TO DO WITH TOMOE-SAMA?!
SO HE REALLY EXISTED?
WHAT DID YOU HEAR FROM SISTER MIZUTAMA?
SO, HOW OLD IS TOMOE-SAMA?
SISTER MIZUTAMA MET HIM ONCE A LONG TIME AGO, WHEN SHE WAS IN TRAINING AT ANOTHER HOUSE.
AKURA-OH CAME TO BUY A GIRL?
NO.

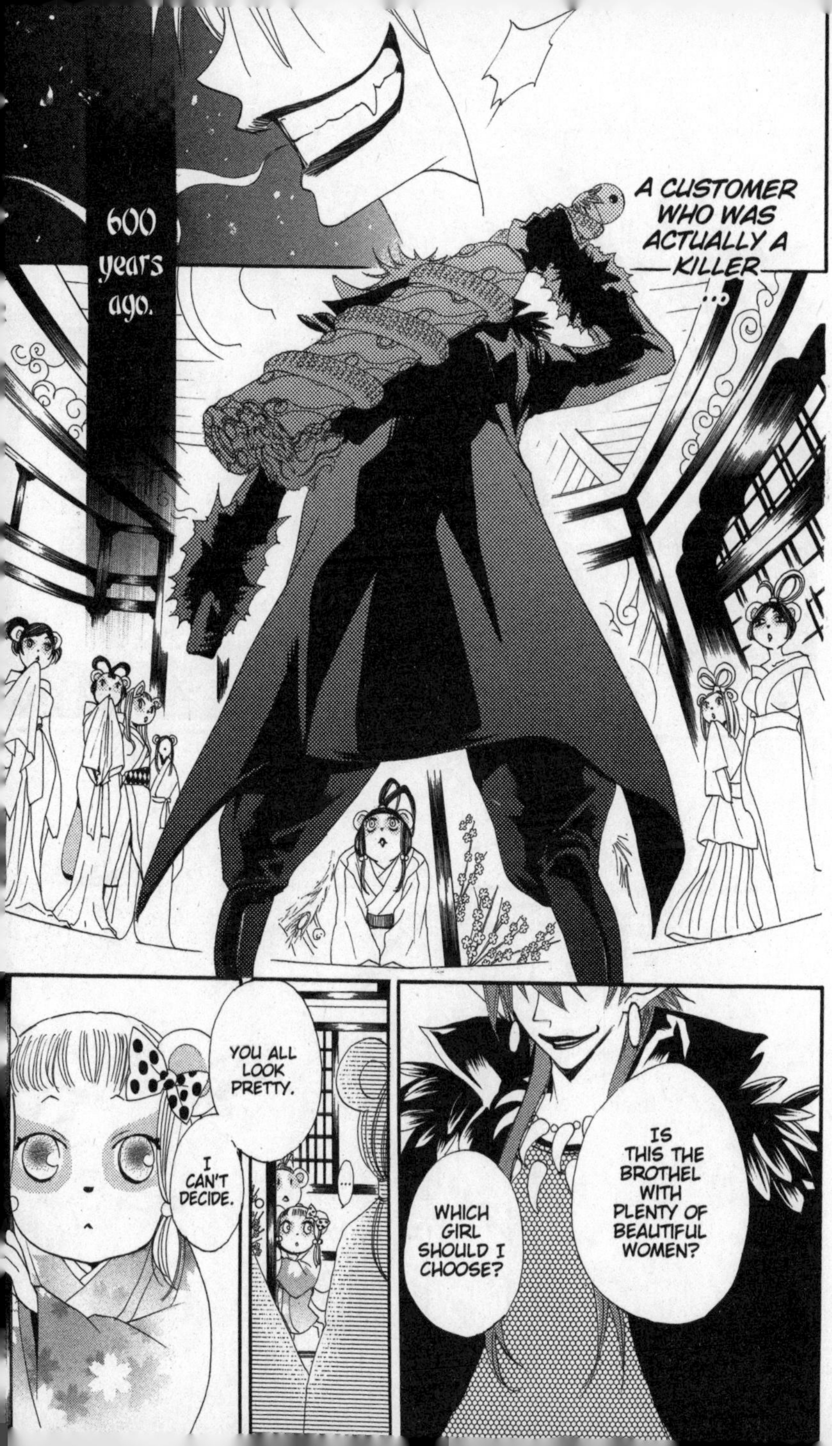
A CUSTOMER WHO WAS ACTUALLY A KILLER...
600 years ago.
IS THIS THE BROTHEL WITH PLENTY OF BEAUTIFUL WOMEN?
WHICH GIRL SHOULD I CHOOSE?
YOU ALL LOOK PRETTY.
I CAN'T DECIDE.
...

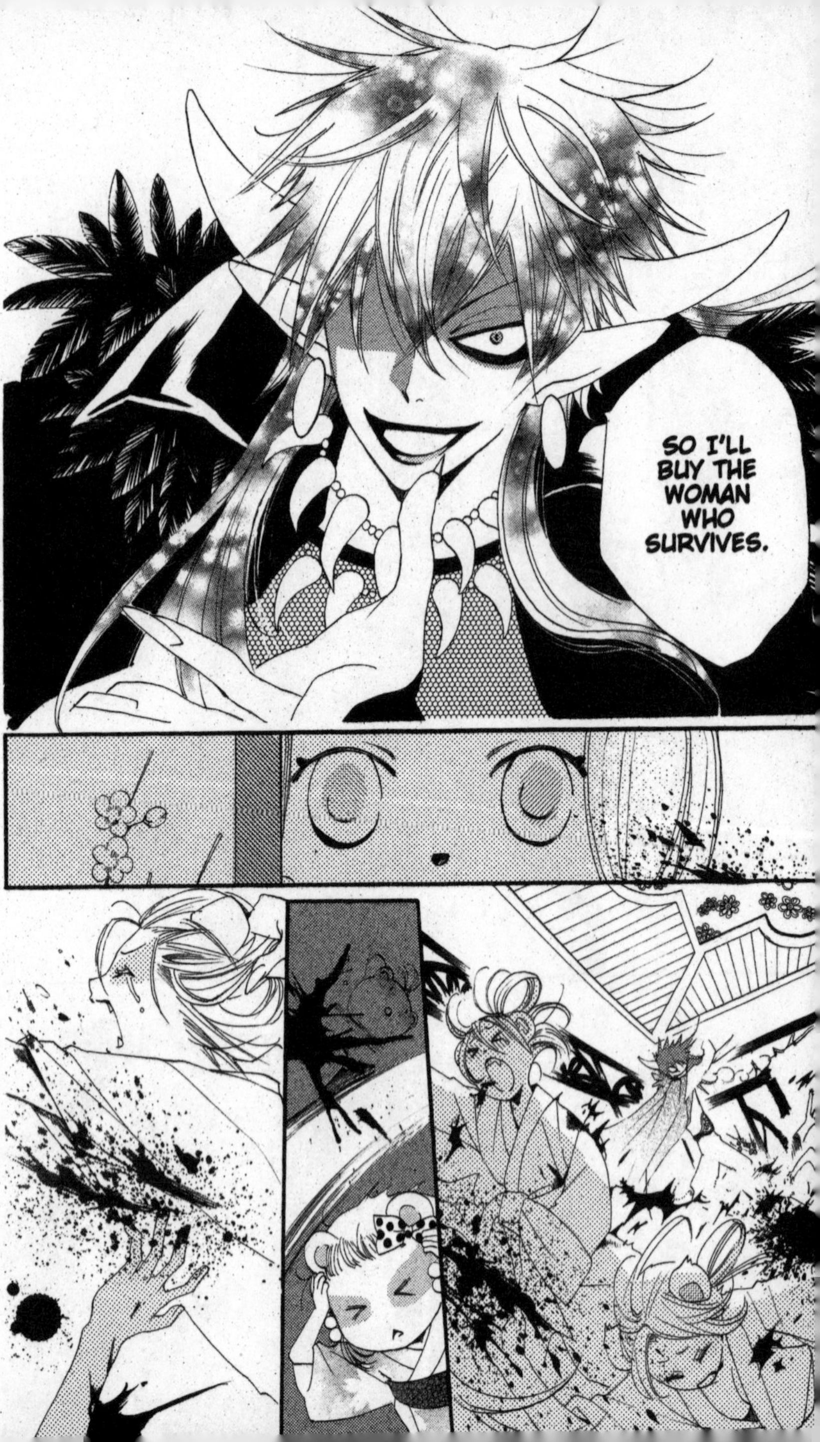
SO I'LL BUY THE WOMAN WHO SURVIVES.

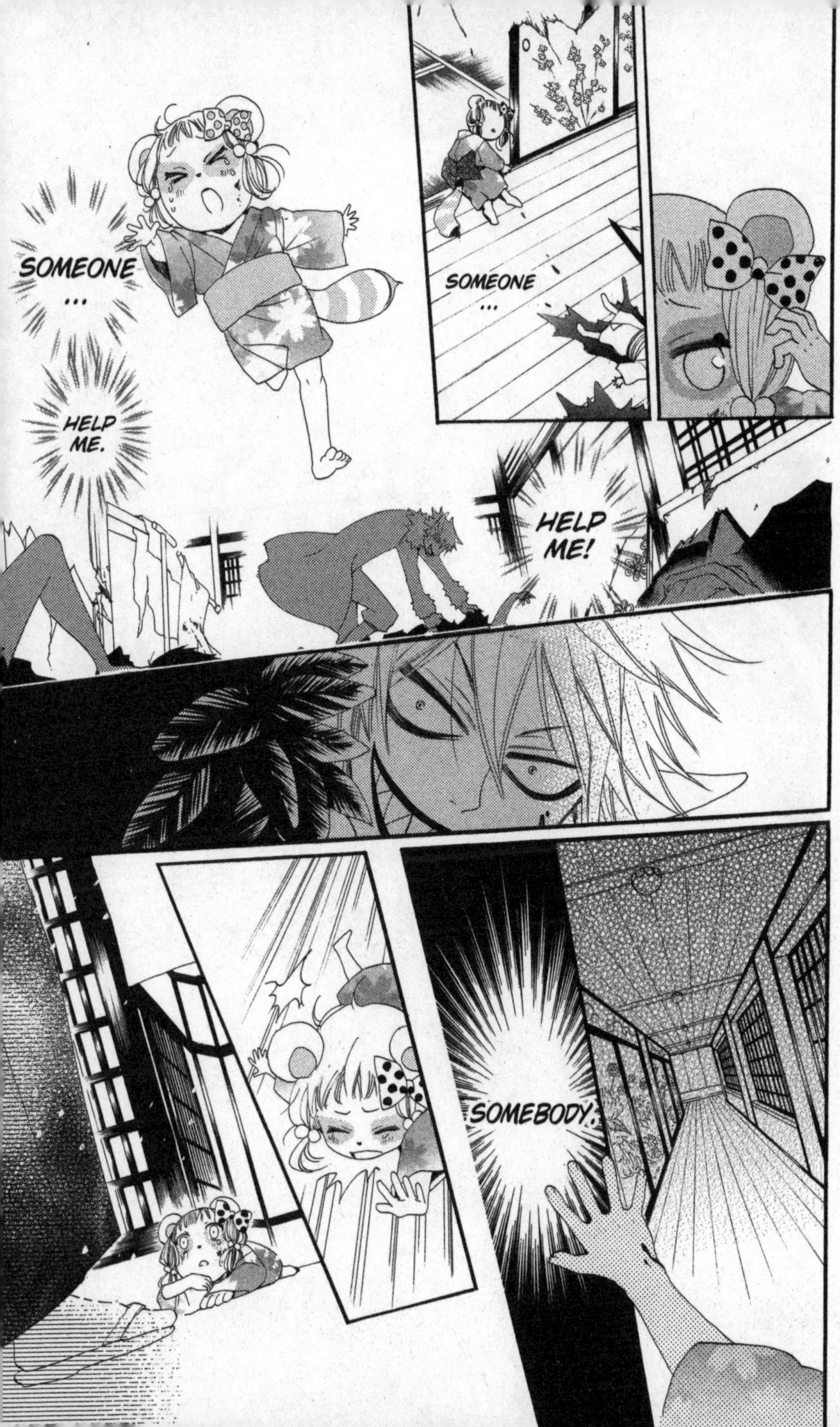
SOMEONE ...
SOMEONE ...
HELP ME.
HELP ME!
SOMEBODY.

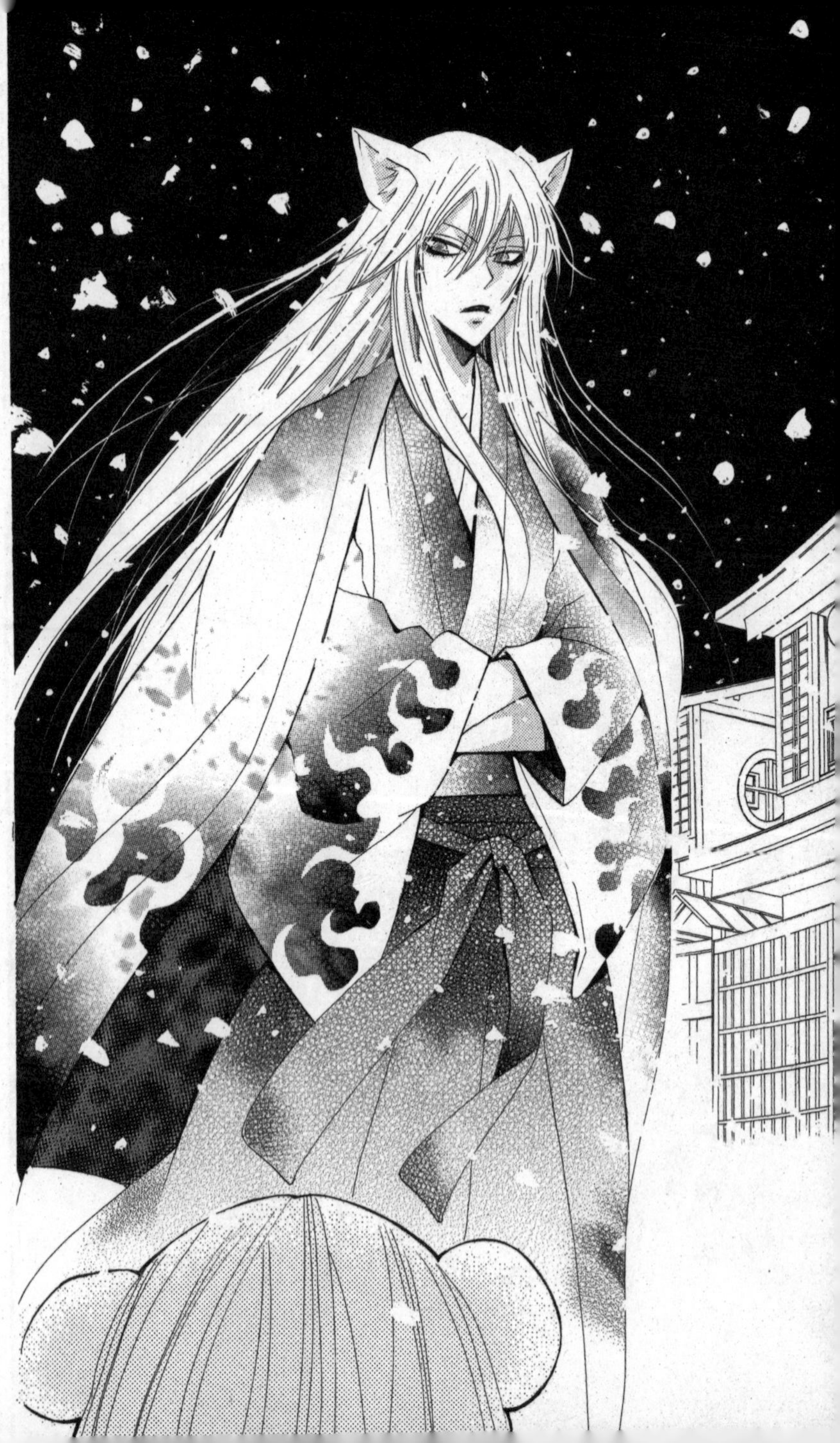

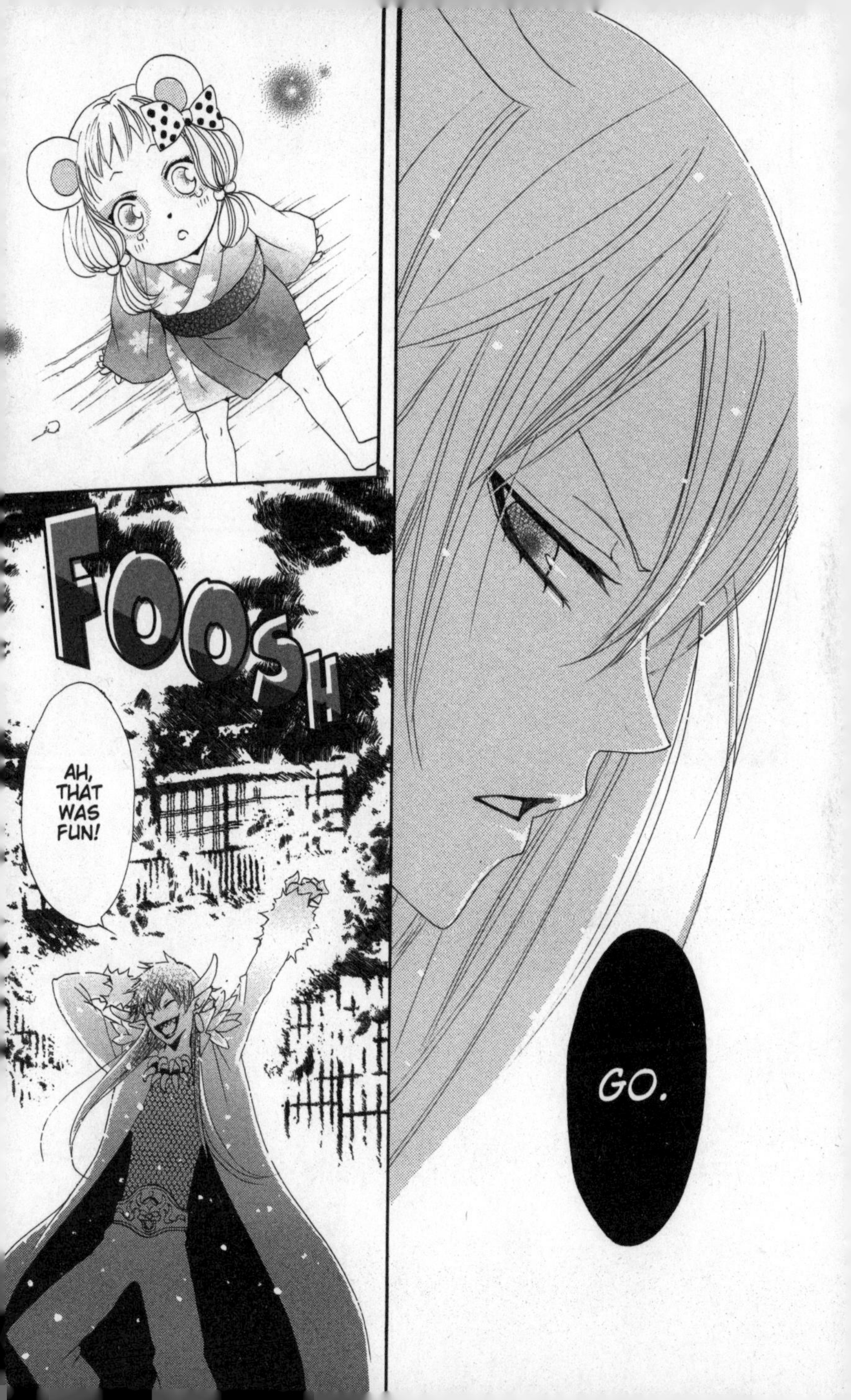
GO.
FOOSH
AH, THAT WAS FUN!

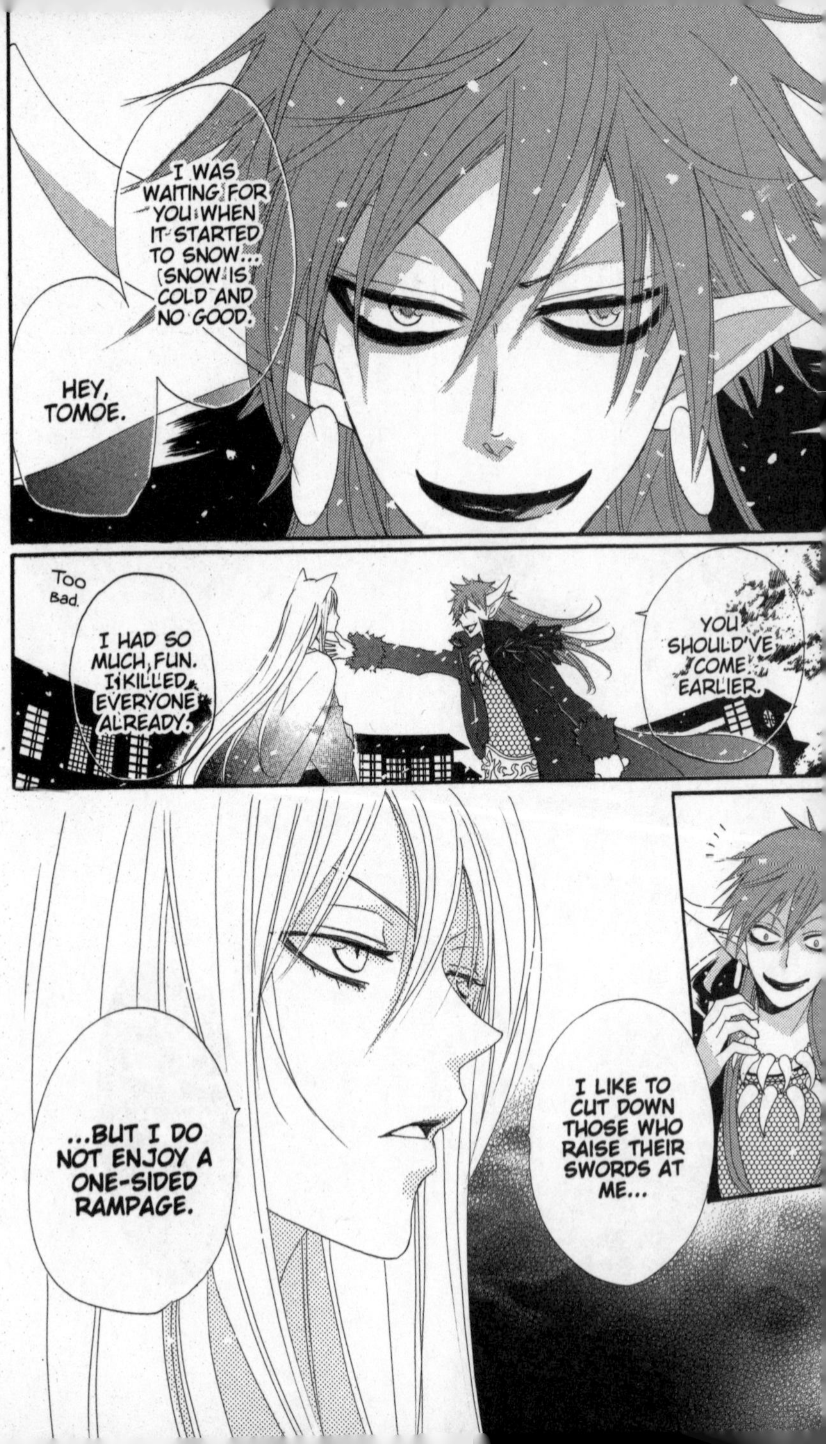
I WAS WAITING FOR YOU WHEN IT STARTED TO SNOW... SNOW IS COLD AND NO GOOD.
HEY, TOMOE.
YOU SHOULD'VE COME EARLIER.
Too Bad.
I HAD SO MUCH FUN. I KILLED EVERYONE ALREADY.
I LIKE TO CUT DOWN THOSE WHO RAISE THEIR SWORDS AT ME...
...BUT I DO NOT ENJOY A ONE-SIDED RAMPAGE.

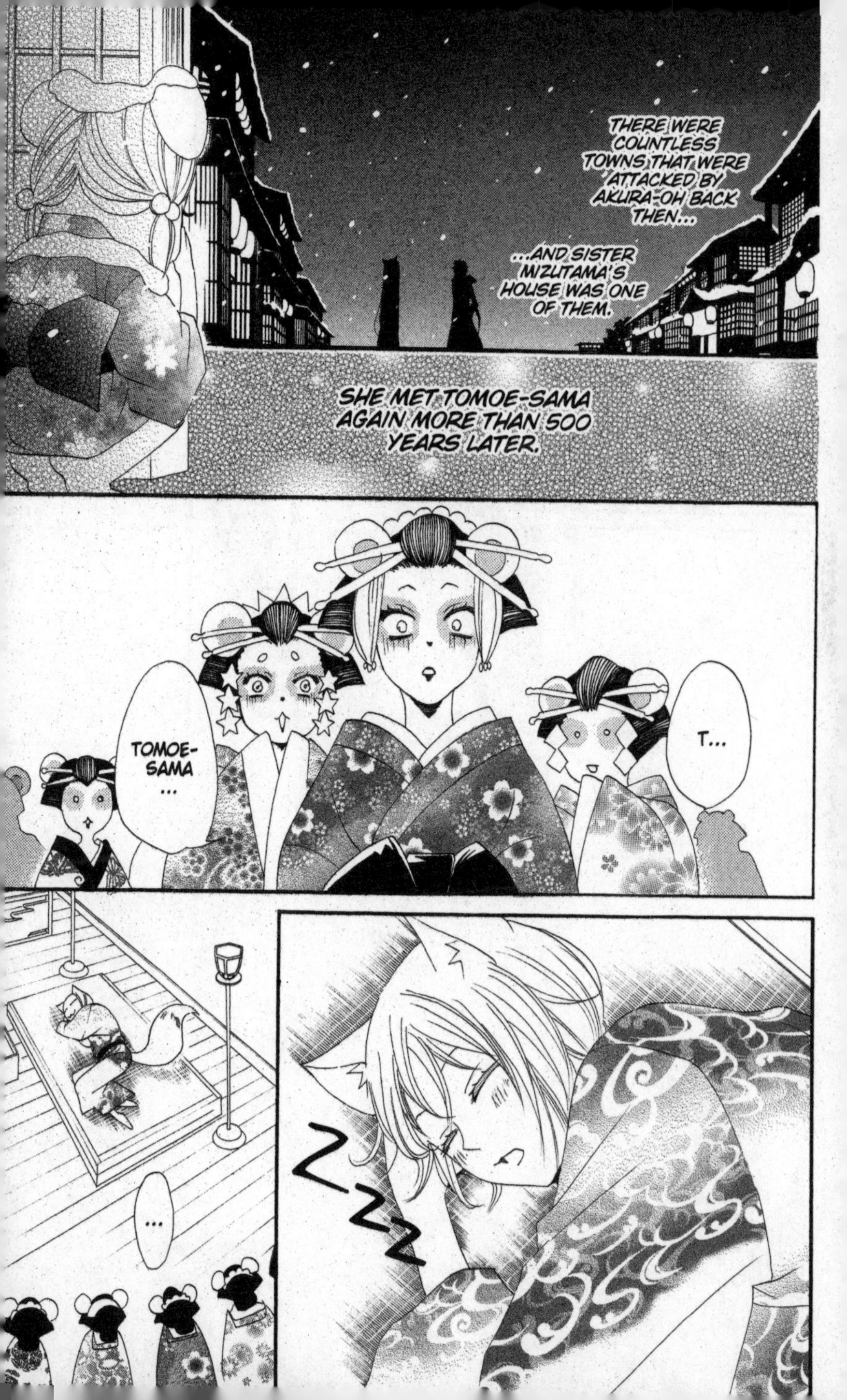
THERE WERE COUNTLESS TOWNS THAT WERE ATTACKED BY AKURA-OH BACK THEN...
...AND SISTER MIZUTAMA'S HOUSE WAS ONE OF THEM.
SHE MET TOMOE-SAMA AGAIN MORE THAN 500 YEARS LATER.
T...
TOMOE-SAMA ...
ZZZ
...

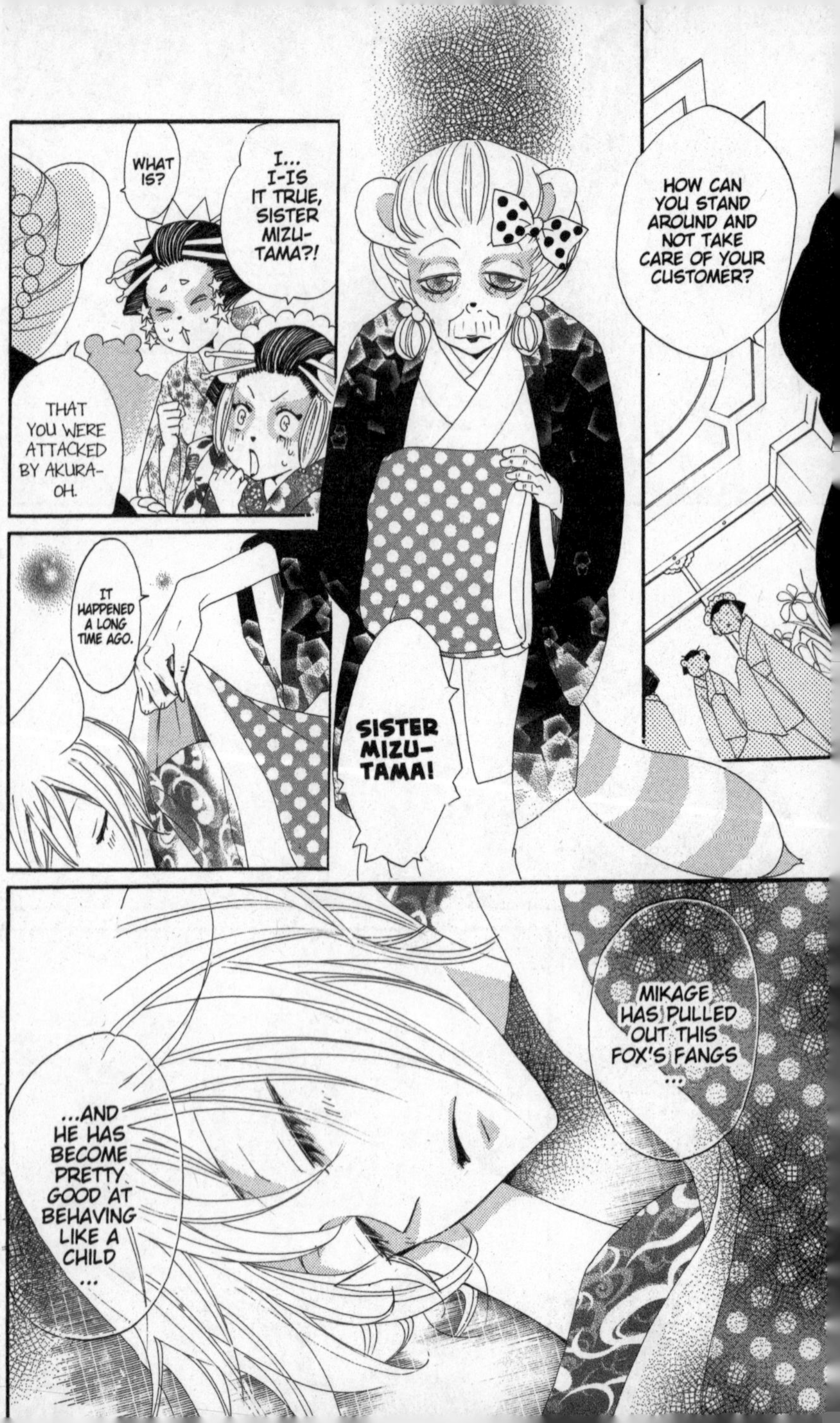
HOW CAN YOU STAND AROUND AND NOT TAKE CARE OF YOUR CUSTOMER?
I... I-IS IT TRUE, SISTER MIZUTAMA?!
WHAT IS?
THAT YOU WERE ATTACKED BY AKURA-OH.
SISTER MIZUTAMA!
IT HAPPENED A LONG TIME AGO.
MIKAGE HAS PULLED OUT THIS FOX'S FANGS ...
...AND HE HAS BECOME PRETTY GOOD AT BEHAVING LIKE A CHILD ...

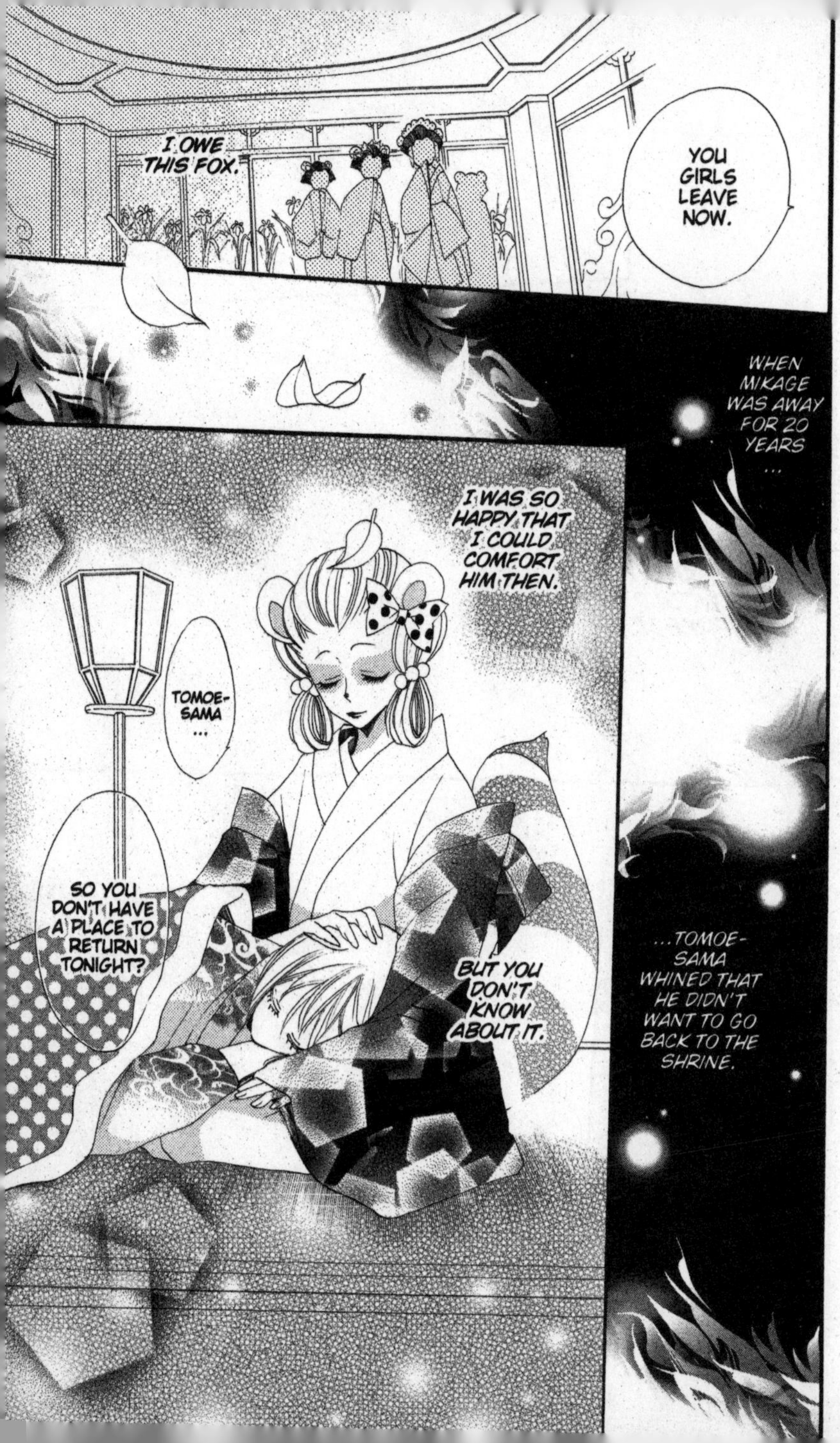
YOU GIRLS LEAVE NOW.
I OWE THIS FOX.
WHEN MIKAGE WAS AWAY FOR 20 YEARS...
...TOMOE-SAMA WHINED THAT HE DIDN'T WANT TO GO BACK TO THE SHRINE.
I WAS SO HAPPY THAT I COULD COMFORT HIM THEN.
TOMOE-SAMA...
SO YOU DON'T HAVE A PLACE TO RETURN TONIGHT?
BUT YOU DON'T KNOW ABOUT IT.

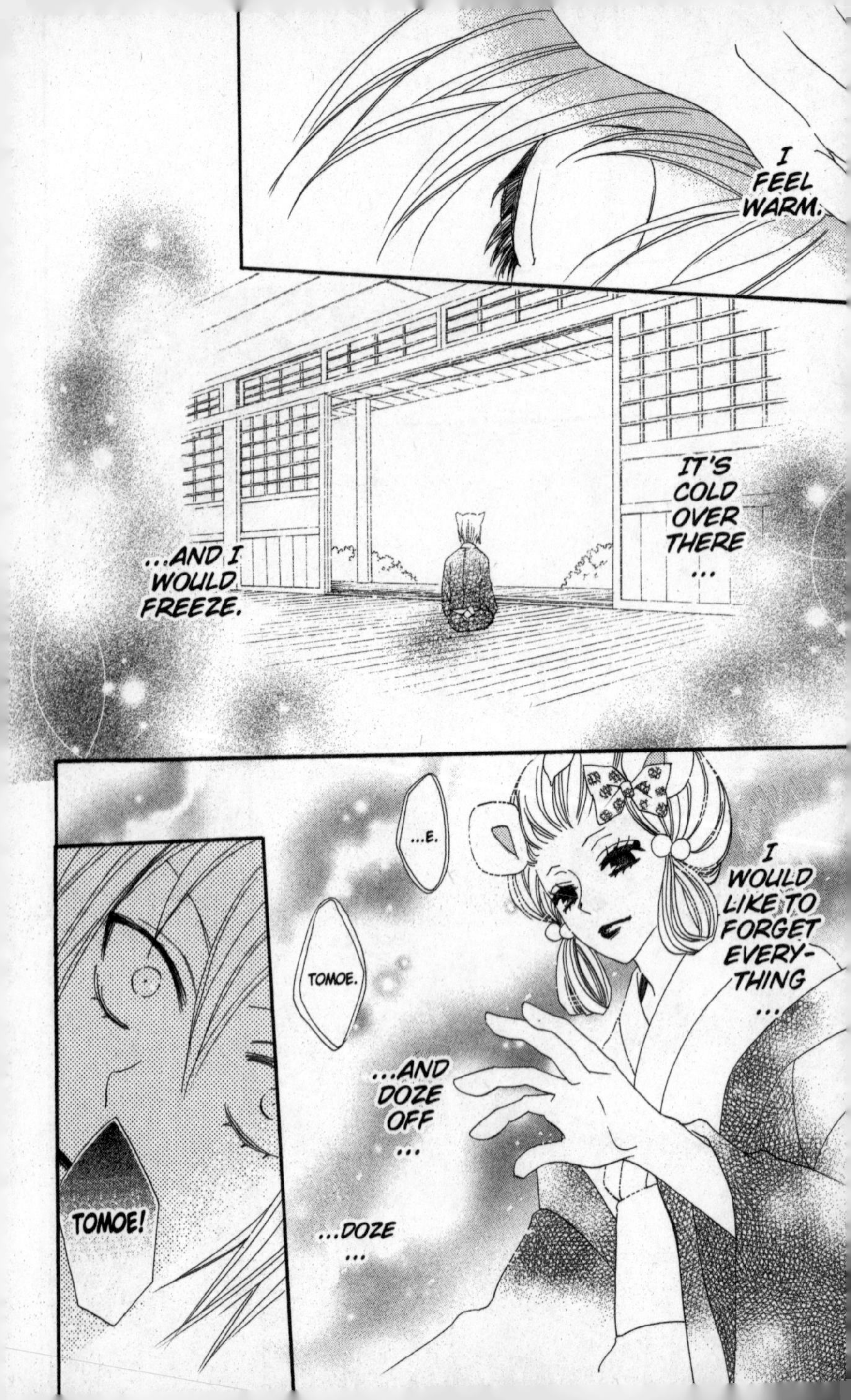
I FEEL WARM.
IT'S COLD OVER THERE...
...AND I WOULD FREEZE.
I WOULD LIKE TO FORGET EVERY-THING...
...E.
TOMOE.
...AND DOZE OFF...
...DOZE...
TOMOE!

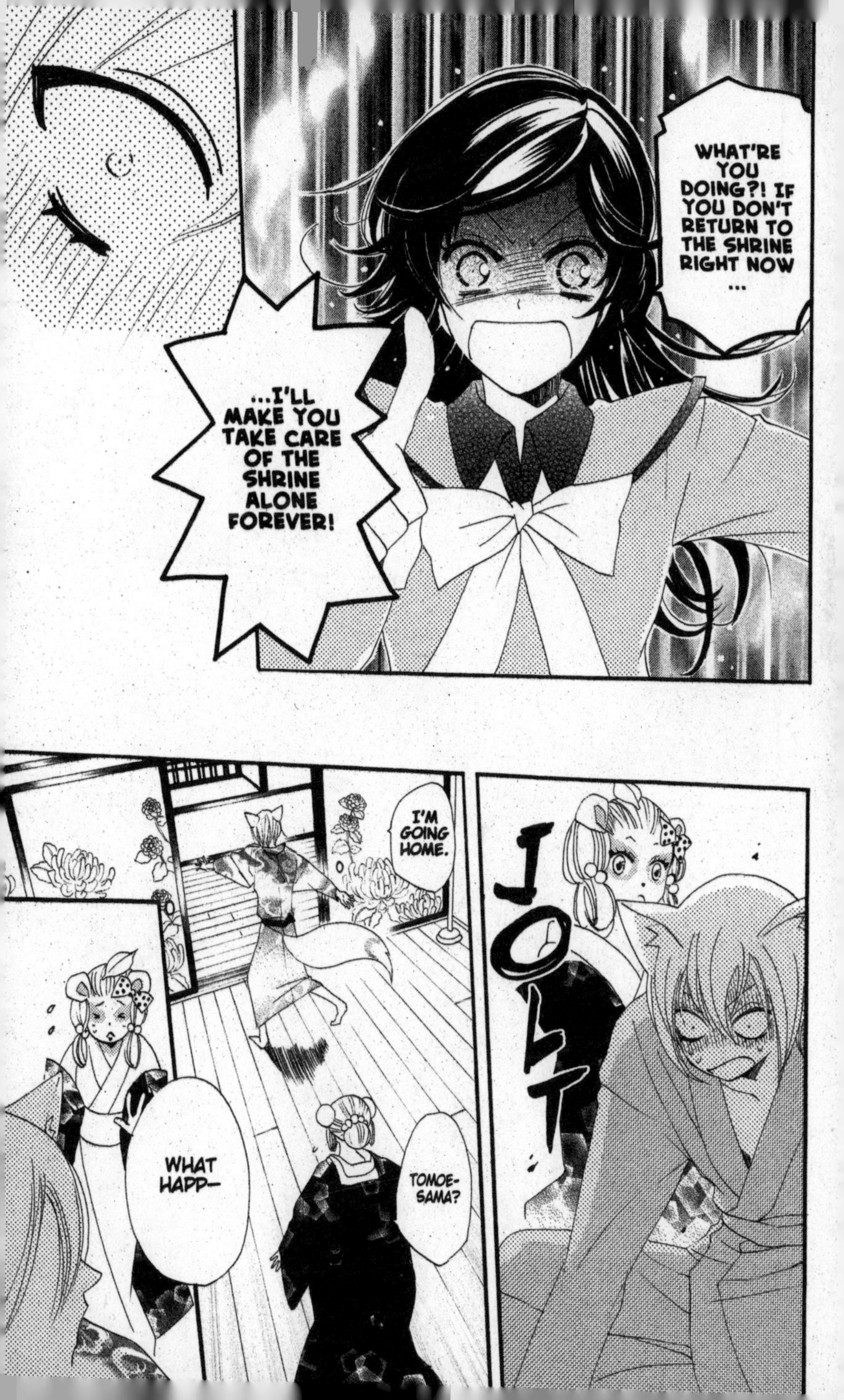
WHAT'RE YOU DOING?! IF YOU DON'T RETURN TO THE SHRINE RIGHT NOW ...
...I'LL MAKE YOU TAKE CARE OF THE SHRINE ALONE FOREVER!
JOLT
I'M GOING HOME.
TOMOE-SAMA?
WHAT HAPP—

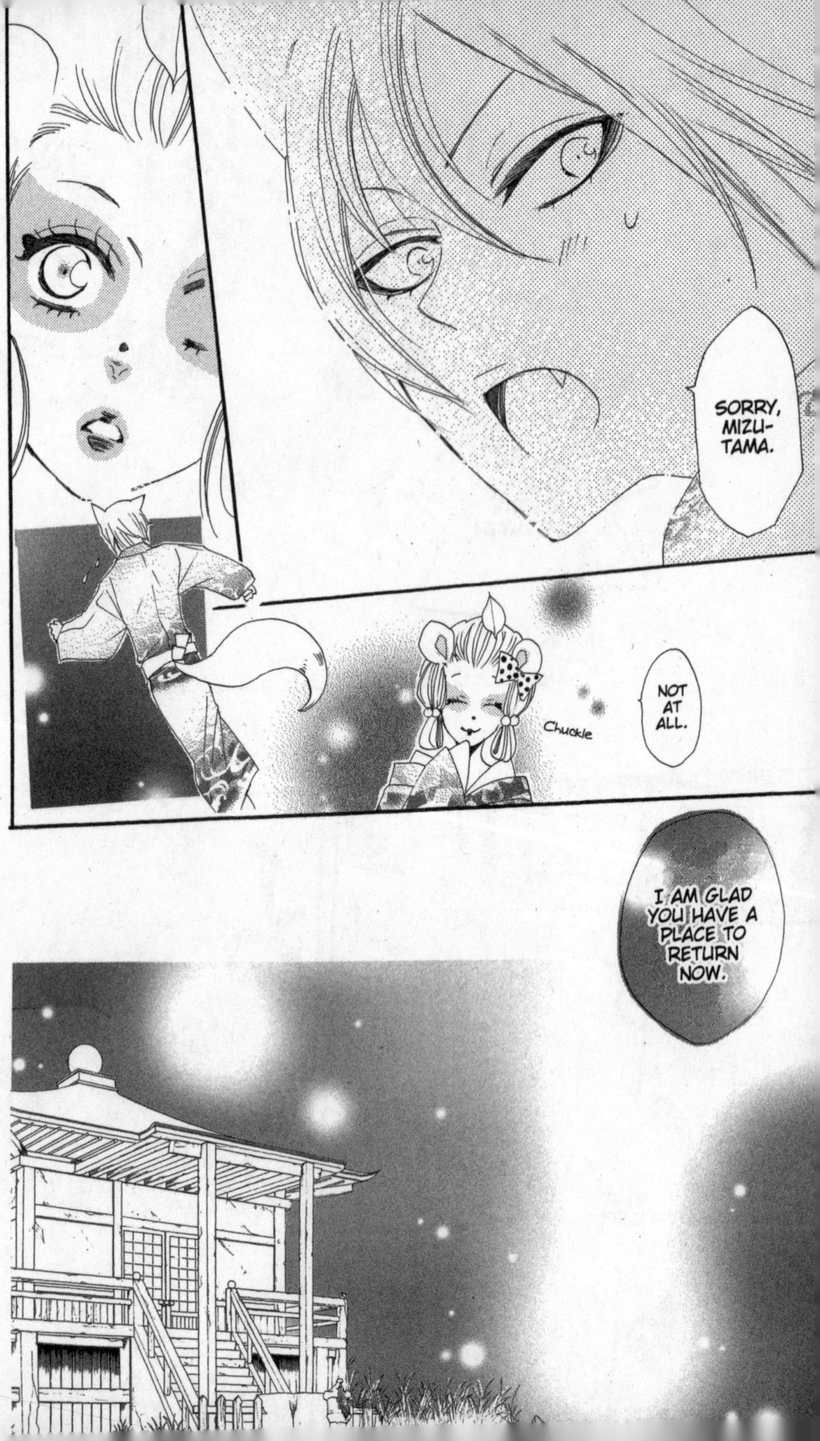
SORRY, MIZU-TAMA.
NOT AT ALL.
Chuckle
I AM GLAD YOU HAVE A PLACE TO RETURN NOW.

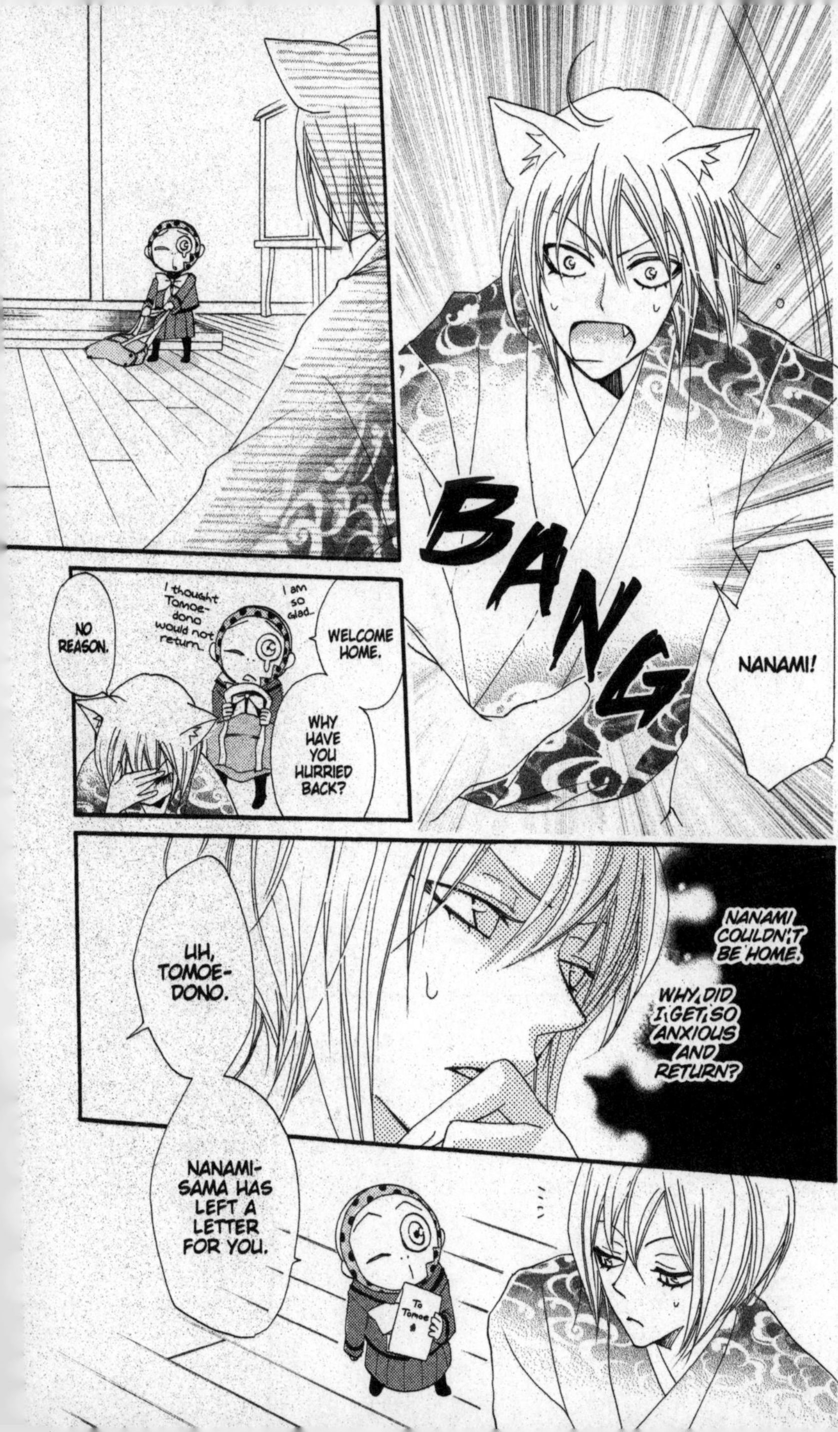
BANG
NANAMI!
WELCOME HOME.
I am so glad...
I thought Tomoe-dono would not return...
WHY HAVE YOU HURRIED BACK?
NO REASON.
NANAMI COULDN'T BE HOME.
WHY DID I GET SO ANXIOUS AND RETURN?
UH, TOMOE-DONO.
NANAMI-SAMA HAS LEFT A LETTER FOR YOU.
To Tomoe

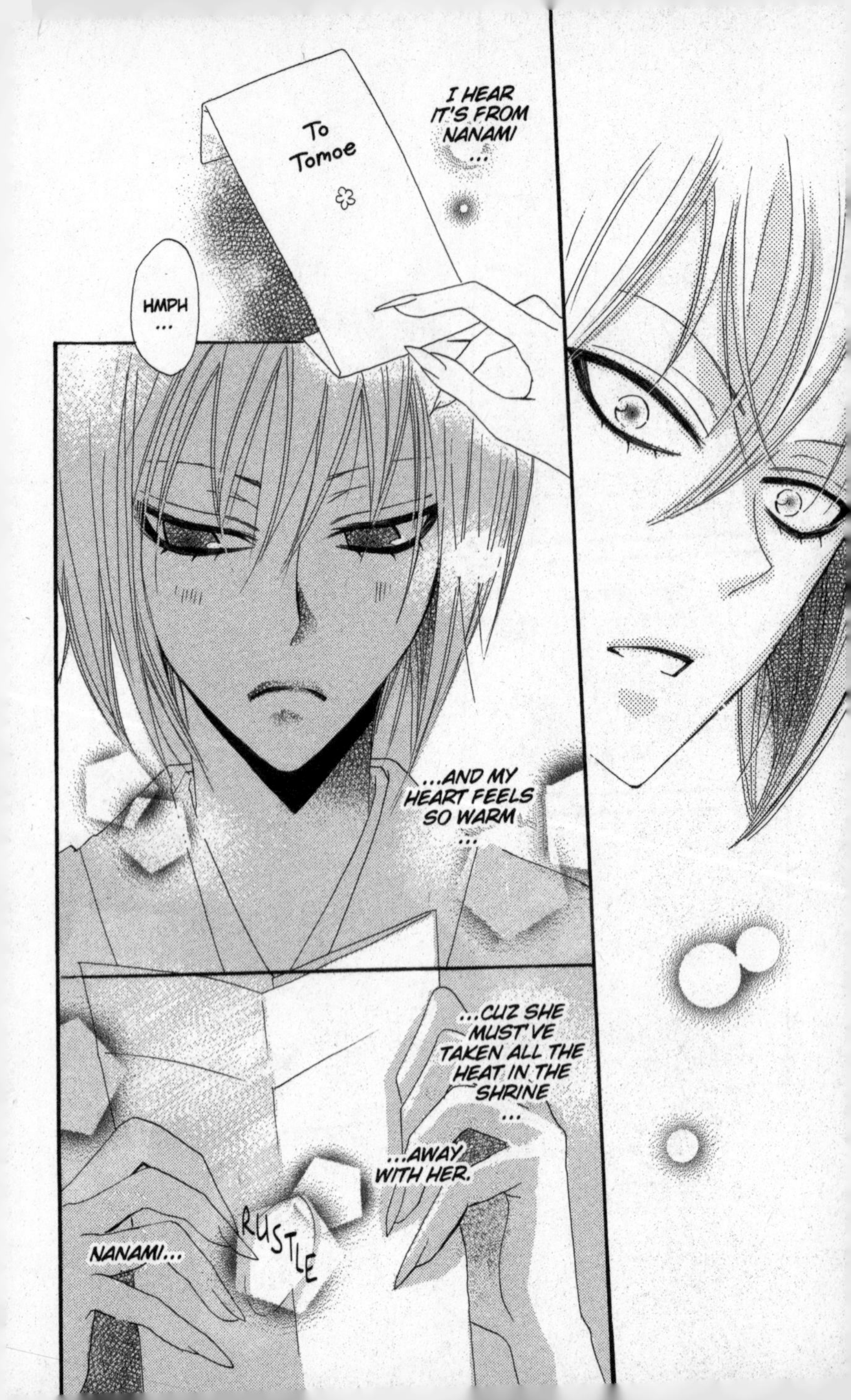
I HEAR IT'S FROM NANAMI ...
To Tomoe
HMPH ...
...AND MY HEART FEELS SO WARM ...
...CUZ SHE MUST'VE TAKEN ALL THE HEAT IN THE SHRINE ...
...AWAY WITH HER.
RUSTLE
NANAMI...

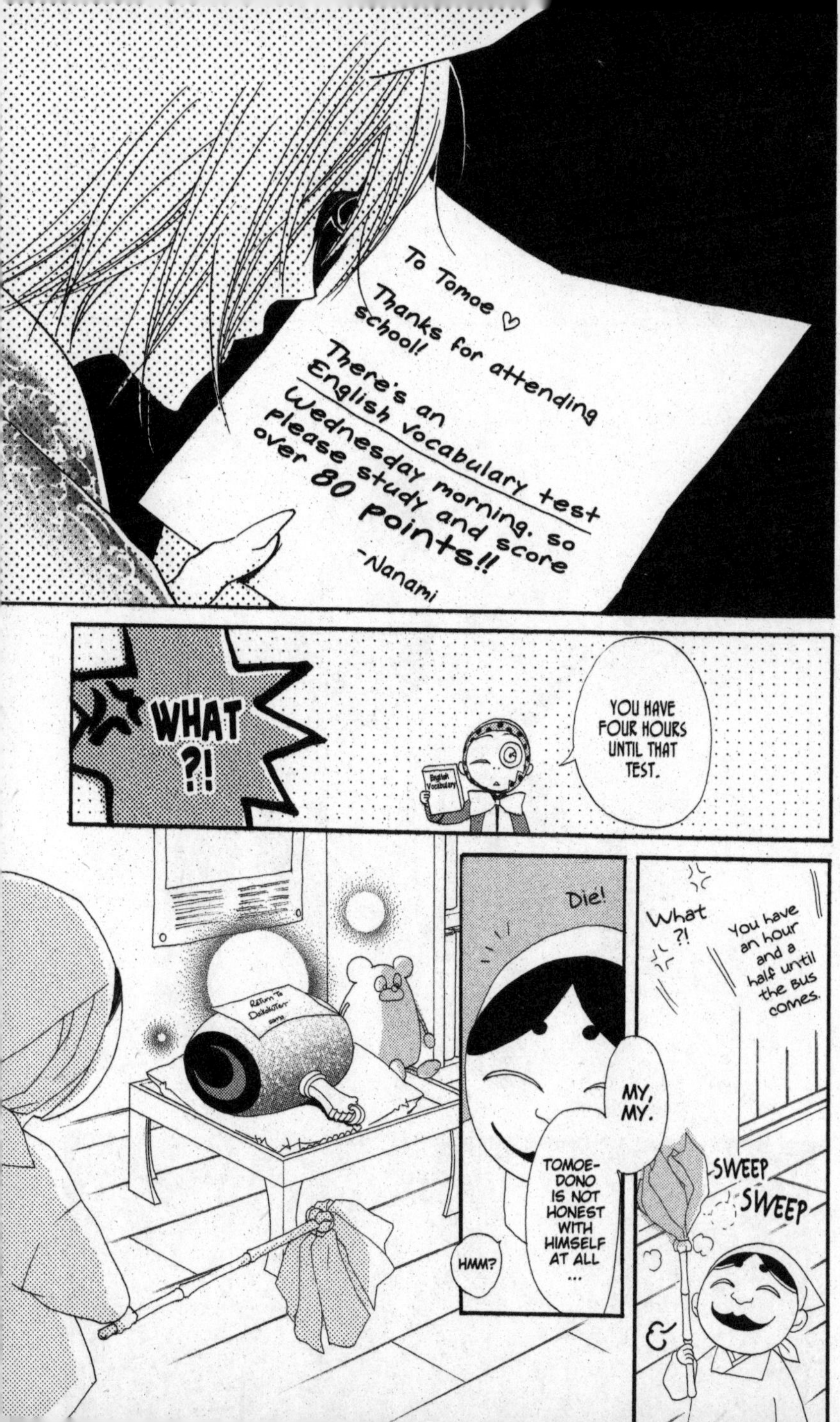
To Tomoe ♡
Thanks for attending school!
There's an English vocabulary test Wednesday morning, so please study and score over 80 points!!
-Nanami
YOU HAVE FOUR HOURS UNTIL THAT TEST.
English Vocabulary
WHAT ?!
You have an hour and a half until the bus comes.
What ?!
SWEEP SWEEP
Die!
MY, MY.
TOMOE-DONO IS NOT HONEST WITH HIMSELF AT ALL ...
HMM?

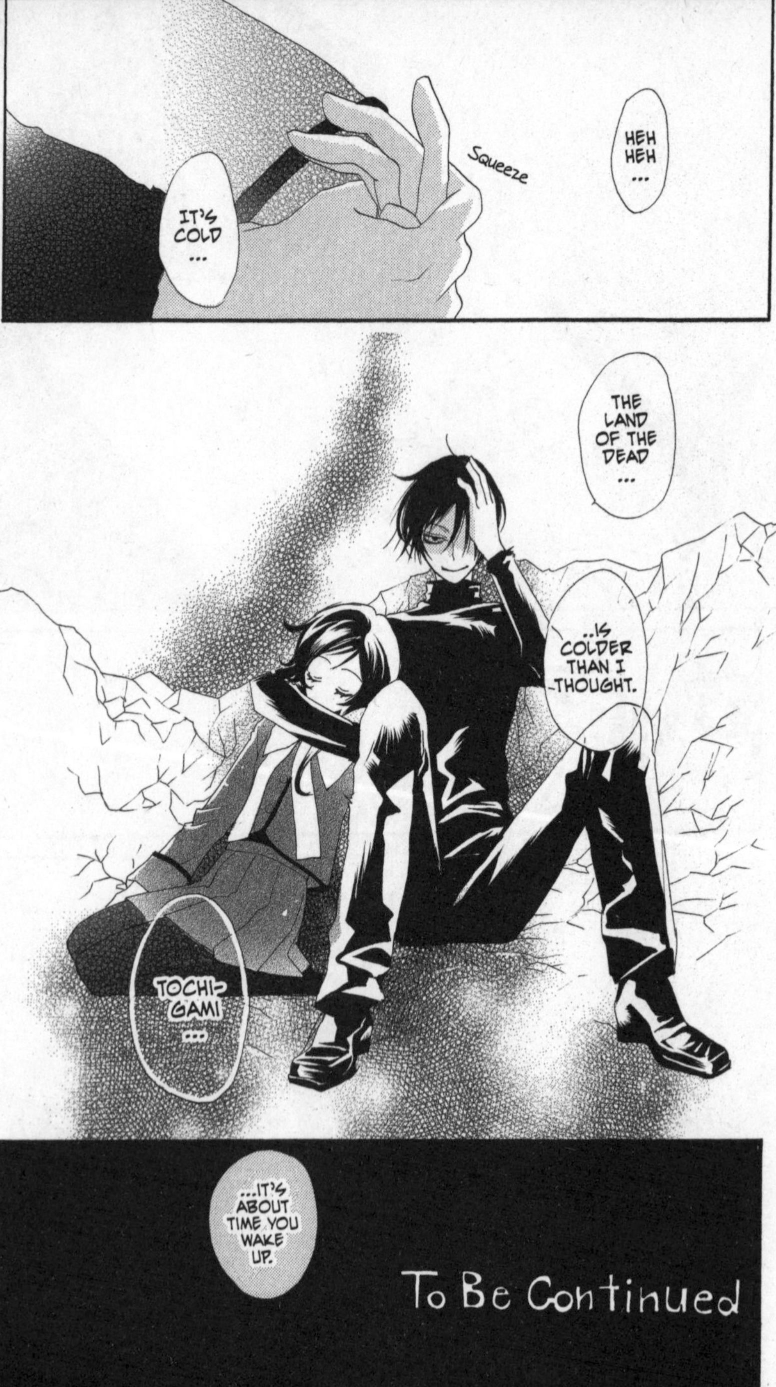
HEH HEH ...
Squeeze
IT'S COLD ...
THE LAND OF THE DEAD ...
...IS COLDER THAN I THOUGHT.
TOCHI-GAMI ...
...IT'S ABOUT TIME YOU WAKE UP.
To Be Continued

Thank you so much!

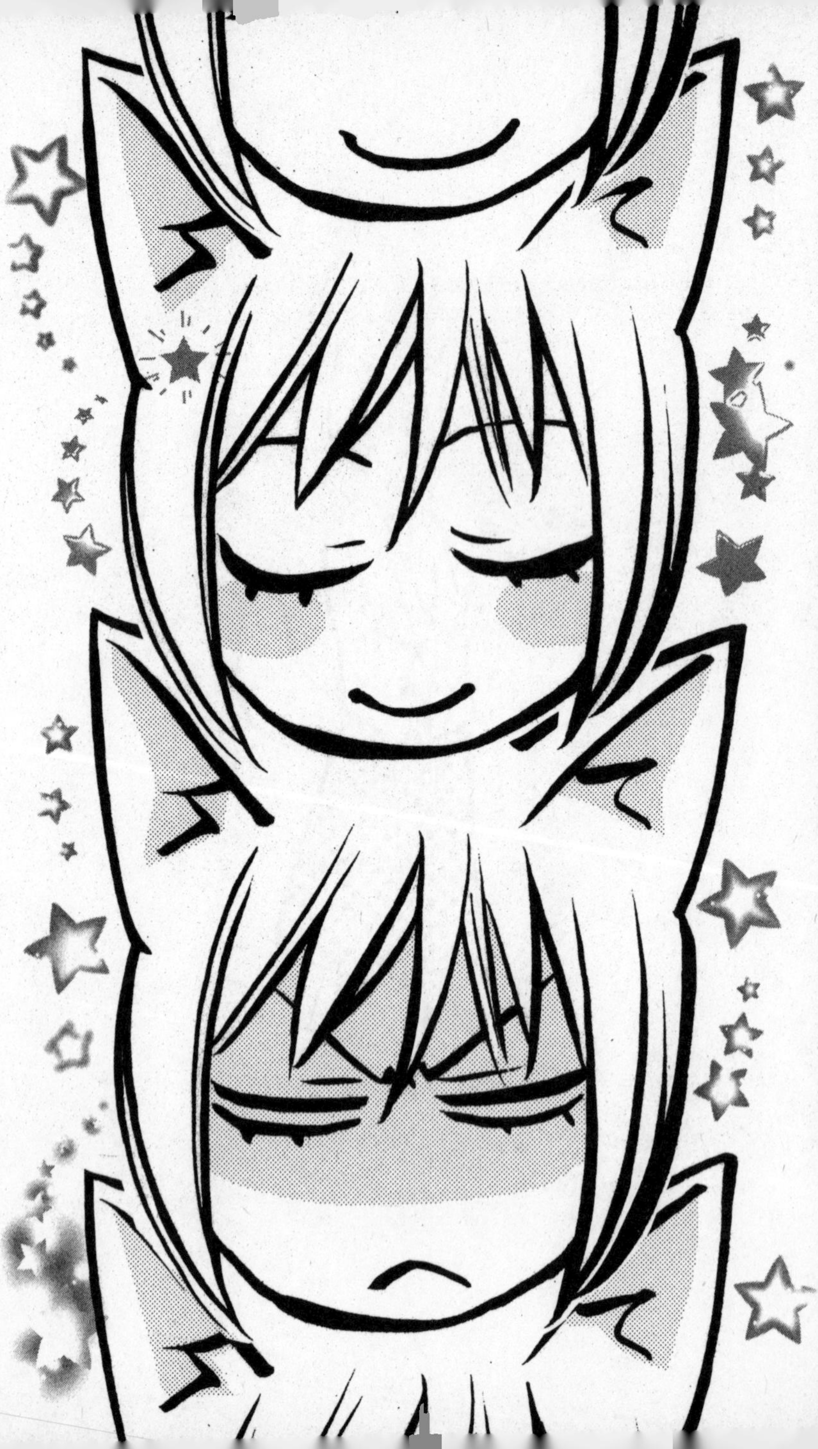

The Otherworld

Ayakashi is an archaic term for yokai.

Kami are Shinto deities or spirits. The word can be used for a range of creatures, from nature spirits to strong and dangerous gods.

Tengu are a type of yokai. They are sometimes associated with excess pride.

Shikigami are spirits that are summoned and employed by *onmyoji* (Yin-Yang sorcerers).

Shinshi are birds, beasts, insects or fish that have a special relationship with a *kami*.

Ookuninushi (also called Daikokusama) is the kami enshrined in Izumo Oyashiro.

Yokai are demons, monsters or goblins.

Honorifics

-chan is a diminutive most often used with babies, children or teenage girls.

-dono roughly means "my lord," although not in the aristocratic sense.

-kun is used by persons of superior rank to their juniors. It can sometimes have a familiar connotation.

-sama is used with people of much higher rank.

-hime means princess, although a Japanese princess is not the same as a Western one and isn't necessarily the daughter of a king.

Notes

Page 11, panel 1: Odaiba
A man-made island in Tokyo Bay that was once used for defense, but now houses a Ferris wheel, a mall, and other amusements.

Page 12, panel 1: 50, 000 yen. 500,000 yen
About $633 US and $6,332 US.

Page 28, panel 2: Talento
A *talento* in Japan usually appears on various TV shows as a regular but may also appear in dramas, sing, or write books and articles.

Page 36, panel 3: Kamuhakari
In October of the lunar calendar, all the kami in Japan gather at Izumo Oyashiro shrine for a one-week convocation. Therefore in the lunar calendar, October is called Kamiarizuki (month-with-kami) in Izumo, and Kannazuki (month-without-kami) in other regions. Festivals are held at Izumo Oyashiro during the Kamuhakari.

Page 70, panel 3: Yogiri-guruma
Literally "night fog carriage."

Page 105, panel 3: Kamimukae festival
The welcoming ceremony to kick off the Kamuhakari. It is held on October 10 (of the lunar calendar) at 7:00 PM on Inasa-no-hama beach.

Page 134, panel 3: Yomotsu-hirasaka
There is actually a "Yomotsu-hirasaka" in Izumo, and it is believed to connect this world to the Land of the Dead.

Page 143, panel 3: Kyoganmon Gate
Kyoganmon literally means "huge rock gate."

Page 167, panel 5: Sasamochi
Mochi (sticky rice cakes) wrapped in sasa (bamboo leaves).

Page 169, panel 1: Yakyuken
Strip rock-paper-scissors.

Julietta Suzuki's debut manga *Hoshi ni Naru Hi* (The Day One Becomes a Star) appeared in the 2004 *Hana to Yume Plus*. Her other books include *Akuma to Dolce* (The Devil and Sweets) and *Karakuri Odette*. Born in December in Fukuoka Prefecture, she enjoys having movies play in the background while she works on her manga.

KAMISAMA KISS

VOL. 7
Shojo Beat Edition

STORY AND ART BY
Julietta Suzuki

English Translation & Adaptation/Tomo Kimura
Touch-up Art & Lettering/Joanna Estep
Design/Yukiko Whitley
Editor/Pancha Diaz

KAMISAMA HAJIMEMASHITA by Julietta Suzuki
© Julietta Suzuki 2010
All rights reserved.
First published in Japan in 2010 by HAKUSENSHA, Inc., Tokyo.
English language translation rights arranged with
HAKUSENSHA, Inc., Tokyo.

Printed in the U.S.A.

Published by VIZ Media, LLC
P.O. Box 77010
San Francisco, CA 94107

10 9 8
First printing, February 2012
Eighth printing, June 2023

viz.com

shojobeat.com

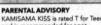